Shojo Beat

Natsume's BOOK of FRIENDS

STORY and ART by
Yuki Midorikawa

VOLUME 27

Natsume's BOOK of FRIENDS

STORY & CHARACTERS

The story so far...

Takashi Natsume has a secret—ever since he was a child, he has been able to see the supernatural. One day, he inherited the *Book of Friends*, a collection of binding contracts with yokai, from his grandmother Reiko. Since then, with his self-proclaimed bodyguard Nyanko Sensei at his side, Natsume has been busy returning names and getting attacked...

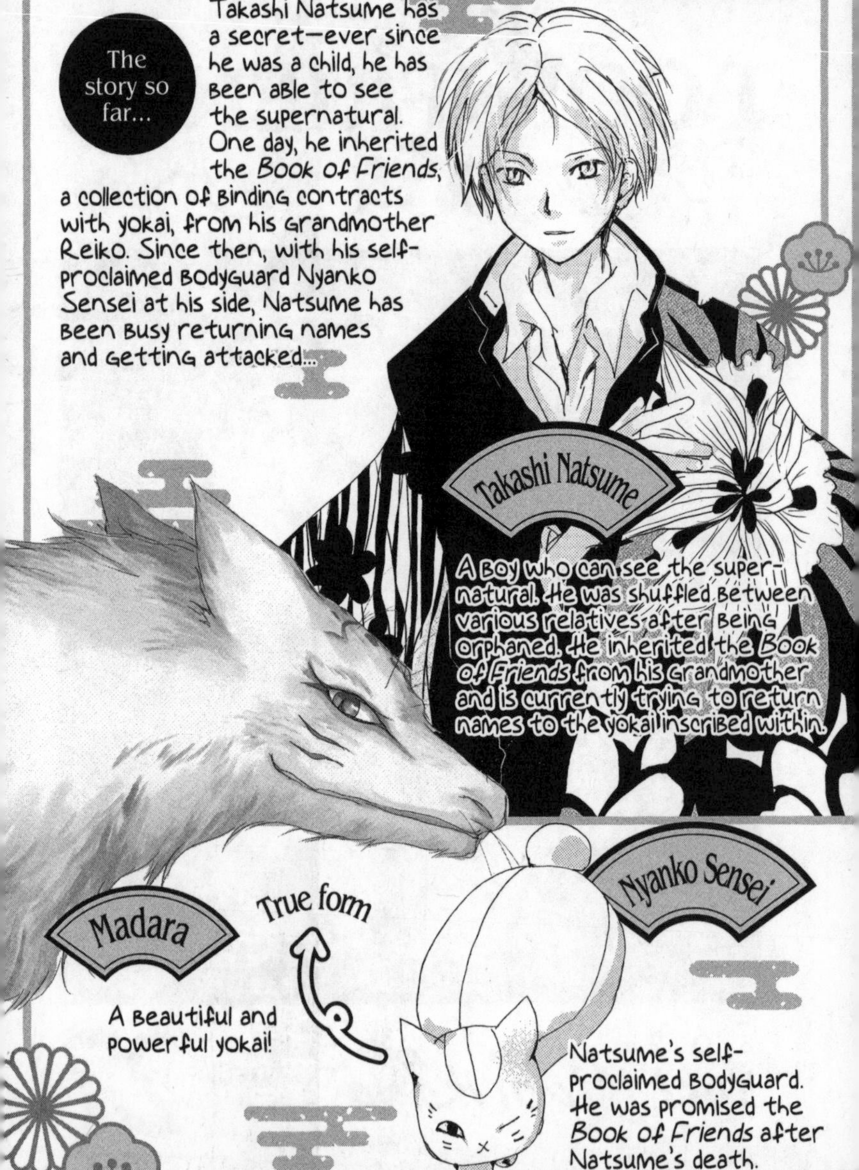

Takashi Natsume
A boy who can see the supernatural. He was shuffled between various relatives after being orphaned. He inherited the *Book of Friends* from his grandmother and is currently trying to return names to the yokai inscribed within.
Nyanko Sensei
True form
Madara
A beautiful and powerful yokai!
Natsume's self-proclaimed bodyguard. He was promised the *Book of Friends* after Natsume's death.

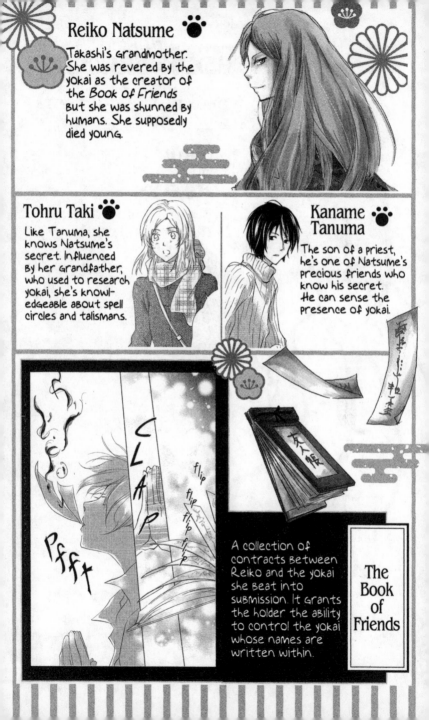

Reiko Natsume

Takashi's grandmother. She was revered by the yokai as the creator of the *Book of Friends* but she was shunned by humans. She supposedly died young.

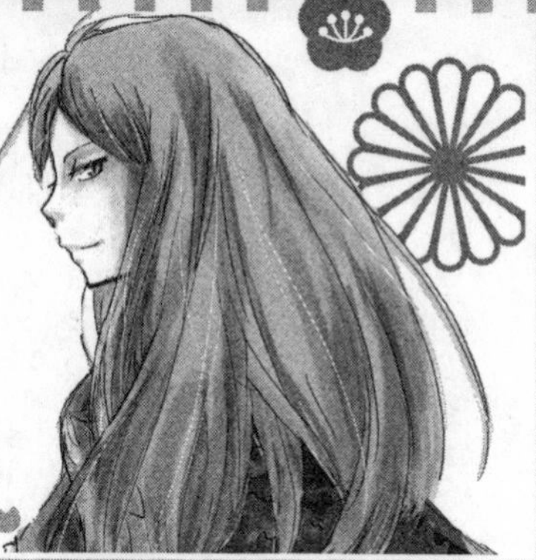

Kaname Tanuma

The son of a priest, he's one of Natsume's precious friends who know his secret. He can sense the presence of yokai.

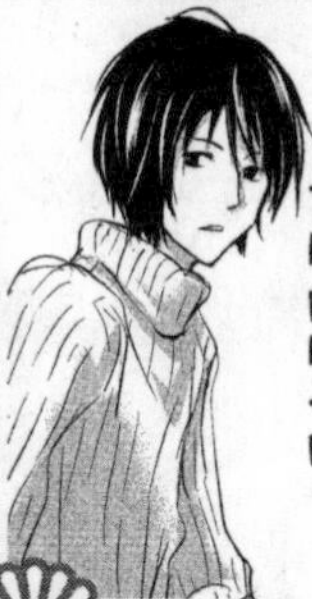

Tohru Taki

Like Tanuma, she knows Natsume's secret. Influenced by her grandfather, who used to research yokai, she's knowledgeable about spell circles and talismans.

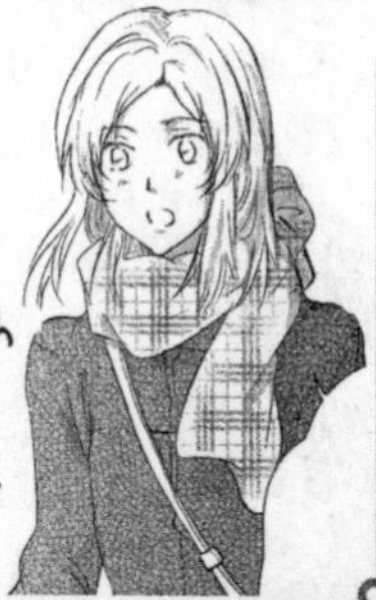

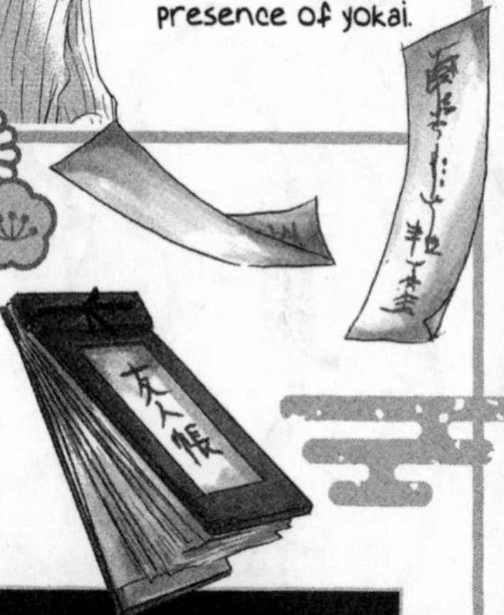
友人帳

The Book of Friends

A collection of contracts between Reiko and the yokai she beat into submission. It grants the holder the ability to control the yokai whose names are written within.

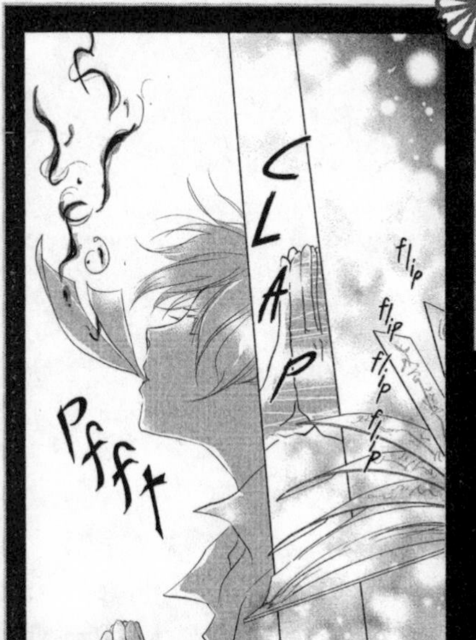
CLAP
flip
flip
flip
flip
Pffft

Natsume's BOOK of FRIENDS

VOLUME 27 CONTENTS

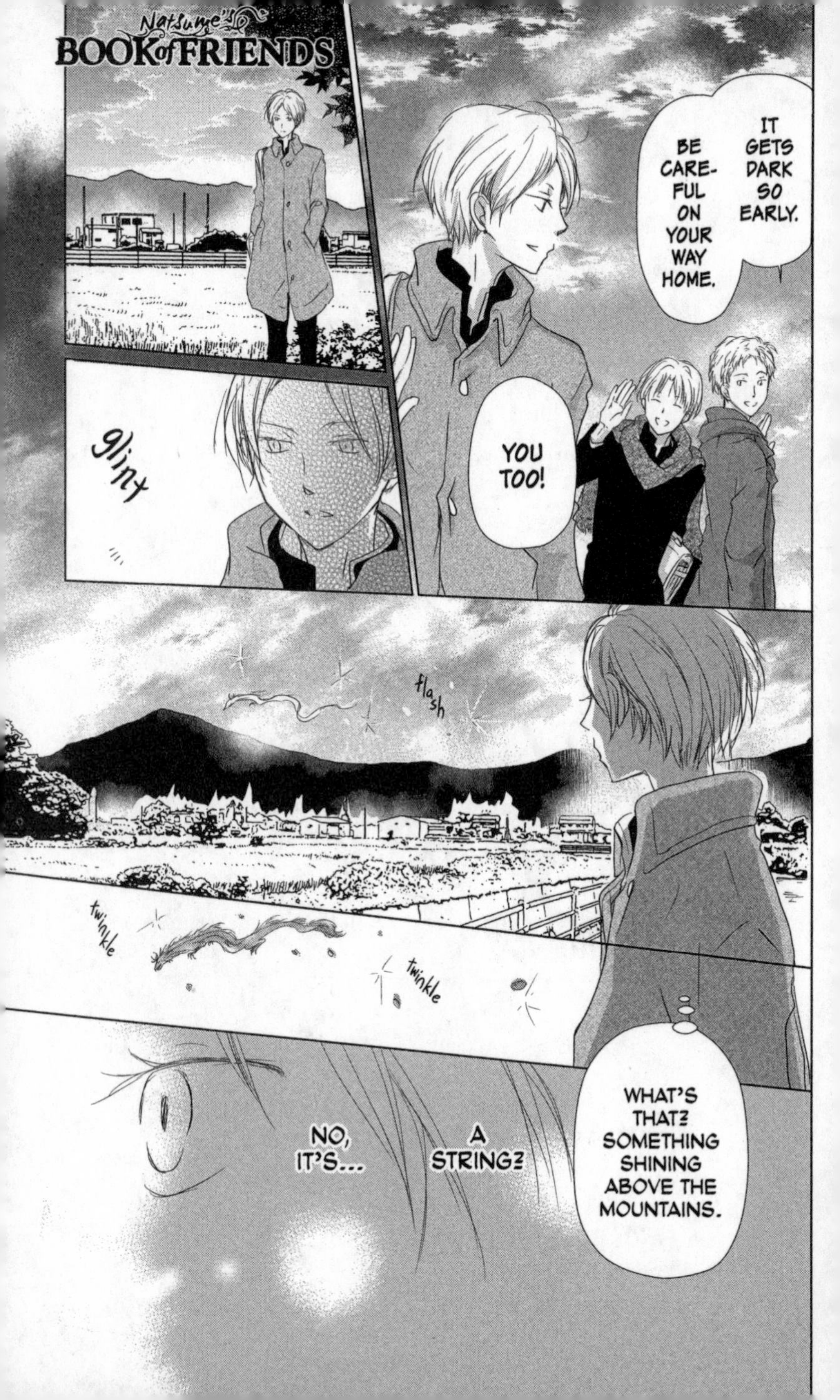
IT GETS DARK SO EARLY.
BE CARE-FUL ON YOUR WAY HOME.
YOU TOO!
glint
flash
twinkle
twinkle
WHAT'S THAT? SOMETHING SHINING ABOVE THE MOUNTAINS.
A STRING?
NO, IT'S...

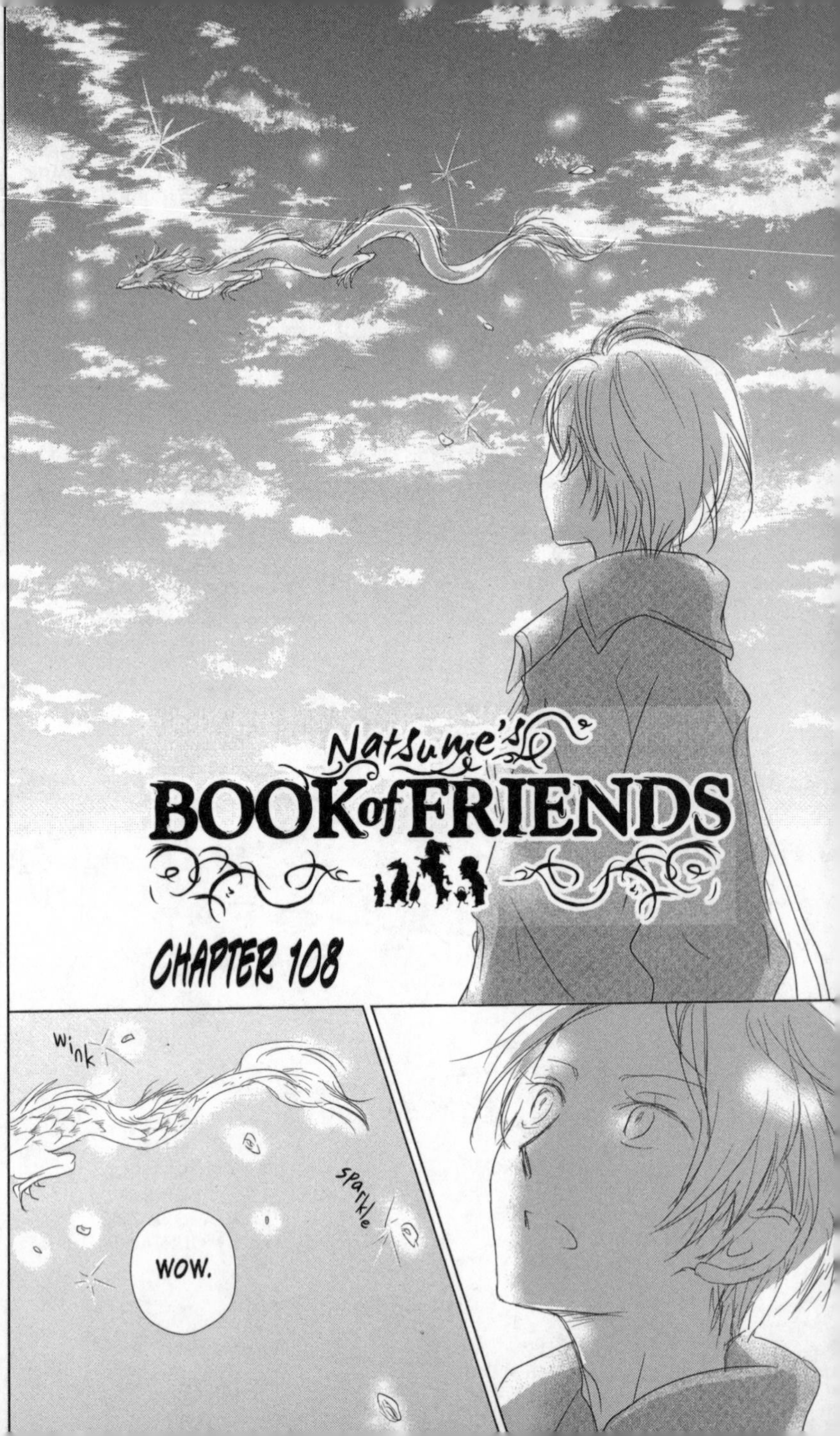
Natsume's
BOOK of FRIENDS
CHAPTER 108
wink
sparkle
WOW.

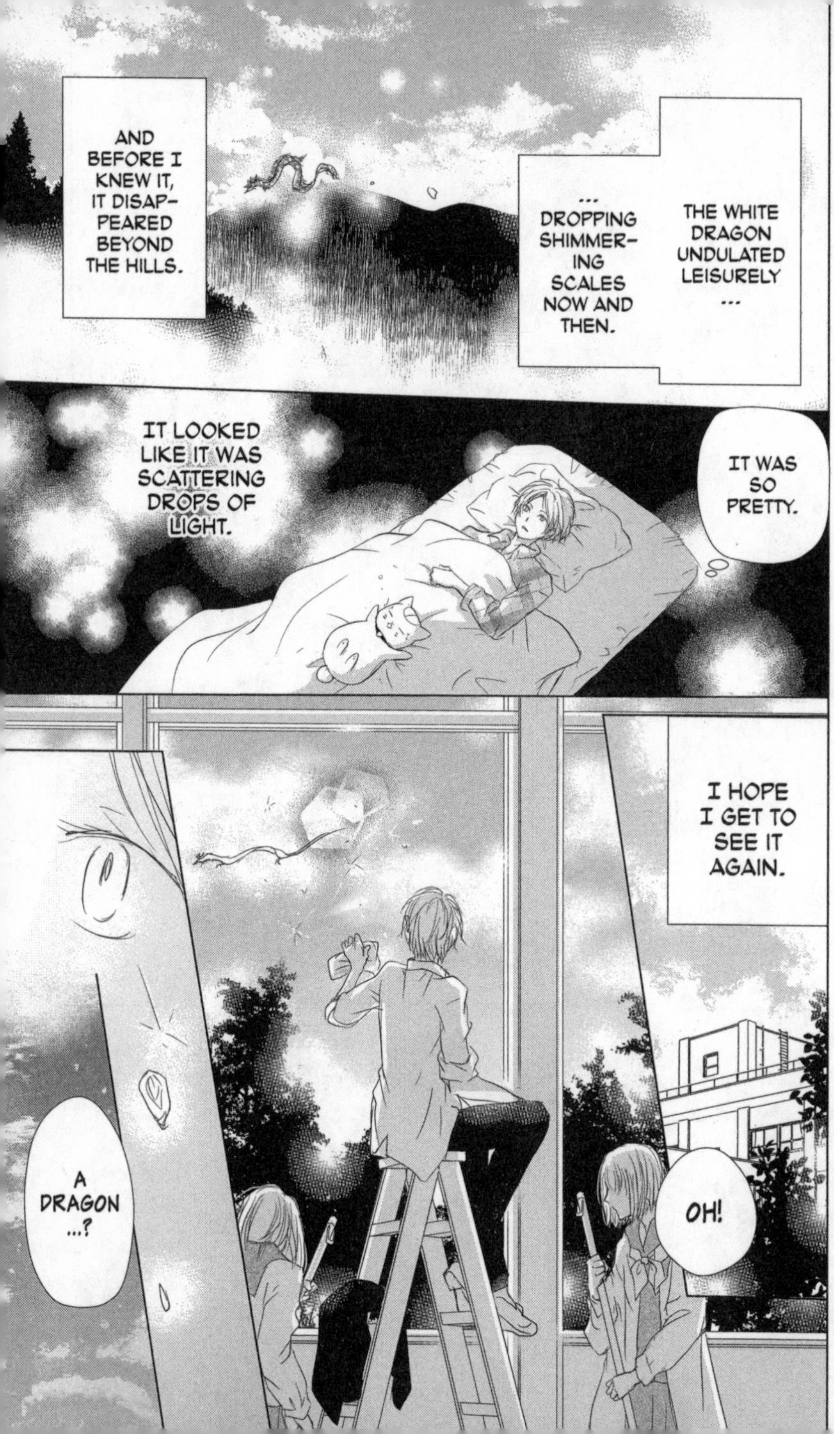
THE WHITE DRAGON UNDULATED LEISURELY ...
... DROPPING SHIMMERING SCALES NOW AND THEN.
AND BEFORE I KNEW IT, IT DISAPPEARED BEYOND THE HILLS.
IT WAS SO PRETTY.
IT LOOKED LIKE IT WAS SCATTERING DROPS OF LIGHT.
I HOPE I GET TO SEE IT AGAIN.
OH!
A DRAGON ...?

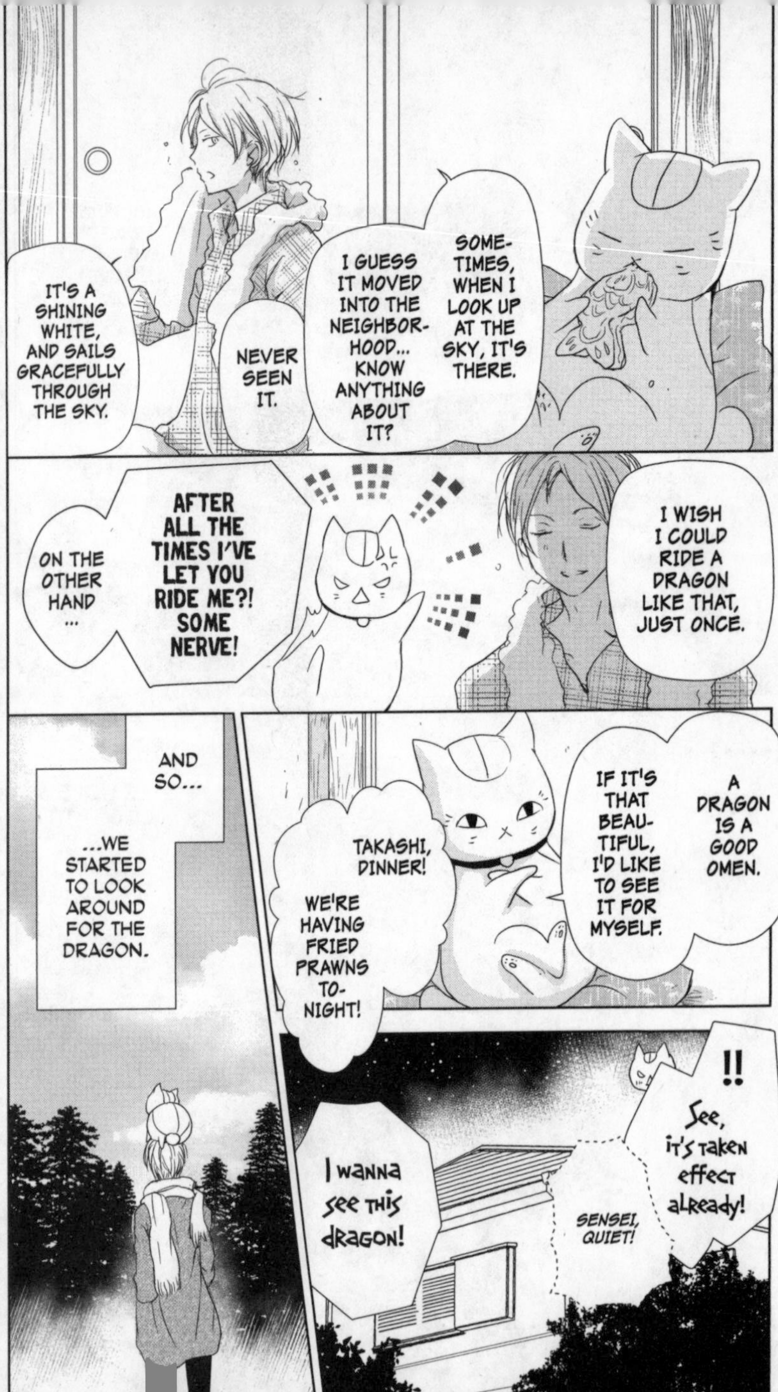
SOME-TIMES, WHEN I LOOK UP AT THE SKY, IT'S THERE.
I GUESS IT MOVED INTO THE NEIGHBOR-HOOD... KNOW ANYTHING ABOUT IT?
NEVER SEEN IT.
IT'S A SHINING WHITE, AND SAILS GRACEFULLY THROUGH THE SKY.
I WISH I COULD RIDE A DRAGON LIKE THAT, JUST ONCE.
AFTER ALL THE TIMES I'VE LET YOU RIDE ME?! SOME NERVE!
ON THE OTHER HAND ...
A DRAGON IS A GOOD OMEN.
IF IT'S THAT BEAU-TIFUL, I'D LIKE TO SEE IT FOR MYSELF.
TAKASHI, DINNER!
WE'RE HAVING FRIED PRAWNS TO-NIGHT!
!!
See, it's taken effect already!
SENSEI, QUIET!
I wanna see this dragon!
AND SO...
...WE STARTED TO LOOK AROUND FOR THE DRAGON.

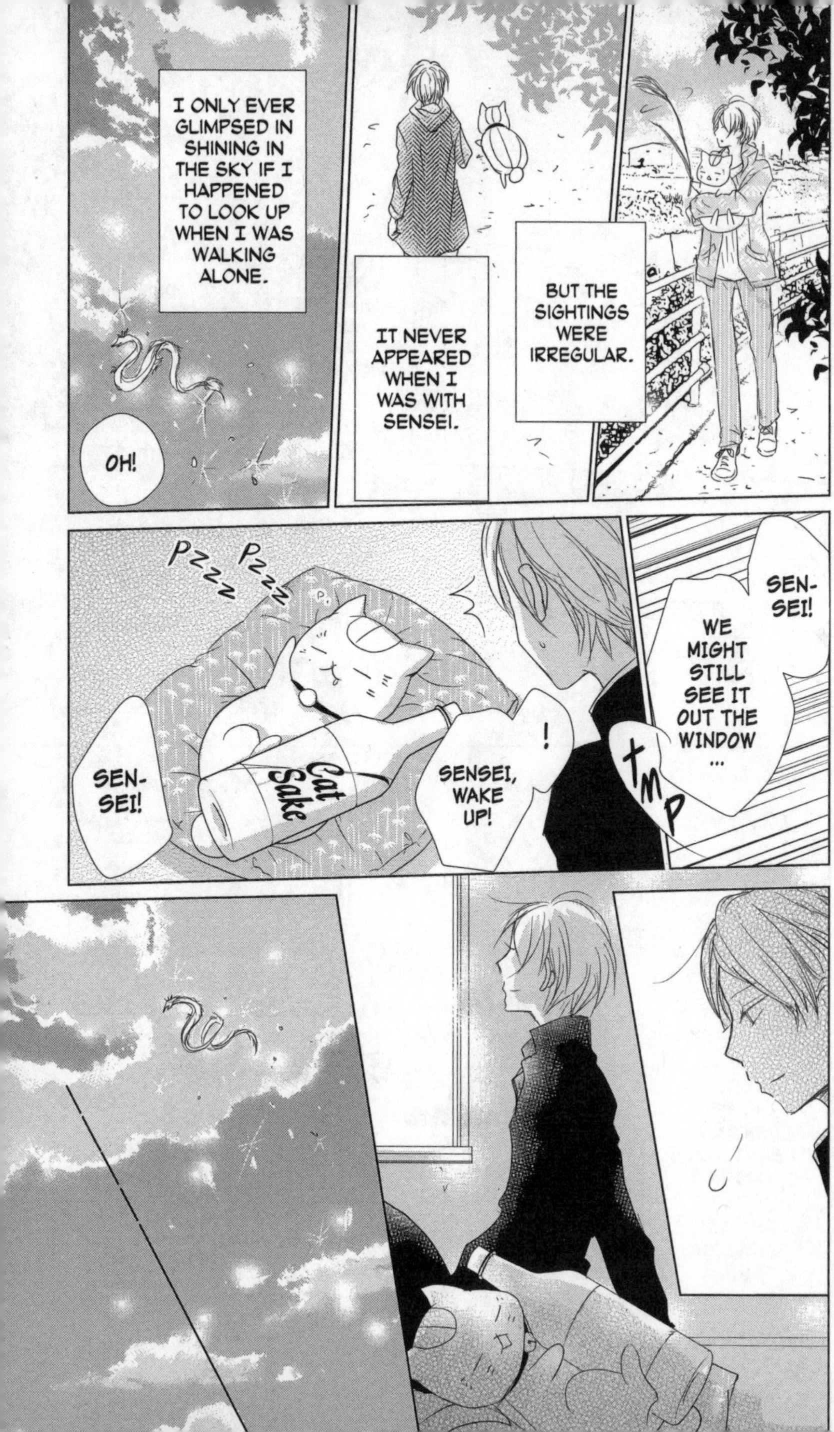
BUT THE SIGHTINGS WERE IRREGULAR.
IT NEVER APPEARED WHEN I WAS WITH SENSEI.
I ONLY EVER GLIMPSED IN SHINING IN THE SKY IF I HAPPENED TO LOOK UP WHEN I WAS WALKING ALONE.
OH!
SEN-SEI!
WE MIGHT STILL SEE IT OUT THE WINDOW ...
TMP
PZZZ PZZZ
!
SENSEI, WAKE UP!
Cat Sake
SEN-SEI!

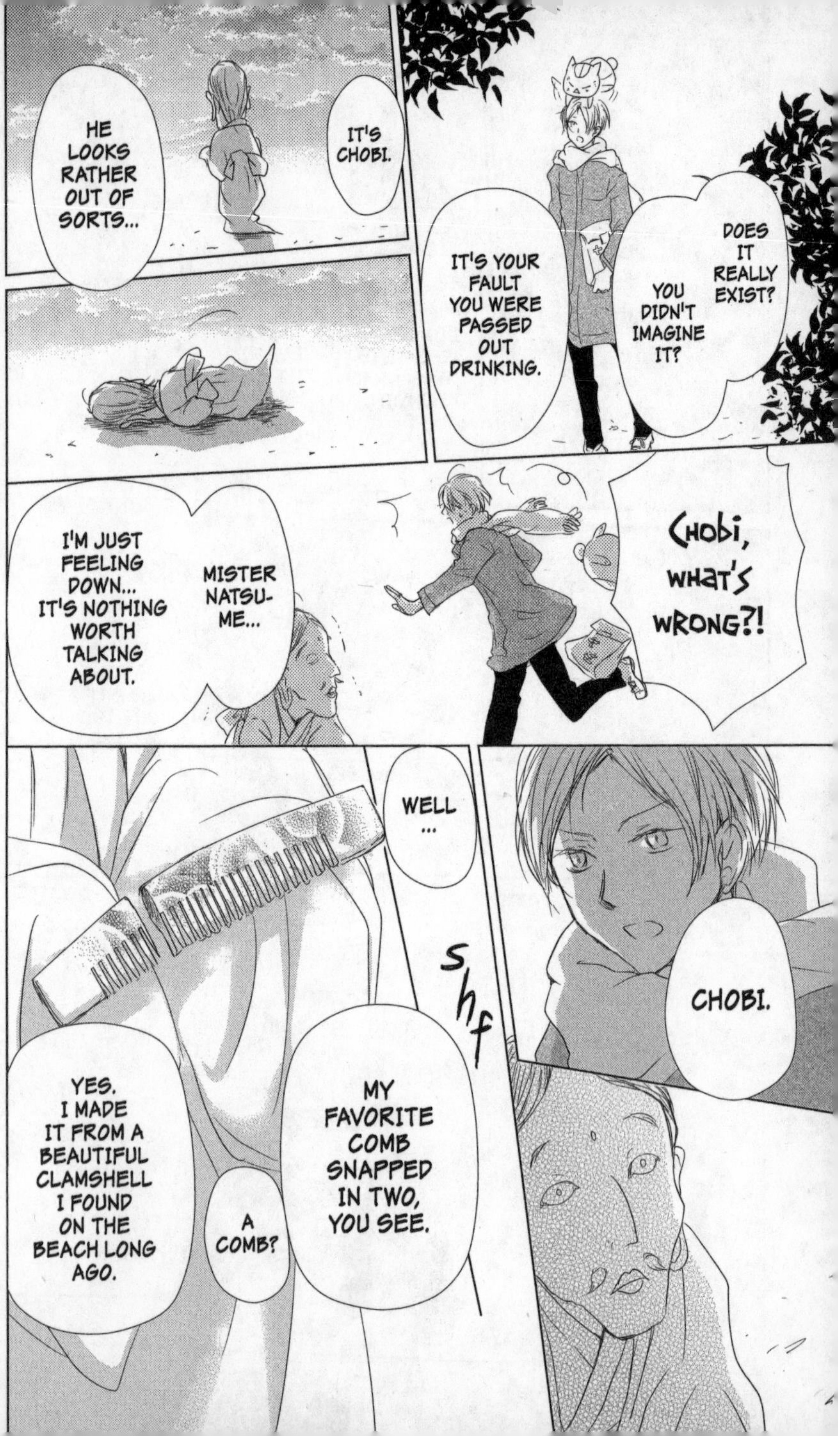
DOES IT REALLY EXIST?
YOU DIDN'T IMAGINE IT?
IT'S YOUR FAULT YOU WERE PASSED OUT DRINKING.
IT'S CHOBI.
HE LOOKS RATHER OUT OF SORTS...
CHOBI, WHAT'S WRONG?!
MISTER NATSU-ME...
I'M JUST FEELING DOWN... IT'S NOTHING WORTH TALKING ABOUT.
CHOBI.
WELL ...
shf
MY FAVORITE COMB SNAPPED IN TWO, YOU SEE.
A COMB?
YES. I MADE IT FROM A BEAUTIFUL CLAMSHELL I FOUND ON THE BEACH LONG AGO.

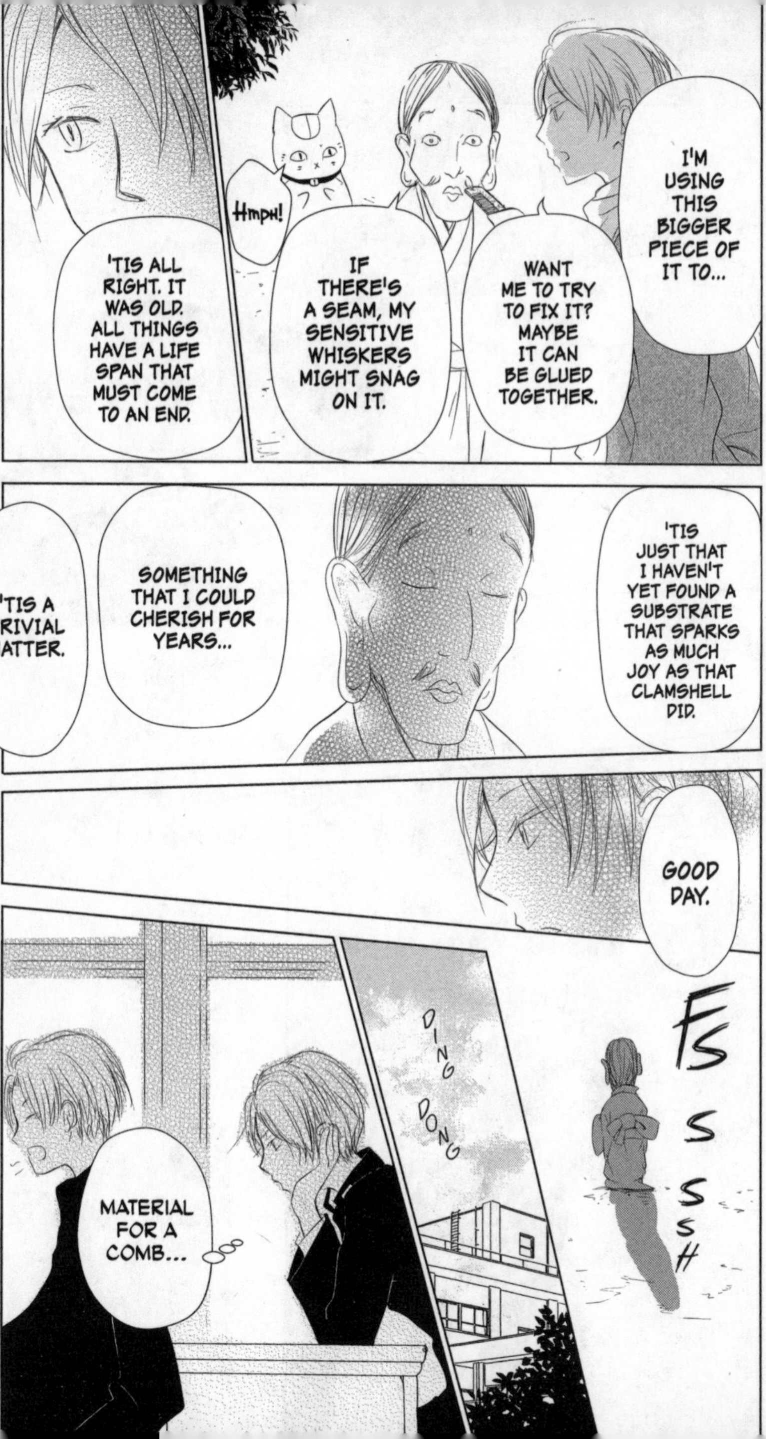
I'M USING THIS BIGGER PIECE OF IT TO...
WANT ME TO TRY TO FIX IT? MAYBE IT CAN BE GLUED TOGETHER.
IF THERE'S A SEAM, MY SENSITIVE WHISKERS MIGHT SNAG ON IT.
Hmph!
'TIS ALL RIGHT. IT WAS OLD. ALL THINGS HAVE A LIFE SPAN THAT MUST COME TO AN END.
'TIS JUST THAT I HAVEN'T YET FOUND A SUBSTRATE THAT SPARKS AS MUCH JOY AS THAT CLAMSHELL DID.
SOMETHING THAT I COULD CHERISH FOR YEARS...
'TIS A TRIVIAL MATTER.
GOOD DAY.
FSSSSH
DING DONG
MATERIAL FOR A COMB...

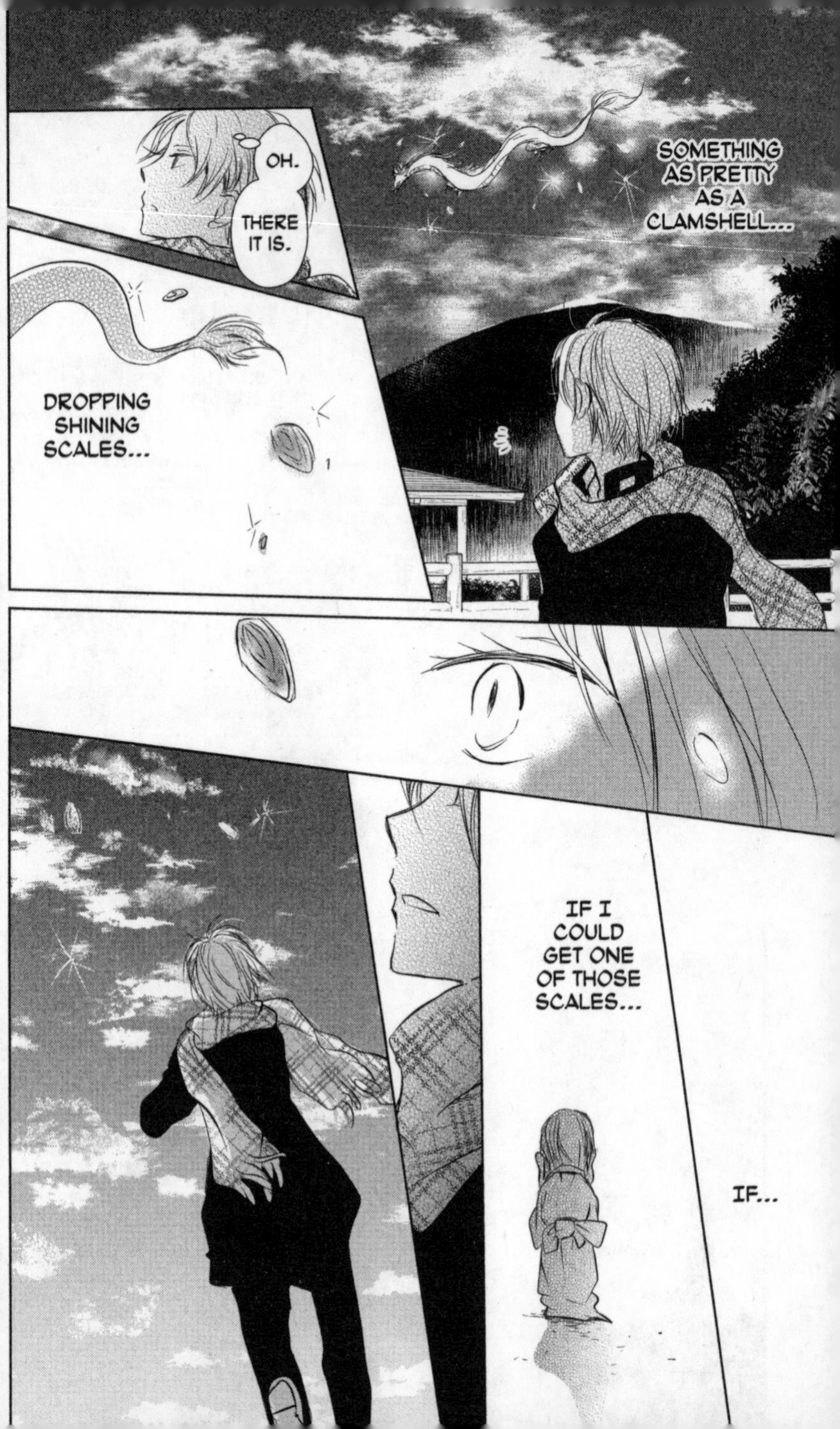
SOMETHING AS PRETTY AS A CLAMSHELL...
OH.
THERE IT IS.
DROPPING SHINING SCALES...
IF I COULD GET ONE OF THOSE SCALES...
IF...

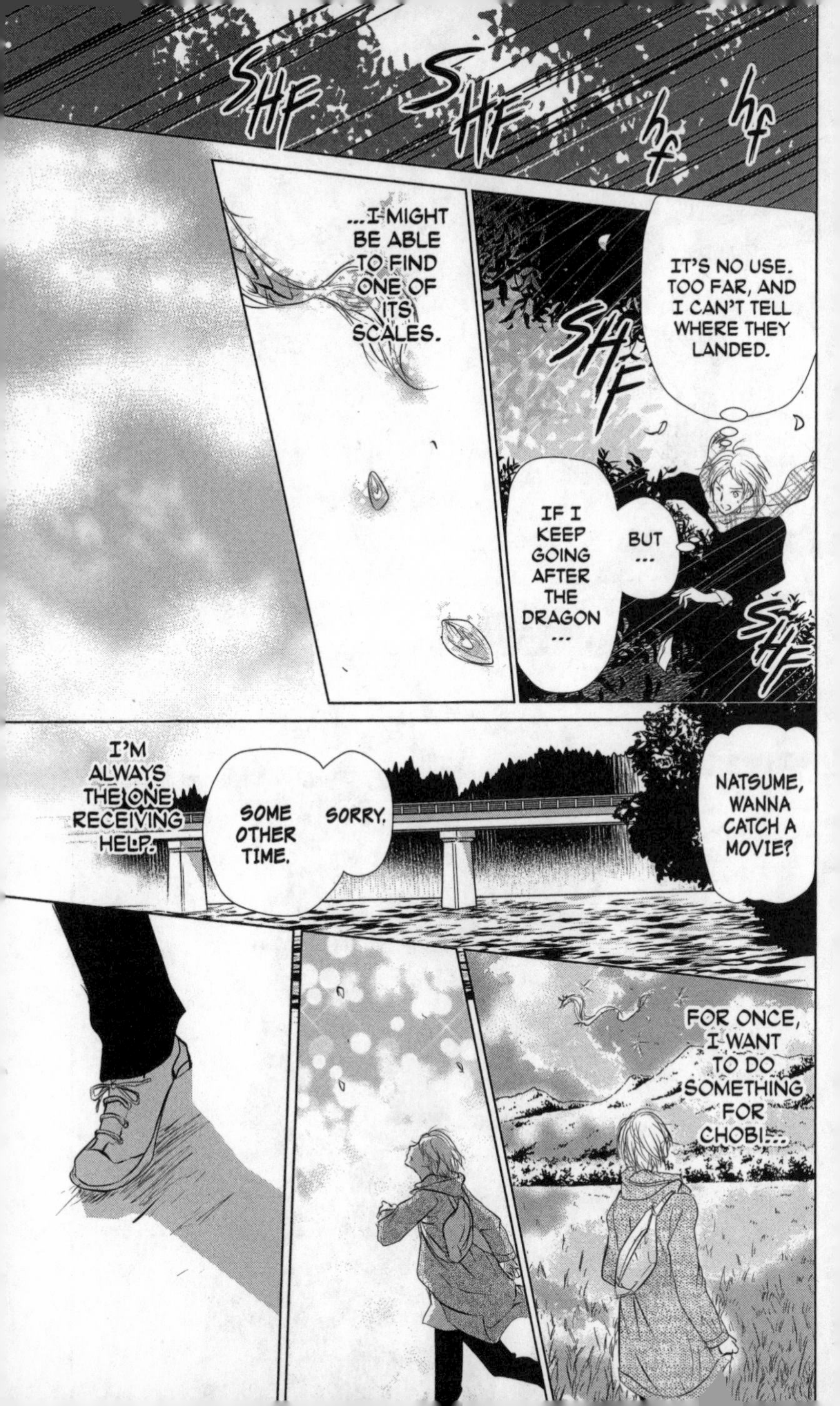
SHF SHF hf hf
IT'S NO USE. TOO FAR, AND I CAN'T TELL WHERE THEY LANDED.
SHF
BUT ...
IF I KEEP GOING AFTER THE DRAGON ...
SHF
...I MIGHT BE ABLE TO FIND ONE OF ITS SCALES.
NATSUME, WANNA CATCH A MOVIE?
SORRY.
SOME OTHER TIME.
I'M ALWAYS THE ONE RECEIVING HELP.
FOR ONCE, I WANT TO DO SOMETHING FOR CHOBI...

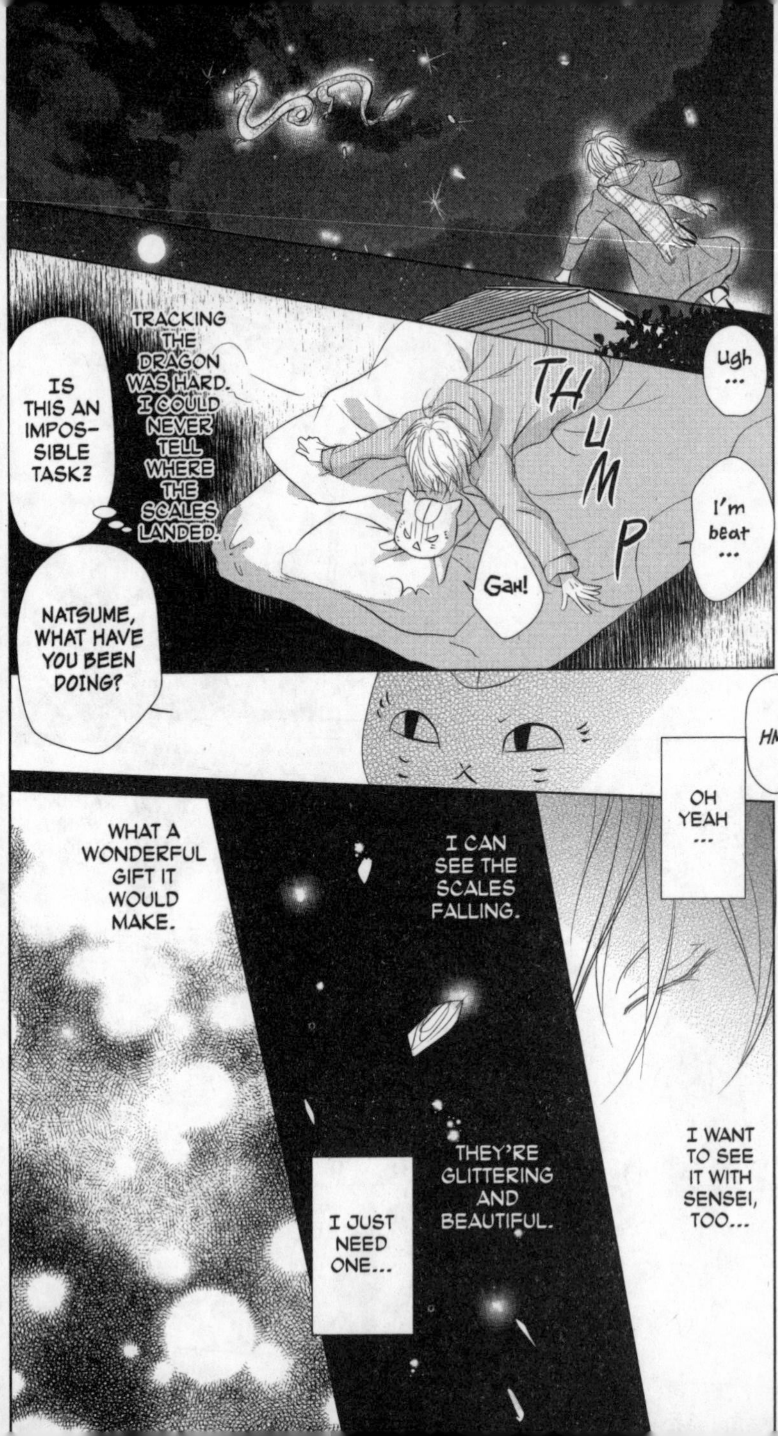

Ugh...
THUMP
I'm beat...
Gah!
TRACKING THE DRAGON WAS HARD. I COULD NEVER TELL WHERE THE SCALES LANDED.
IS THIS AN IMPOSSIBLE TASK?
NATSUME, WHAT HAVE YOU BEEN DOING?
HM?
OH YEAH...
I WANT TO SEE IT WITH SENSEI, TOO...
I CAN SEE THE SCALES FALLING.
THEY'RE GLITTERING AND BEAUTIFUL.
I JUST NEED ONE...
WHAT A WONDERFUL GIFT IT WOULD MAKE.

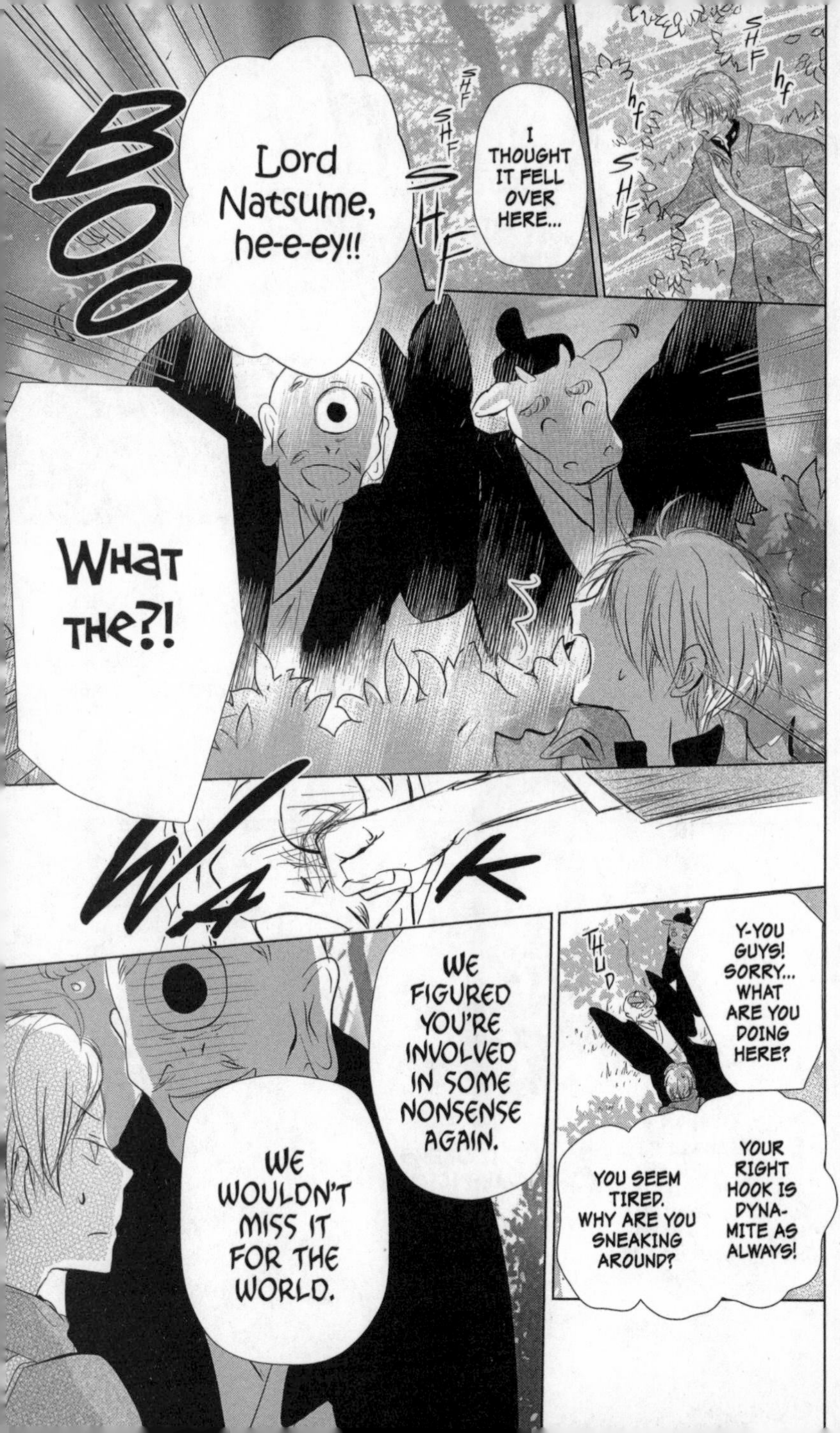
SHF
hf
hf
SHF
SHF
I THOUGHT IT FELL OVER HERE...
SHF
BOO
Lord Natsume, he-e-ey!!
What the?!
WAK
THUD
Y-YOU GUYS! SORRY... WHAT ARE YOU DOING HERE?
YOUR RIGHT HOOK IS DYNA-MITE AS ALWAYS!
YOU SEEM TIRED. WHY ARE YOU SNEAKING AROUND?
WE FIGURED YOU'RE INVOLVED IN SOME NONSENSE AGAIN.
WE WOULDN'T MISS IT FOR THE WORLD.

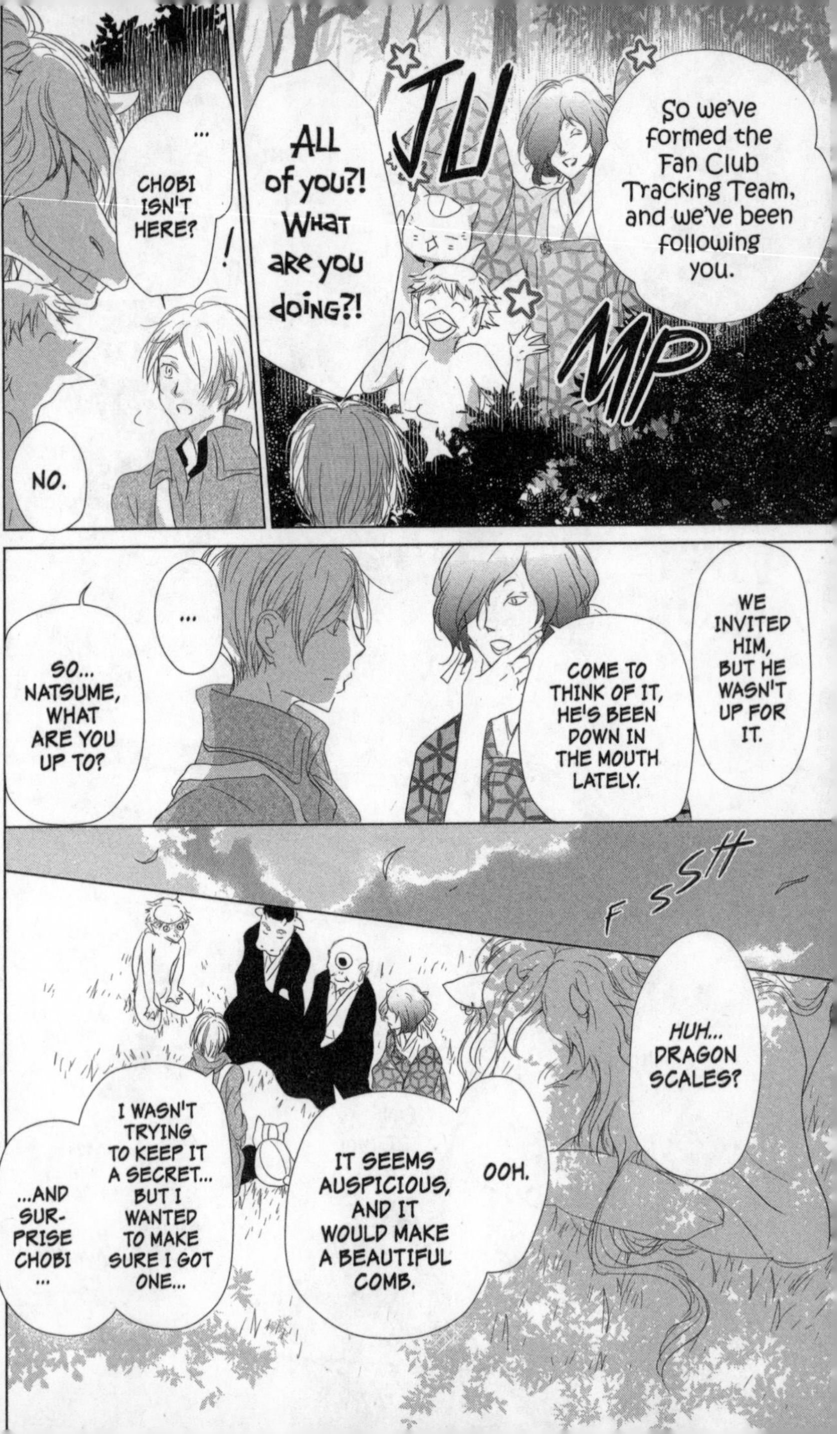
JU MP
All of you?! What are you doing?!
So we've formed the Fan Club Tracking Team, and we've been following you.
...
CHOBI ISN'T HERE?
!
NO.
WE INVITED HIM, BUT HE WASN'T UP FOR IT.
COME TO THINK OF IT, HE'S BEEN DOWN IN THE MOUTH LATELY.
...
SO... NATSUME, WHAT ARE YOU UP TO?
FSSH
HUH... DRAGON SCALES?
OOH.
IT SEEMS AUSPICIOUS, AND IT WOULD MAKE A BEAUTIFUL COMB.
I WASN'T TRYING TO KEEP IT A SECRET... BUT I WANTED TO MAKE SURE I GOT ONE...
...AND SUR-PRISE CHOBI ...

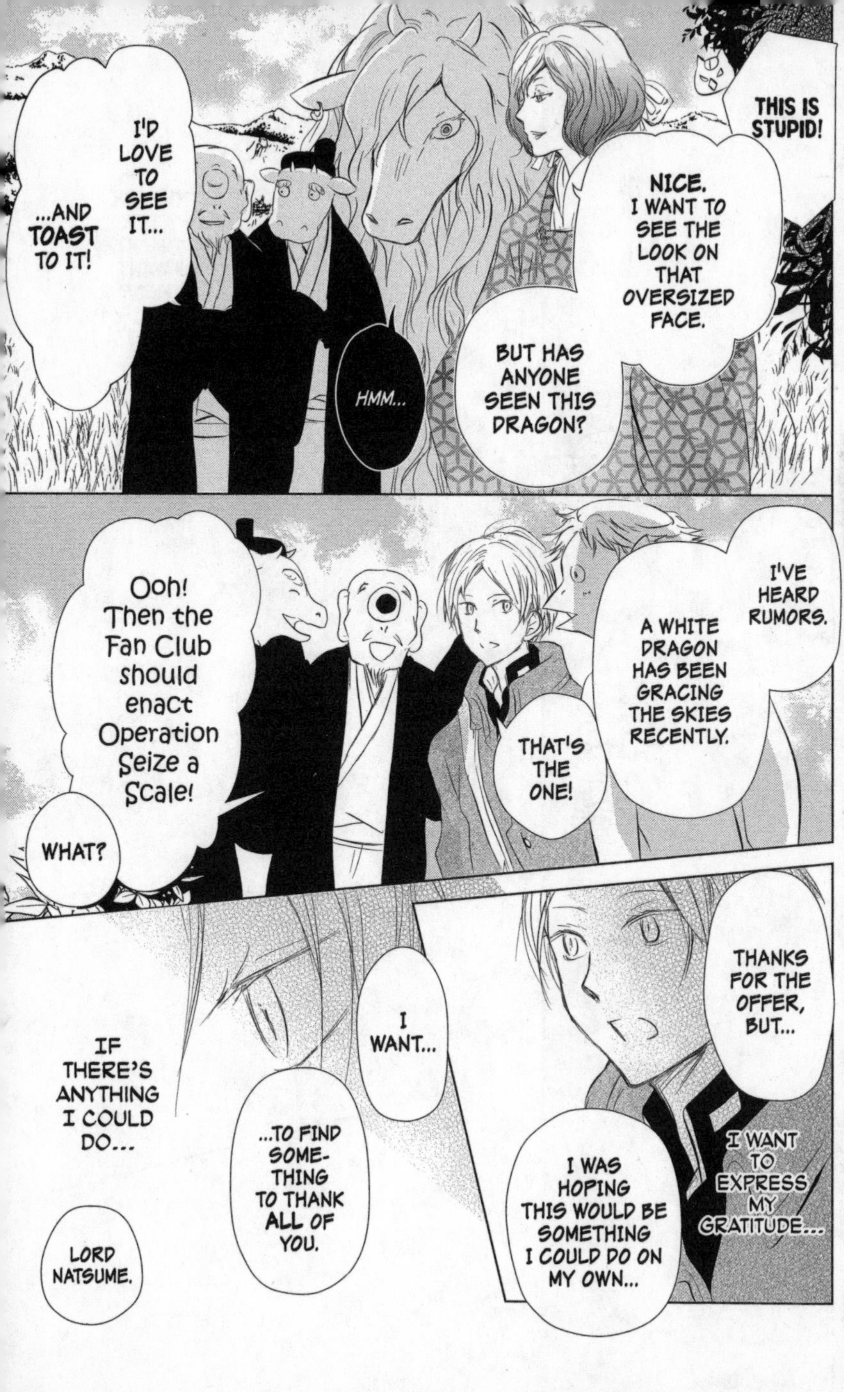
THIS IS STUPID!
NICE. I WANT TO SEE THE LOOK ON THAT OVERSIZED FACE.
I'D LOVE TO SEE IT...
...AND TOAST TO IT!
BUT HAS ANYONE SEEN THIS DRAGON?
HMM...
I'VE HEARD RUMORS.
A WHITE DRAGON HAS BEEN GRACING THE SKIES RECENTLY.
THAT'S THE ONE!
Ooh! Then the Fan Club should enact Operation Seize a Scale!
WHAT?
THANKS FOR THE OFFER, BUT...
I WANT TO EXPRESS MY GRATITUDE...
I WAS HOPING THIS WOULD BE SOMETHING I COULD DO ON MY OWN...
I WANT...
...TO FIND SOME-THING TO THANK ALL OF YOU.
IF THERE'S ANYTHING I COULD DO...
LORD NATSUME.

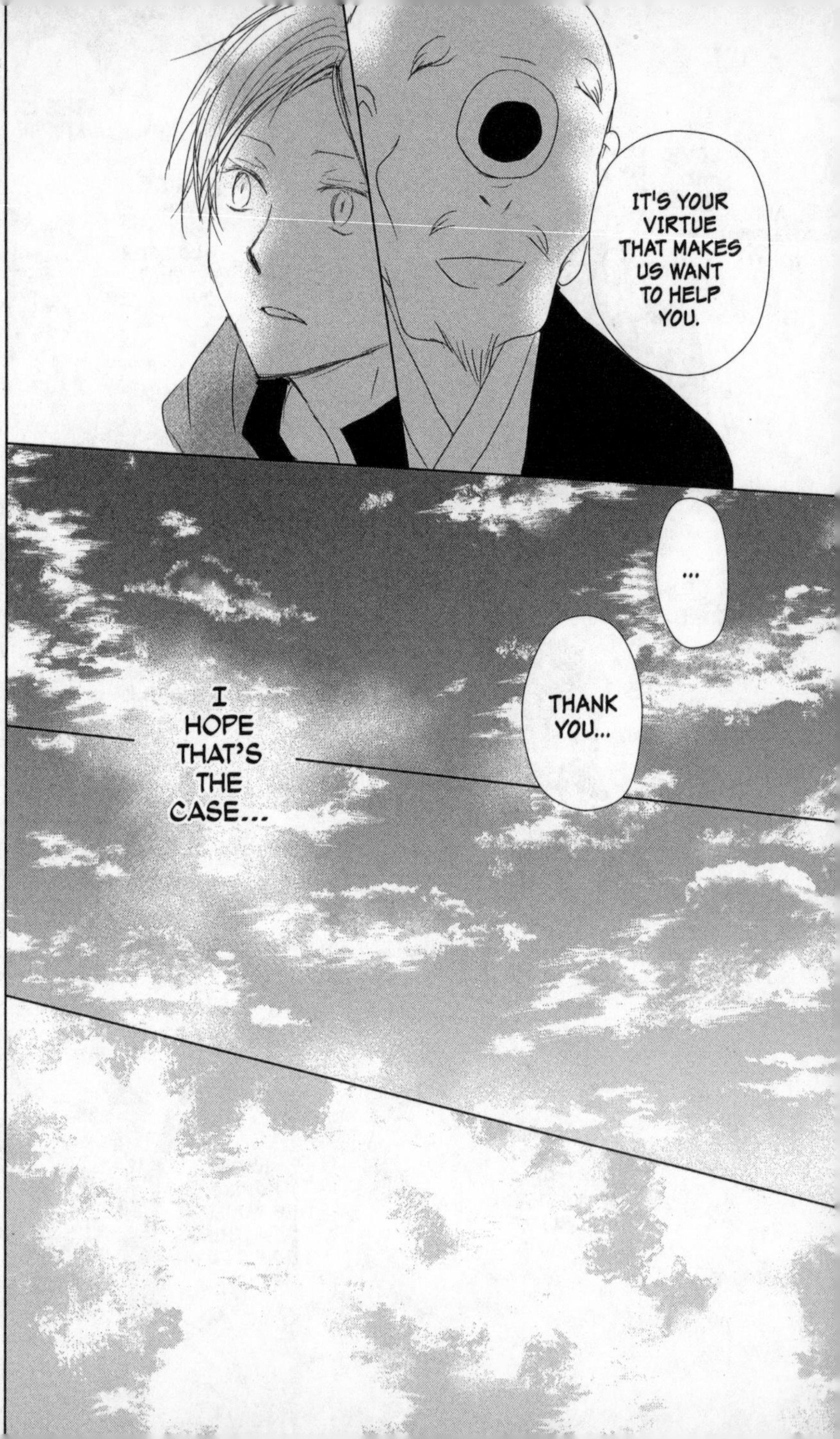
IT'S YOUR VIRTUE THAT MAKES US WANT TO HELP YOU.
...
THANK YOU...
I HOPE THAT'S THE CASE...

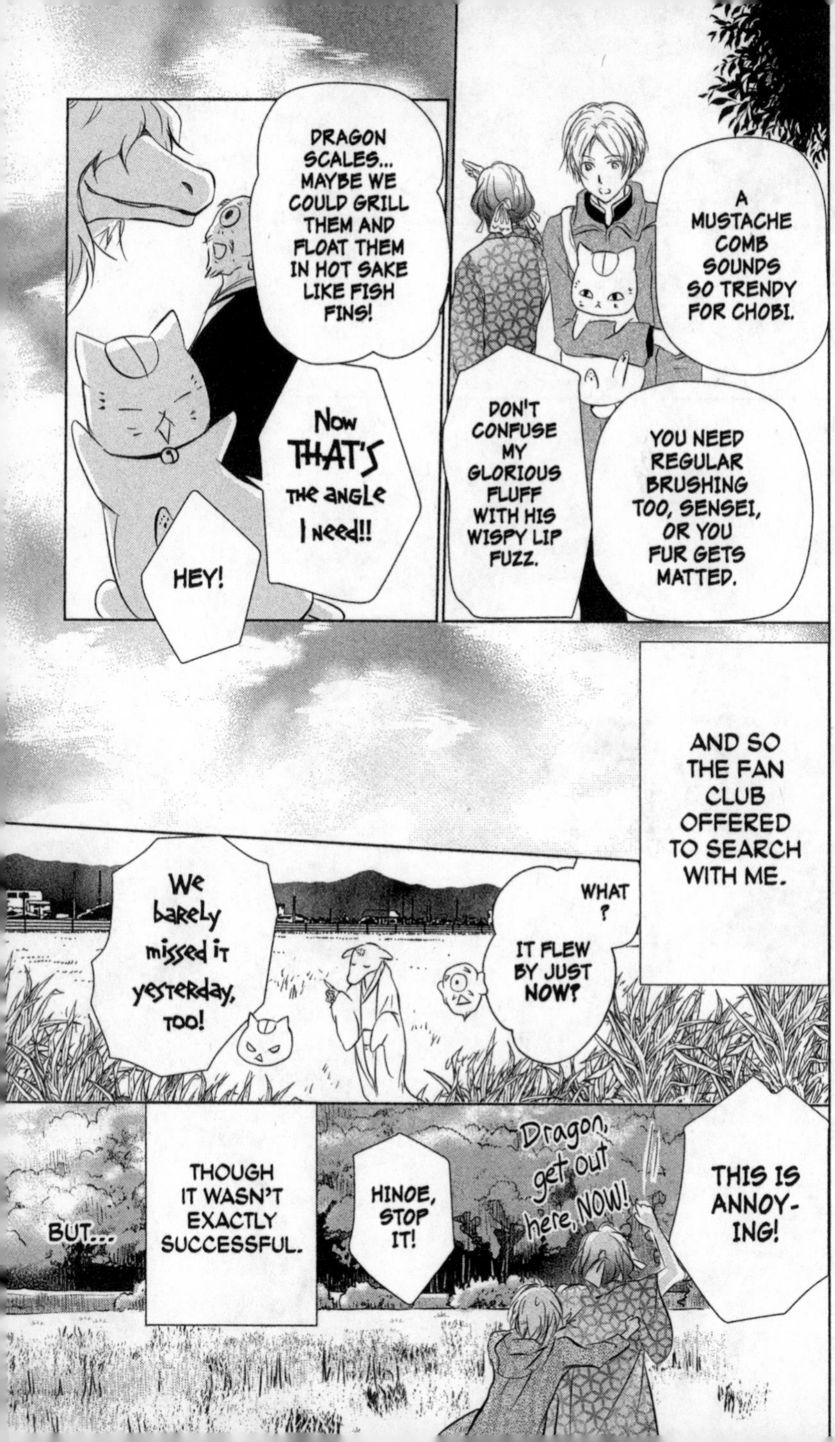
A MUSTACHE COMB SOUNDS SO TRENDY FOR CHOBI.
YOU NEED REGULAR BRUSHING TOO, SENSEI, OR YOU FUR GETS MATTED.
DON'T CONFUSE MY GLORIOUS FLUFF WITH HIS WISPY LIP FUZZ.
DRAGON SCALES... MAYBE WE COULD GRILL THEM AND FLOAT THEM IN HOT SAKE LIKE FISH FINS!
Now THAT'S the angle I need!!
HEY!
AND SO THE FAN CLUB OFFERED TO SEARCH WITH ME.
WHAT?
IT FLEW BY JUST NOW?
We barely missed it yesterday, too!
THIS IS ANNOY-ING!
Dragon, get out here, NOW!
HINOE, STOP IT!
THOUGH IT WASN'T EXACTLY SUCCESSFUL.
BUT...

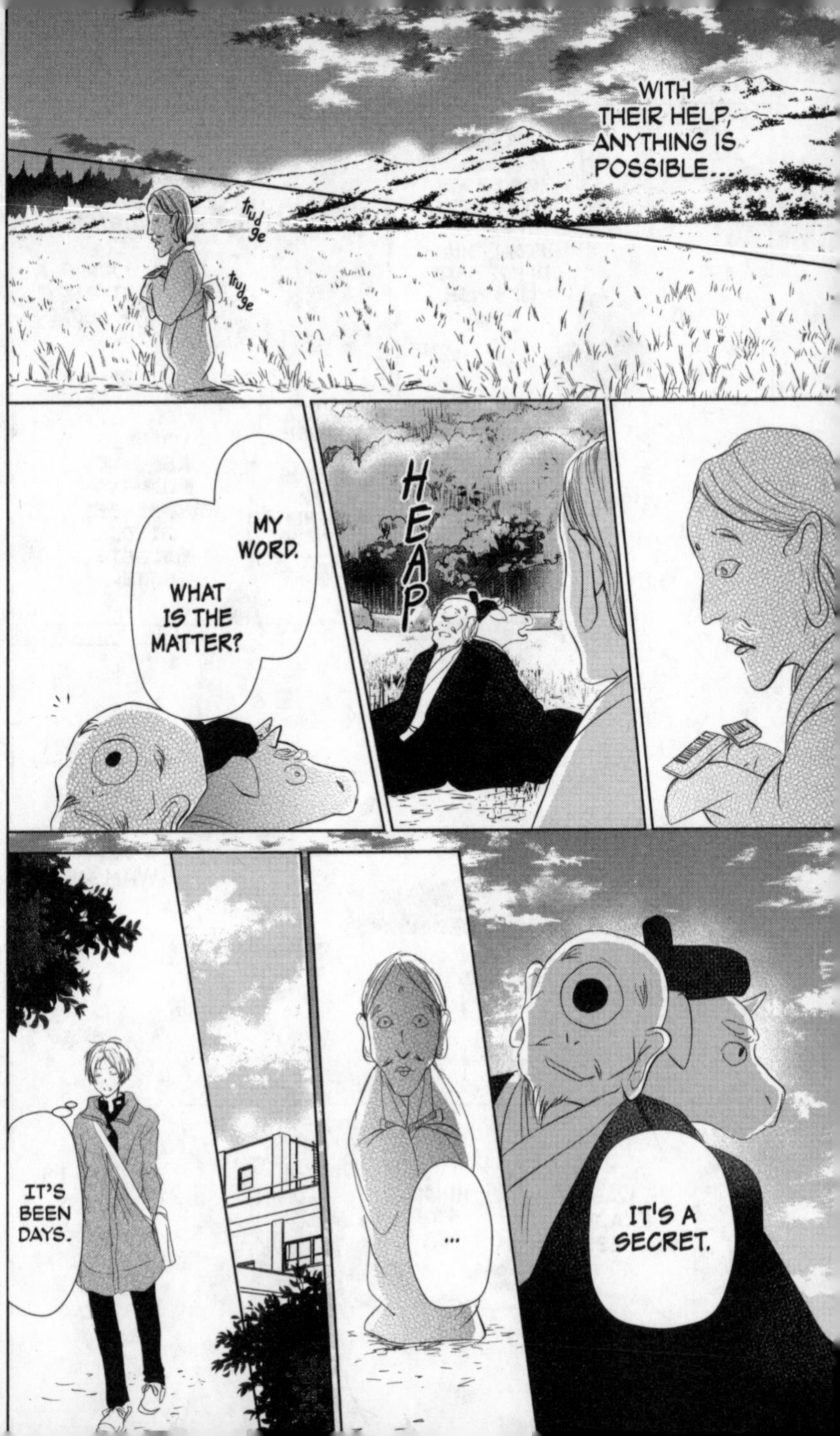
WITH THEIR HELP, ANYTHING IS POSSIBLE...
trudge
trudge
HEAP
MY WORD.
WHAT IS THE MATTER?
IT'S A SECRET.
...
IT'S BEEN DAYS.

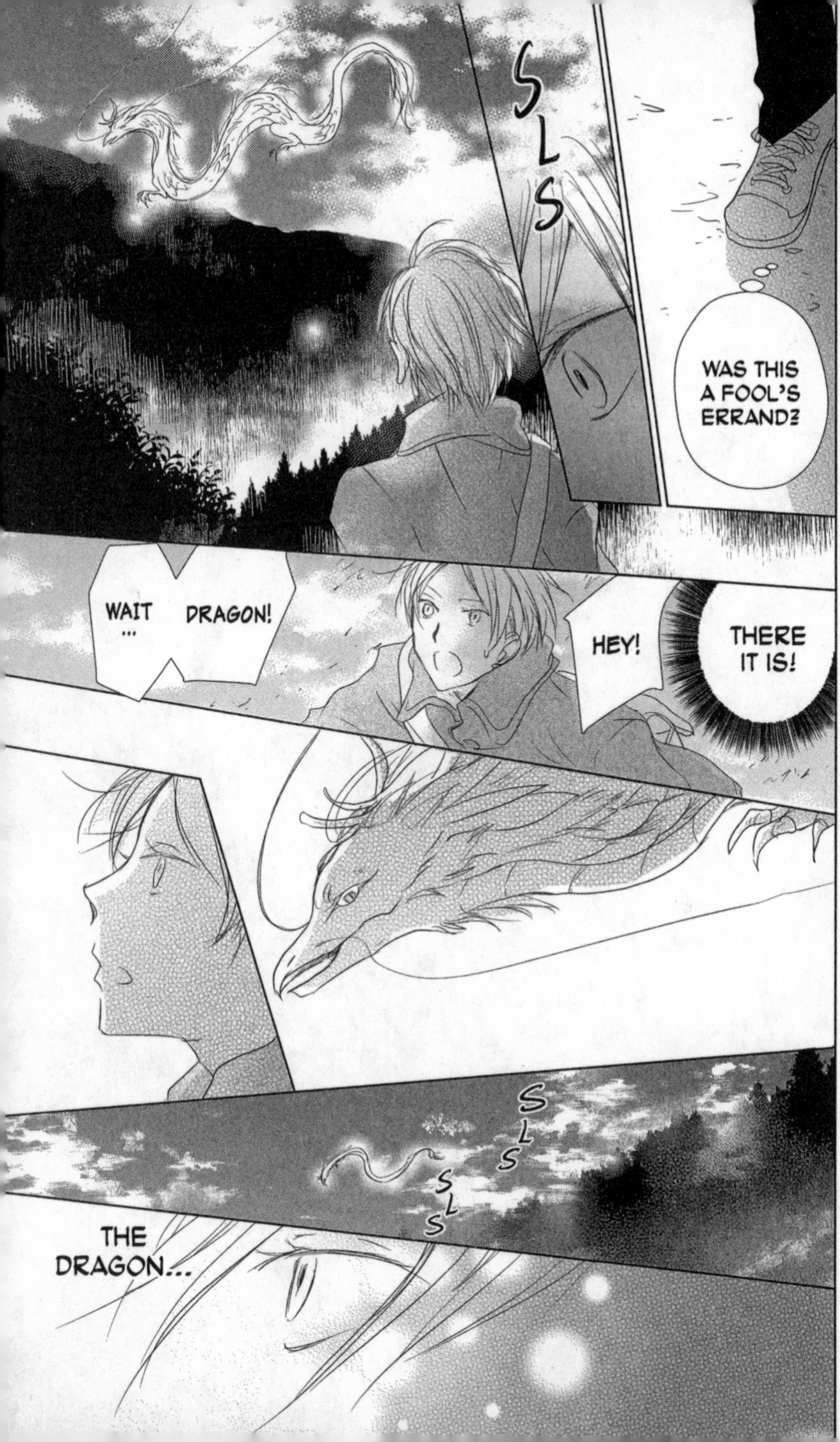
WAS THIS A FOOL'S ERRAND?
SLS
THERE IT IS!
HEY!
WAIT ... DRAGON!
SLS
SLS
THE DRAGON...

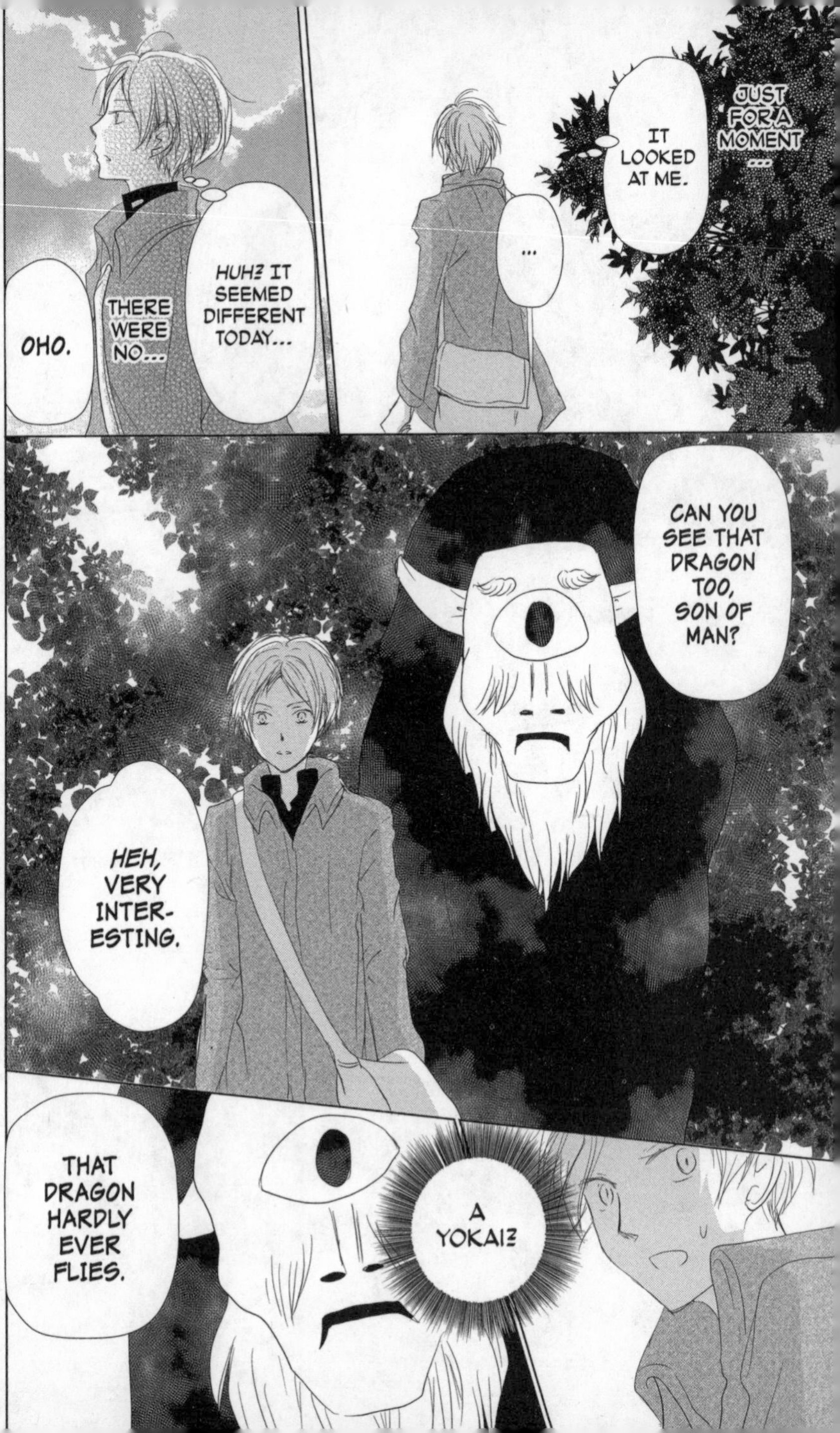
JUST FOR A MOMENT...
IT LOOKED AT ME.
...
HUH? IT SEEMED DIFFERENT TODAY...
THERE WERE NO...
OHO.
CAN YOU SEE THAT DRAGON TOO, SON OF MAN?
HEH, VERY INTER-ESTING.
A YOKAI?
THAT DRAGON HARDLY EVER FLIES.

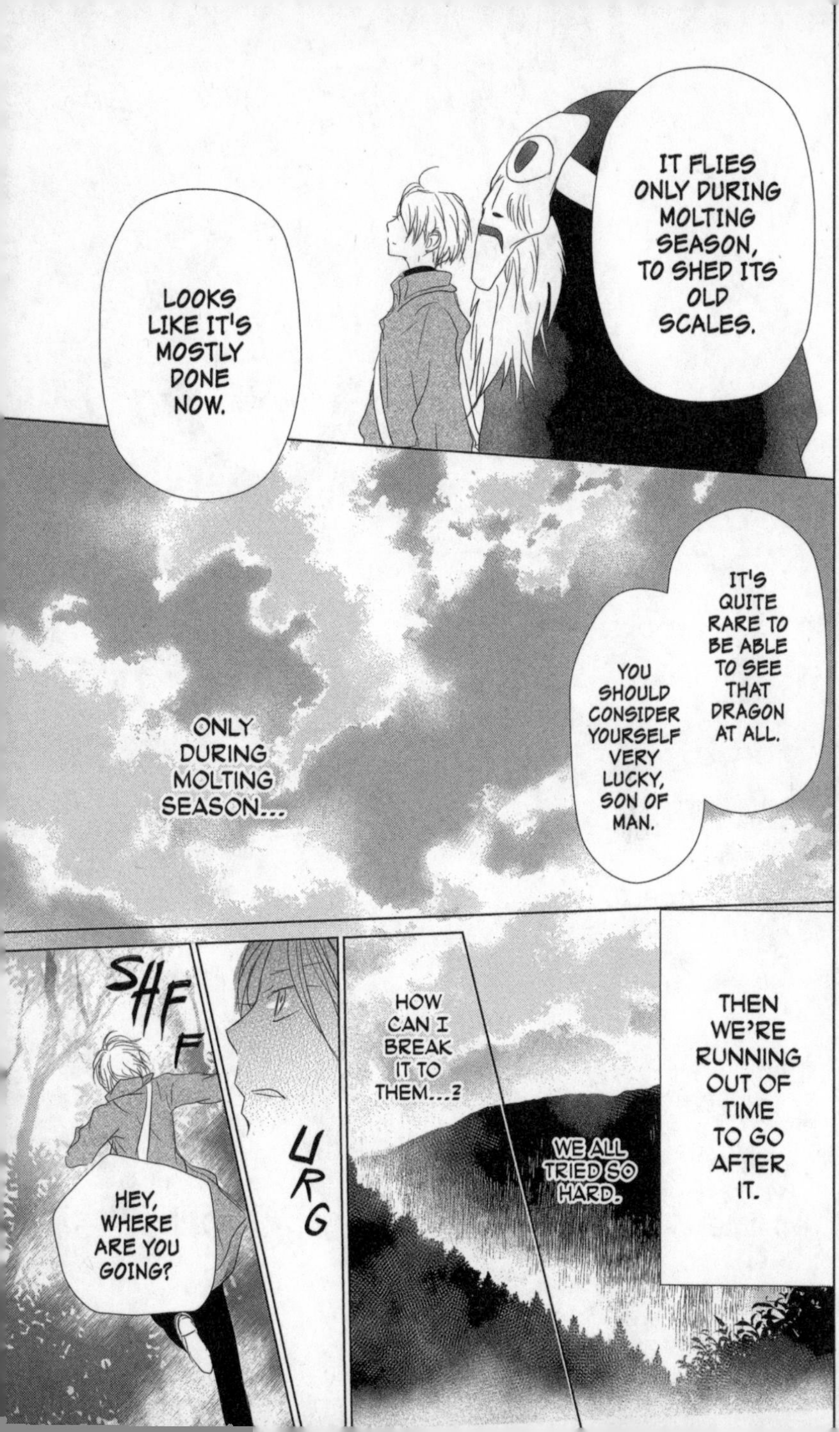
IT FLIES ONLY DURING MOLTING SEASON, TO SHED ITS OLD SCALES.
LOOKS LIKE IT'S MOSTLY DONE NOW.
IT'S QUITE RARE TO BE ABLE TO SEE THAT DRAGON AT ALL.
YOU SHOULD CONSIDER YOURSELF VERY LUCKY, SON OF MAN.
ONLY DURING MOLTING SEASON...
THEN WE'RE RUNNING OUT OF TIME TO GO AFTER IT.
HOW CAN I BREAK IT TO THEM...?
WE ALL TRIED SO HARD.
URG
SHFF
HEY, WHERE ARE YOU GOING?

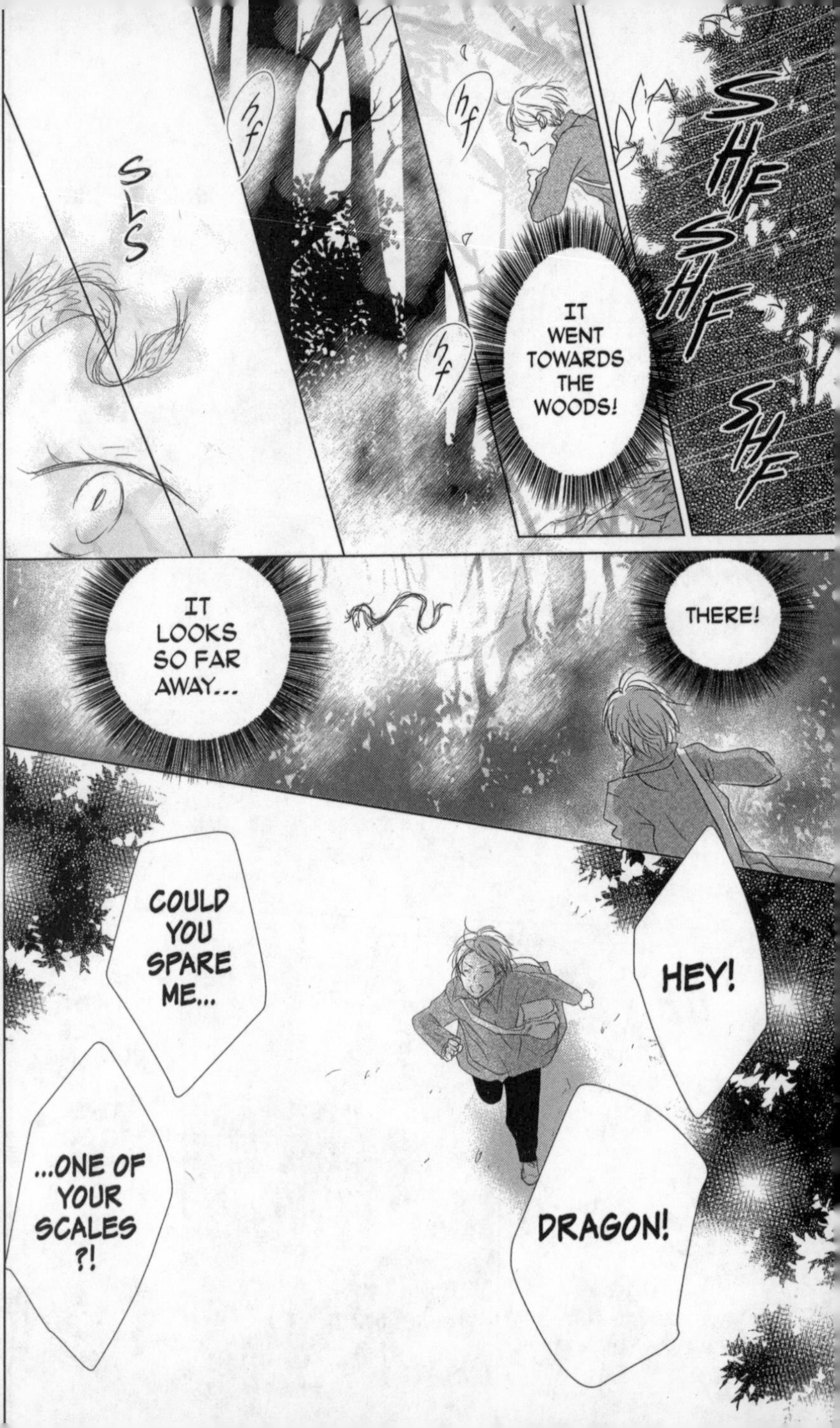
SHF SHF SHF
hf
IT WENT TOWARDS THE WOODS!
hf
hf
SLS
THERE!
IT LOOKS SO FAR AWAY...
HEY!
DRAGON!
COULD YOU SPARE ME...
...ONE OF YOUR SCALES?!

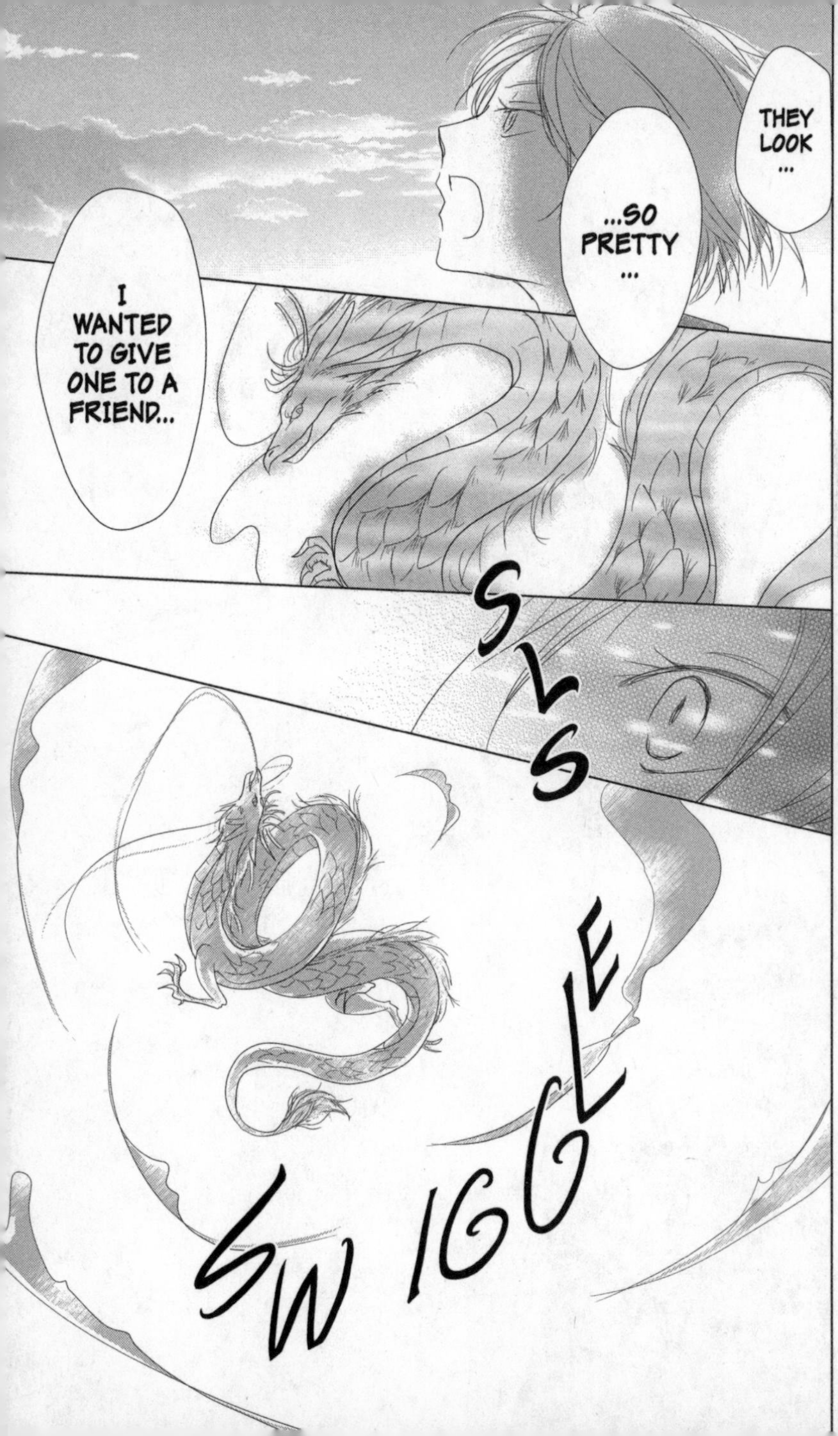
THEY LOOK ...
...SO PRETTY ...
I WANTED TO GIVE ONE TO A FRIEND...
SLSS
SWIGGLE

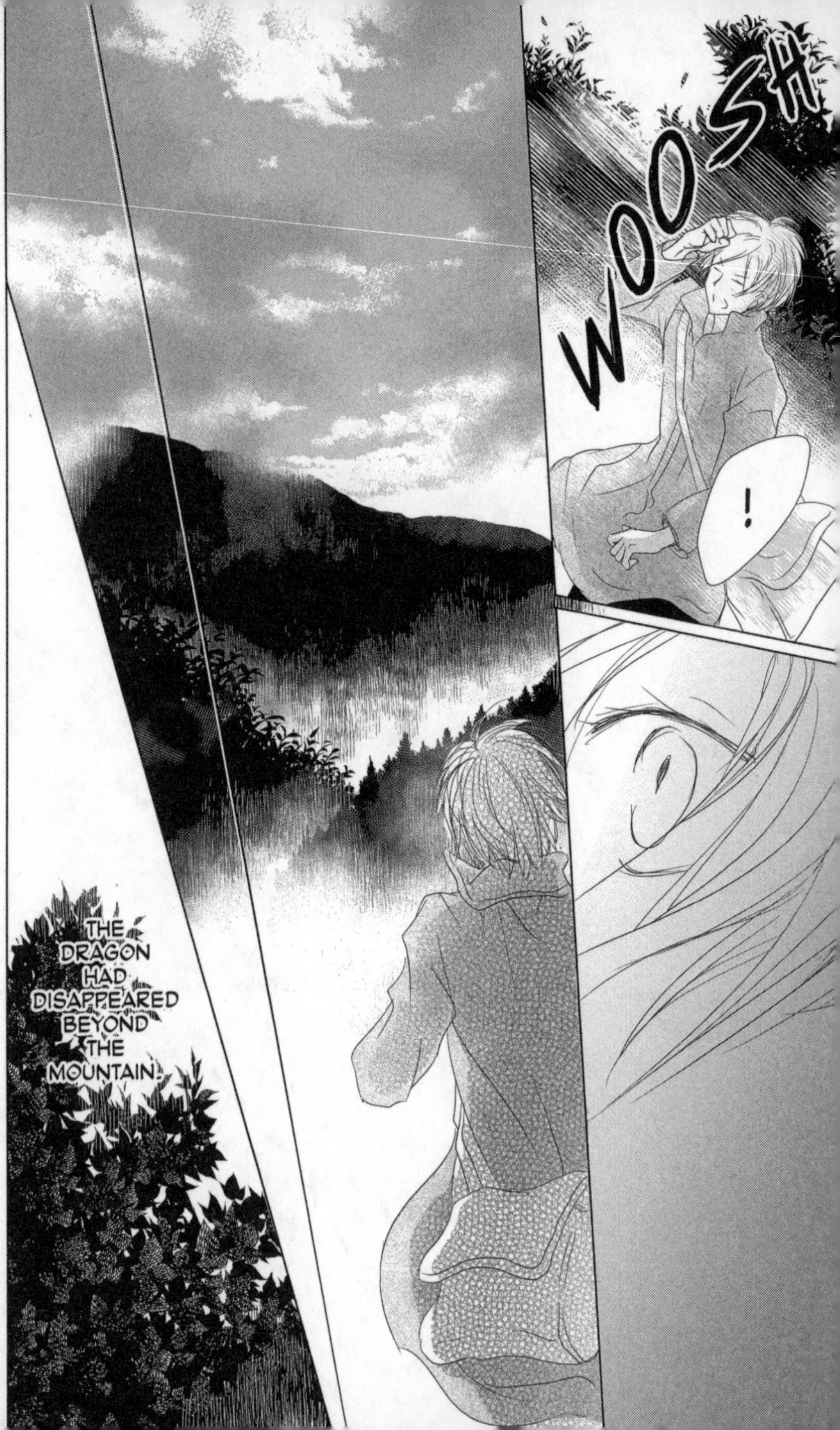
WOOSH
!
THE DRAGON HAD DISAPPEARED BEYOND THE MOUNTAIN.

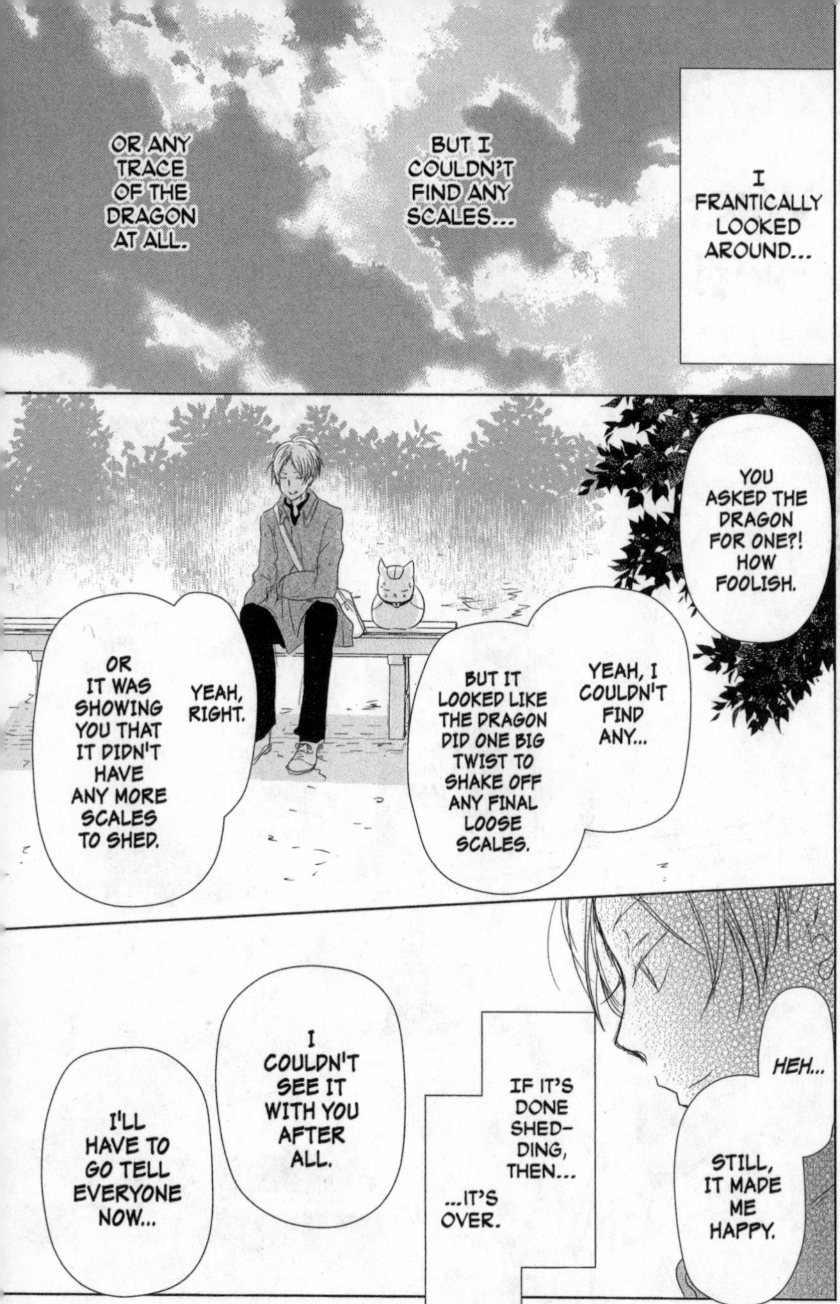
I FRANTICALLY LOOKED AROUND...
BUT I COULDN'T FIND ANY SCALES...
OR ANY TRACE OF THE DRAGON AT ALL.
YOU ASKED THE DRAGON FOR ONE?! HOW FOOLISH.
YEAH, I COULDN'T FIND ANY...
BUT IT LOOKED LIKE THE DRAGON DID ONE BIG TWIST TO SHAKE OFF ANY FINAL LOOSE SCALES.
YEAH, RIGHT.
OR IT WAS SHOWING YOU THAT IT DIDN'T HAVE ANY MORE SCALES TO SHED.
HEH...
STILL, IT MADE ME HAPPY.
IF IT'S DONE SHEDDING, THEN...
...IT'S OVER.
I COULDN'T SEE IT WITH YOU AFTER ALL.
I'LL HAVE TO GO TELL EVERYONE NOW...

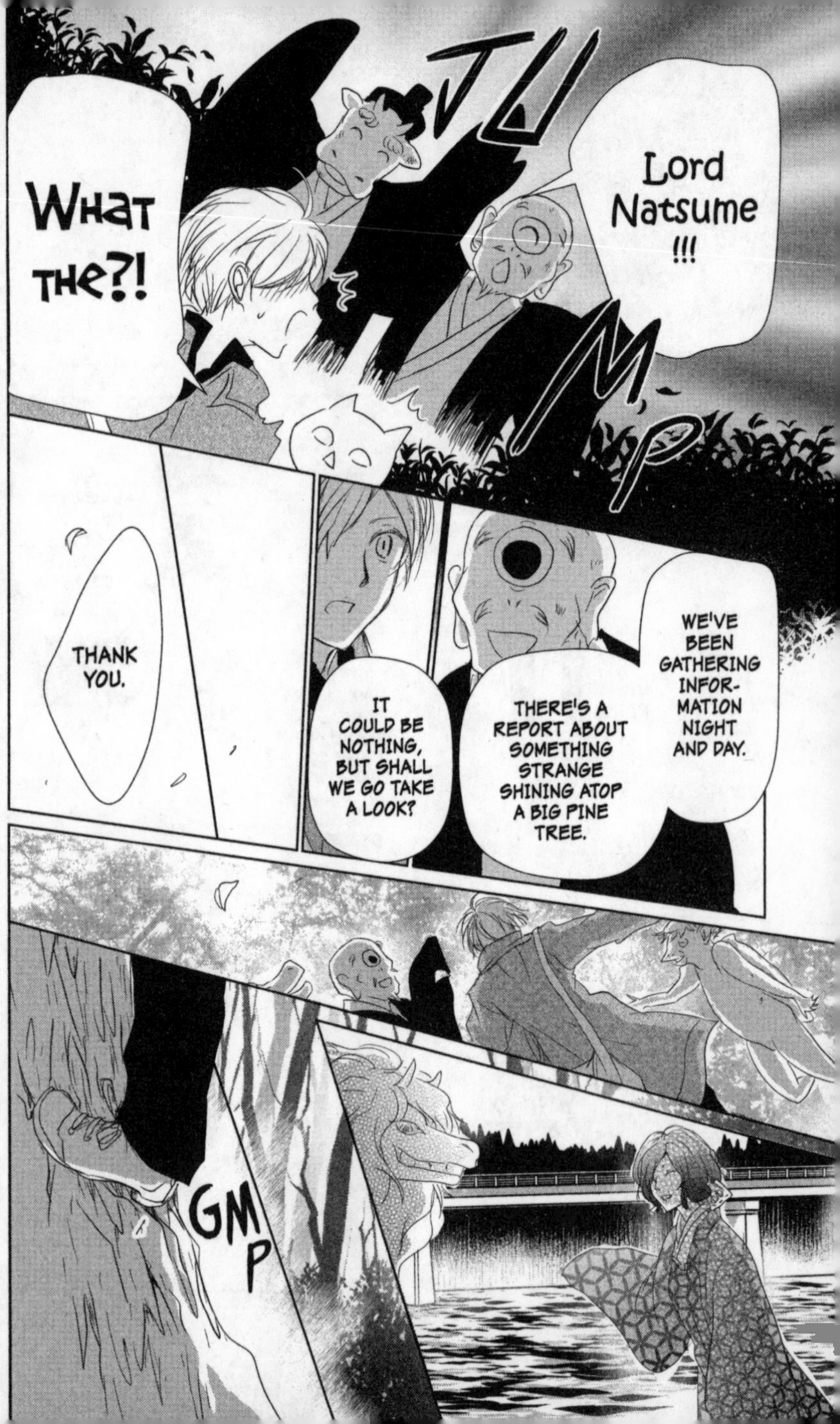
Lord Natsume !!!
JUMP
What the?!
We've been gathering information night and day.
There's a report about something strange shining atop a big pine tree.
It could be nothing, but shall we go take a look?
Thank you.
GMP

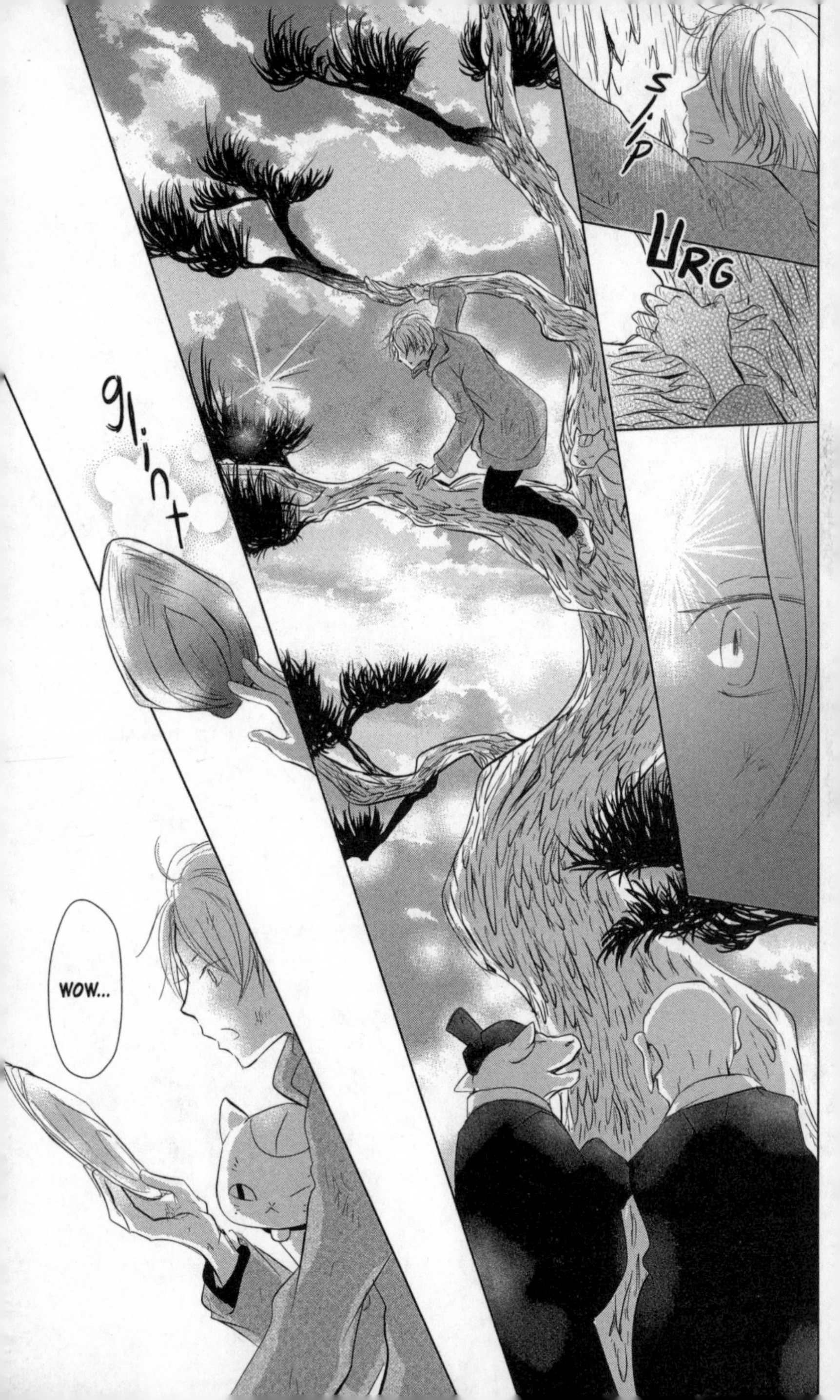
SLIP
URG
glint
WOW...

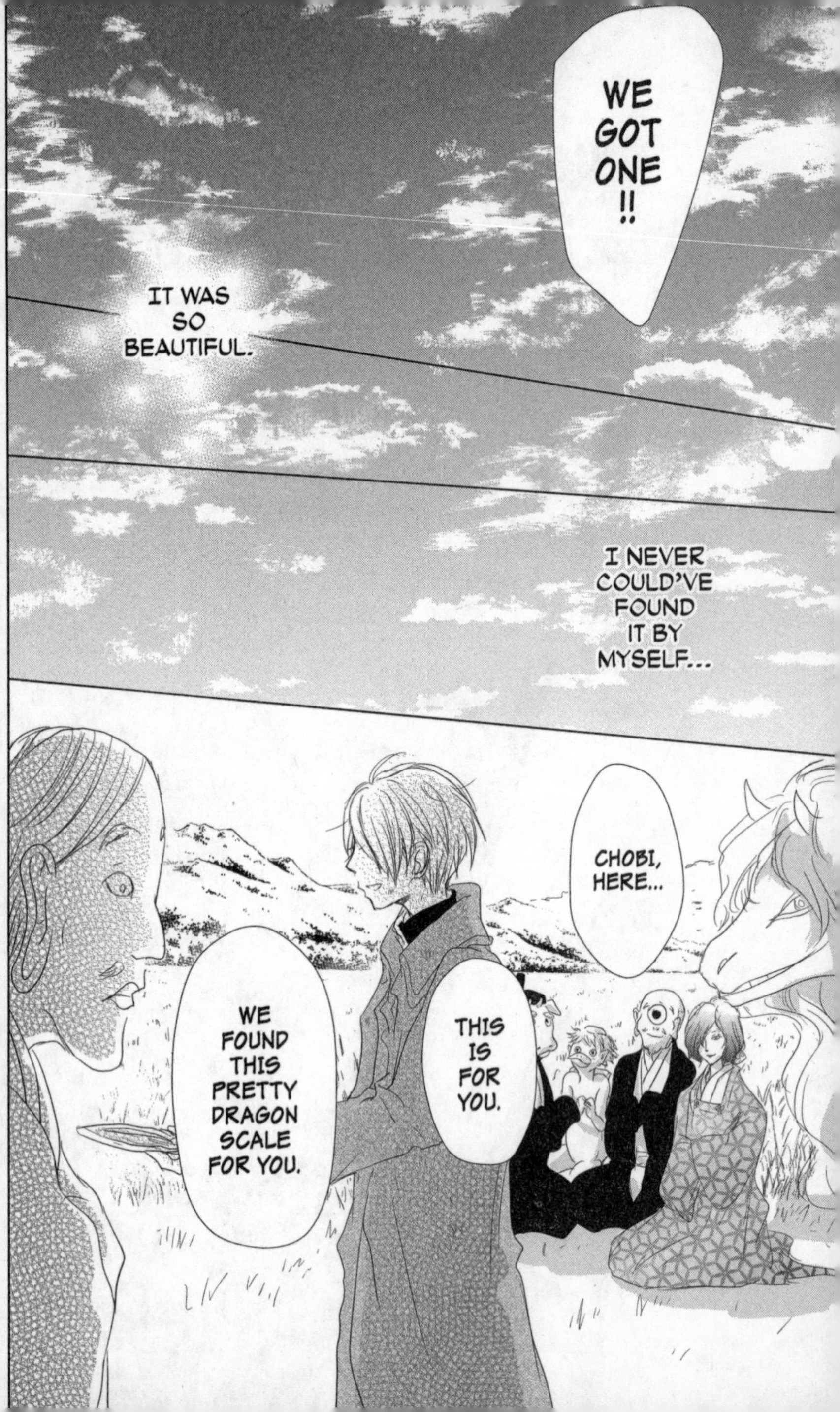
WE GOT ONE!!
IT WAS SO BEAUTIFUL.
I NEVER COULD'VE FOUND IT BY MYSELF...
CHOBI, HERE...
THIS IS FOR YOU.
WE FOUND THIS PRETTY DRAGON SCALE FOR YOU.

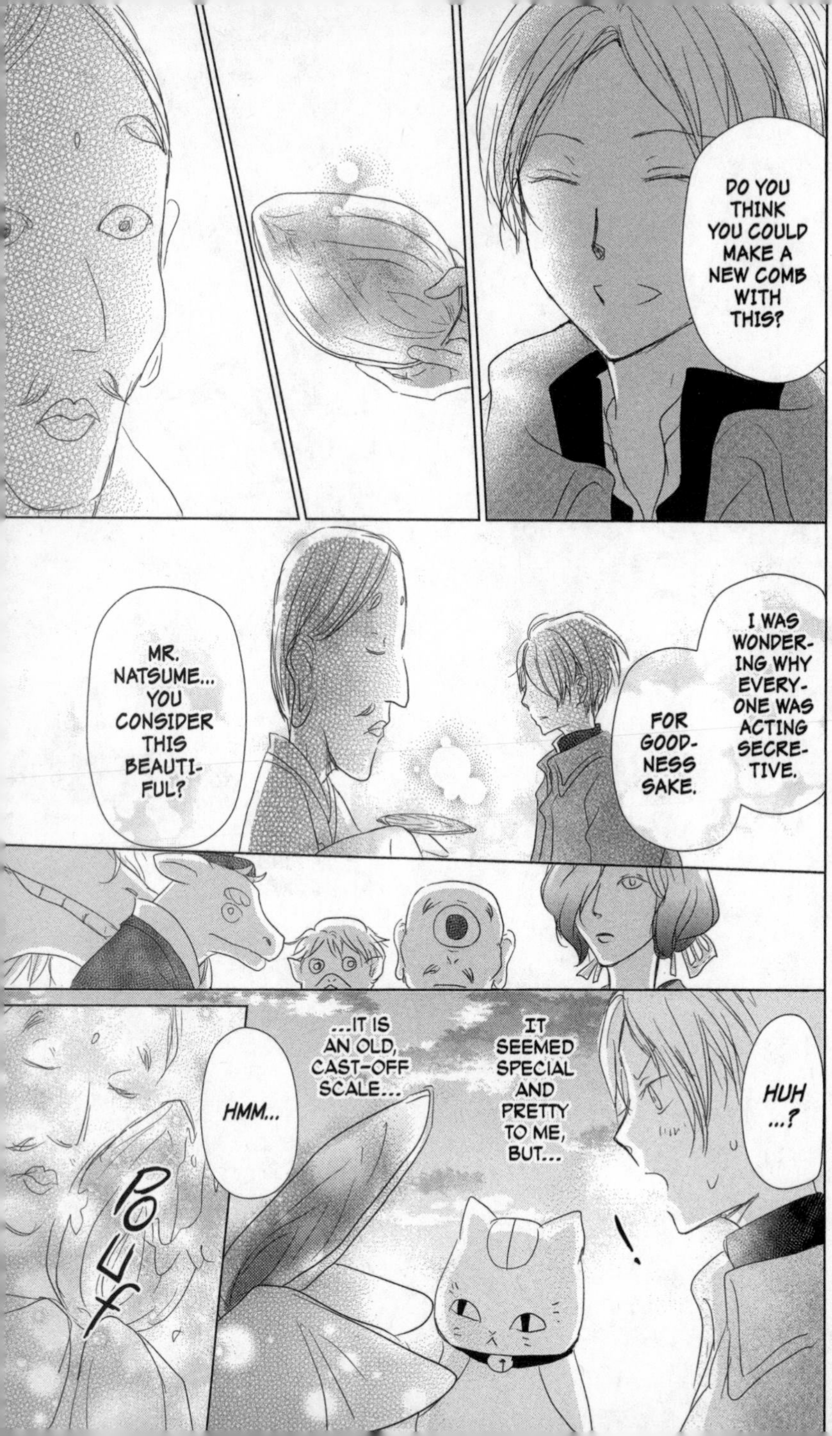
DO YOU THINK YOU COULD MAKE A NEW COMB WITH THIS?
I WAS WONDERING WHY EVERYONE WAS ACTING SECRETIVE.
FOR GOODNESS SAKE.
MR. NATSUME... YOU CONSIDER THIS BEAUTIFUL?
HUH ...?
IT SEEMED SPECIAL AND PRETTY TO ME, BUT...
...IT IS AN OLD, CAST-OFF SCALE...
HMM...
POUF

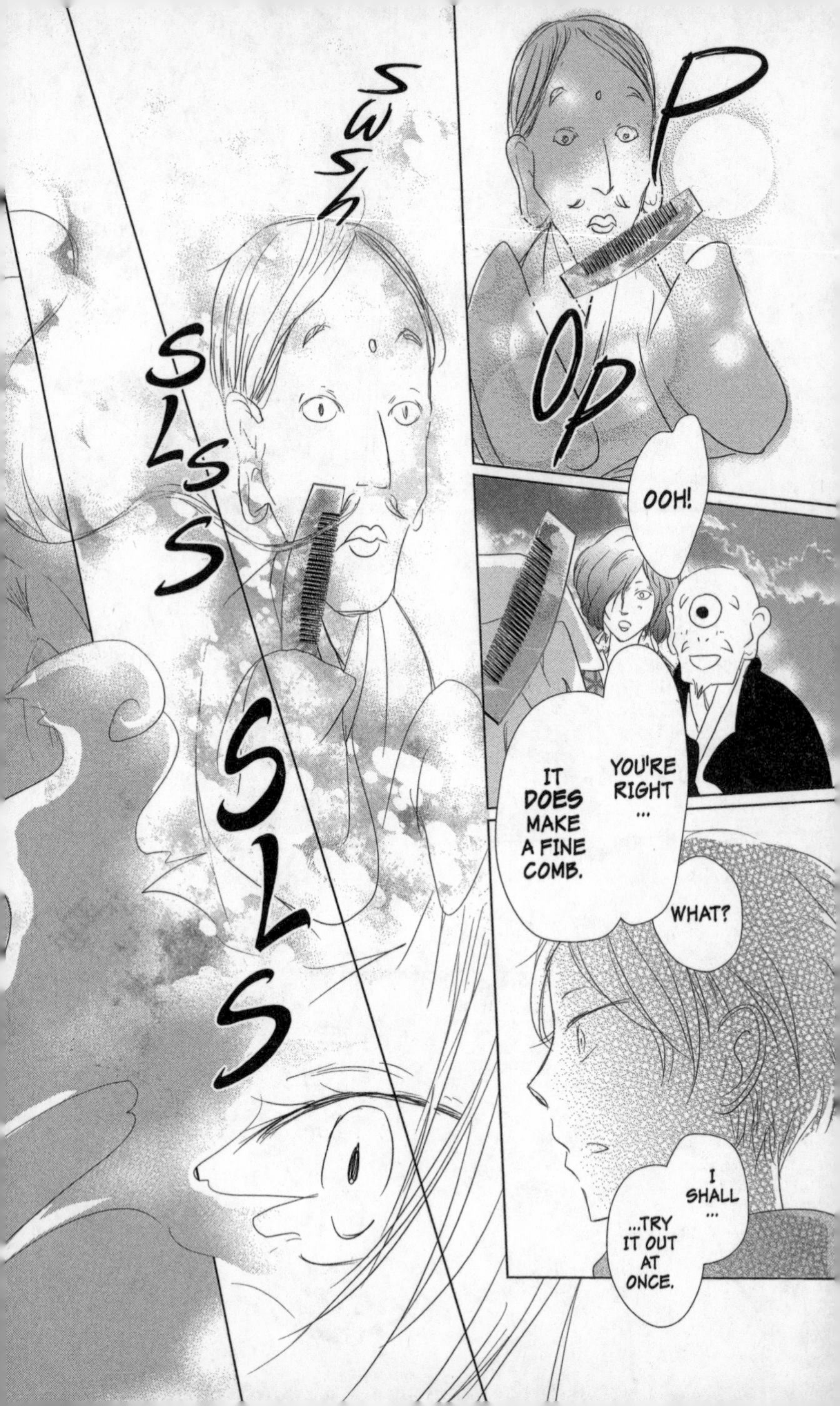
POP
OOH!
YOU'RE RIGHT ...
IT DOES MAKE A FINE COMB.
WHAT?
I SHALL ...
...TRY IT OUT AT ONCE.
SWSH
SLSS
SLS

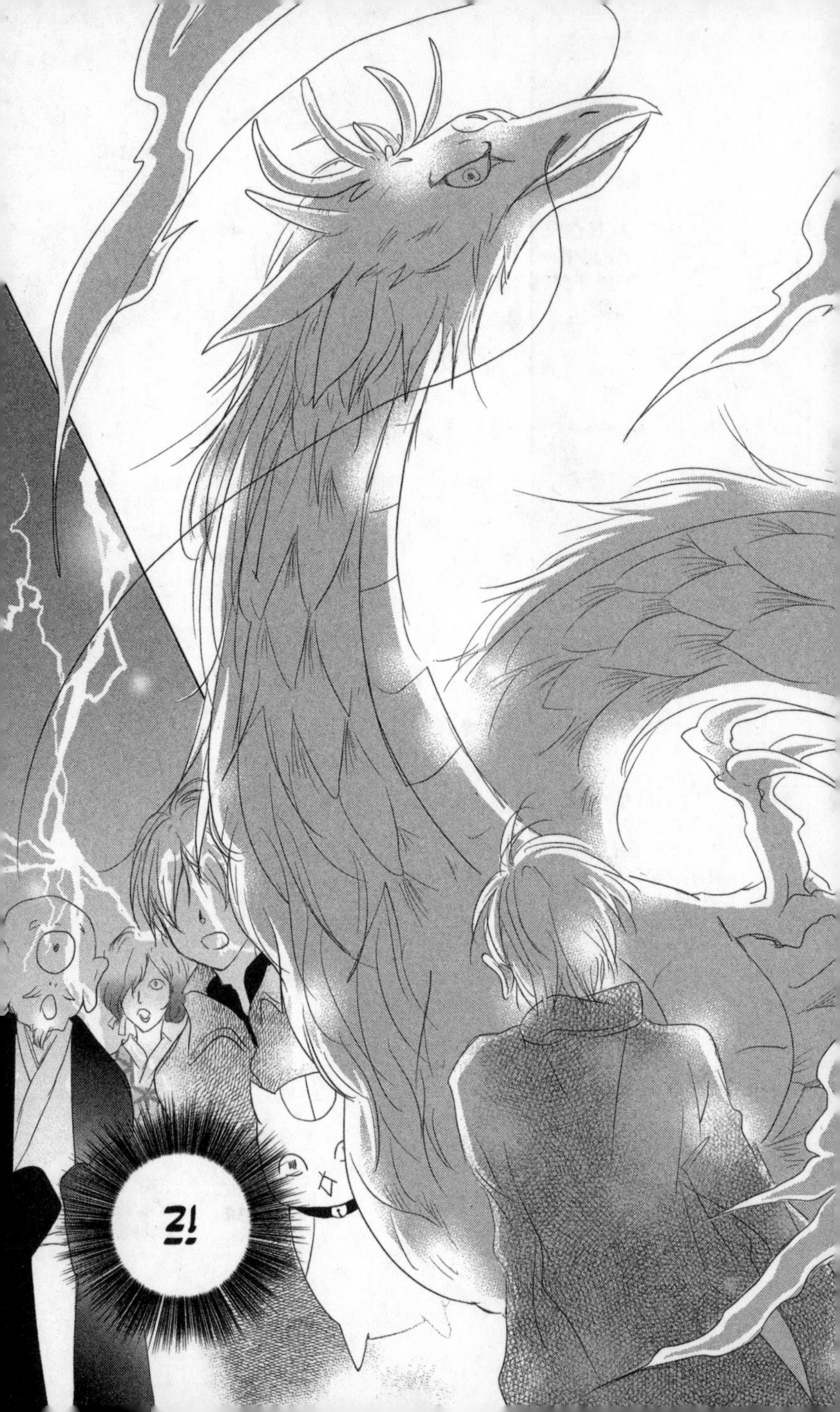
!?

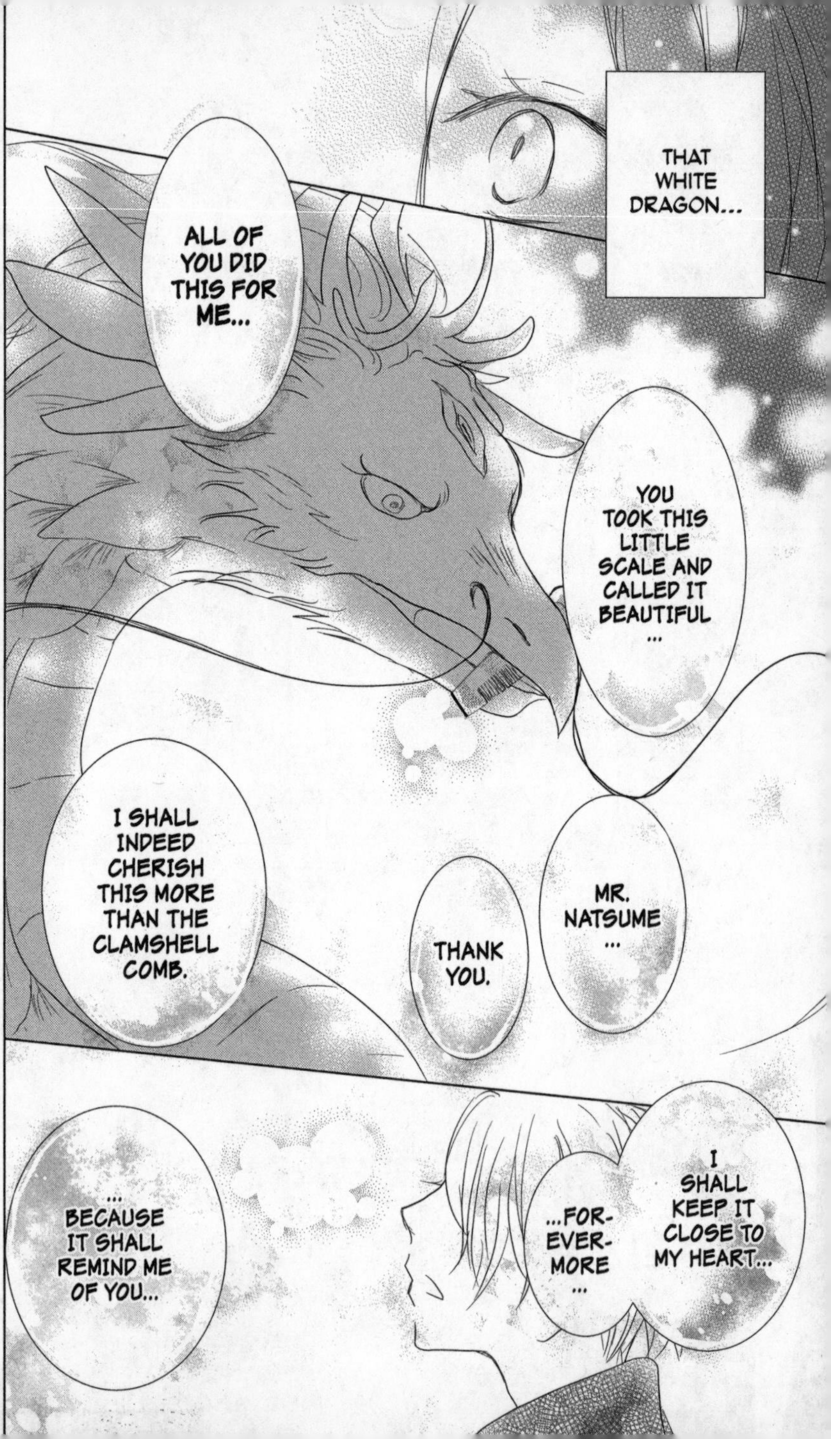
THAT WHITE DRAGON...
ALL OF YOU DID THIS FOR ME...
YOU TOOK THIS LITTLE SCALE AND CALLED IT BEAUTIFUL...
MR. NATSUME...
THANK YOU.
I SHALL INDEED CHERISH THIS MORE THAN THE CLAMSHELL COMB.
I SHALL KEEP IT CLOSE TO MY HEART...
...FOR-EVER-MORE...
...BECAUSE IT SHALL REMIND ME OF YOU...

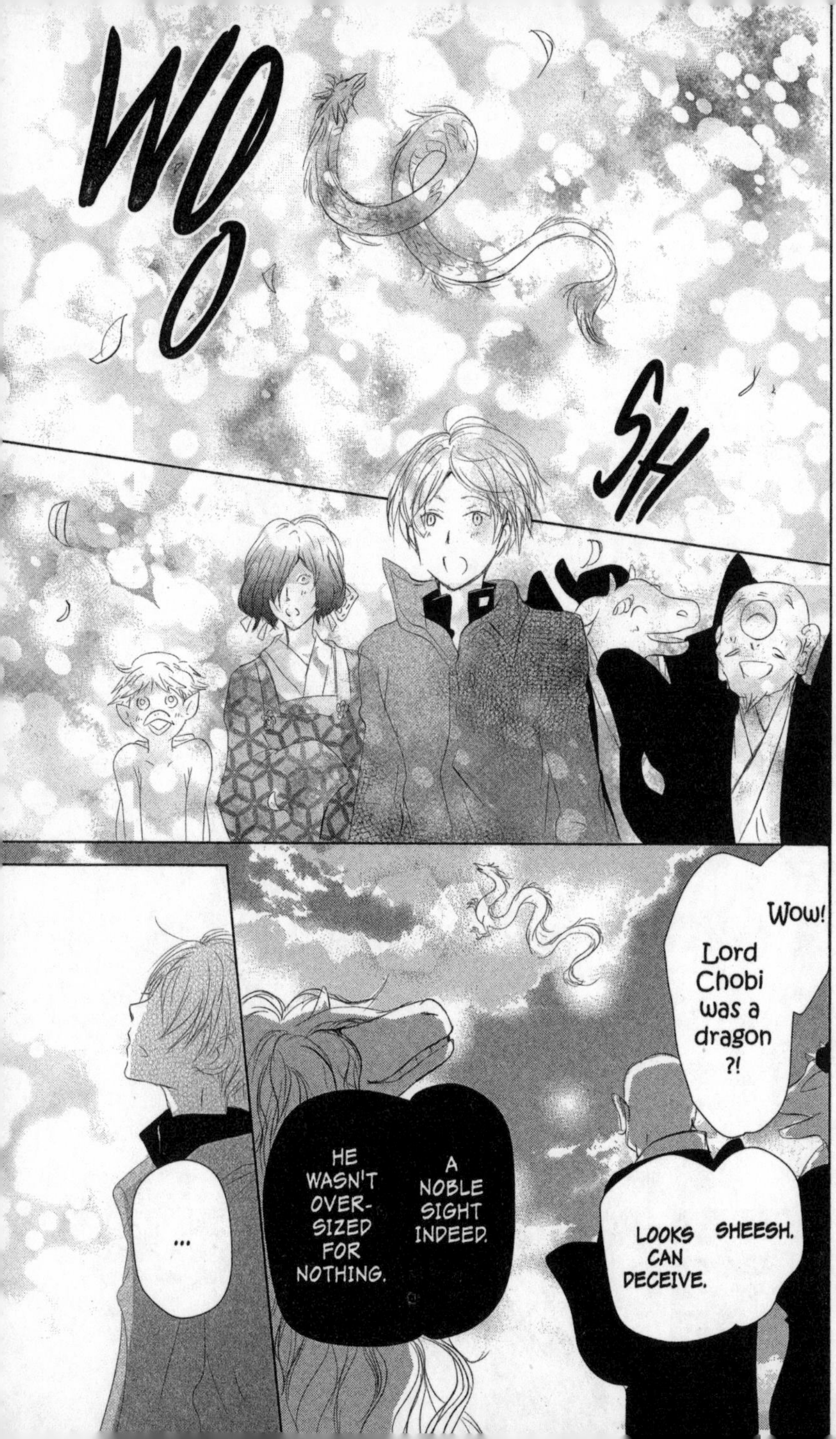
WOOSH
Wow!
Lord Chobi was a dragon?!
SHEESH.
LOOKS CAN DECEIVE.
A NOBLE SIGHT INDEED.
HE WASN'T OVER-SIZED FOR NOTHING.
...

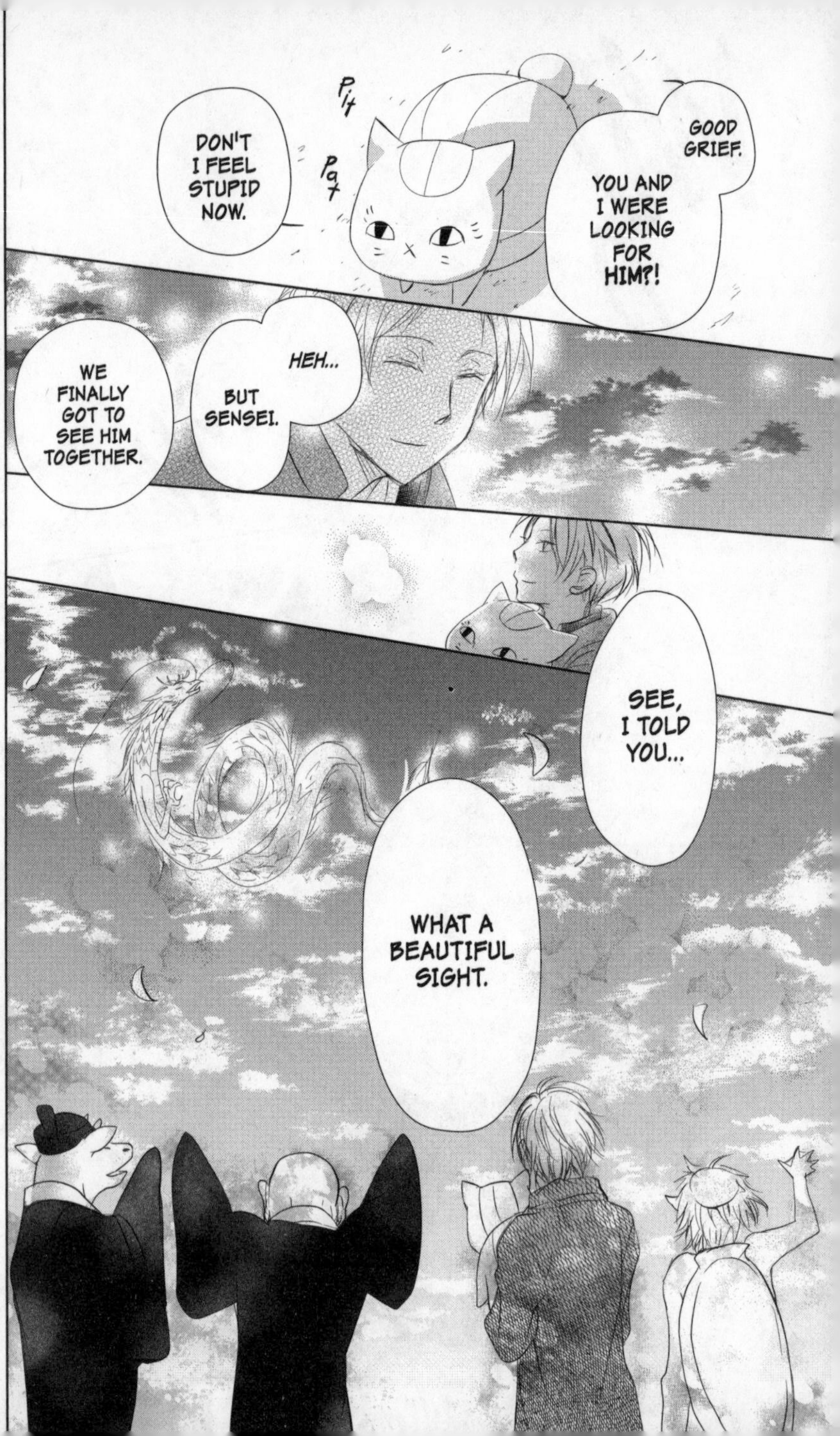
GOOD GRIEF.
YOU AND I WERE LOOKING FOR HIM?!
Pit
Pat
DON'T I FEEL STUPID NOW.
HEH...
BUT SENSEI.
WE FINALLY GOT TO SEE HIM TOGETHER.
SEE, I TOLD YOU...
WHAT A BEAUTIFUL SIGHT.

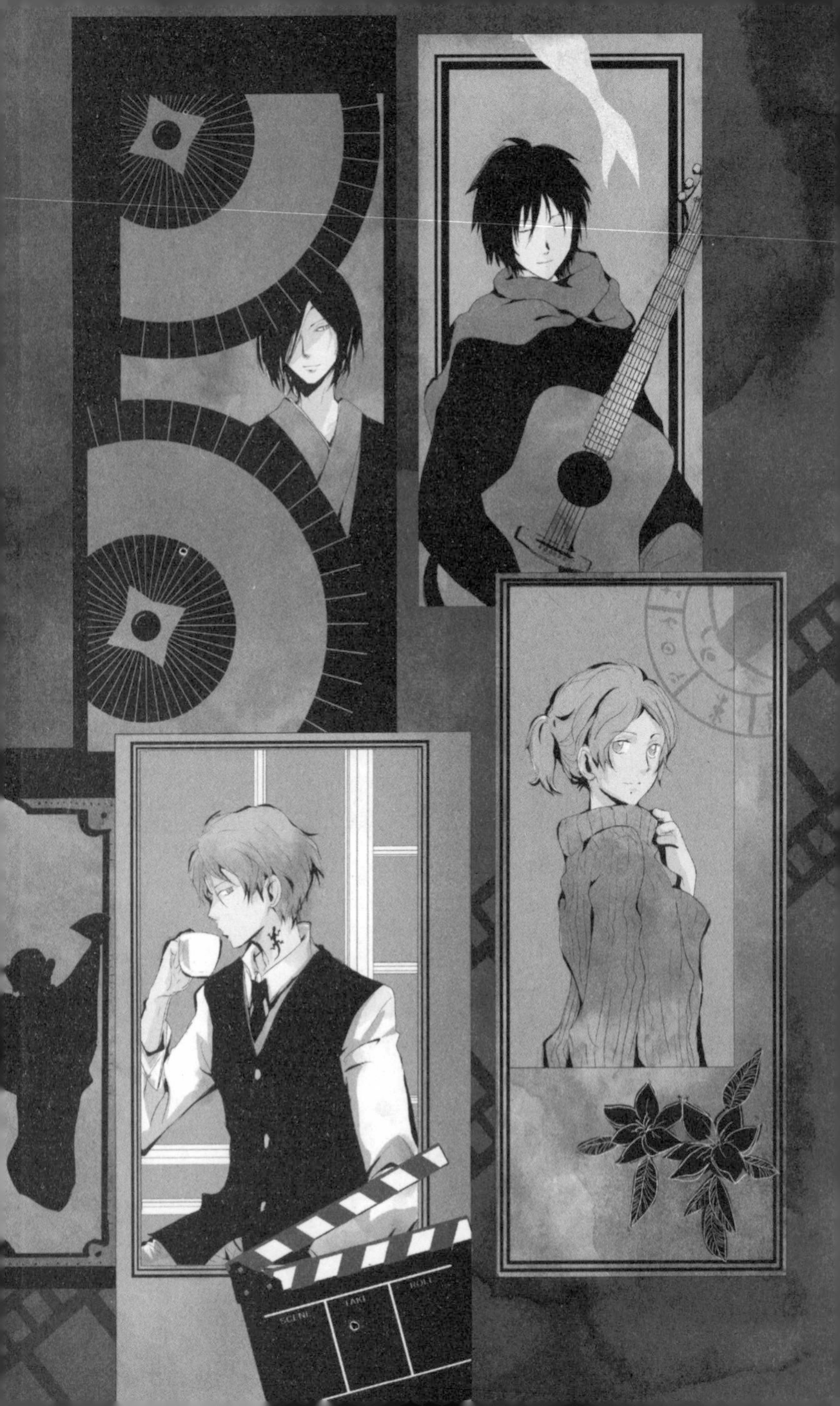
SCENE
TAKE
ROLL

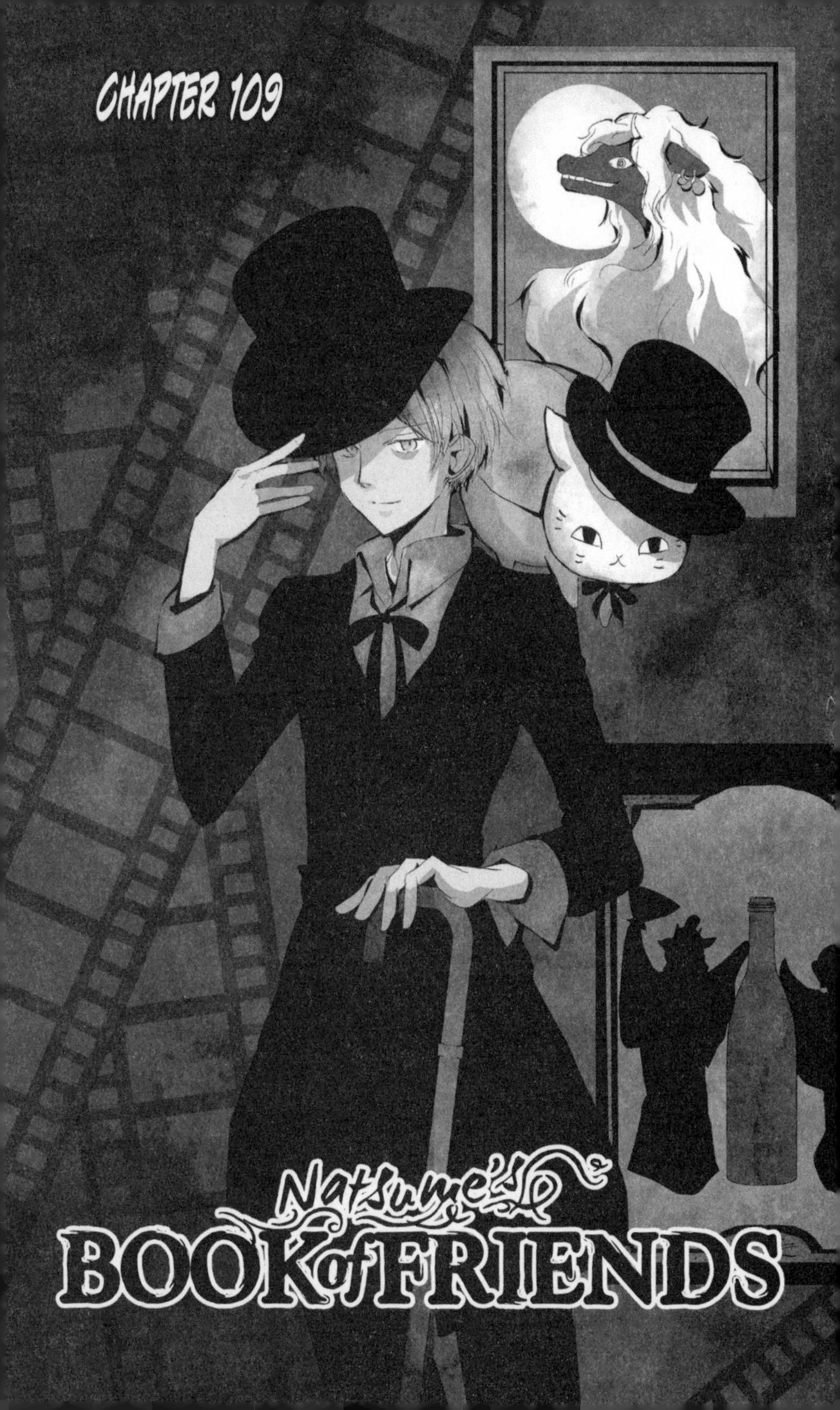
CHAPTER 109
Natsume's
BOOK of FRIENDS

The town of Hitoyoshi and the village of Kuma in Kumamoto Prefecture were picked as inspirations for the town where Natsume lives, and the locations were filmed as reference for the anime *Natsume's Book of Friends*. Unfortunately, they were devastated by a flood in July 2020. Director Ohmori and the *Natsume's Book of Friends* production committee, the anime company Shuka Inc., the voice actors, and Hakusensha Publishing collaborated with Kumamoto Prefecture and produced a short PR video called "Fun Times in Hitoyoshi and Kuma" to help raise funds for the relief effort.

Natsume and Nyanko Sensei travel through beautiful and nostalgic locations (before the flood damage). It's a two-minute, 43-second love letter to an area hopeful for reconstruction, and you can search for it on YouTube.

All the sights are so familiar to me. I hope seeing Natsume and Nyanko Sensei frolic in the lush and colorful landscape makes you want to go visit one day. Thank you so much for such a wonderful anime.

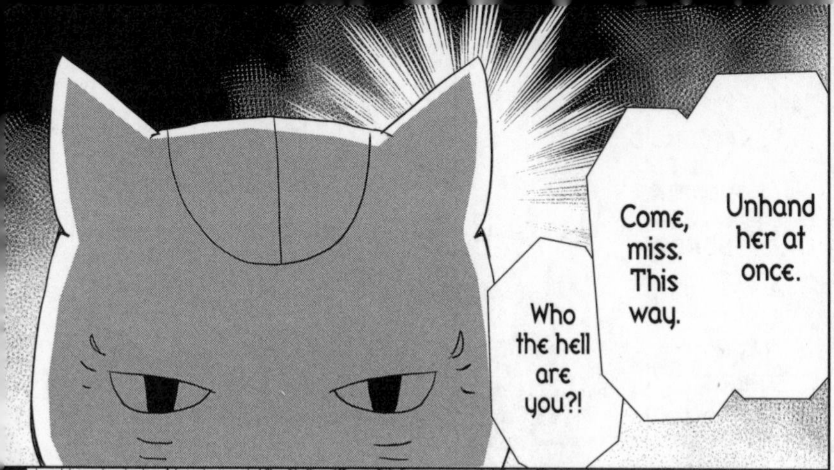
Unhand her at once.
Come, miss. This way.
Who the hell are you?!

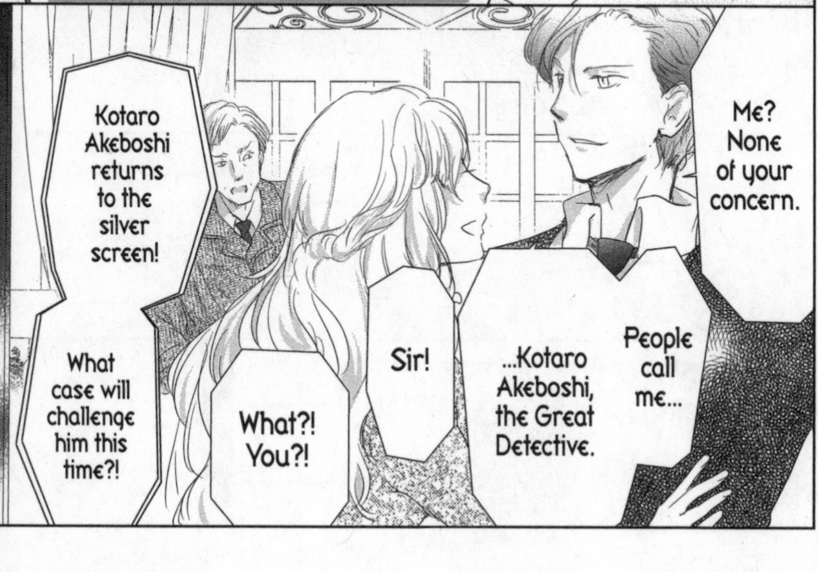
Me? None of your concern.
People call me...
...Kotaro Akeboshi, the Great Detective.
Sir!
What?! You?!
Kotaro Akeboshi returns to the silver screen!
What case will challenge him this time?!

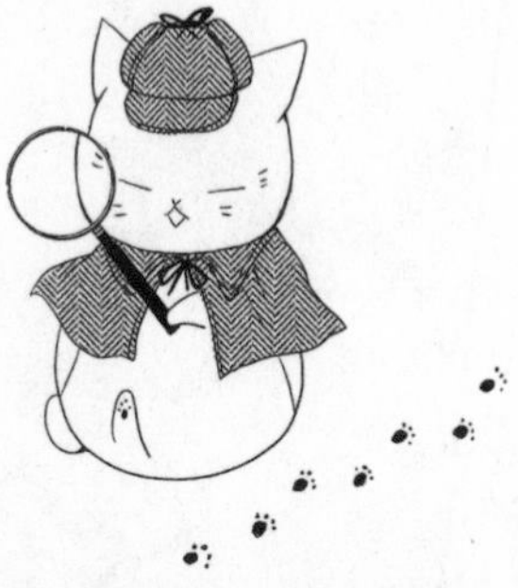

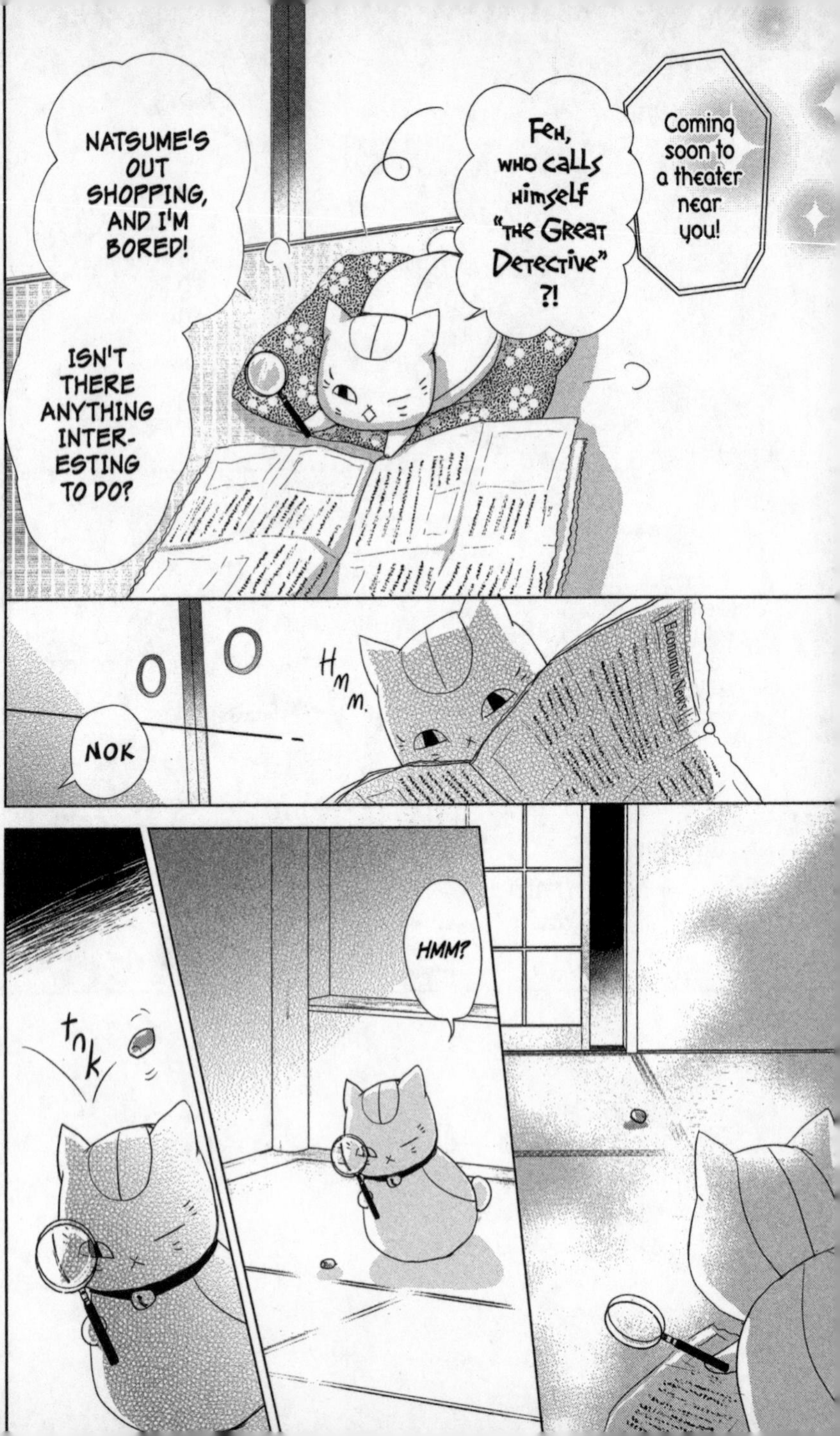

Coming soon to a theater near you!
Feh, who calls himself "the Great Detective" ?!
NATSUME'S OUT SHOPPING, AND I'M BORED!
ISN'T THERE ANYTHING INTER-ESTING TO DO?
Economic News
Hmm.
NOK
HMM?
tnk

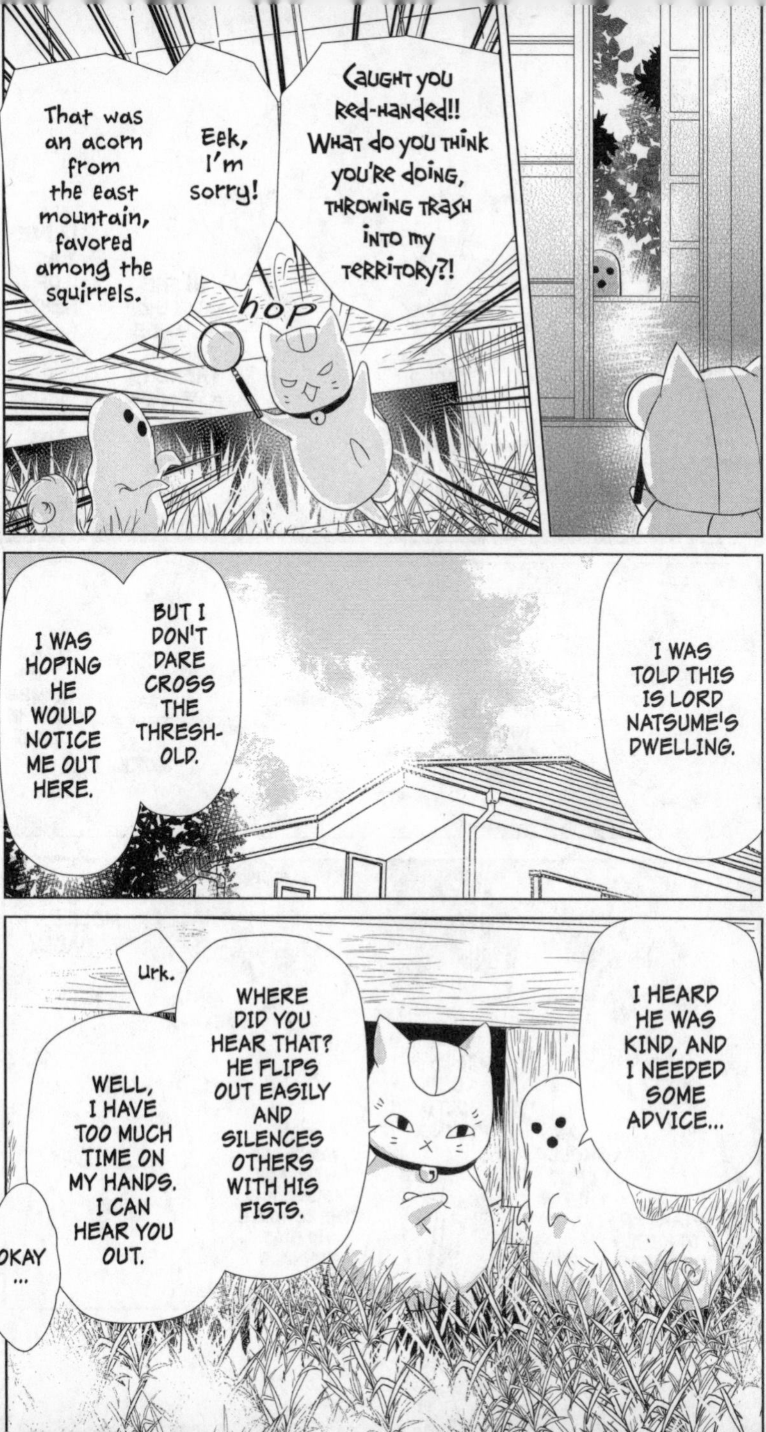

Caught you red-handed!! What do you think you're doing, throwing trash into my territory?!
Eek, I'm sorry!
That was an acorn from the east mountain, favored among the squirrels.
hop
I WAS TOLD THIS IS LORD NATSUME'S DWELLING.
BUT I DON'T DARE CROSS THE THRESH-OLD.
I WAS HOPING HE WOULD NOTICE ME OUT HERE.
I HEARD HE WAS KIND, AND I NEEDED SOME ADVICE...
WHERE DID YOU HEAR THAT? HE FLIPS OUT EASILY AND SILENCES OTHERS WITH HIS FISTS.
Urk.
WELL, I HAVE TOO MUCH TIME ON MY HANDS. I CAN HEAR YOU OUT.
OKAY ...

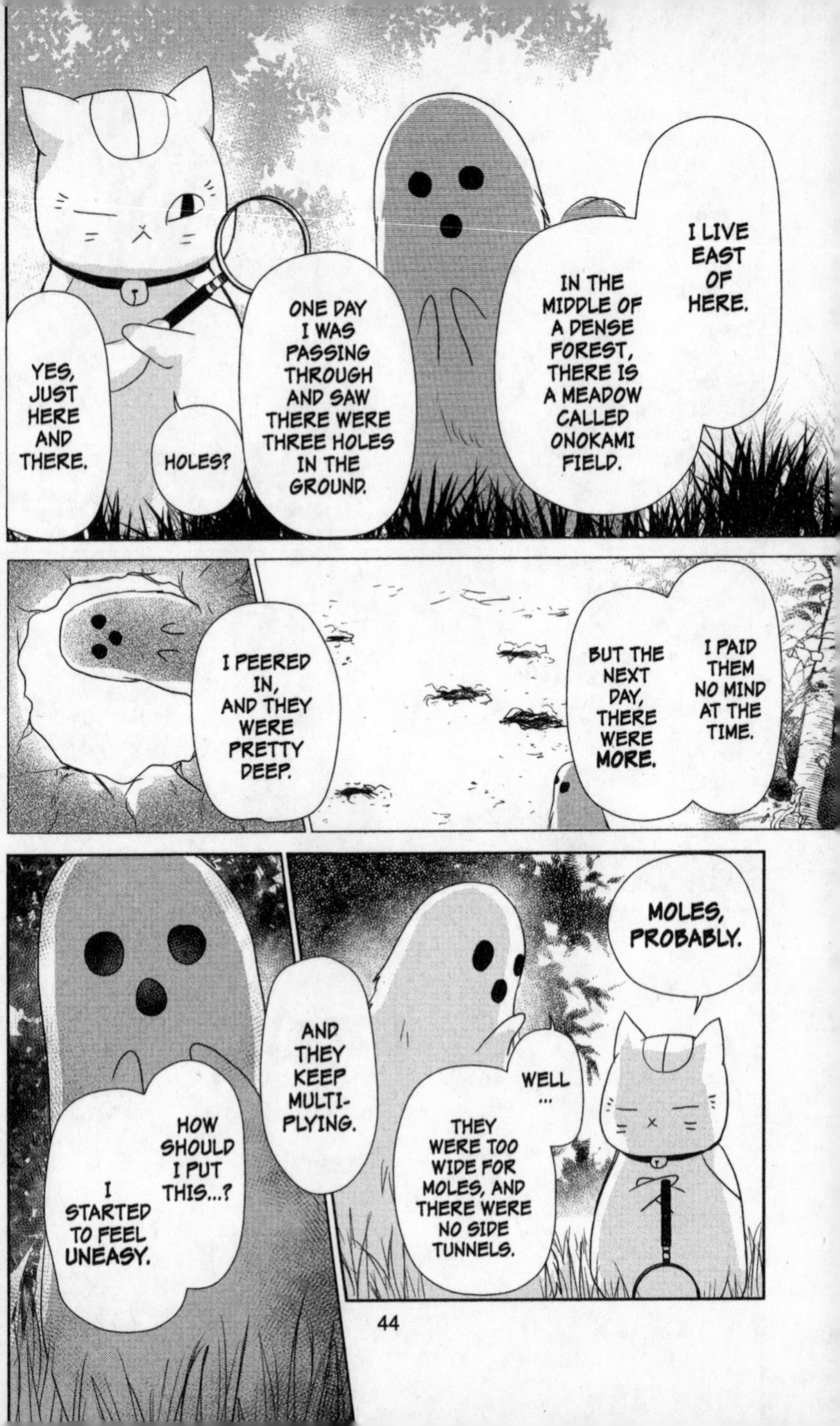
I LIVE EAST OF HERE.
IN THE MIDDLE OF A DENSE FOREST, THERE IS A MEADOW CALLED ONOKAMI FIELD.
ONE DAY I WAS PASSING THROUGH AND SAW THERE WERE THREE HOLES IN THE GROUND.
HOLES?
YES, JUST HERE AND THERE.
I PAID THEM NO MIND AT THE TIME.
BUT THE NEXT DAY, THERE WERE MORE.
I PEERED IN, AND THEY WERE PRETTY DEEP.
MOLES, PROBABLY.
WELL...
THEY WERE TOO WIDE FOR MOLES, AND THERE WERE NO SIDE TUNNELS.
AND THEY KEEP MULTI-PLYING.
HOW SHOULD I PUT THIS...?
I STARTED TO FEEL UNEASY.

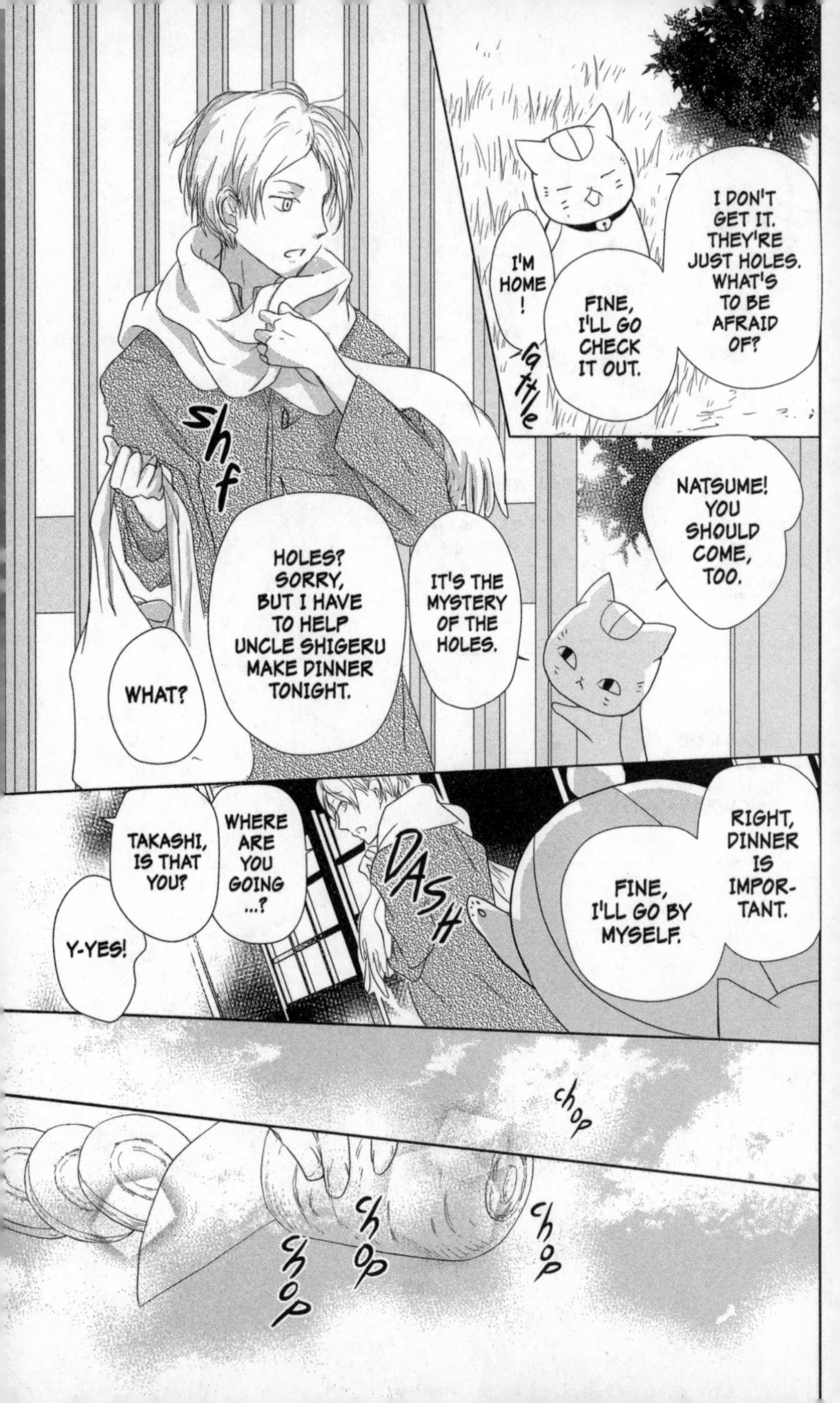
I DON'T GET IT. THEY'RE JUST HOLES. WHAT'S TO BE AFRAID OF?
FINE, I'LL GO CHECK IT OUT.
I'M HOME!
rattle
NATSUME! YOU SHOULD COME, TOO.
IT'S THE MYSTERY OF THE HOLES.
HOLES? SORRY, BUT I HAVE TO HELP UNCLE SHIGERU MAKE DINNER TONIGHT.
shf
WHAT?
RIGHT, DINNER IS IMPOR-TANT.
FINE, I'LL GO BY MYSELF.
DASH
WHERE ARE YOU GOING ...?
TAKASHI, IS THAT YOU?
Y-YES!
chop
chop
chop
chop

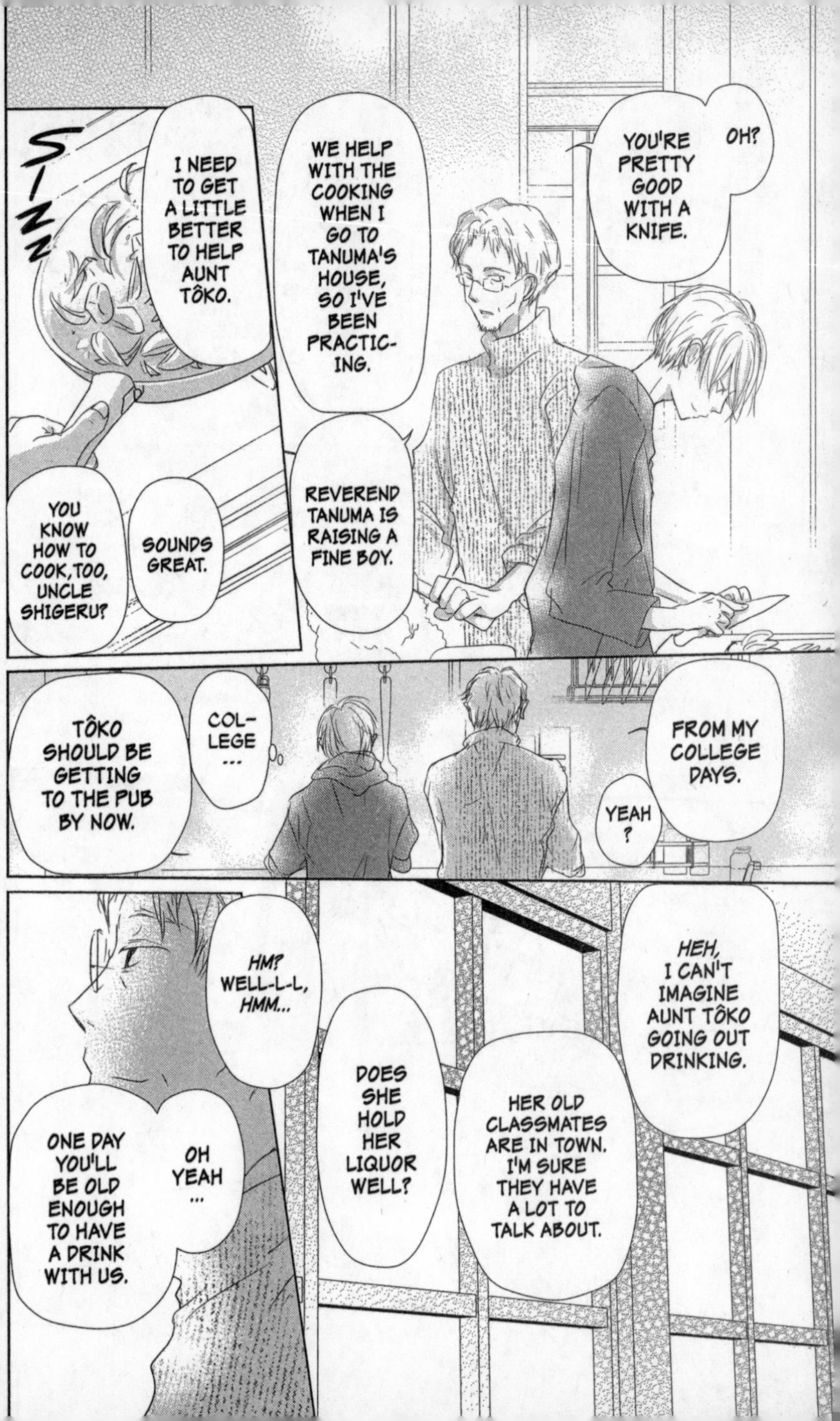
OH?
YOU'RE PRETTY GOOD WITH A KNIFE.
WE HELP WITH THE COOKING WHEN I GO TO TANUMA'S HOUSE, SO I'VE BEEN PRACTIC-ING.
REVEREND TANUMA IS RAISING A FINE BOY.
SIZZ
I NEED TO GET A LITTLE BETTER TO HELP AUNT TÔKO.
SOUNDS GREAT.
YOU KNOW HOW TO COOK, TOO, UNCLE SHIGERU?
FROM MY COLLEGE DAYS.
YEAH?
COL-LEGE...
TÔKO SHOULD BE GETTING TO THE PUB BY NOW.
HEH, I CAN'T IMAGINE AUNT TÔKO GOING OUT DRINKING.
HER OLD CLASSMATES ARE IN TOWN. I'M SURE THEY HAVE A LOT TO TALK ABOUT.
DOES SHE HOLD HER LIQUOR WELL?
HM? WELL-L-L, HMM...
OH YEAH...
ONE DAY YOU'LL BE OLD ENOUGH TO HAVE A DRINK WITH US.

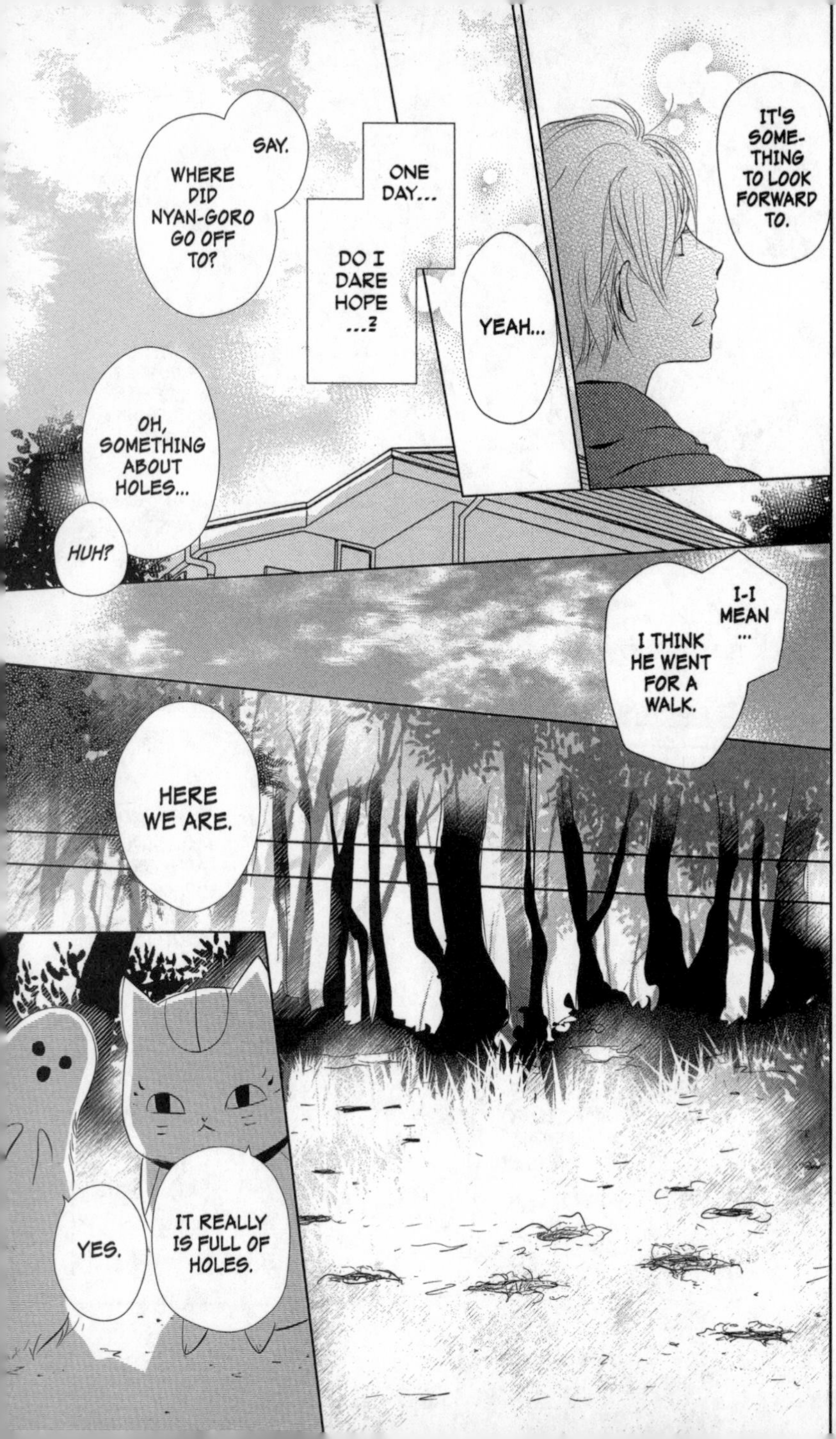
IT'S SOMETHING TO LOOK FORWARD TO.
YEAH...
ONE DAY...
DO I DARE HOPE...?
SAY.
WHERE DID NYAN-GORO GO OFF TO?
OH, SOMETHING ABOUT HOLES...
HUH?
I-I MEAN...
I THINK HE WENT FOR A WALK.
HERE WE ARE.
IT REALLY IS FULL OF HOLES.
YES.

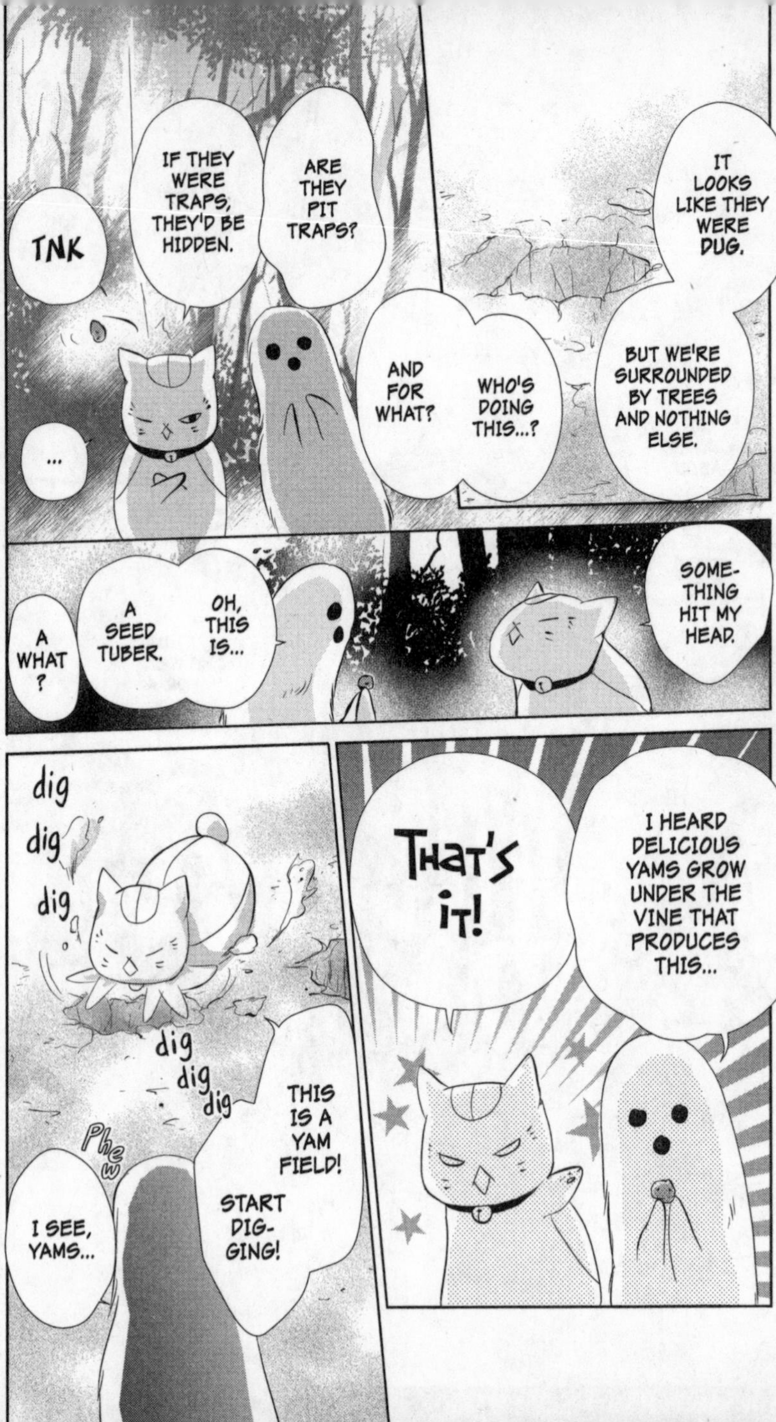
IT LOOKS LIKE THEY WERE DUG.
BUT WE'RE SURROUNDED BY TREES AND NOTHING ELSE.
WHO'S DOING THIS...?
AND FOR WHAT?
ARE THEY PIT TRAPS?
IF THEY WERE TRAPS, THEY'D BE HIDDEN.
TNK
...
SOME-THING HIT MY HEAD.
OH, THIS IS...
A SEED TUBER.
A WHAT?
I HEARD DELICIOUS YAMS GROW UNDER THE VINE THAT PRODUCES THIS...
THAT'S IT!
dig dig dig
dig dig dig
THIS IS A YAM FIELD!
START DIG-GING!
Phew
I SEE, YAMS...

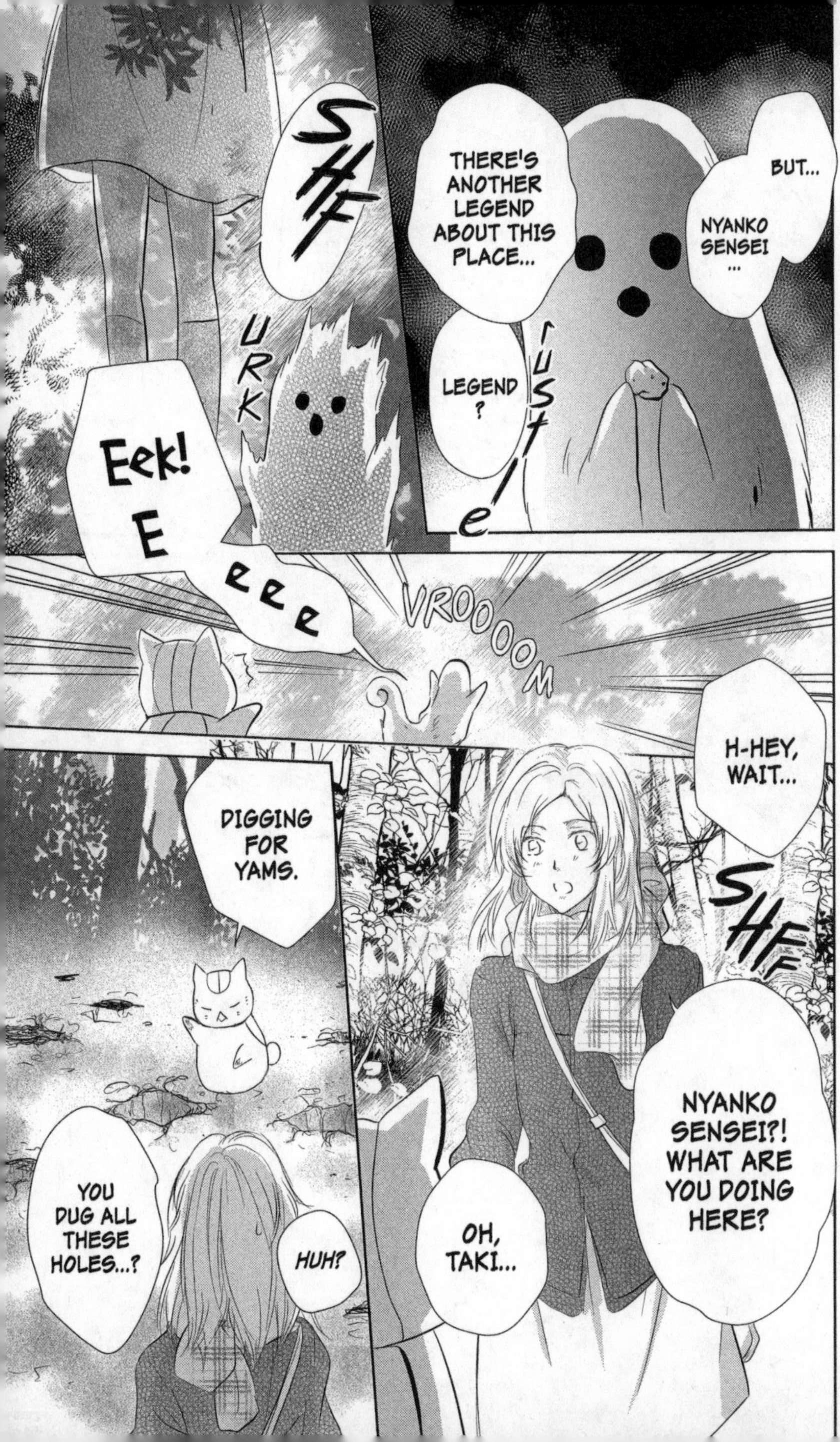
BUT...
NYANKO SENSEI ...
THERE'S ANOTHER LEGEND ABOUT THIS PLACE...
RUSTLE
LEGEND?
SHF
URK
Eek! E eee
VROOOOOM
H-HEY, WAIT...
SHF
NYANKO SENSEI?! WHAT ARE YOU DOING HERE?
OH, TAKI...
DIGGING FOR YAMS.
HUH?
YOU DUG ALL THESE HOLES...?

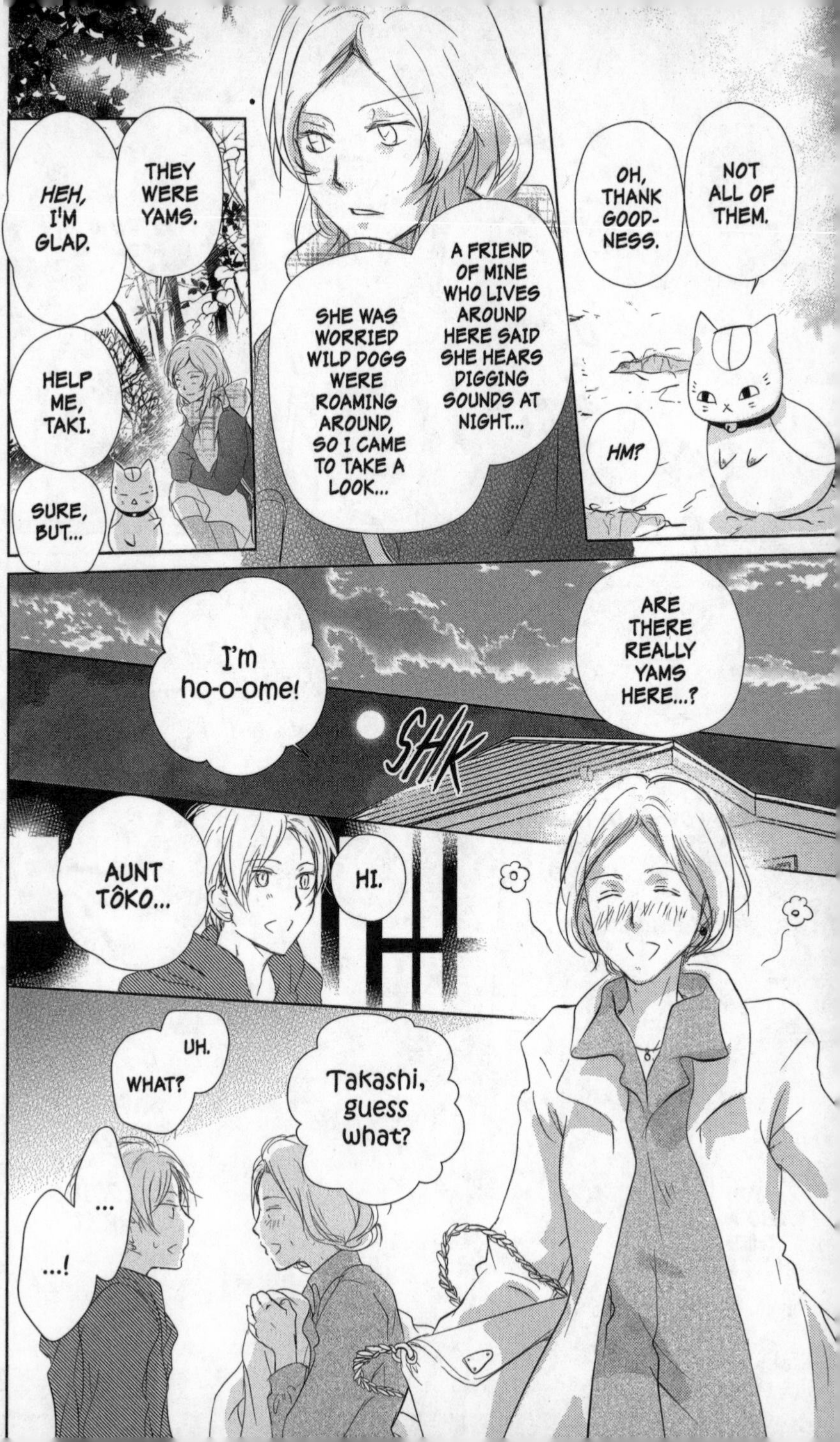
NOT ALL OF THEM.
OH, THANK GOOD-NESS.
HM?
A FRIEND OF MINE WHO LIVES AROUND HERE SAID SHE HEARS DIGGING SOUNDS AT NIGHT...
SHE WAS WORRIED WILD DOGS WERE ROAMING AROUND, SO I CAME TO TAKE A LOOK...
THEY WERE YAMS.
HEH, I'M GLAD.
HELP ME, TAKI.
SURE, BUT...
ARE THERE REALLY YAMS HERE...?
I'm ho-o-ome!
SHK
HI.
AUNT TÔKO...
Takashi, guess what?
UH.
WHAT?
...
...!

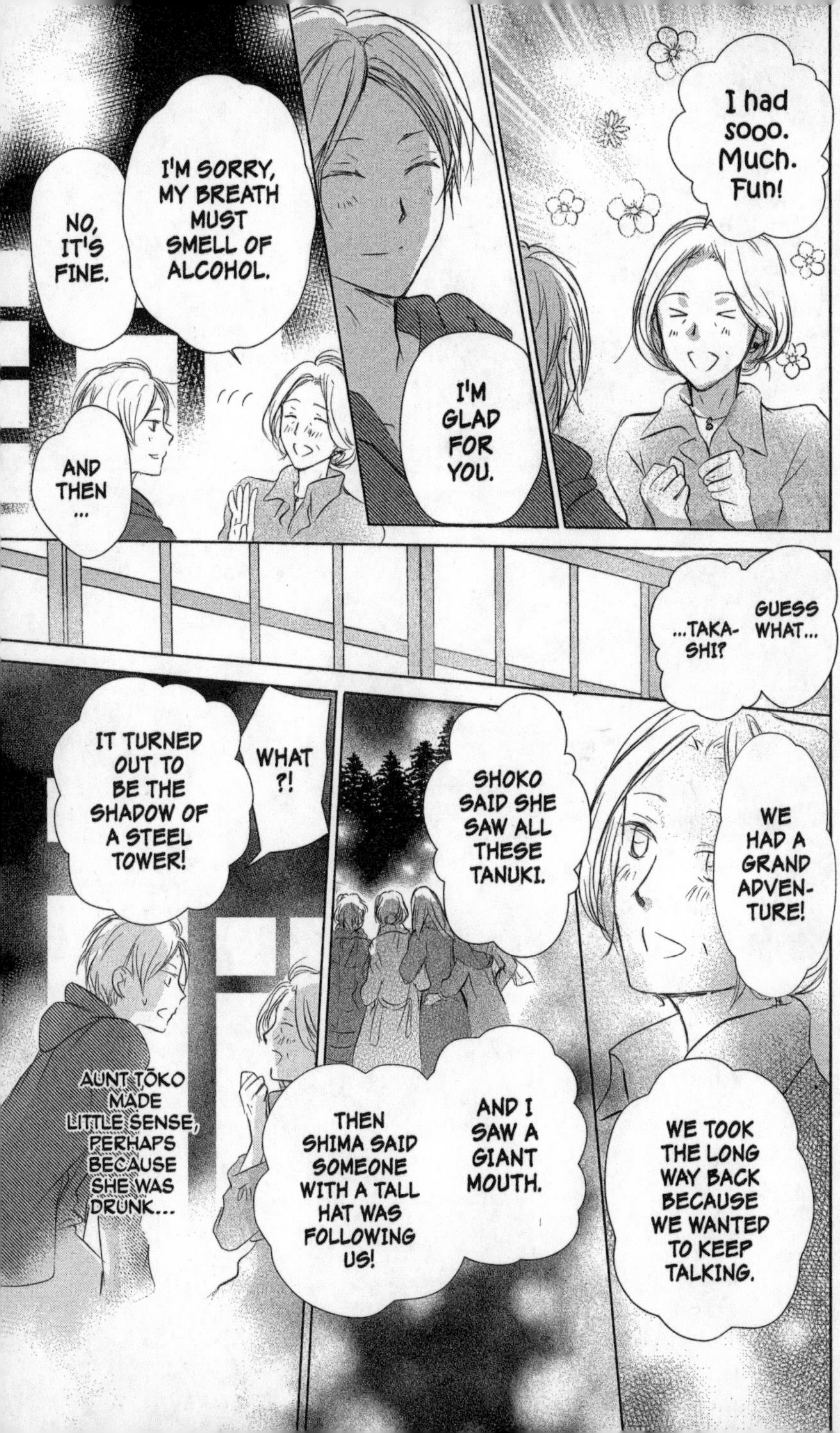
I had sooo. Much. Fun!
I'M GLAD FOR YOU.
I'M SORRY, MY BREATH MUST SMELL OF ALCOHOL.
NO, IT'S FINE.
AND THEN ...
GUESS WHAT...
...TAKA-SHI?
WE HAD A GRAND ADVEN-TURE!
WE TOOK THE LONG WAY BACK BECAUSE WE WANTED TO KEEP TALKING.
SHOKO SAID SHE SAW ALL THESE TANUKI.
AND I SAW A GIANT MOUTH.
THEN SHIMA SAID SOMEONE WITH A TALL HAT WAS FOLLOWING US!
WHAT ?!
IT TURNED OUT TO BE THE SHADOW OF A STEEL TOWER!
AUNT TŌKO MADE LITTLE SENSE, PERHAPS BECAUSE SHE WAS DRUNK...

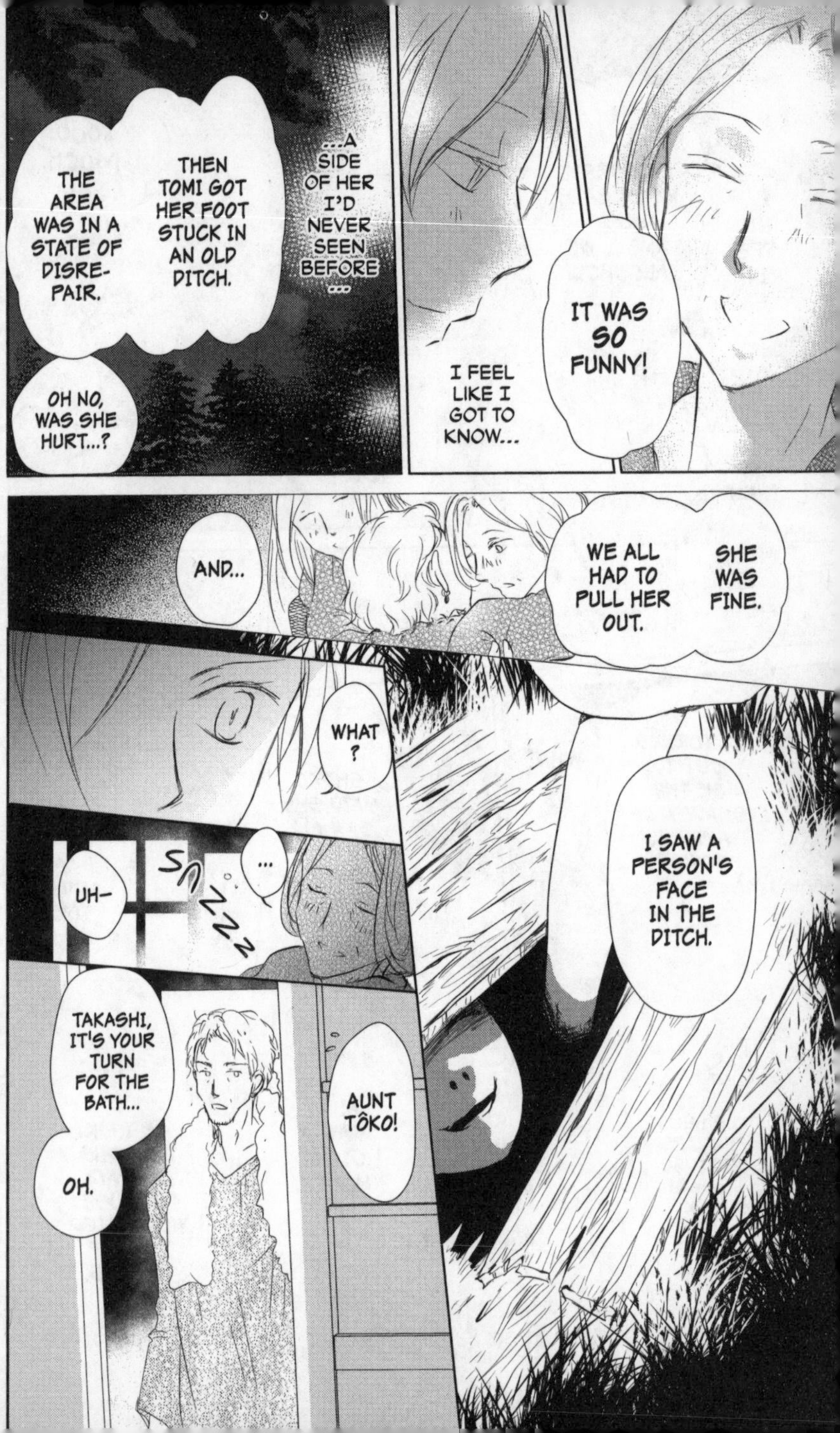
IT WAS SO FUNNY!
I FEEL LIKE I GOT TO KNOW...
...A SIDE OF HER I'D NEVER SEEN BEFORE...
THEN TOMI GOT HER FOOT STUCK IN AN OLD DITCH.
THE AREA WAS IN A STATE OF DISREPAIR.
OH NO, WAS SHE HURT...?
SHE WAS FINE.
WE ALL HAD TO PULL HER OUT.
AND...
I SAW A PERSON'S FACE IN THE DITCH.
WHAT?
...
SUZZZ
UH-
AUNT TÔKO!
TAKASHI, IT'S YOUR TURN FOR THE BATH...
OH.

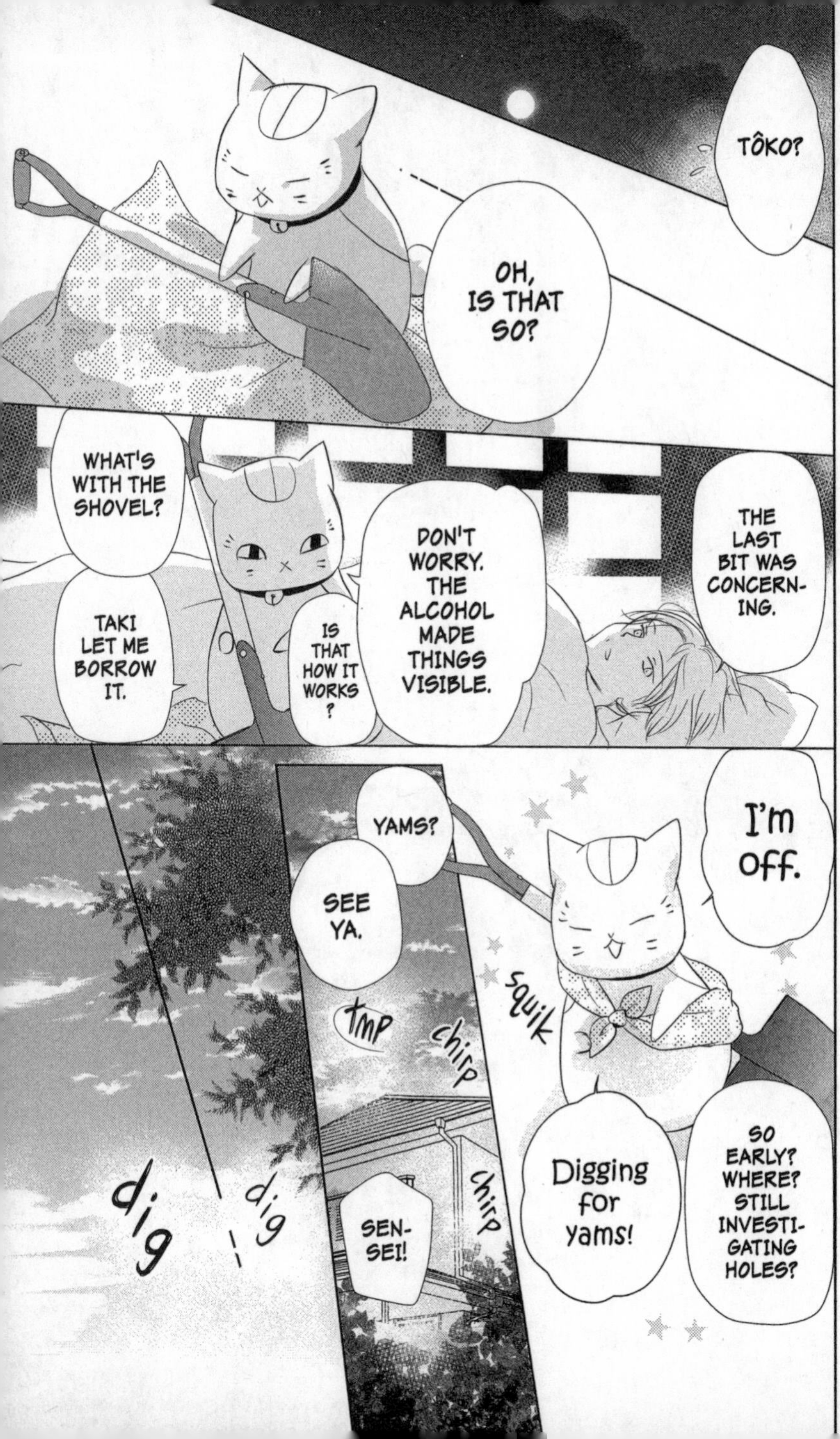
TÔKO?
OH, IS THAT SO?
THE LAST BIT WAS CONCERNING.
DON'T WORRY. THE ALCOHOL MADE THINGS VISIBLE.
IS THAT HOW IT WORKS?
WHAT'S WITH THE SHOVEL?
TAKI LET ME BORROW IT.
I'm off.
SO EARLY? WHERE? STILL INVESTIGATING HOLES?
squik
Digging for yams!
YAMS?
SEE YA.
tmp
chirp
chirp
SEN-SEI!
dig
dig

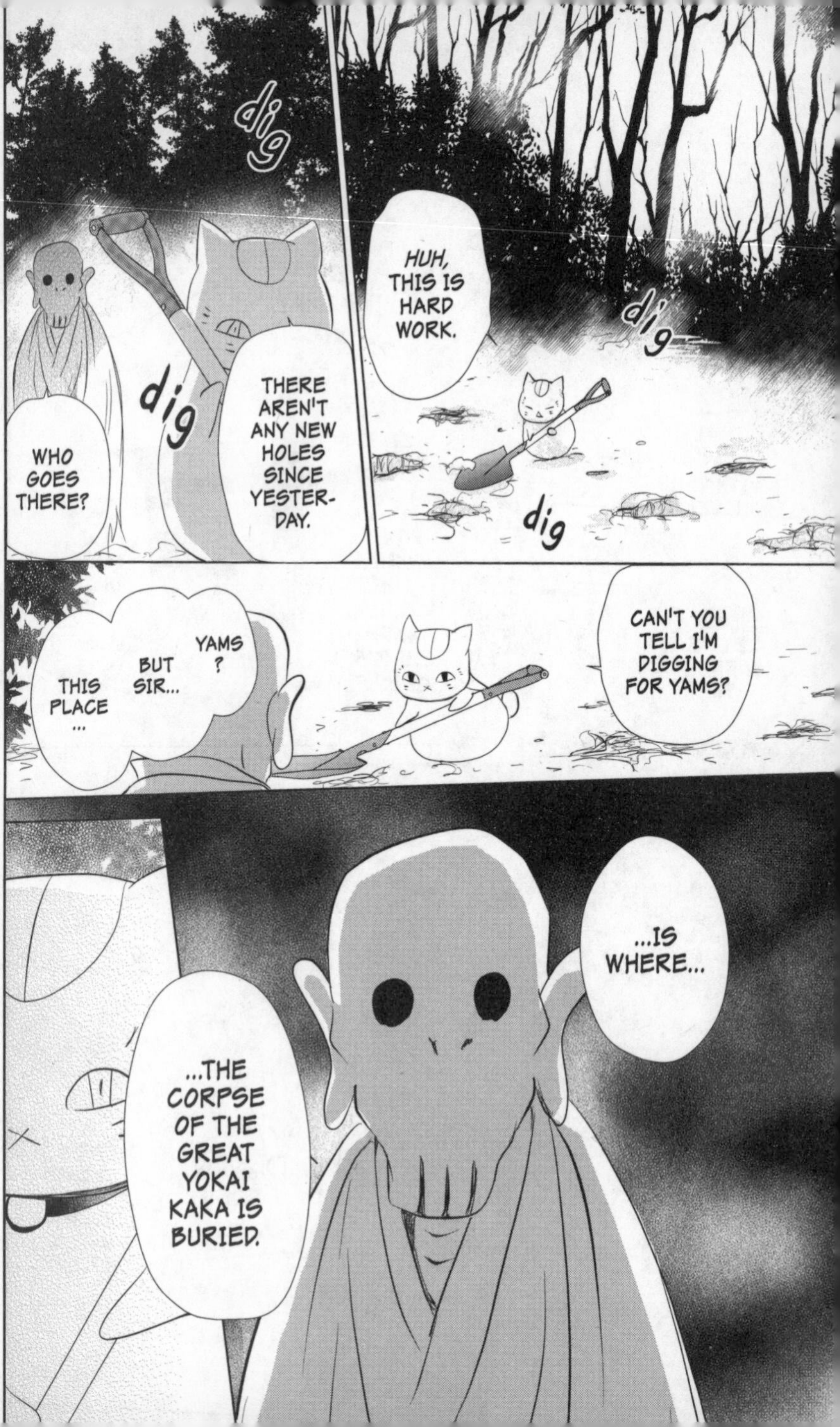
dig
HUH, THIS IS HARD WORK.
dig
dig
THERE AREN'T ANY NEW HOLES SINCE YESTER-DAY.
dig
WHO GOES THERE?
CAN'T YOU TELL I'M DIGGING FOR YAMS?
YAMS?
BUT SIR...
THIS PLACE...
...IS WHERE...
...THE CORPSE OF THE GREAT YOKAI KAKA IS BURIED.

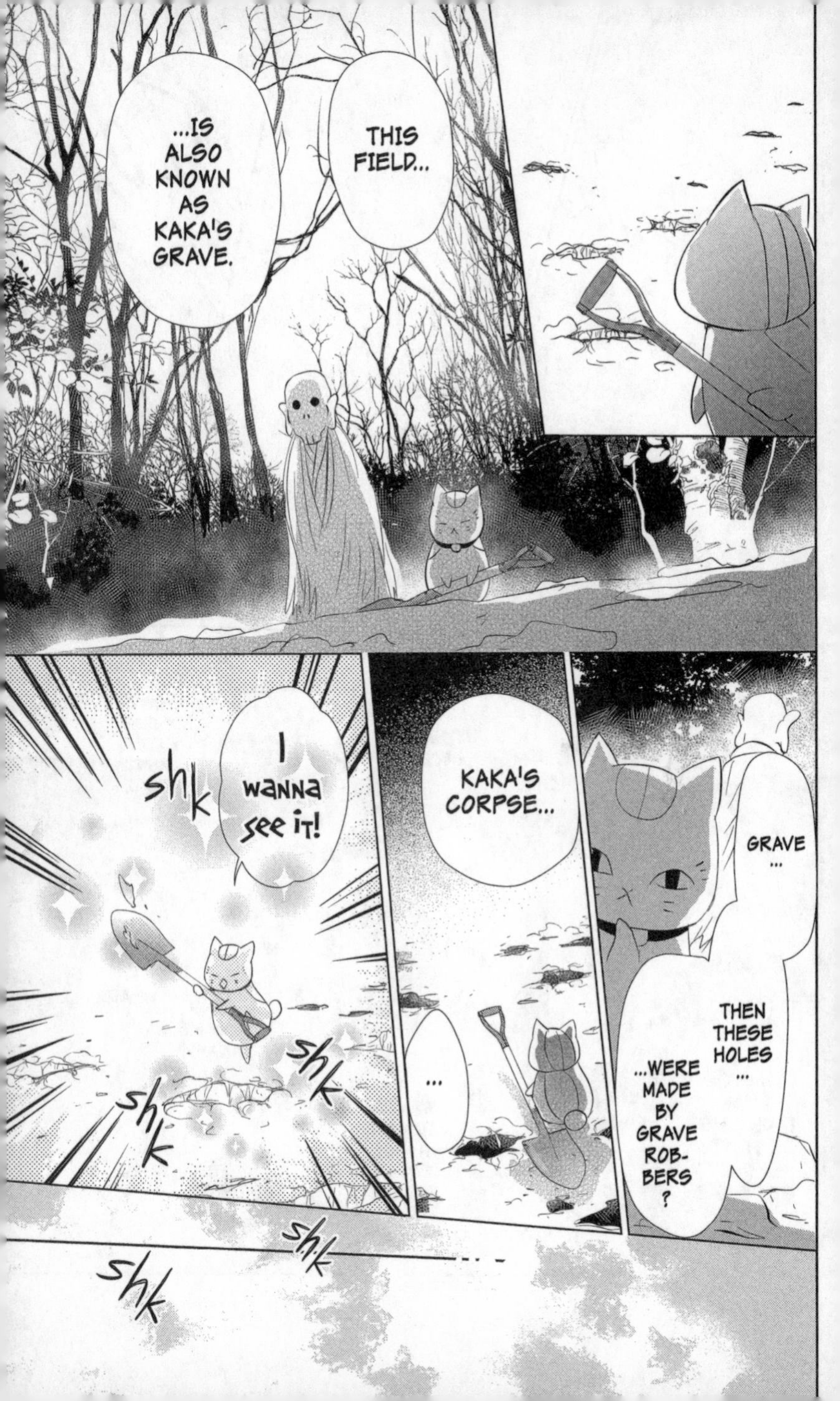

THIS FIELD...
...IS ALSO KNOWN AS KAKA'S GRAVE.
GRAVE ...
THEN THESE HOLES ...
...WERE MADE BY GRAVE ROB-BERS?
KAKA'S CORPSE...
...
I wanna see it!
shk
shk
shk
shk
shk

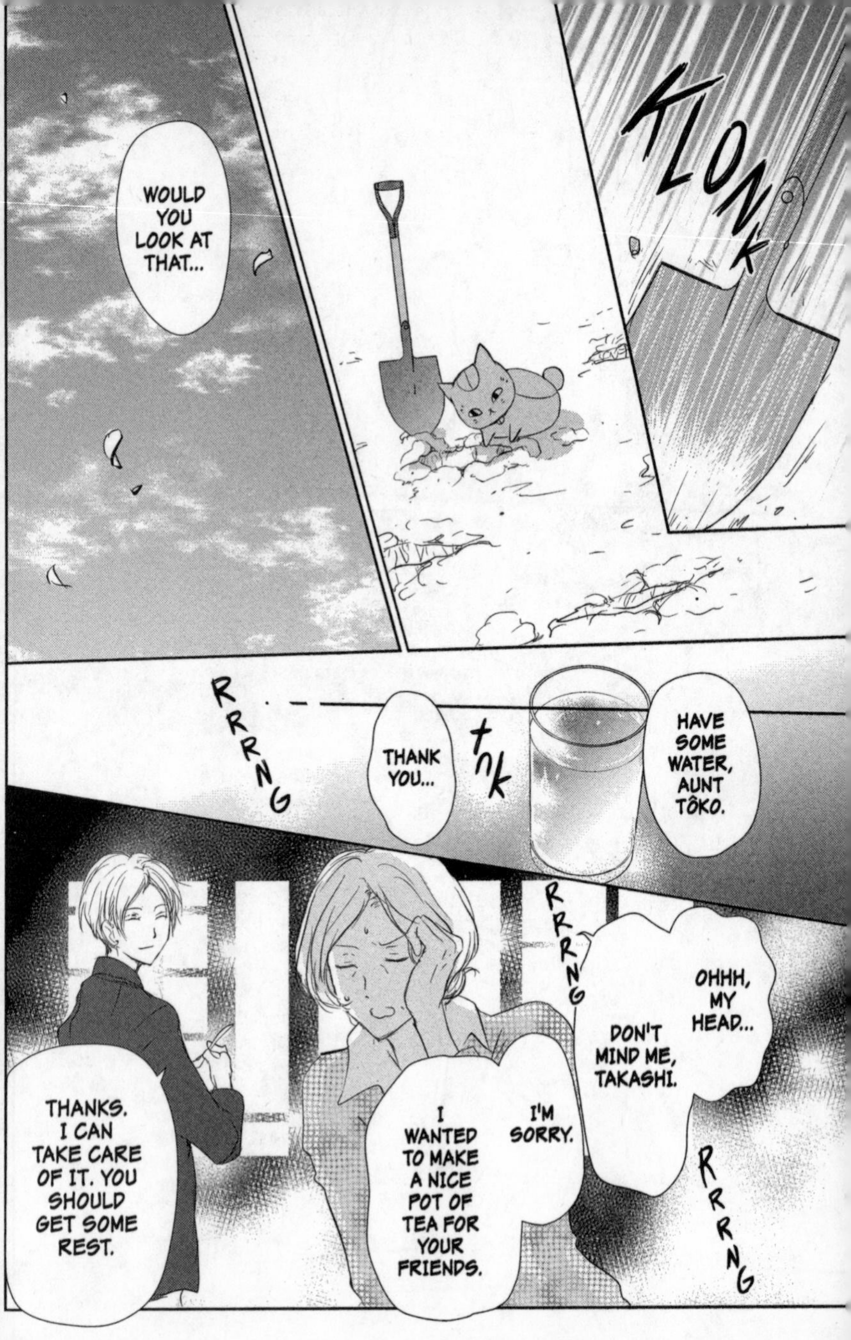
KLONK
WOULD YOU LOOK AT THAT...
HAVE SOME WATER, AUNT TÔKO.
tnk
THANK YOU...
RRRNG
RRRNG
OHHH, MY HEAD...
DON'T MIND ME, TAKASHI.
I'M SORRY.
I WANTED TO MAKE A NICE POT OF TEA FOR YOUR FRIENDS.
RRRNG
THANKS. I CAN TAKE CARE OF IT. YOU SHOULD GET SOME REST.

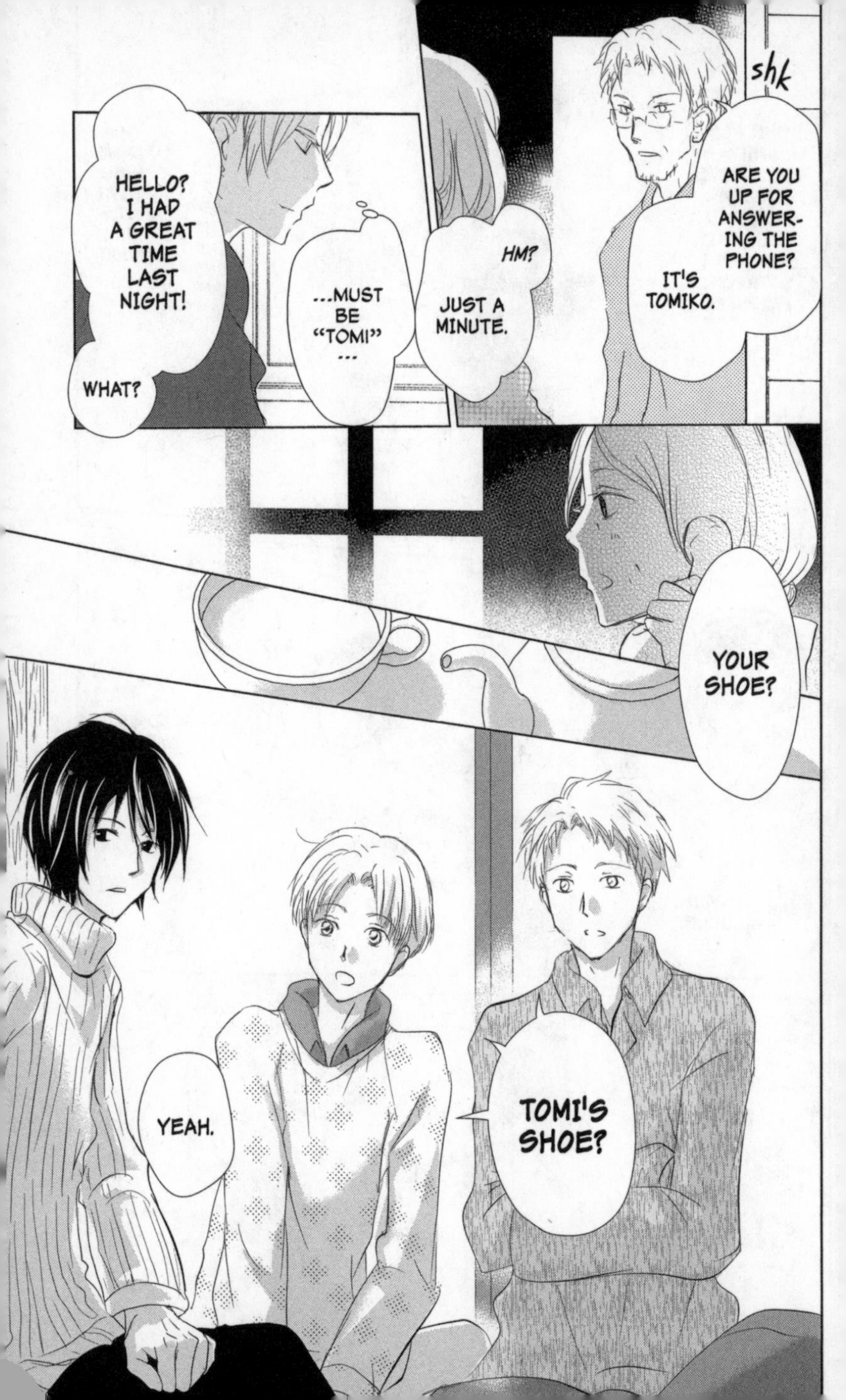
shk
ARE YOU UP FOR ANSWERING THE PHONE?
IT'S TOMIKO.
HM?
JUST A MINUTE.
...MUST BE "TOMI"...
HELLO? I HAD A GREAT TIME LAST NIGHT!
WHAT?
YOUR SHOE?
TOMI'S SHOE?
YEAH.

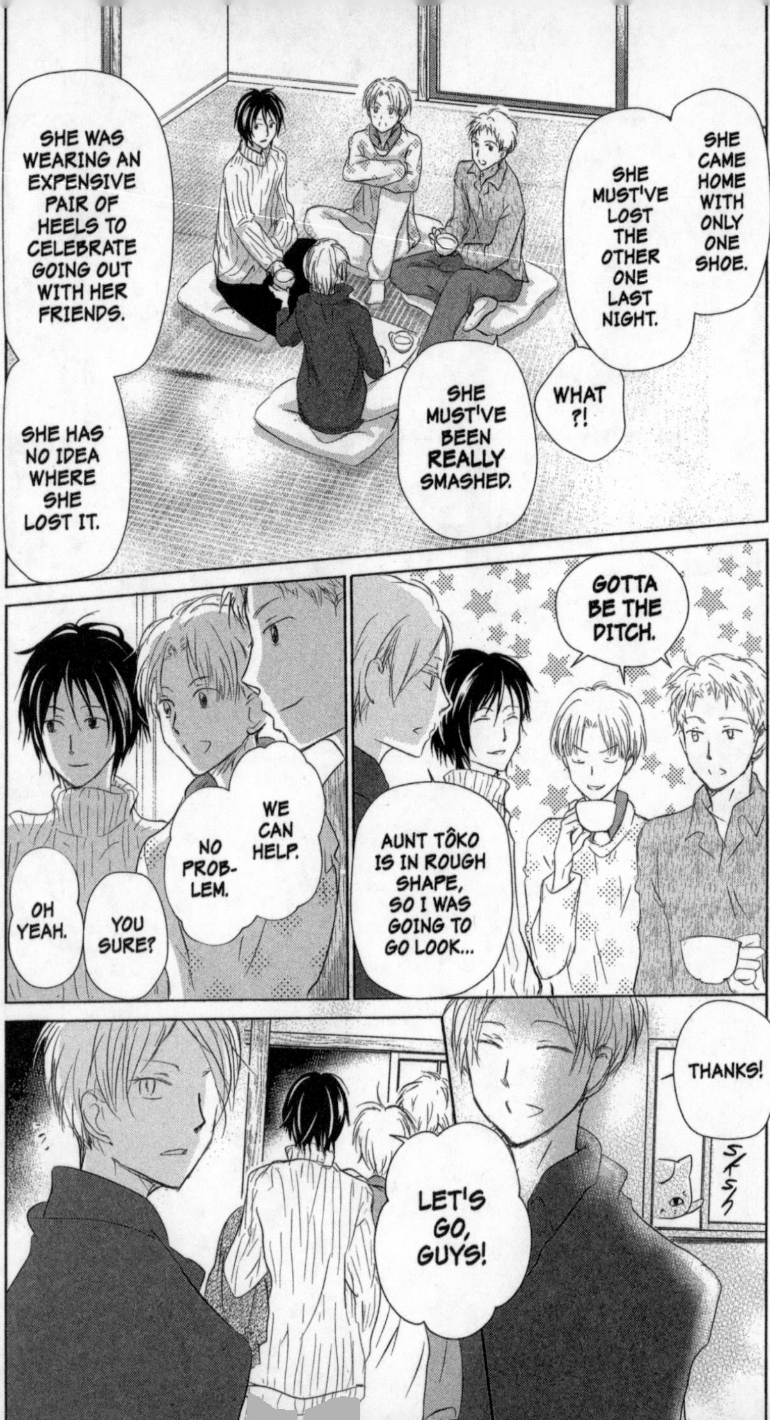
SHE CAME HOME WITH ONLY ONE SHOE.
SHE MUST'VE LOST THE OTHER ONE LAST NIGHT.
WHAT?!
SHE MUST'VE BEEN REALLY SMASHED.
SHE WAS WEARING AN EXPENSIVE PAIR OF HEELS TO CELEBRATE GOING OUT WITH HER FRIENDS.
SHE HAS NO IDEA WHERE SHE LOST IT.
GOTTA BE THE DITCH.
AUNT TÔKO IS IN ROUGH SHAPE, SO I WAS GOING TO GO LOOK...
WE CAN HELP.
NO PROB-LEM.
YOU SURE?
OH YEAH.
THANKS!
SKSH
LET'S GO, GUYS!

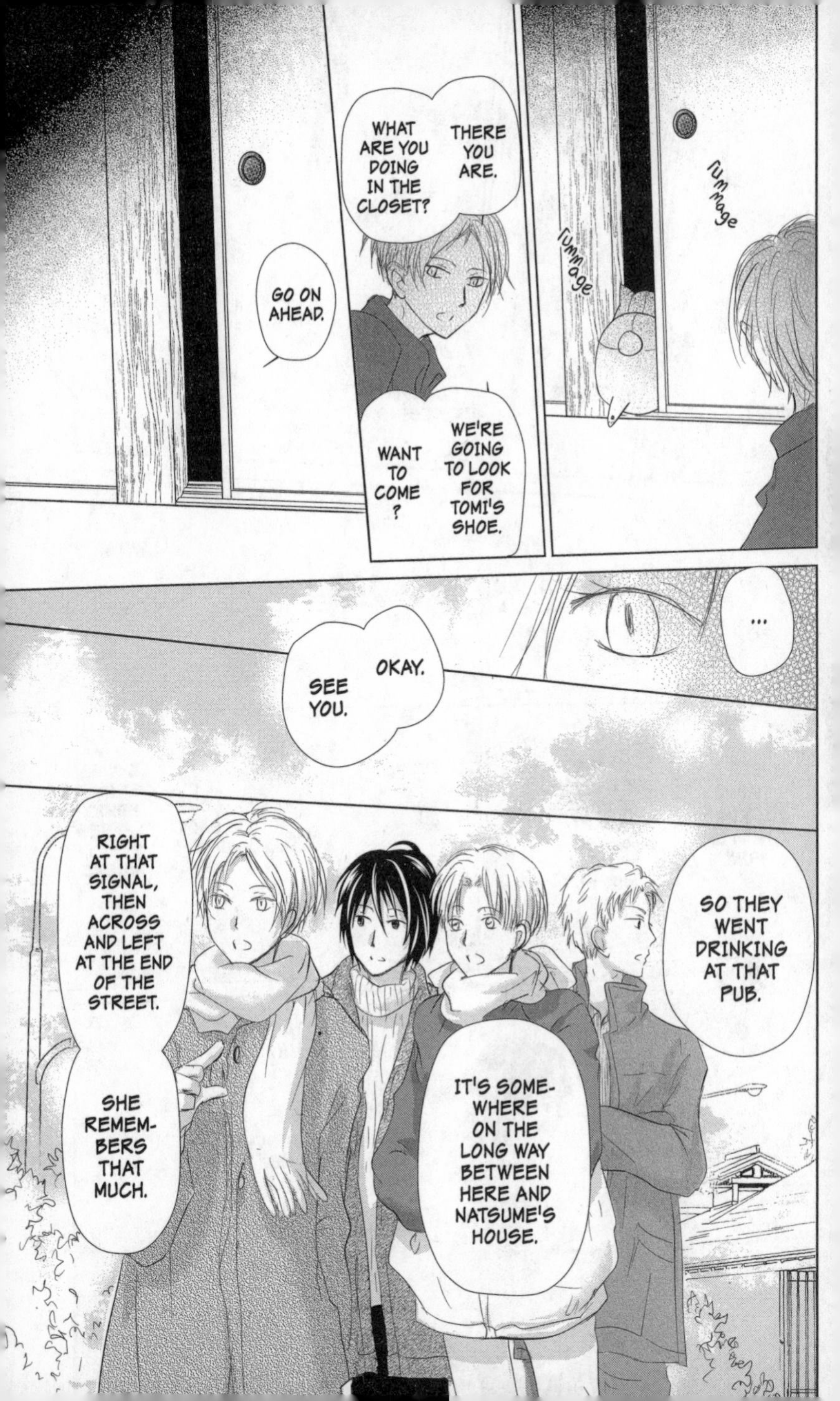
rummage
rummage
THERE YOU ARE.
WHAT ARE YOU DOING IN THE CLOSET?
WE'RE GOING TO LOOK FOR TOMI'S SHOE.
WANT TO COME?
GO ON AHEAD.
...
OKAY. SEE YOU.
SO THEY WENT DRINKING AT THAT PUB.
IT'S SOME-WHERE ON THE LONG WAY BETWEEN HERE AND NATSUME'S HOUSE.
RIGHT AT THAT SIGNAL, THEN ACROSS AND LEFT AT THE END OF THE STREET.
SHE REMEMBERS THAT MUCH.

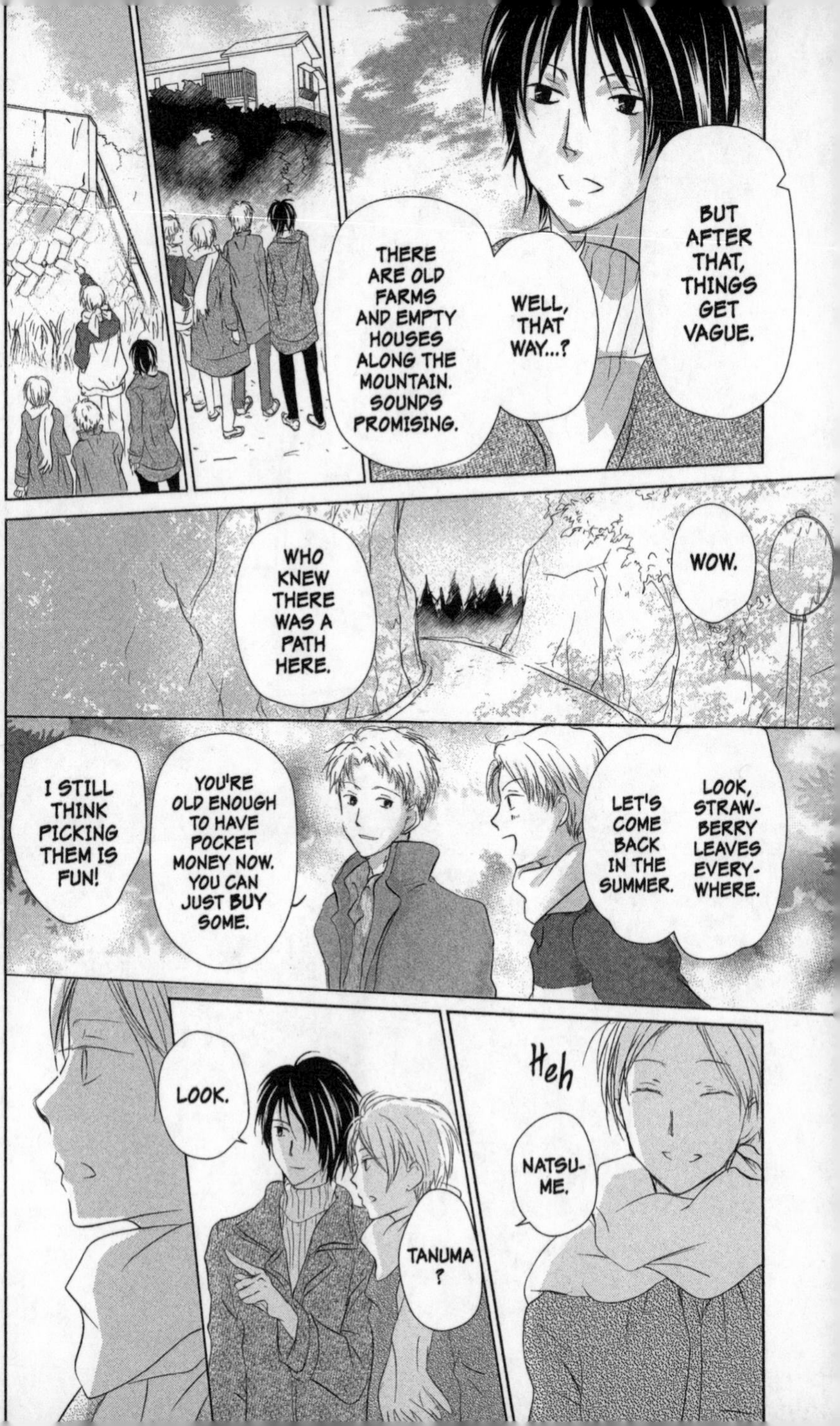
BUT AFTER THAT, THINGS GET VAGUE.
WELL, THAT WAY...?
THERE ARE OLD FARMS AND EMPTY HOUSES ALONG THE MOUNTAIN. SOUNDS PROMISING.
WOW.
WHO KNEW THERE WAS A PATH HERE.
LOOK, STRAW-BERRY LEAVES EVERY-WHERE.
LET'S COME BACK IN THE SUMMER.
YOU'RE OLD ENOUGH TO HAVE POCKET MONEY NOW. YOU CAN JUST BUY SOME.
I STILL THINK PICKING THEM IS FUN!
Heh
NATSU-ME.
LOOK.
TANUMA?

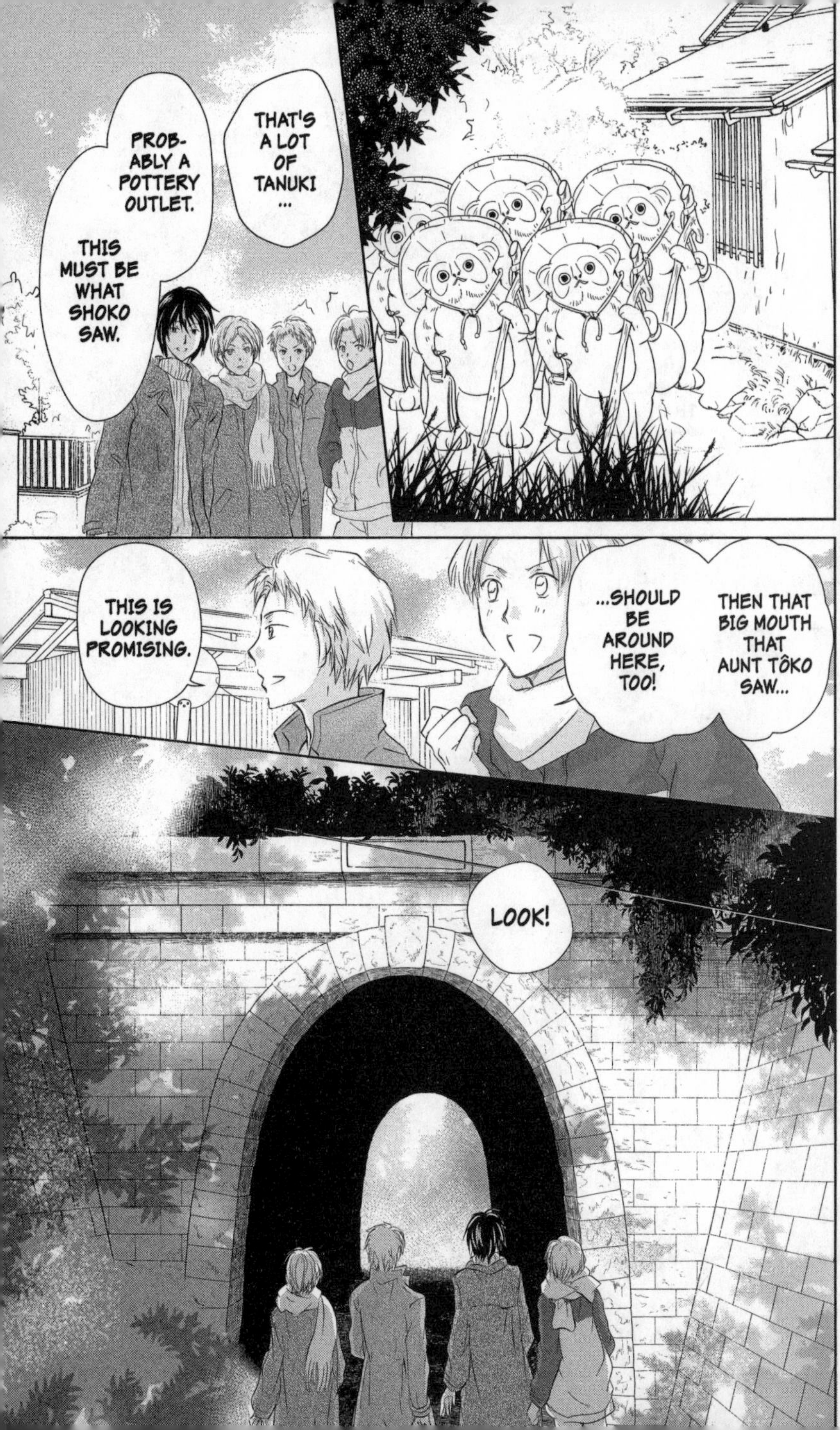
THAT'S A LOT OF TANUKI...
PROB-ABLY A POTTERY OUTLET.
THIS MUST BE WHAT SHOKO SAW.
THEN THAT BIG MOUTH THAT AUNT TÔKO SAW...
...SHOULD BE AROUND HERE, TOO!
THIS IS LOOKING PROMISING.
LOOK!

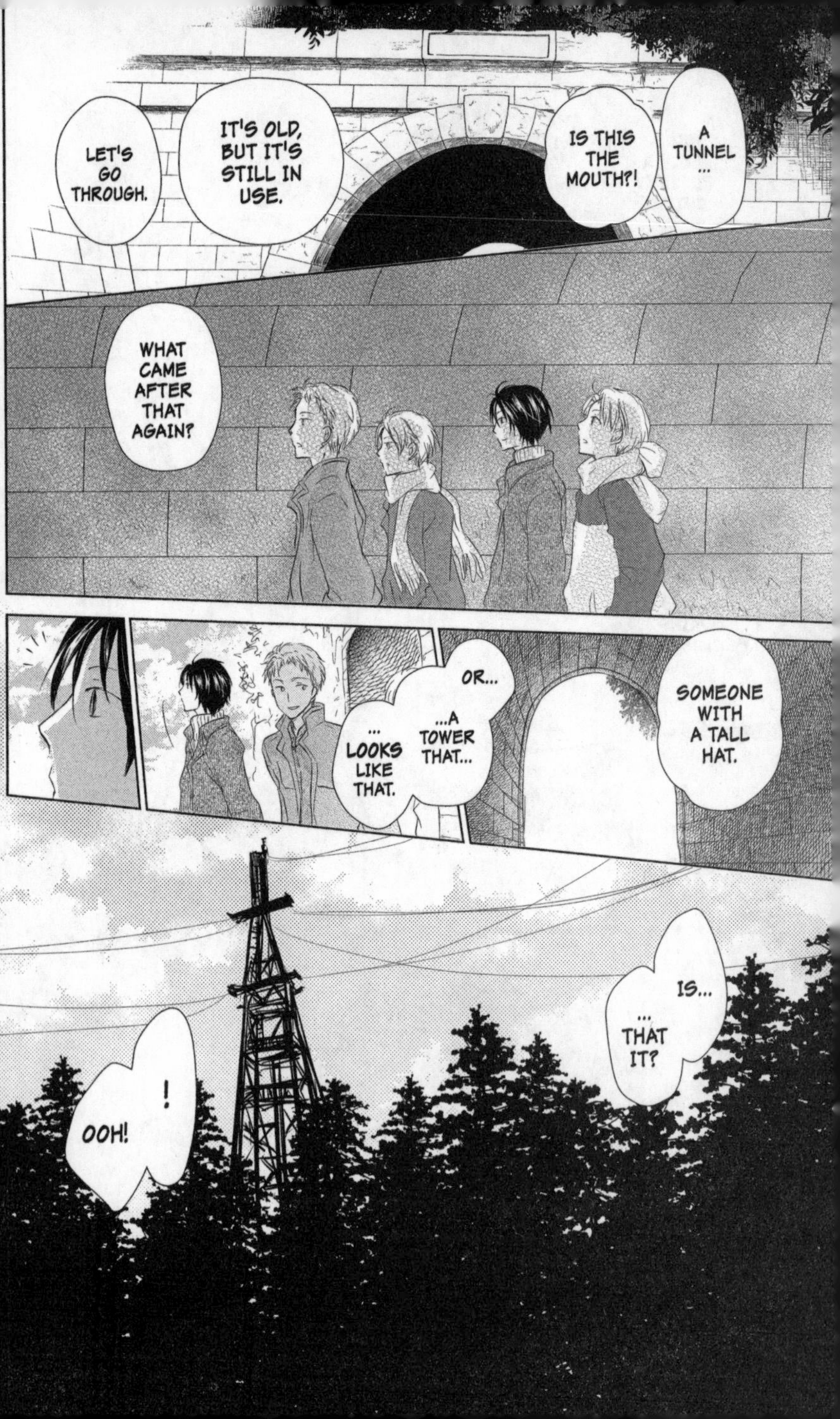
A TUNNEL ...
IS THIS THE MOUTH?!
IT'S OLD, BUT IT'S STILL IN USE.
LET'S GO THROUGH.
WHAT CAME AFTER THAT AGAIN?
SOMEONE WITH A TALL HAT.
OR...
...A TOWER THAT...
... LOOKS LIKE THAT.
IS...
... THAT IT?
!
OOH!

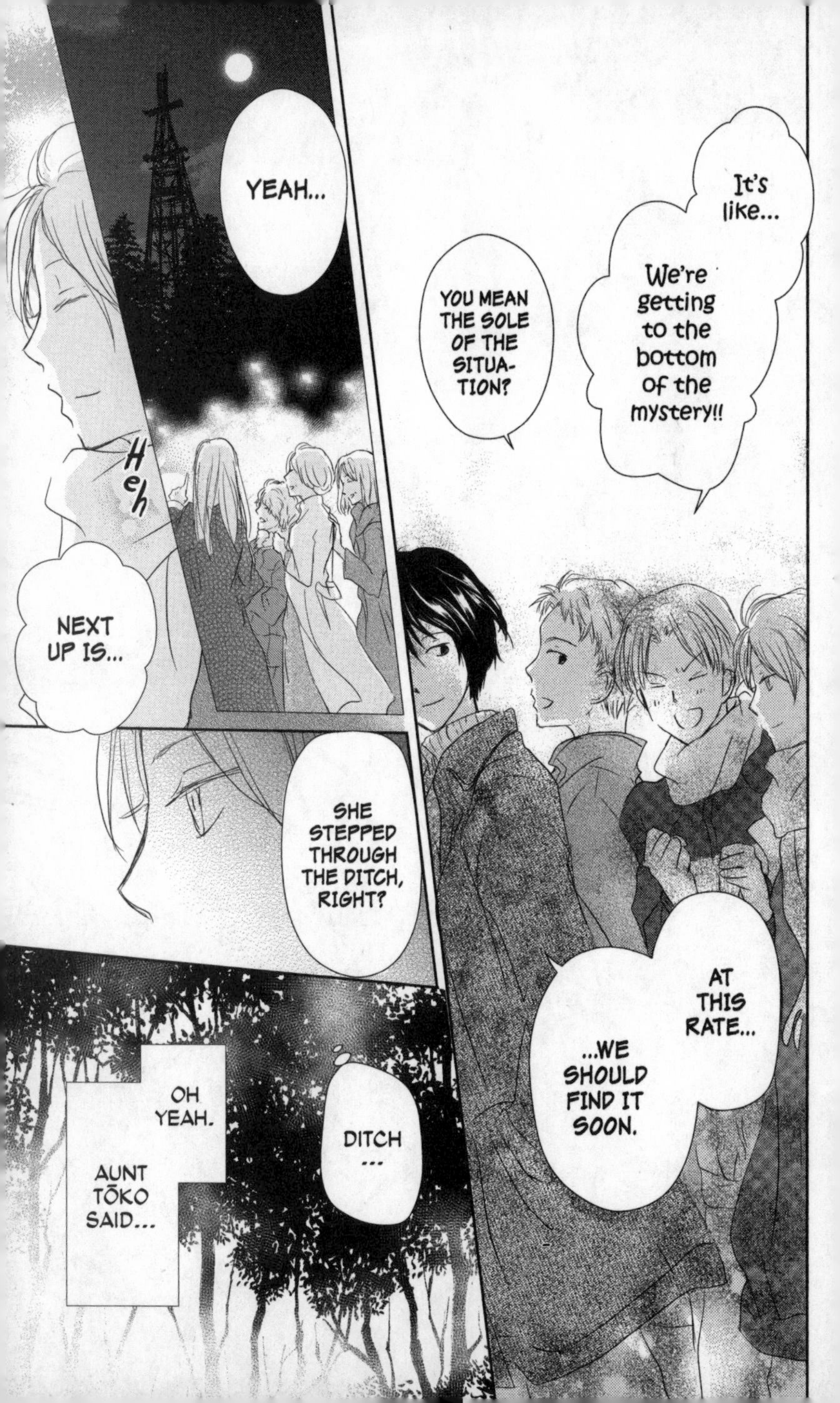
It's like...
We're getting to the bottom of the mystery!!
YOU MEAN THE SOLE OF THE SITUATION?
AT THIS RATE...
...WE SHOULD FIND IT SOON.
YEAH...
Heh
NEXT UP IS...
SHE STEPPED THROUGH THE DITCH, RIGHT?
DITCH...
OH YEAH.
AUNT TŌKO SAID...

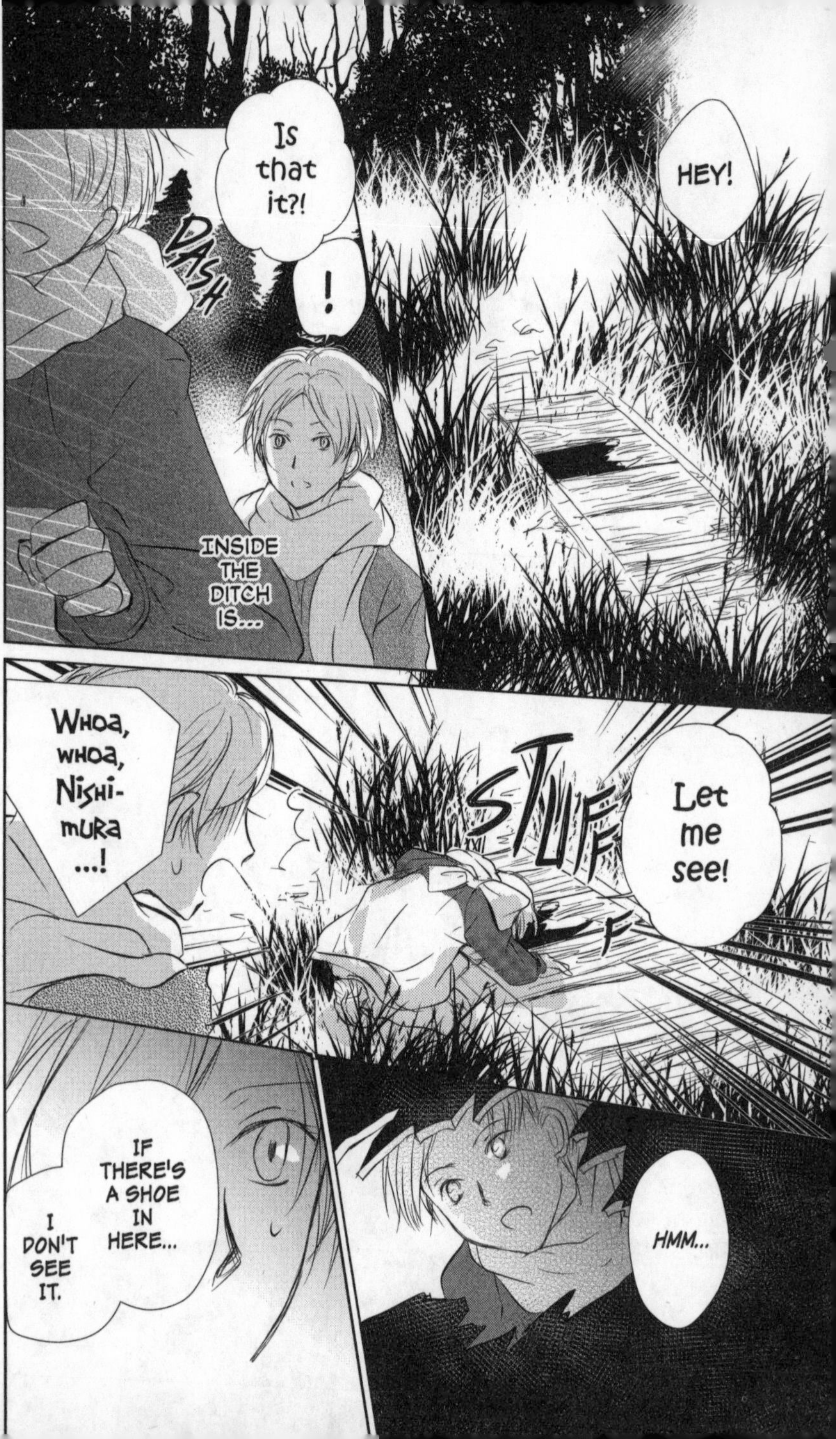
HEY!
Is that it?!
DASH
!
INSIDE THE DITCH IS...
Let me see!
STUFF
Whoa, whoa, Nishimura...!
HMM...
IF THERE'S A SHOE IN HERE...
I DON'T SEE IT.

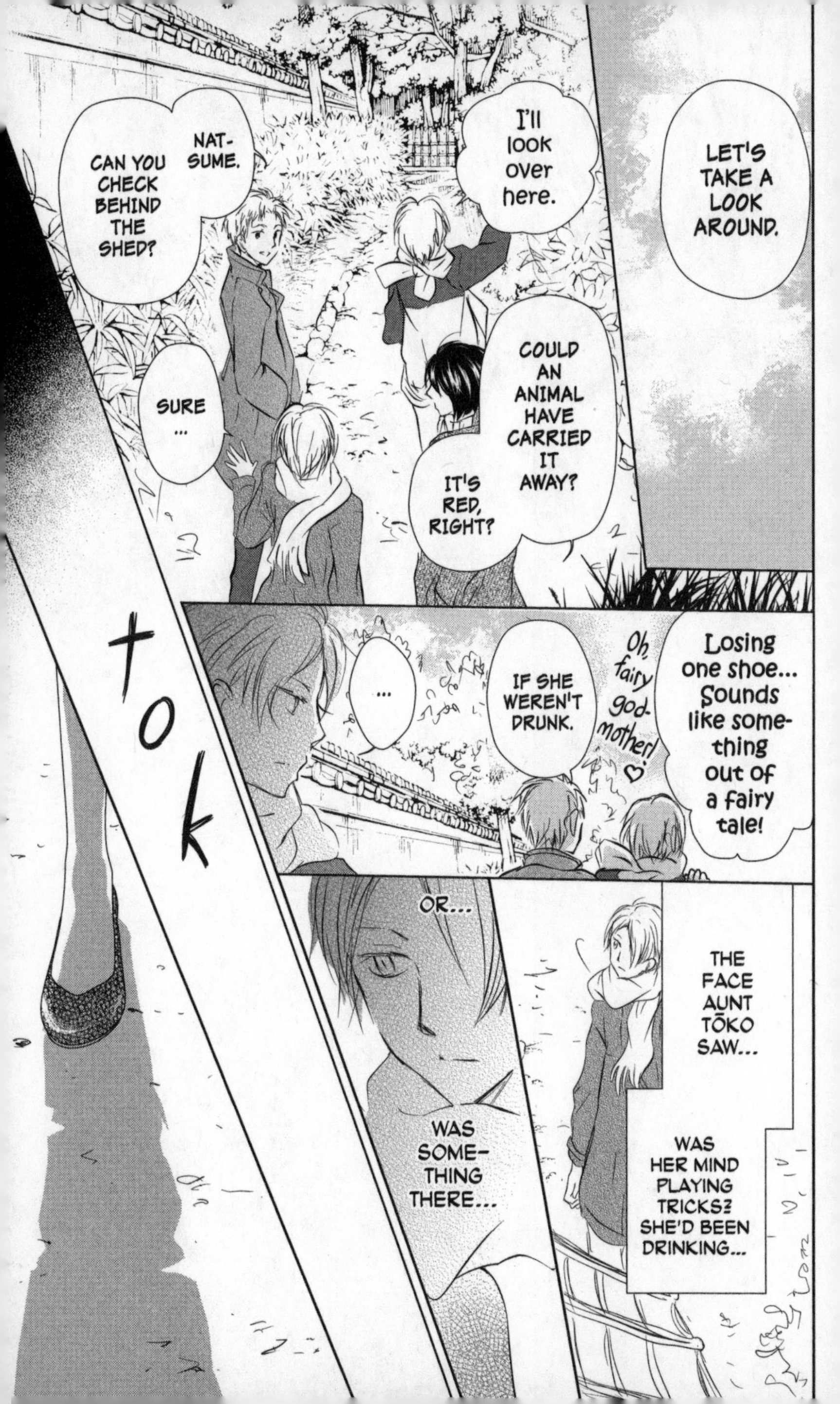
LET'S TAKE A LOOK AROUND.
I'll look over here.
NAT-SUME.
CAN YOU CHECK BEHIND THE SHED?
COULD AN ANIMAL HAVE CARRIED IT AWAY?
IT'S RED, RIGHT?
SURE ...
Losing one shoe... Sounds like some-thing out of a fairy tale!
Oh, fairy god-mother! ♡
IF SHE WEREN'T DRUNK.
...
THE FACE AUNT TŌKO SAW...
WAS HER MIND PLAYING TRICKS? SHE'D BEEN DRINKING...
OR...
WAS SOME-THING THERE...
tok

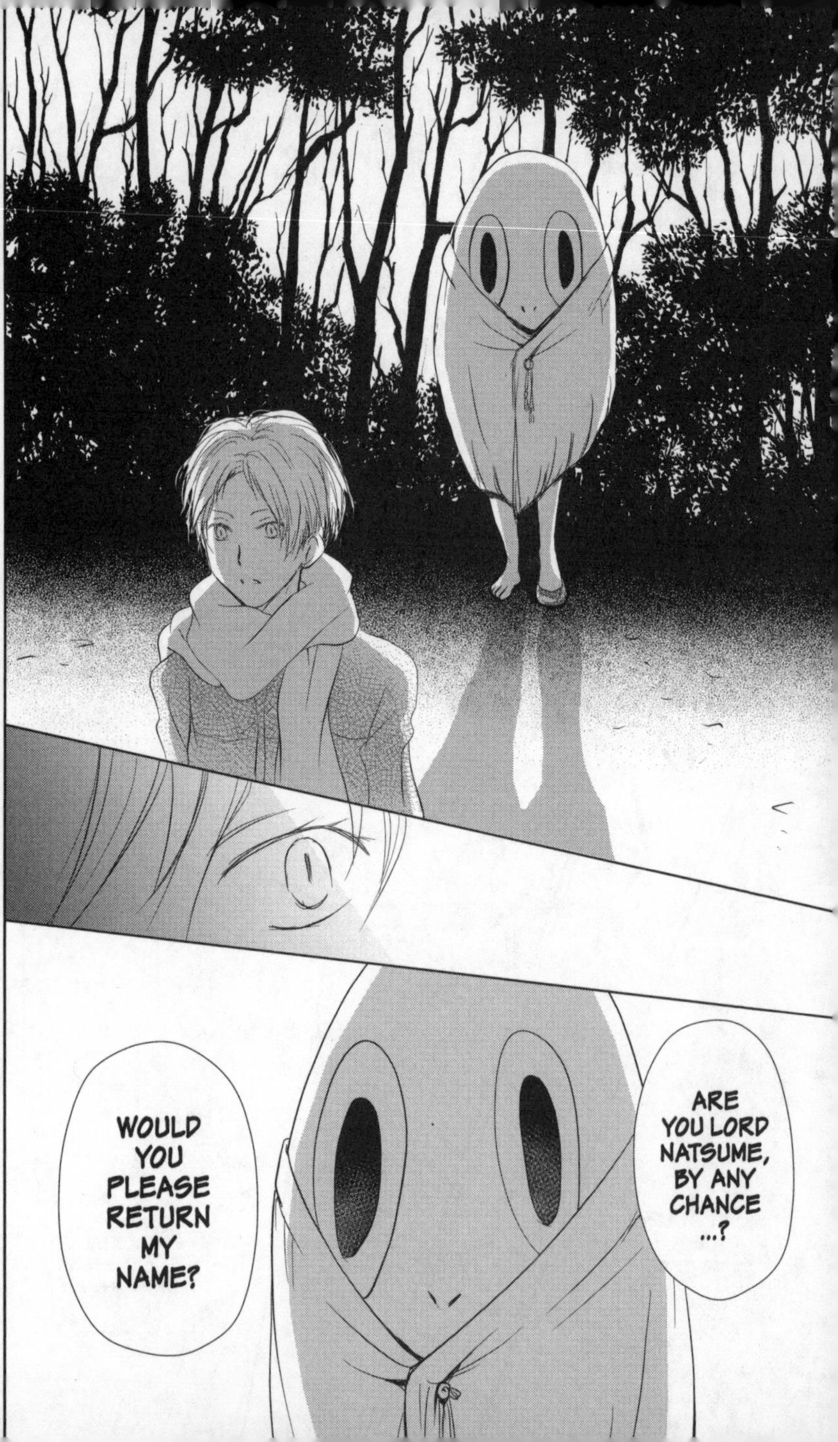
ARE YOU LORD NATSUME, BY ANY CHANCE ...?
WOULD YOU PLEASE RETURN MY NAME?

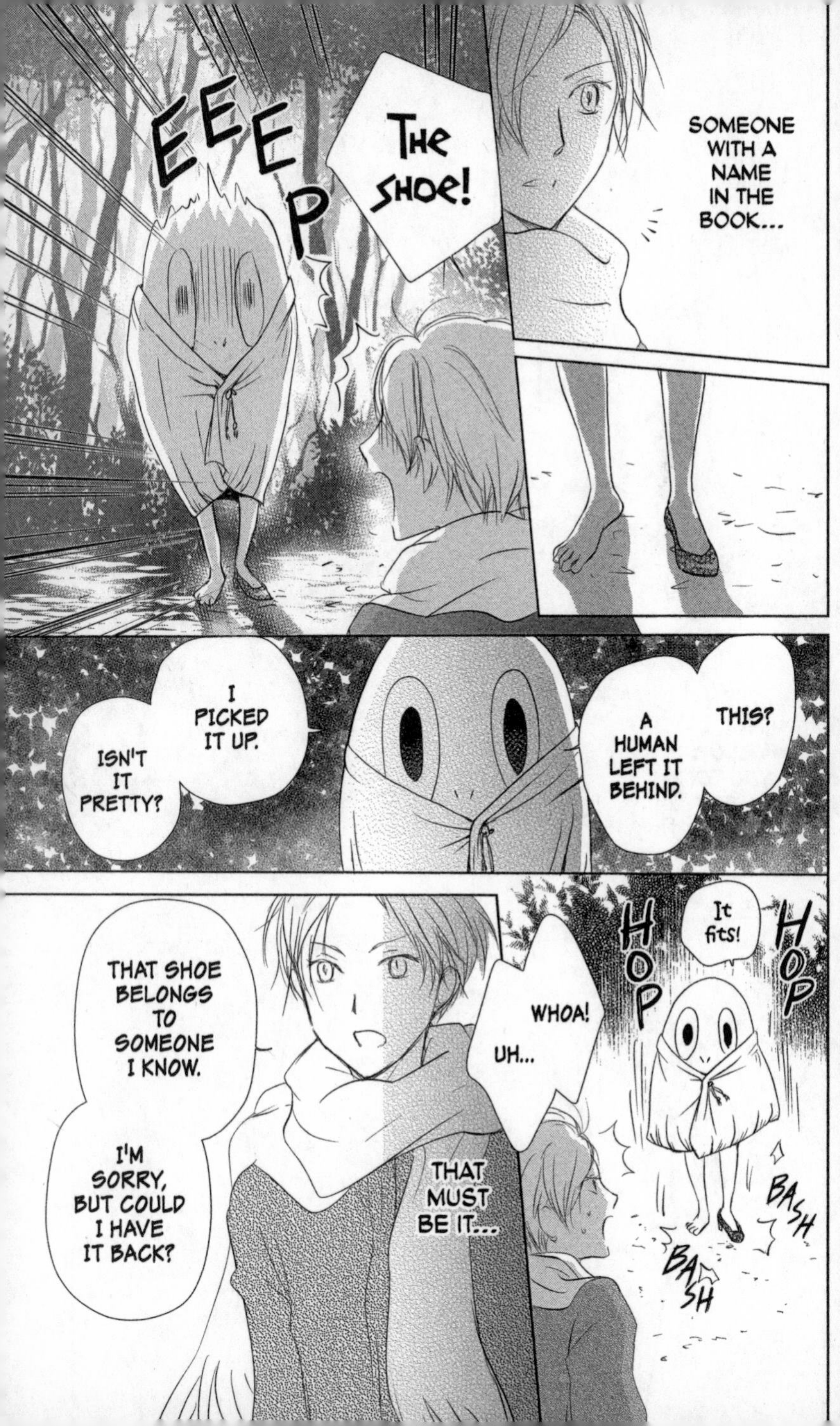
SOMEONE WITH A NAME IN THE BOOK...
THE SHOE!
EEEP
THIS?
A HUMAN LEFT IT BEHIND.
I PICKED IT UP.
ISN'T IT PRETTY?
HOP
It fits!
HOP
BASH
BASH
WHOA!
UH...
THAT MUST BE IT...
THAT SHOE BELONGS TO SOMEONE I KNOW.
I'M SORRY, BUT COULD I HAVE IT BACK?

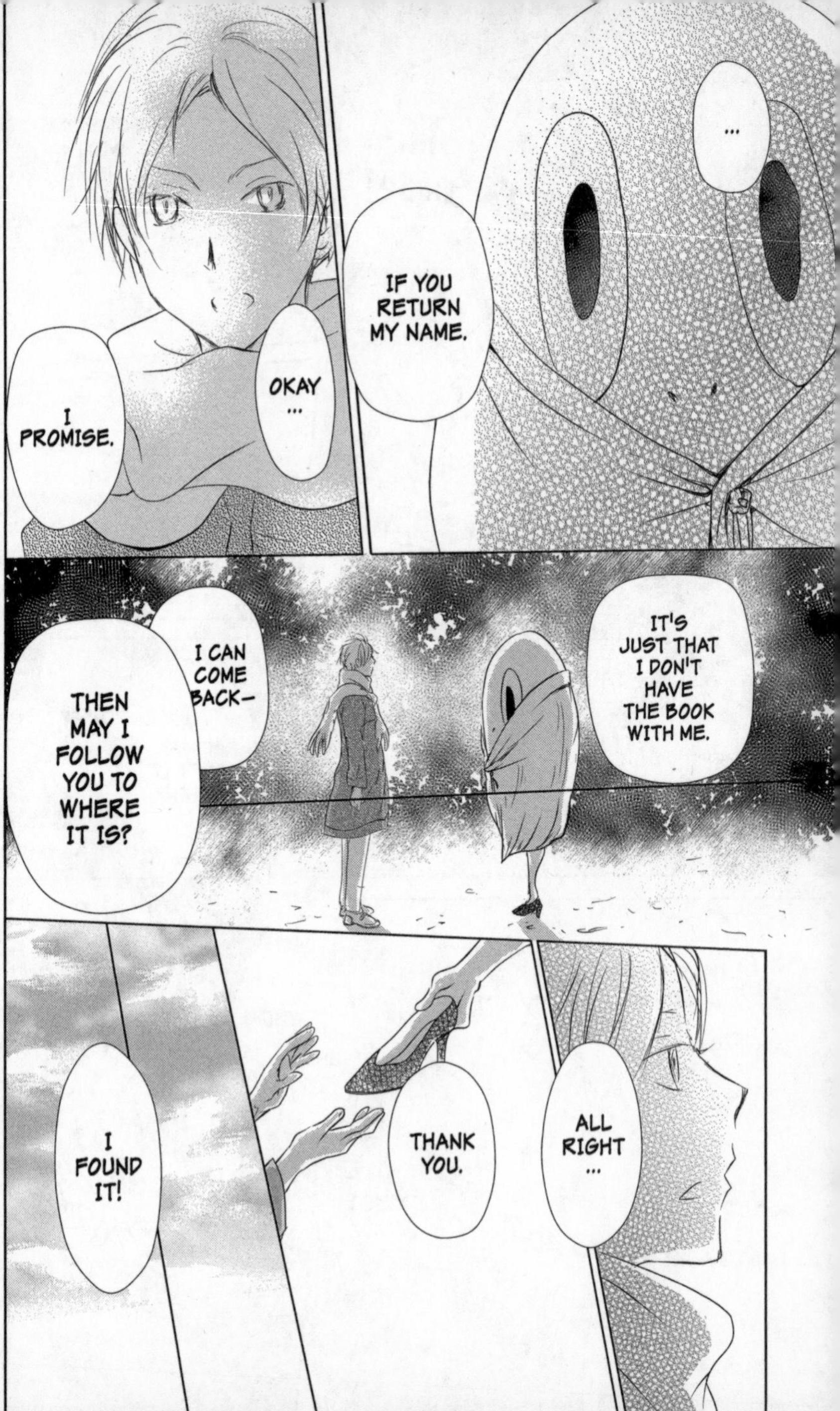
...
IF YOU RETURN MY NAME.
OKAY ...
I PROMISE.
IT'S JUST THAT I DON'T HAVE THE BOOK WITH ME.
I CAN COME BACK—
THEN MAY I FOLLOW YOU TO WHERE IT IS?
ALL RIGHT ...
THANK YOU.
I FOUND IT!

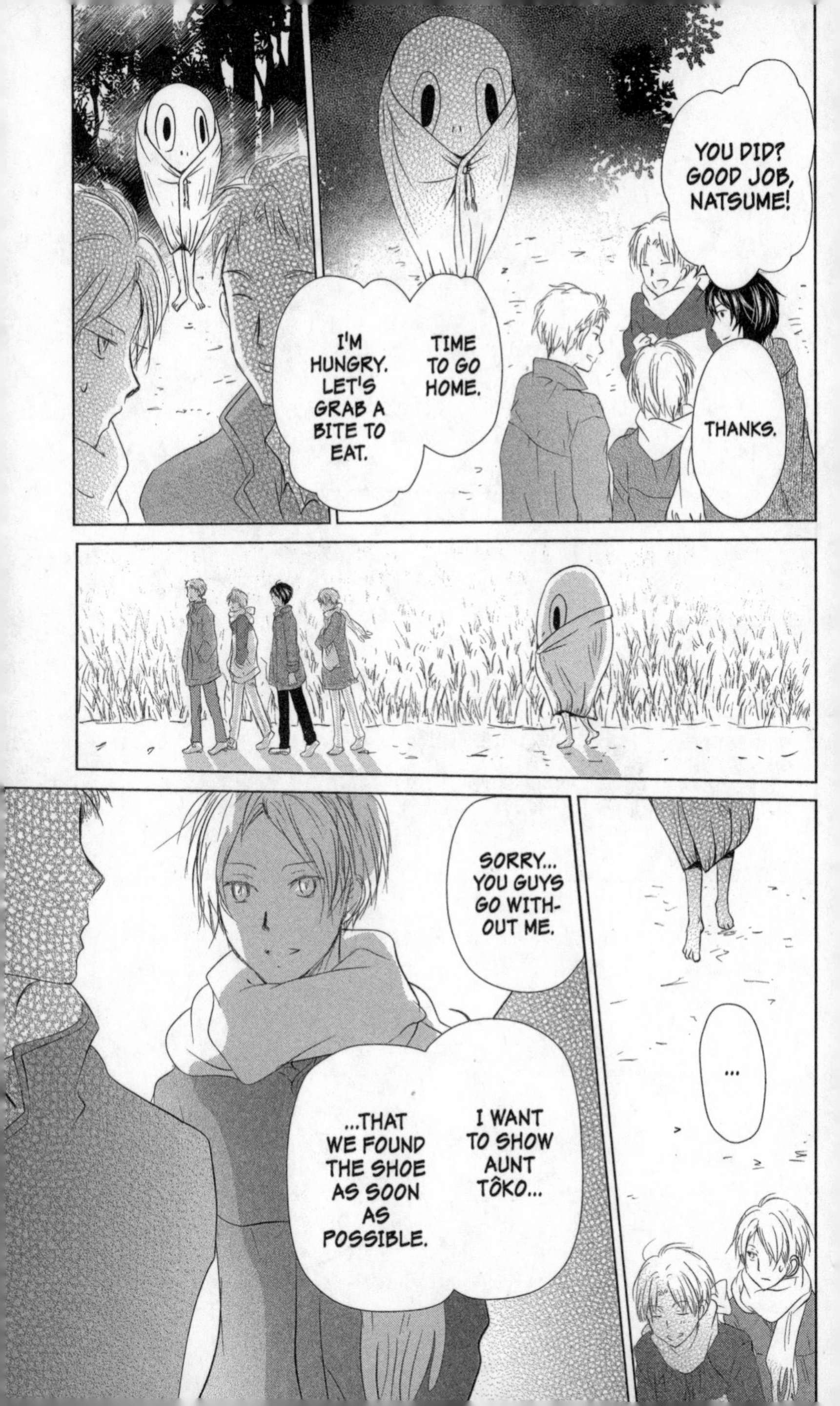
YOU DID? GOOD JOB, NATSUME!
THANKS.
TIME TO GO HOME.
I'M HUNGRY. LET'S GRAB A BITE TO EAT.
...
SORRY... YOU GUYS GO WITH-OUT ME.
I WANT TO SHOW AUNT TÔKO...
...THAT WE FOUND THE SHOE AS SOON AS POSSIBLE.

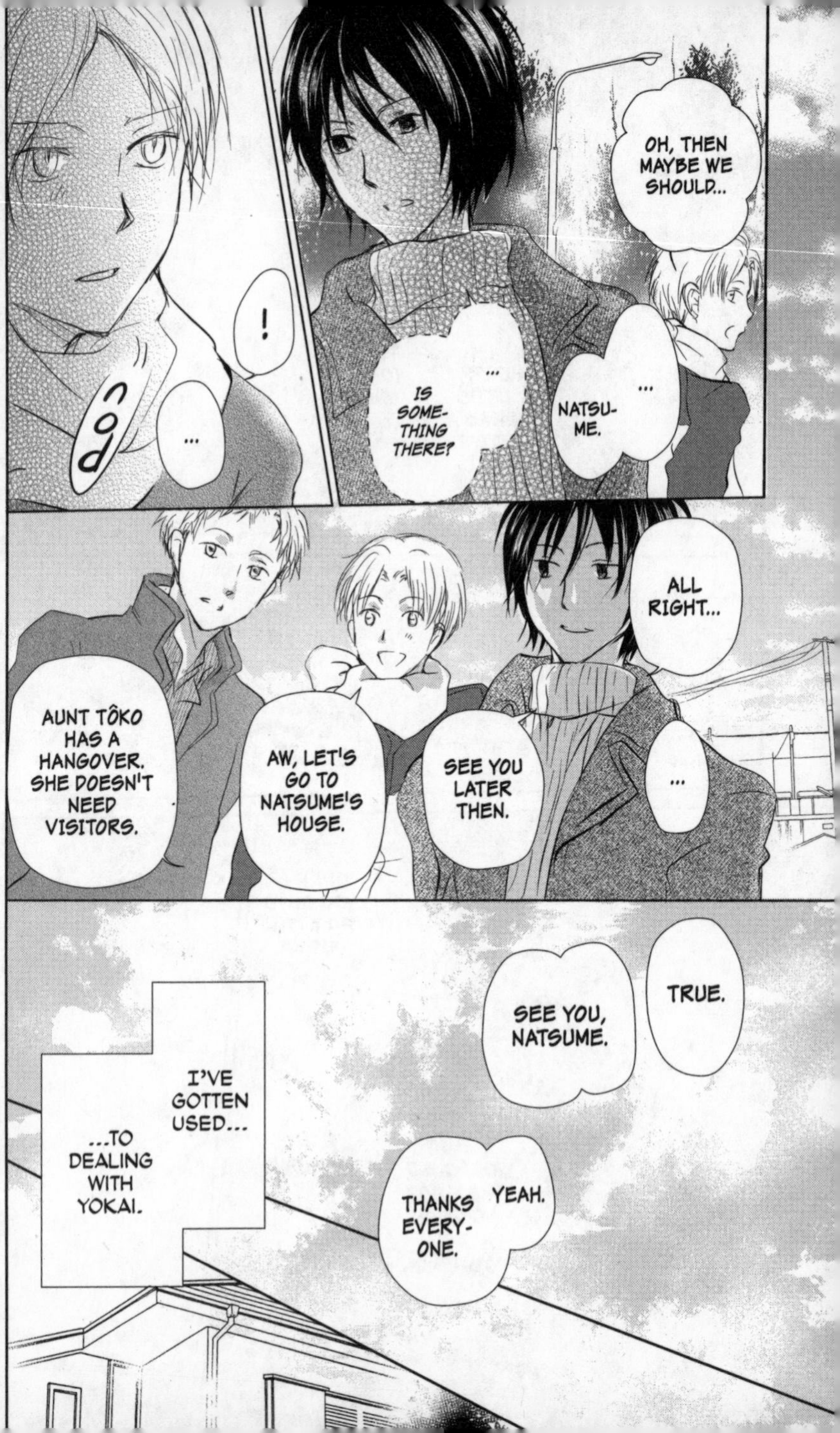
OH, THEN MAYBE WE SHOULD...
...
NATSU-ME.
...
IS SOME-THING THERE?
!
...
ALL RIGHT...
...
SEE YOU LATER THEN.
AW, LET'S GO TO NATSUME'S HOUSE.
AUNT TÔKO HAS A HANGOVER. SHE DOESN'T NEED VISITORS.
TRUE.
SEE YOU, NATSUME.
YEAH.
THANKS EVERY-ONE.
I'VE GOTTEN USED...
...TO DEALING WITH YOKAI.

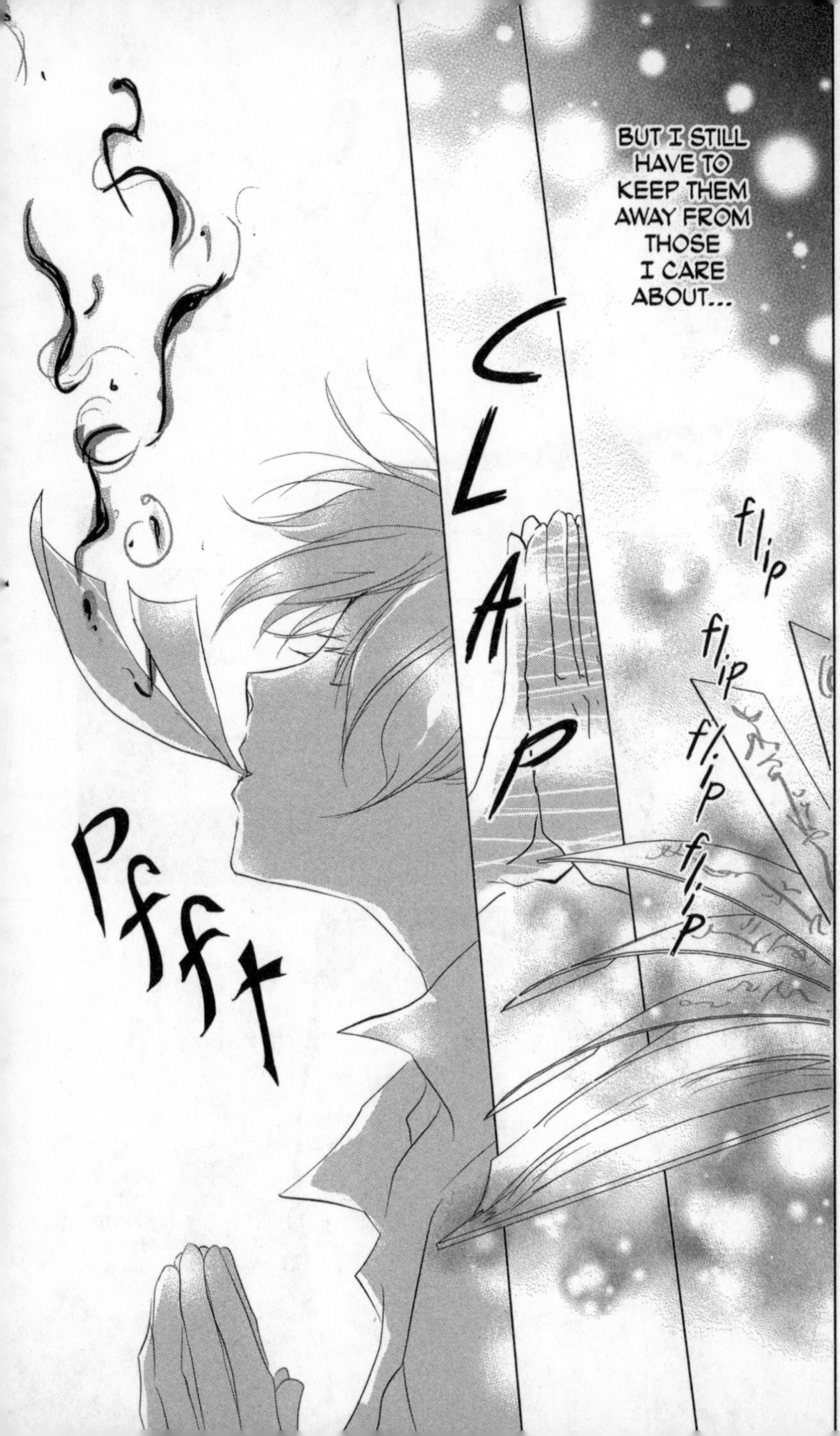
BUT I STILL HAVE TO KEEP THEM AWAY FROM THOSE I CARE ABOUT...
flip flip flip flip
CLAP
Pffft

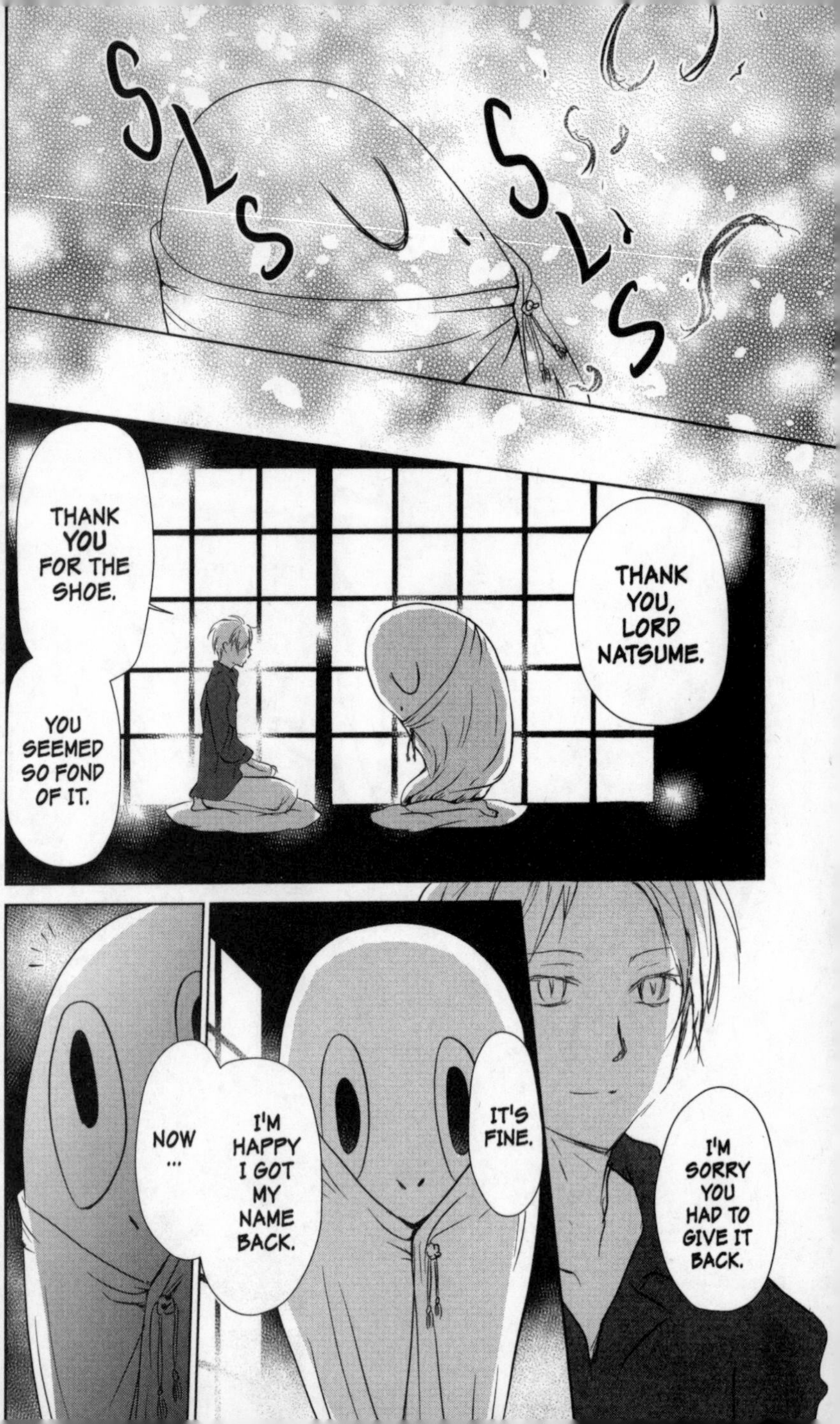
SLS
SLS
THANK YOU, LORD NATSUME.
THANK YOU FOR THE SHOE.
YOU SEEMED SO FOND OF IT.
I'M SORRY YOU HAD TO GIVE IT BACK.
IT'S FINE.
I'M HAPPY I GOT MY NAME BACK.
NOW ...

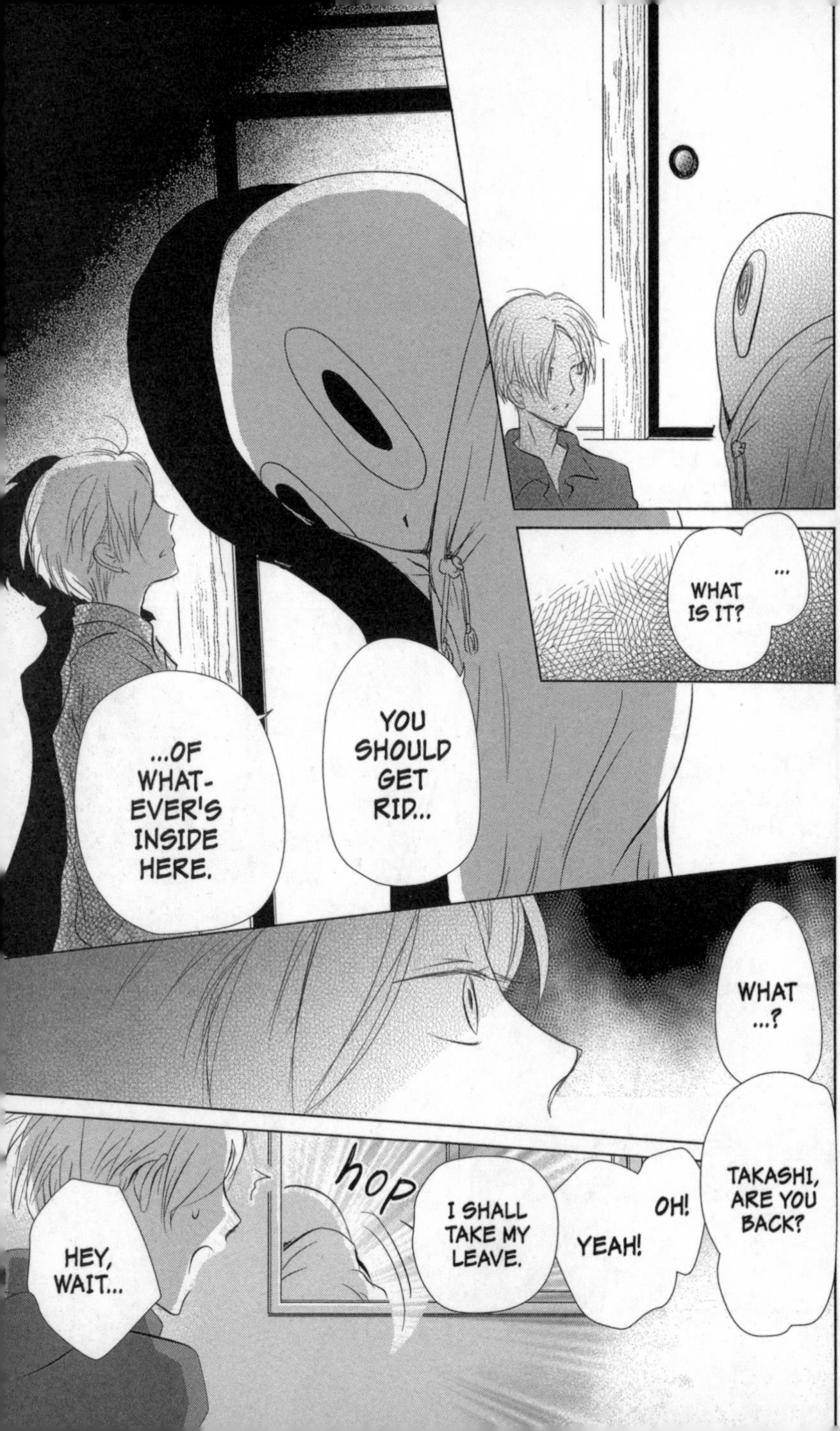
...
WHAT IS IT?
YOU SHOULD GET RID...
...OF WHATEVER'S INSIDE HERE.
WHAT ...?
TAKASHI, ARE YOU BACK?
OH!
YEAH!
hop
I SHALL TAKE MY LEAVE.
HEY, WAIT...

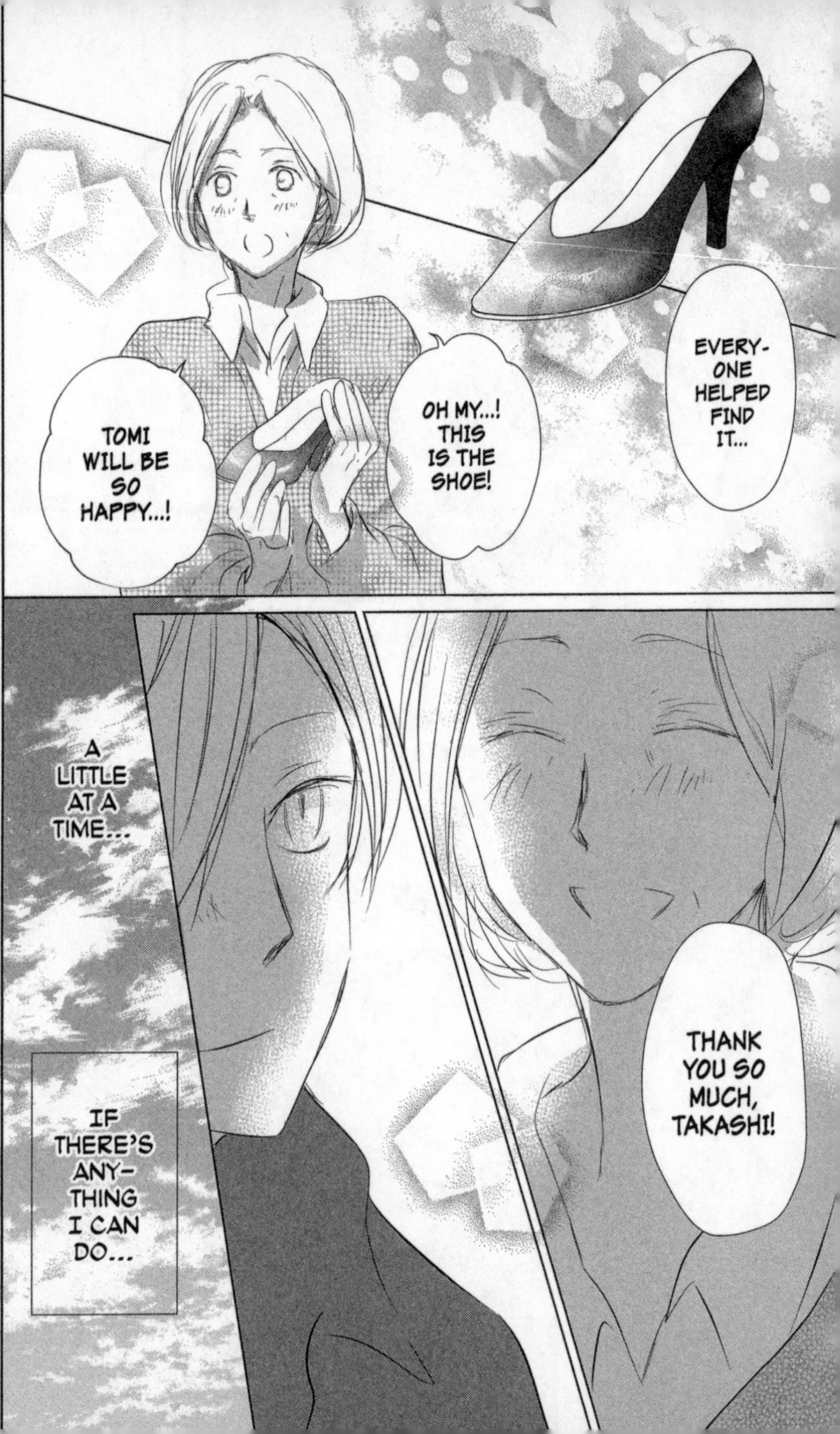

EVERY-ONE HELPED FIND IT...
OH MY...! THIS IS THE SHOE!
TOMI WILL BE SO HAPPY...!
THANK YOU SO MUCH, TAKASHI!
A LITTLE AT A TIME...
IF THERE'S ANY-THING I CAN DO...

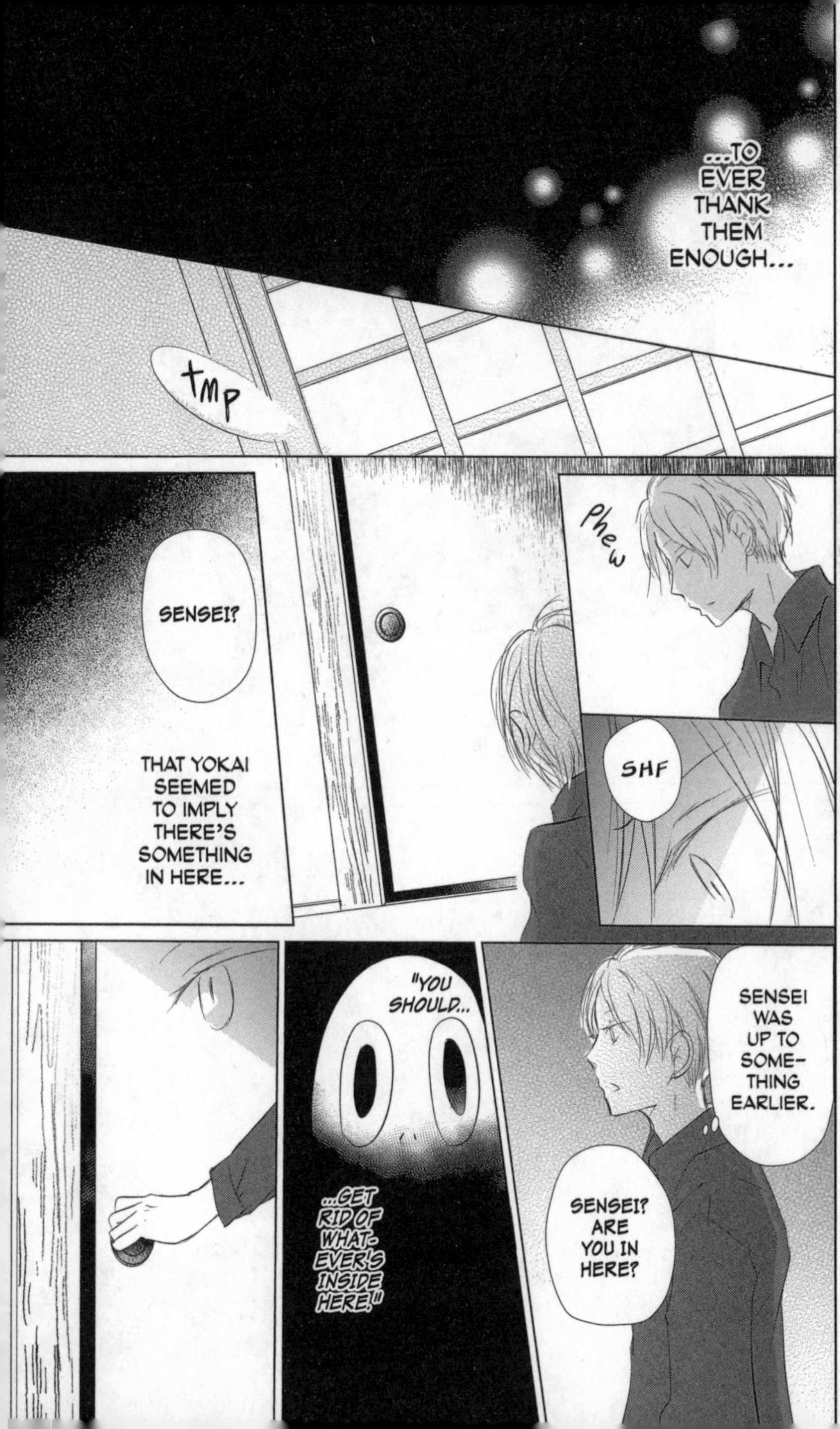
...TO EVER THANK THEM ENOUGH...
tmp
Phew
SHF
SENSEI?
THAT YOKAI SEEMED TO IMPLY THERE'S SOMETHING IN HERE...
SENSEI WAS UP TO SOME-THING EARLIER.
SENSEI? ARE YOU IN HERE?
"YOU SHOULD...
...GET RID OF WHAT-EVER'S INSIDE HERE."

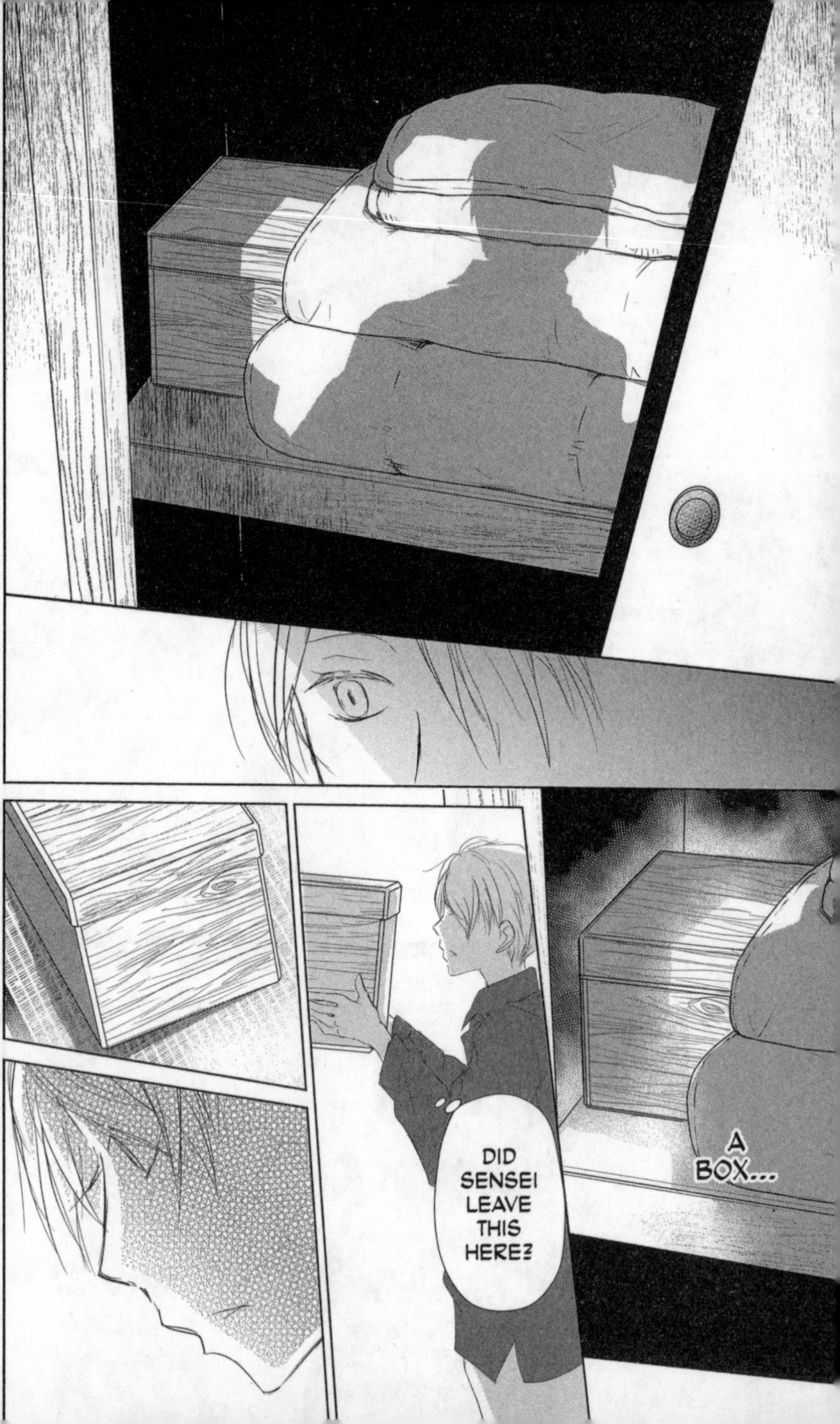
A BOX...
DID SENSEI LEAVE THIS HERE?

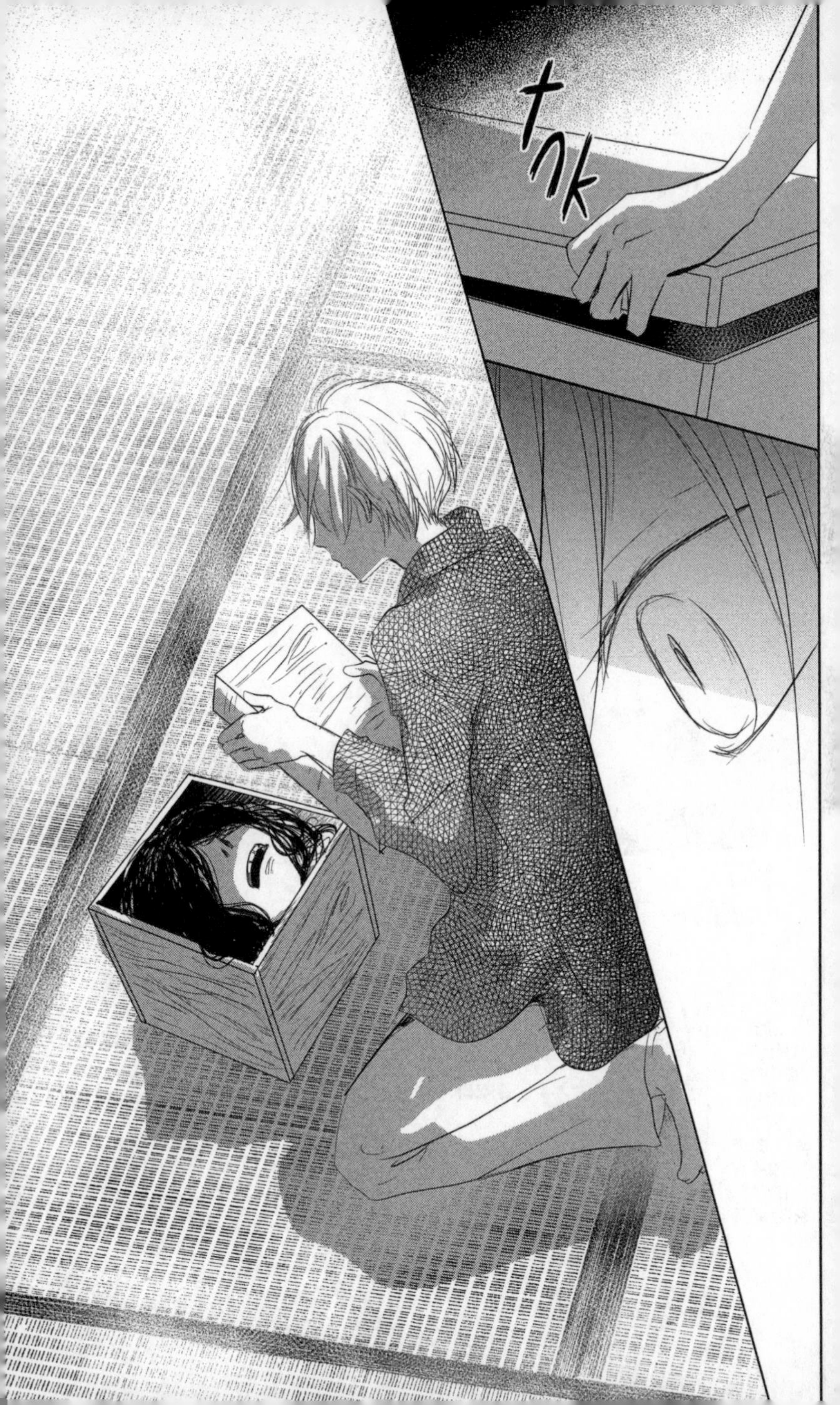
TNK

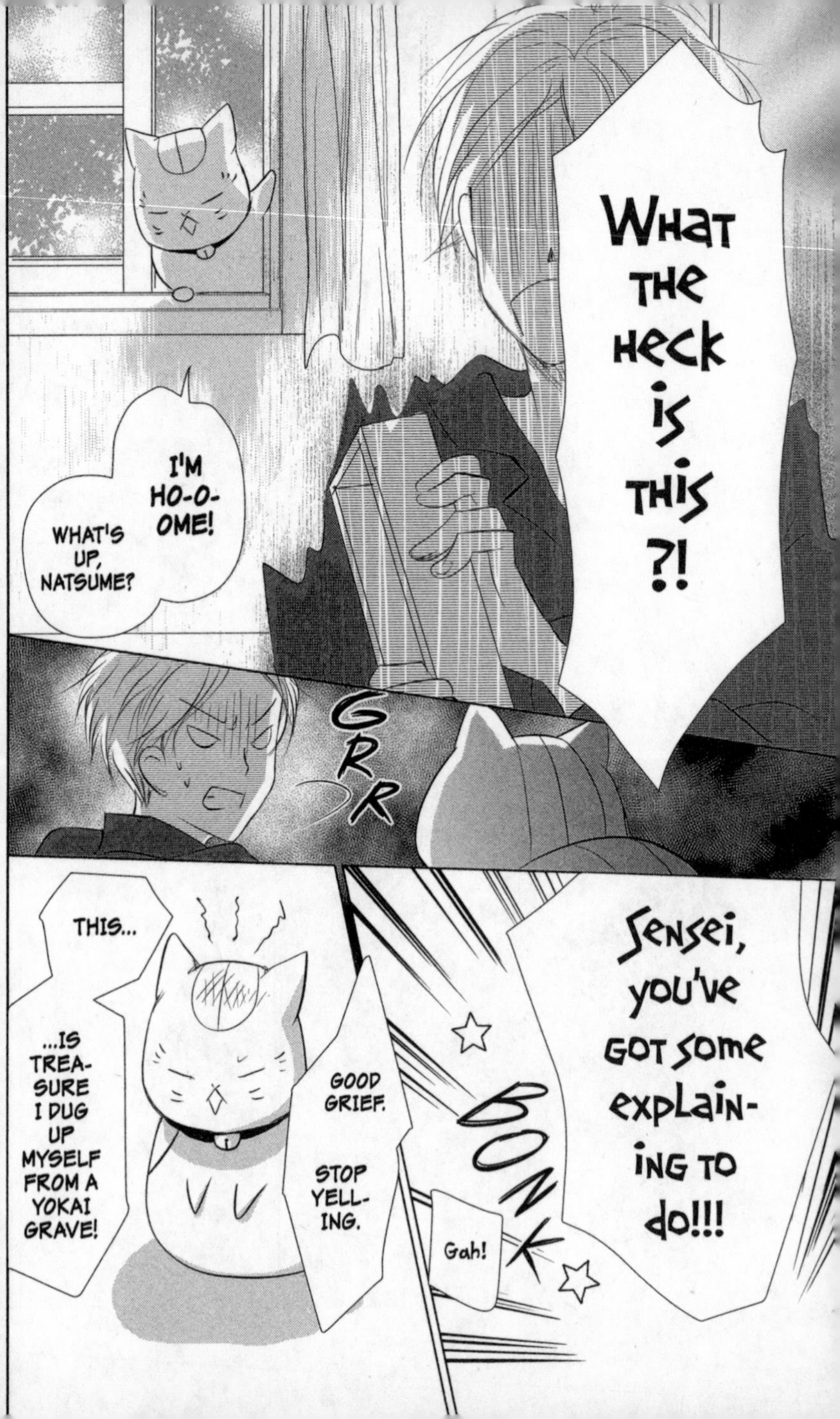
What the heck is this?!
I'M HO-O-OME!
WHAT'S UP, NATSUME?
GRR
Sensei, you've got some explaining to do!!!
BONK
Gah!
GOOD GRIEF.
STOP YELLING.
THIS...
...IS TREASURE I DUG UP MYSELF FROM A YOKAI GRAVE!

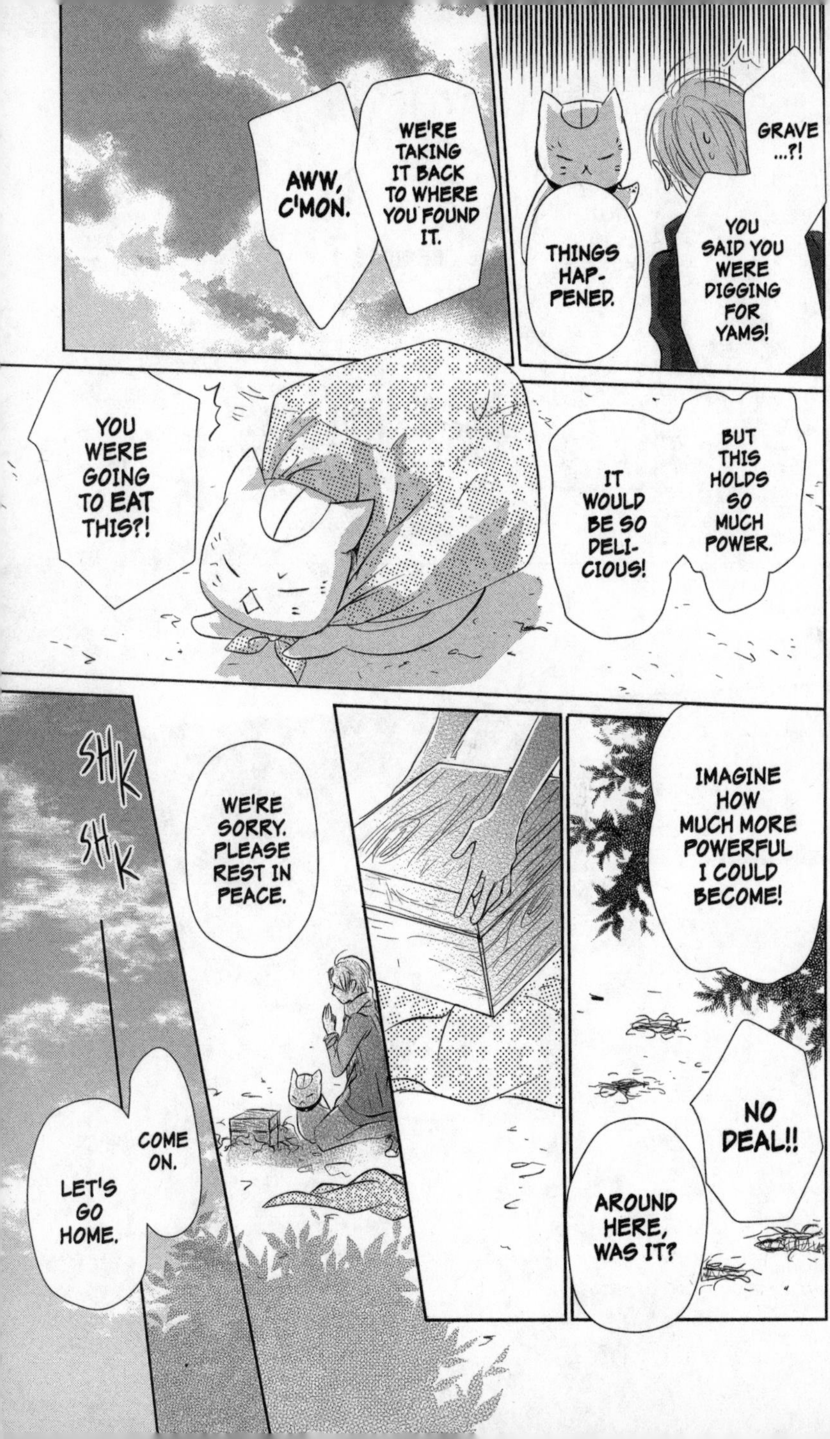
GRAVE ...?!
YOU SAID YOU WERE DIGGING FOR YAMS!
THINGS HAPPENED.
WE'RE TAKING IT BACK TO WHERE YOU FOUND IT.
AWW, C'MON.
BUT THIS HOLDS SO MUCH POWER.
IT WOULD BE SO DELICIOUS!
YOU WERE GOING TO EAT THIS?!
IMAGINE HOW MUCH MORE POWERFUL I COULD BECOME!
NO DEAL!!
AROUND HERE, WAS IT?
WE'RE SORRY. PLEASE REST IN PEACE.
SHK
SHK
COME ON.
LET'S GO HOME.

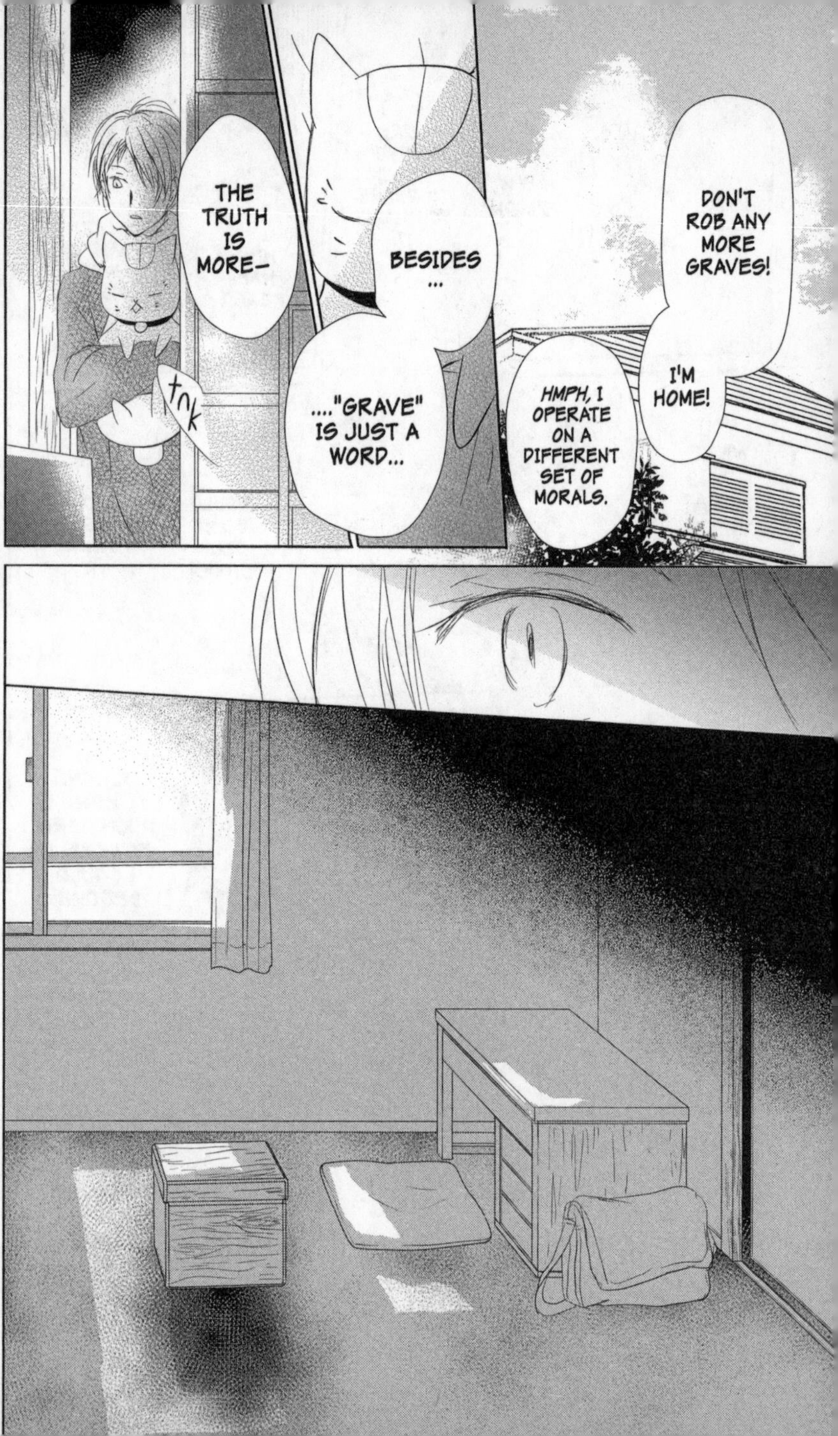
DON'T ROB ANY MORE GRAVES!
I'M HOME!
HMPH, I OPERATE ON A DIFFERENT SET OF MORALS.
BESIDES...
...."GRAVE" IS JUST A WORD...
THE TRUTH IS MORE–
tnk

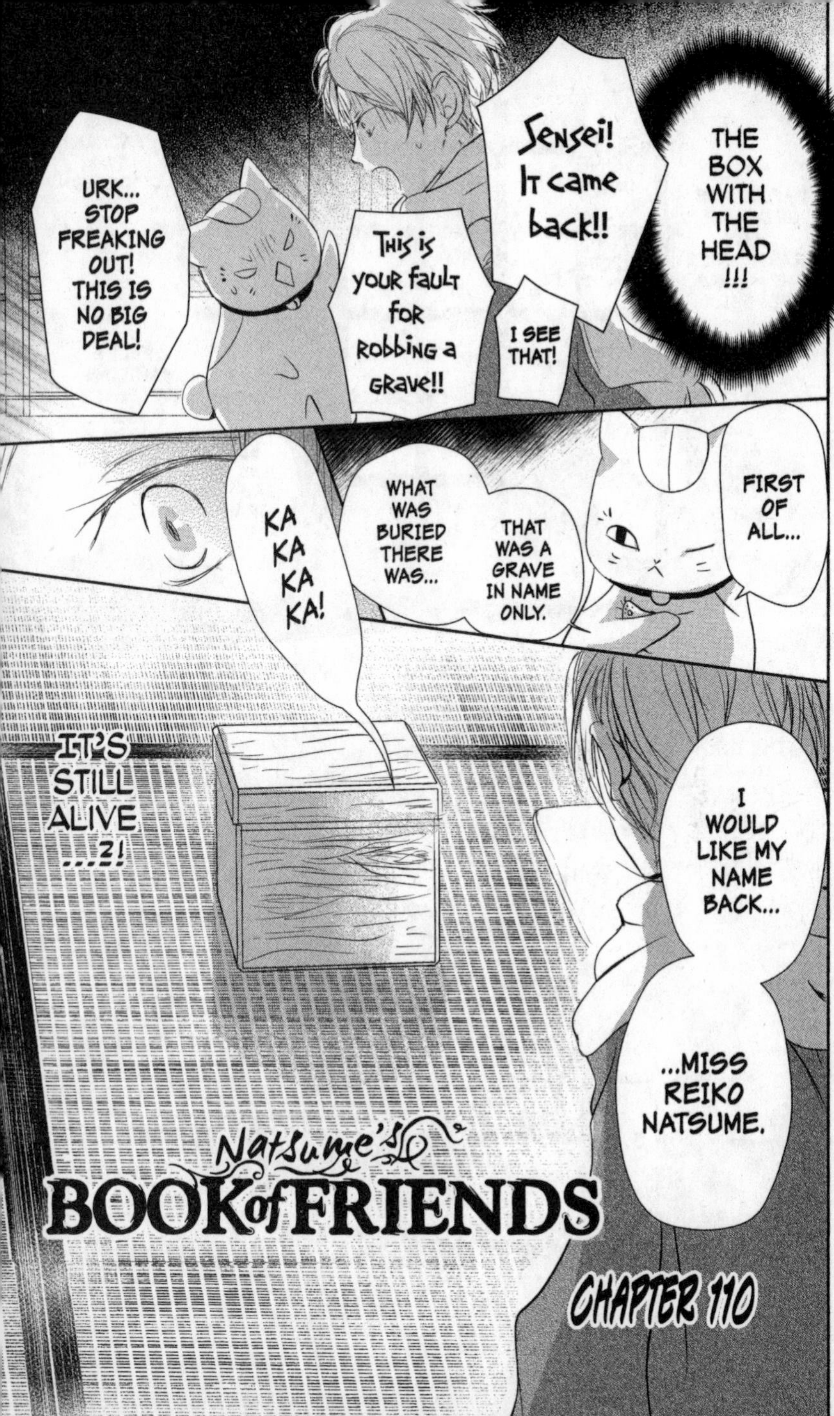
THE BOX WITH THE HEAD!!!
Sensei! It came back!!
I SEE THAT!
This is your fault for robbing a grave!!
URK... STOP FREAKING OUT! THIS IS NO BIG DEAL!
FIRST OF ALL...
THAT WAS A GRAVE IN NAME ONLY.
WHAT WAS BURIED THERE WAS...
KA KA KA KA!
I WOULD LIKE MY NAME BACK...
...MISS REIKO NATSUME.
IT'S STILL ALIVE...?!
Natsume's BOOK of FRIENDS
CHAPTER 110

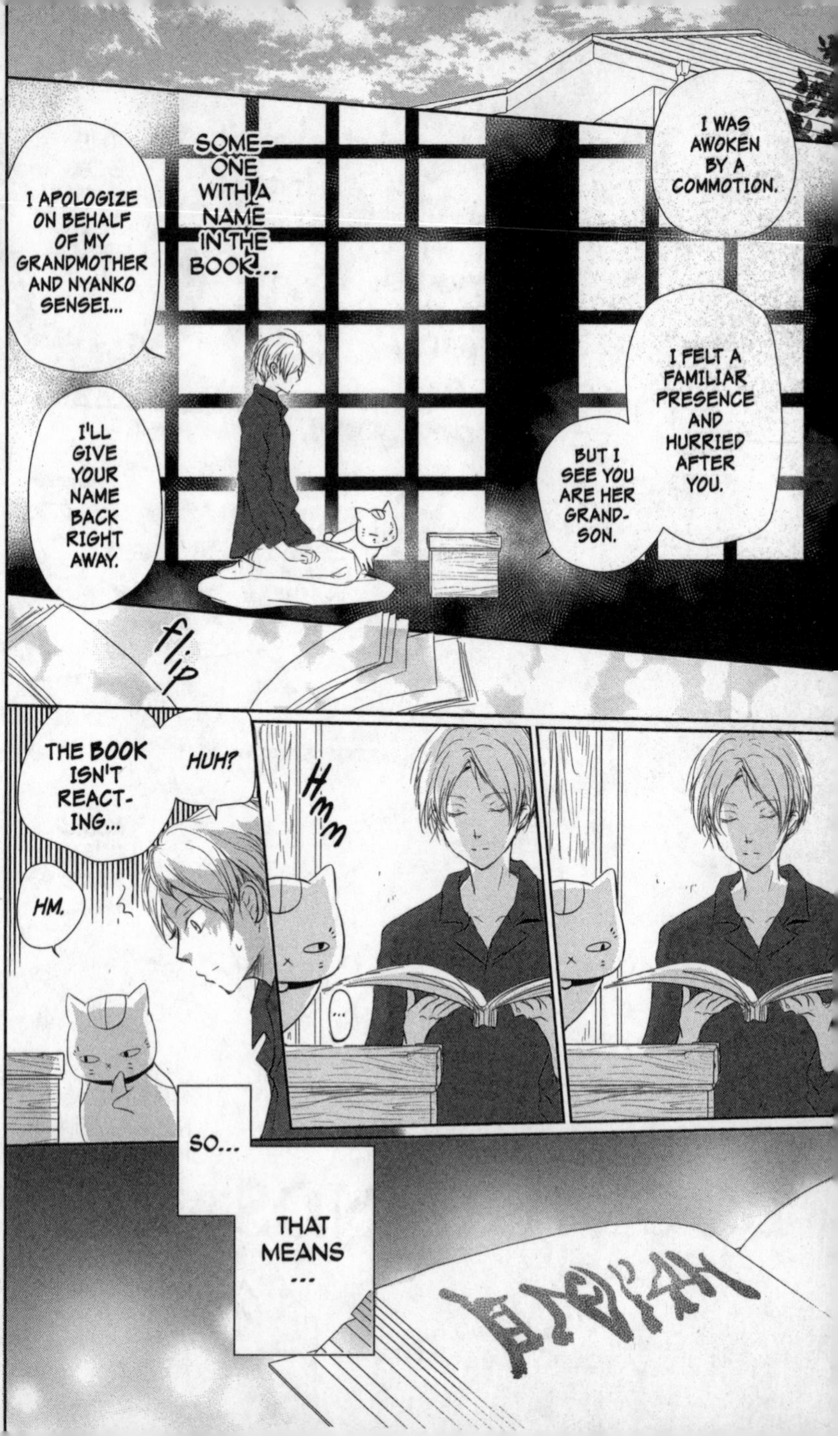
I WAS AWOKEN BY A COMMOTION.
I FELT A FAMILIAR PRESENCE AND HURRIED AFTER YOU.
BUT I SEE YOU ARE HER GRAND-SON.
SOME-ONE WITH A NAME IN THE BOOK...
I APOLOGIZE ON BEHALF OF MY GRANDMOTHER AND NYANKO SENSEI...
I'LL GIVE YOUR NAME BACK RIGHT AWAY.
flip
Hmm
...
HUH?
THE BOOK ISN'T REACT-ING...
HM.
SO...
THAT MEANS ...

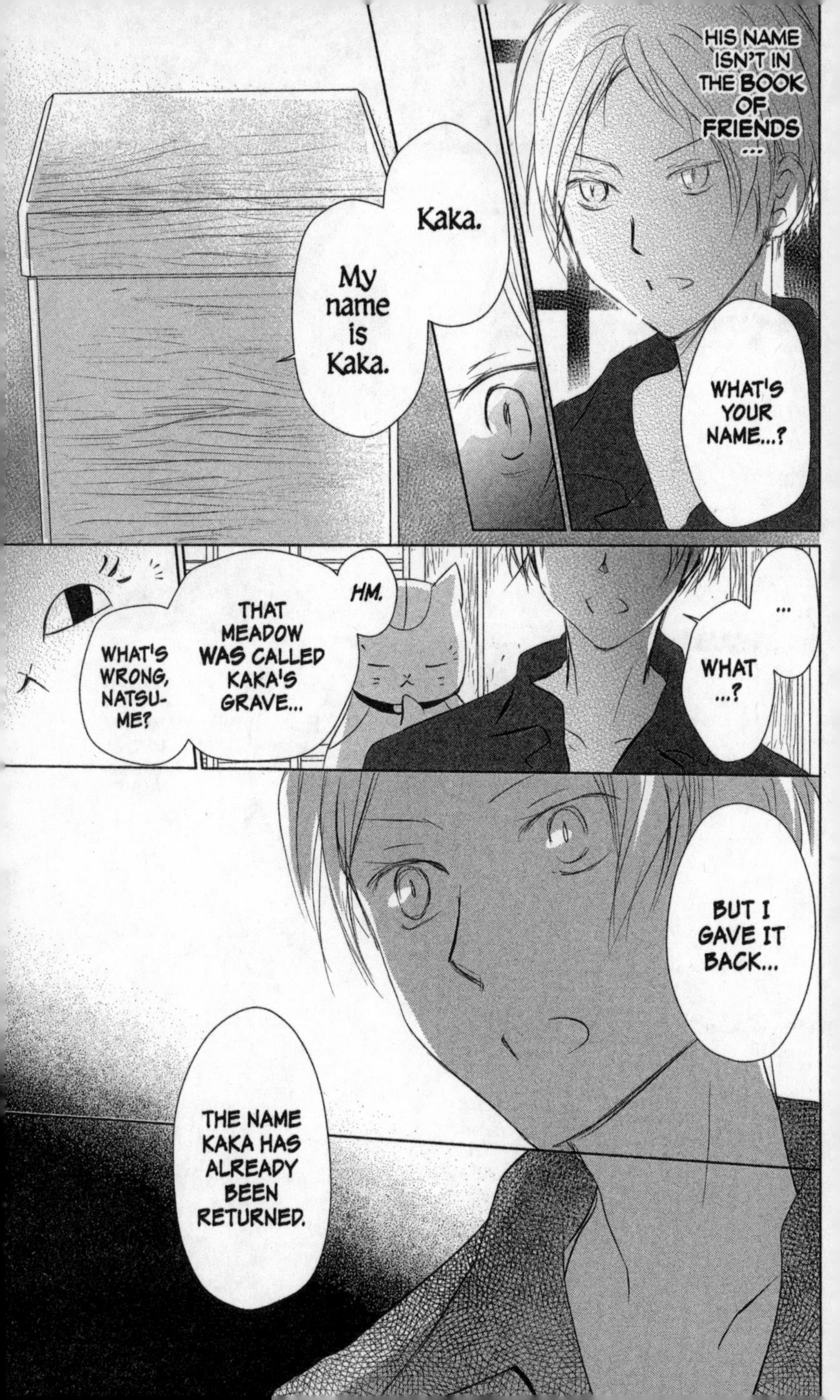
HIS NAME ISN'T IN THE BOOK OF FRIENDS...
WHAT'S YOUR NAME...?
Kaka.
My name is Kaka.
... WHAT ...?
HM.
THAT MEADOW WAS CALLED KAKA'S GRAVE...
WHAT'S WRONG, NATSUME?
BUT I GAVE IT BACK...
THE NAME KAKA HAS ALREADY BEEN RETURNED.

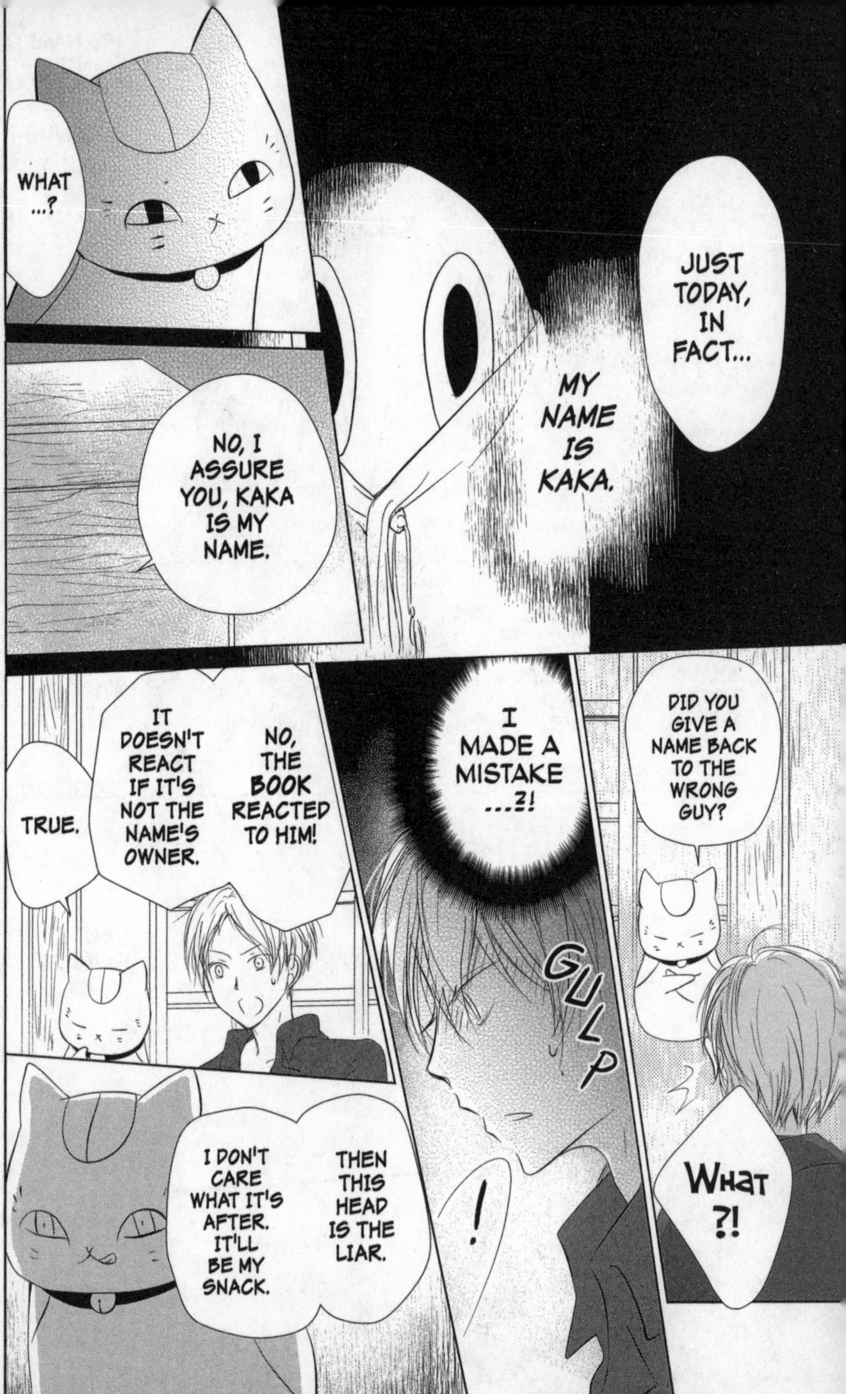
JUST TODAY, IN FACT...
MY NAME IS KAKA.
WHAT ...?
NO, I ASSURE YOU, KAKA IS MY NAME.
DID YOU GIVE A NAME BACK TO THE WRONG GUY?
WHAT ?!
I MADE A MISTAKE ...?!
GULP
!
NO, THE BOOK REACTED TO HIM!
IT DOESN'T REACT IF IT'S NOT THE NAME'S OWNER.
TRUE.
THEN THIS HEAD IS THE LIAR.
I DON'T CARE WHAT IT'S AFTER. IT'LL BE MY SNACK.

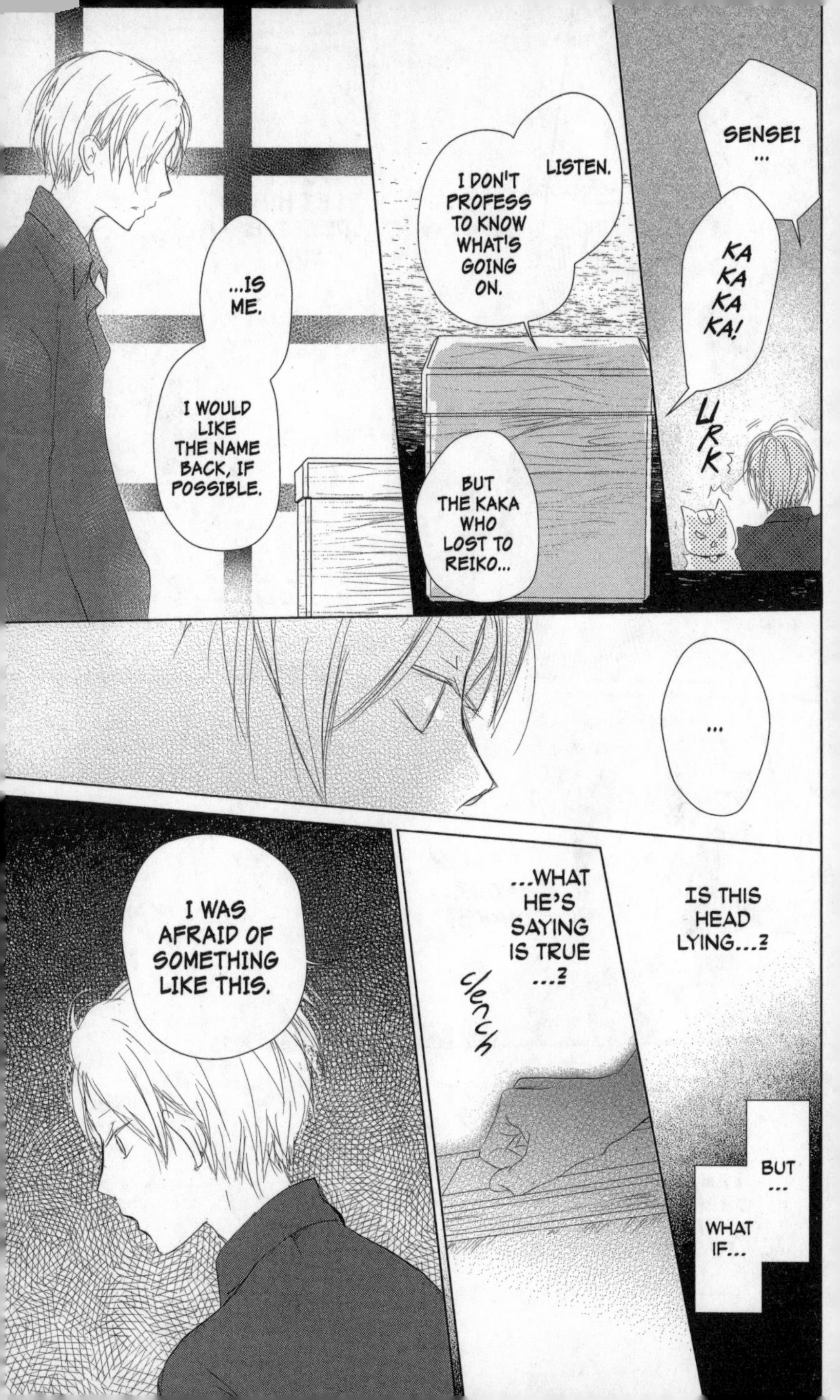
SENSEI ...
KA KA KA KA!
URK
LISTEN.
I DON'T PROFESS TO KNOW WHAT'S GOING ON.
BUT THE KAKA WHO LOST TO REIKO...
...IS ME.
I WOULD LIKE THE NAME BACK, IF POSSIBLE.
...
IS THIS HEAD LYING...?
BUT... WHAT IF...
...WHAT HE'S SAYING IS TRUE...?
clench
I WAS AFRAID OF SOMETHING LIKE THIS.

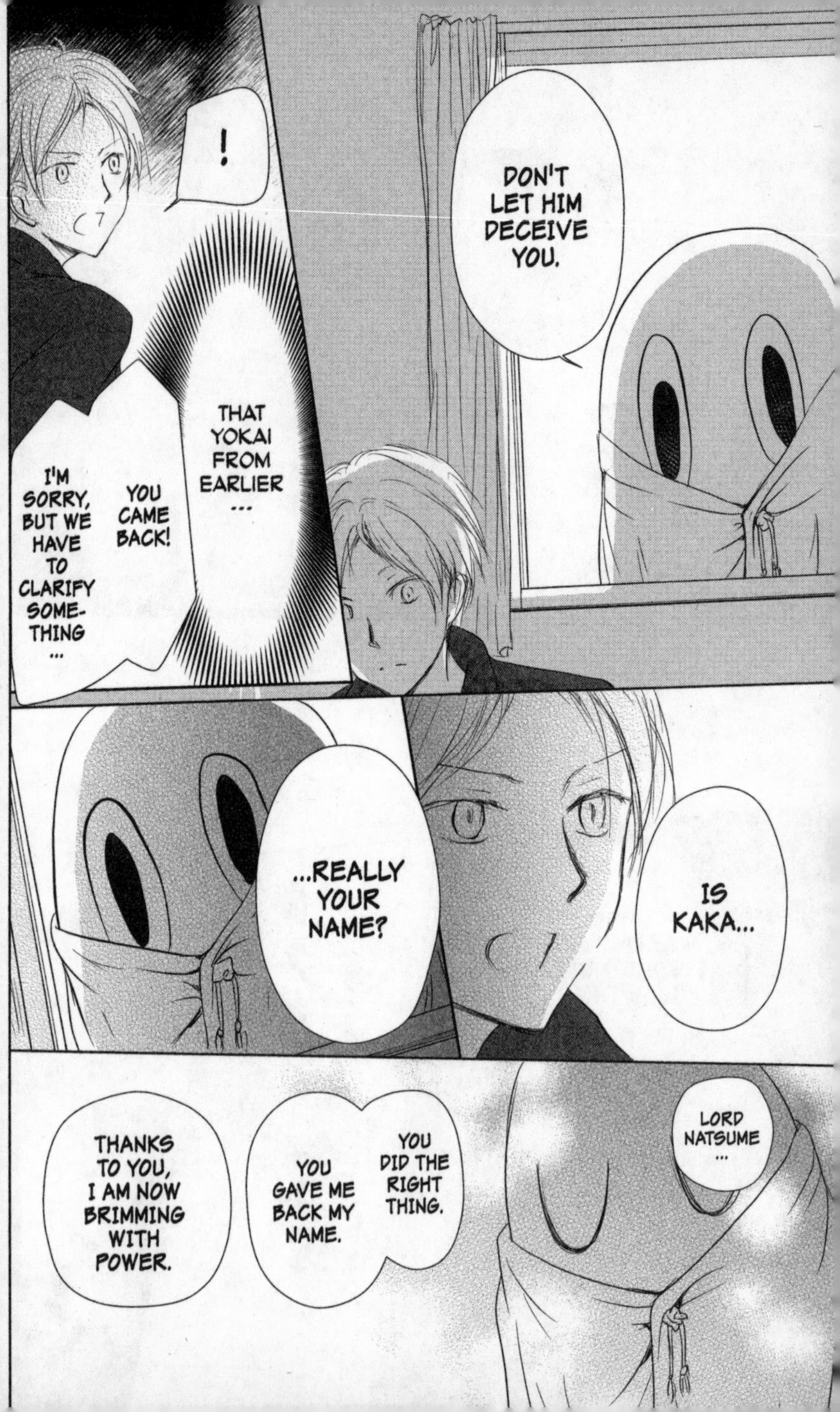
DON'T LET HIM DECEIVE YOU.
!
THAT YOKAI FROM EARLIER...
YOU CAME BACK!
I'M SORRY, BUT WE HAVE TO CLARIFY SOME-THING...
IS KAKA...
...REALLY YOUR NAME?
LORD NATSUME...
YOU DID THE RIGHT THING.
YOU GAVE ME BACK MY NAME.
THANKS TO YOU, I AM NOW BRIMMING WITH POWER.

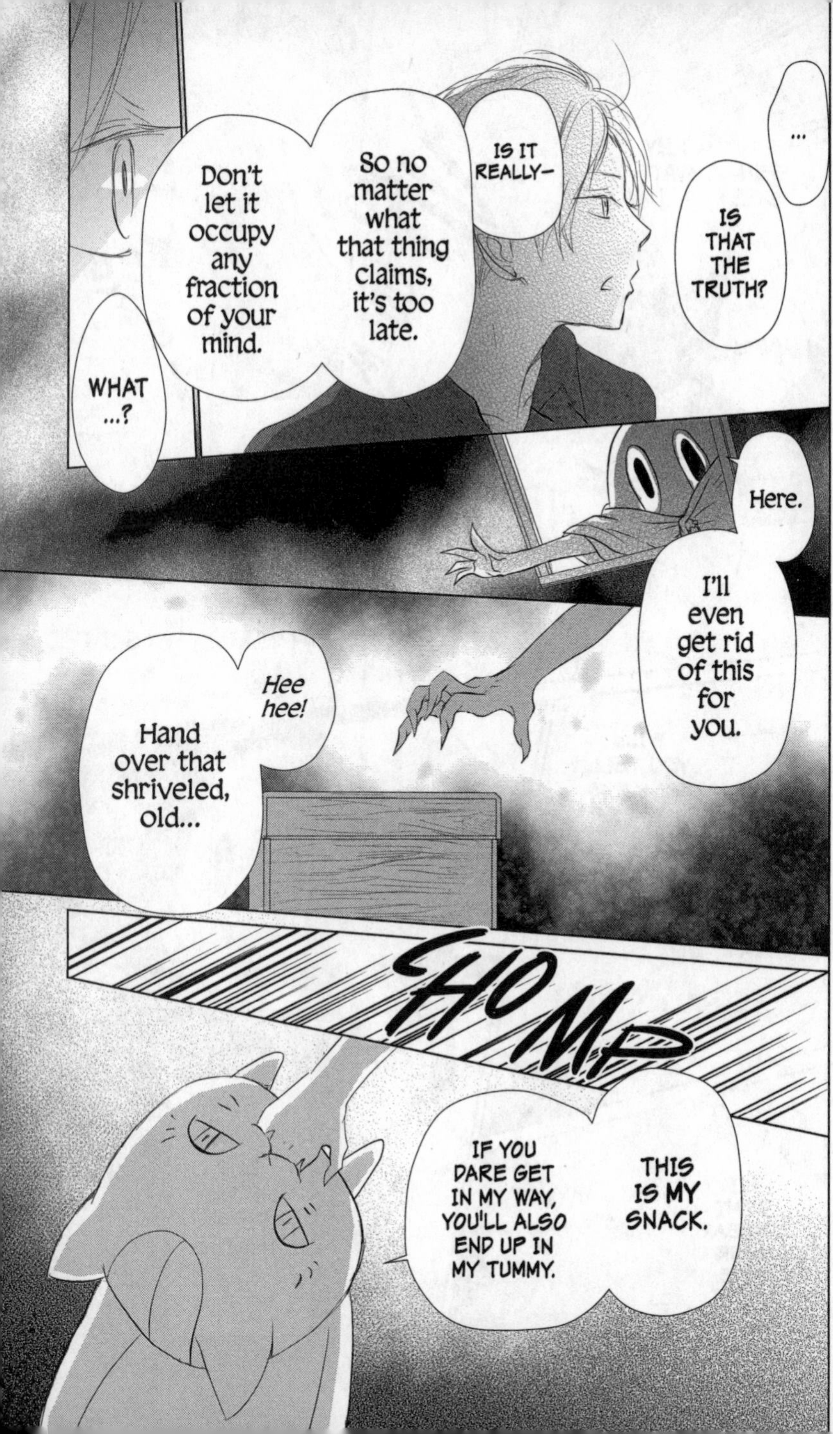
...
IS THAT THE TRUTH?
IS IT REALLY—
So no matter what that thing claims, it's too late.
Don't let it occupy any fraction of your mind.
WHAT ...?
Here.
I'll even get rid of this for you.
Hee hee!
Hand over that shriveled, old...
CHOMP
THIS IS MY SNACK.
IF YOU DARE GET IN MY WAY, YOU'LL ALSO END UP IN MY TUMMY.

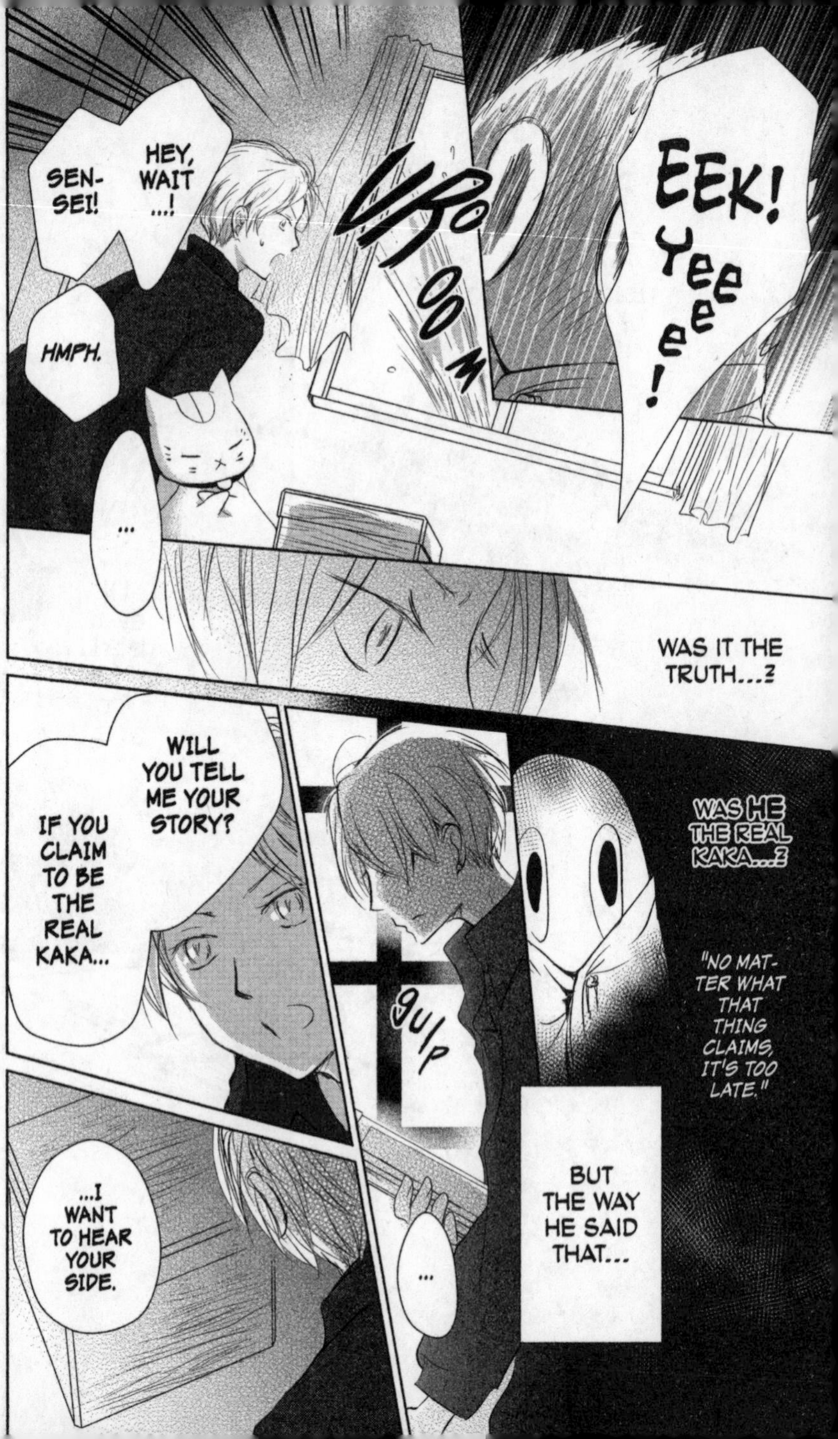
EEK! Yeeeee!
VROOOM
HEY, WAIT...!
SEN-SEI!
HMPH.
...
WAS IT THE TRUTH...?
WAS HE THE REAL KAKA...?
"NO MATTER WHAT THAT THING CLAIMS, IT'S TOO LATE."
BUT THE WAY HE SAID THAT...
gulp
WILL YOU TELL ME YOUR STORY?
IF YOU CLAIM TO BE THE REAL KAKA...
...I WANT TO HEAR YOUR SIDE.
...

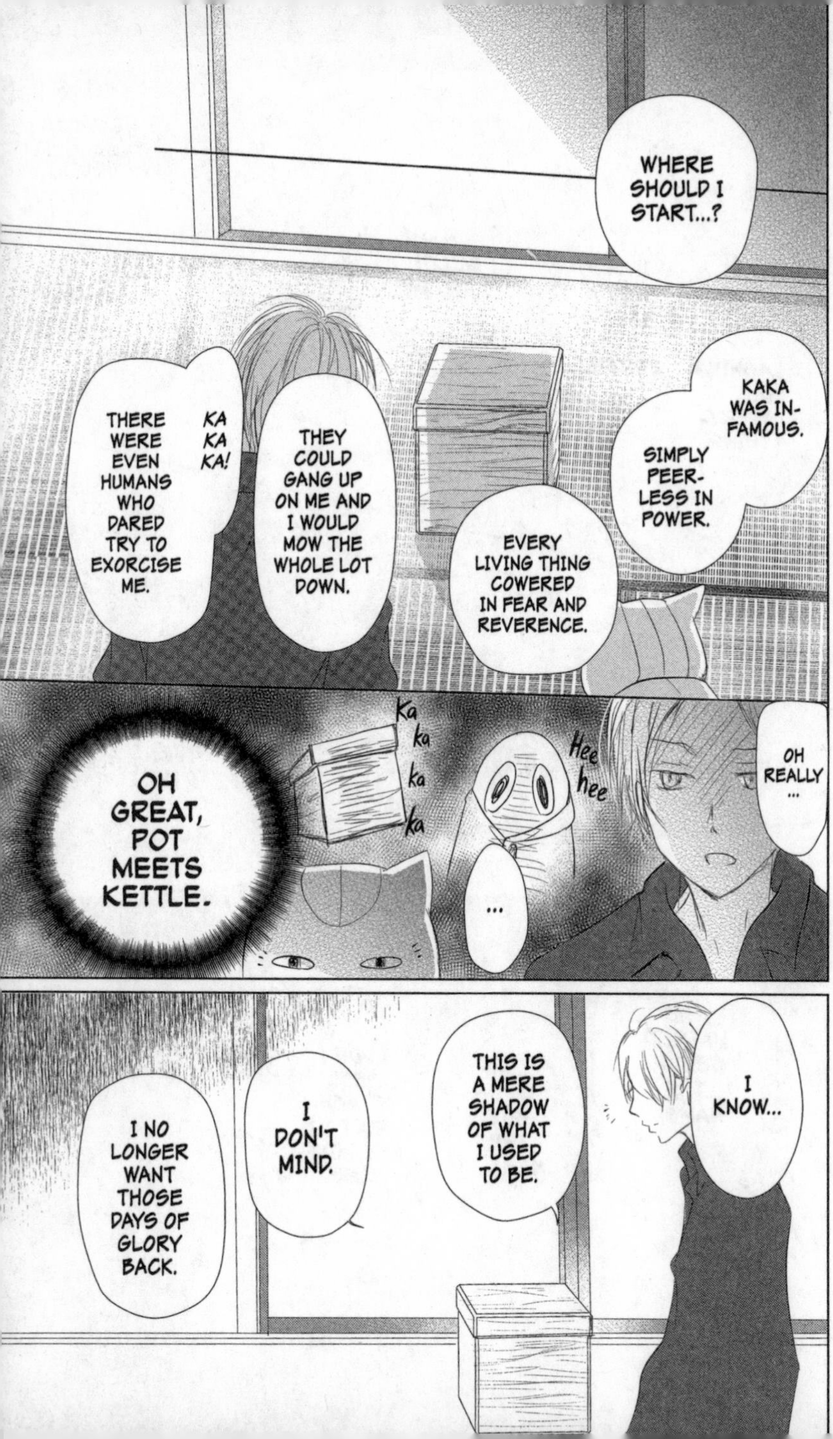
WHERE SHOULD I START...?
KAKA WAS IN-FAMOUS.
SIMPLY PEER-LESS IN POWER.
EVERY LIVING THING COWERED IN FEAR AND REVERENCE.
THEY COULD GANG UP ON ME AND I WOULD MOW THE WHOLE LOT DOWN.
KA KA KA!
THERE WERE EVEN HUMANS WHO DARED TRY TO EXORCISE ME.
OH REALLY ...
Hee hee
Ka ka ka ka
...
OH GREAT, POT MEETS KETTLE.
I KNOW...
THIS IS A MERE SHADOW OF WHAT I USED TO BE.
I DON'T MIND.
I NO LONGER WANT THOSE DAYS OF GLORY BACK.

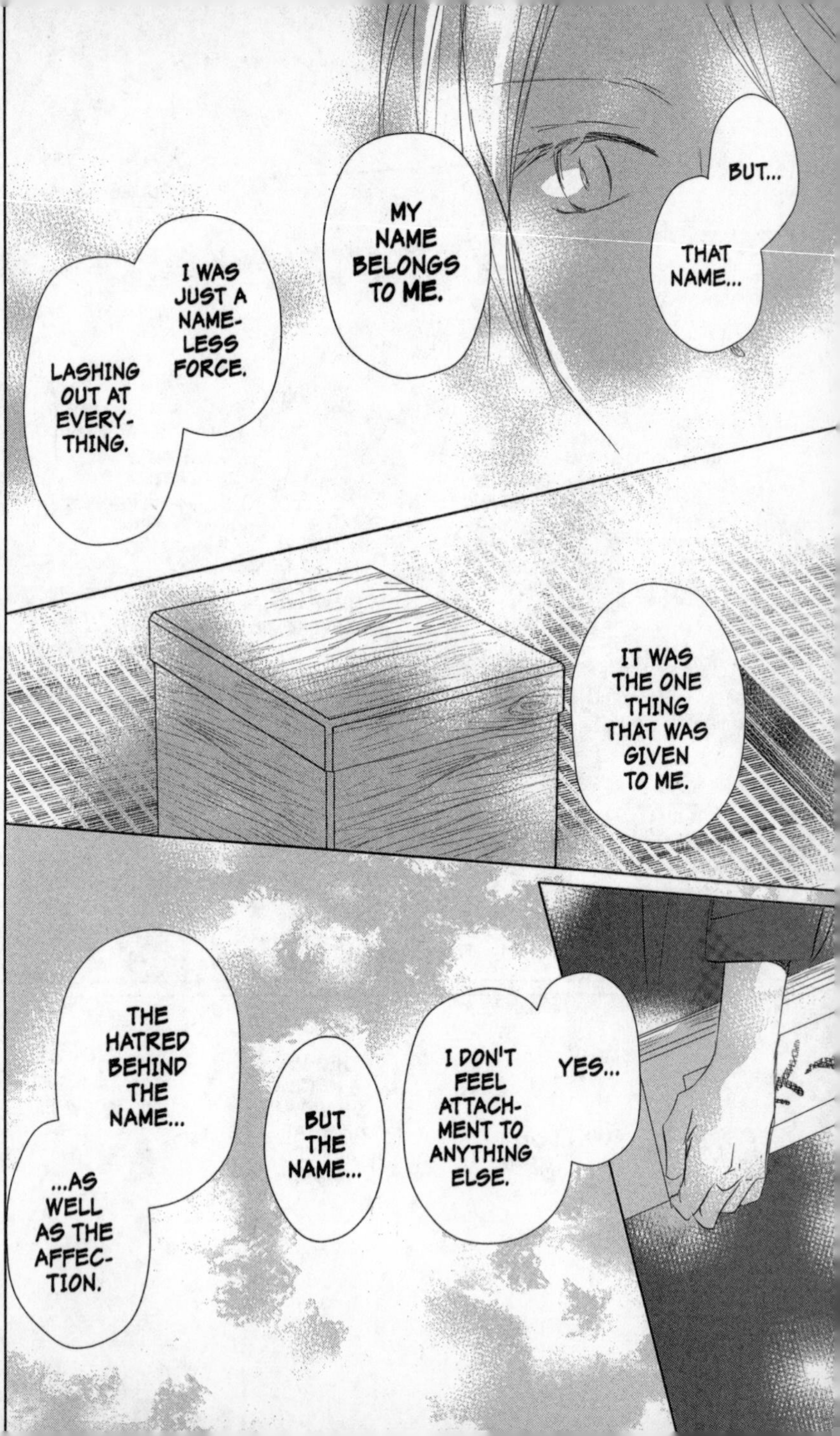
BUT...
THAT NAME...
MY NAME BELONGS TO ME.
I WAS JUST A NAMELESS FORCE.
LASHING OUT AT EVERYTHING.
IT WAS THE ONE THING THAT WAS GIVEN TO ME.
YES...
I DON'T FEEL ATTACHMENT TO ANYTHING ELSE.
BUT THE NAME...
THE HATRED BEHIND THE NAME...
...AS WELL AS THE AFFECTION.

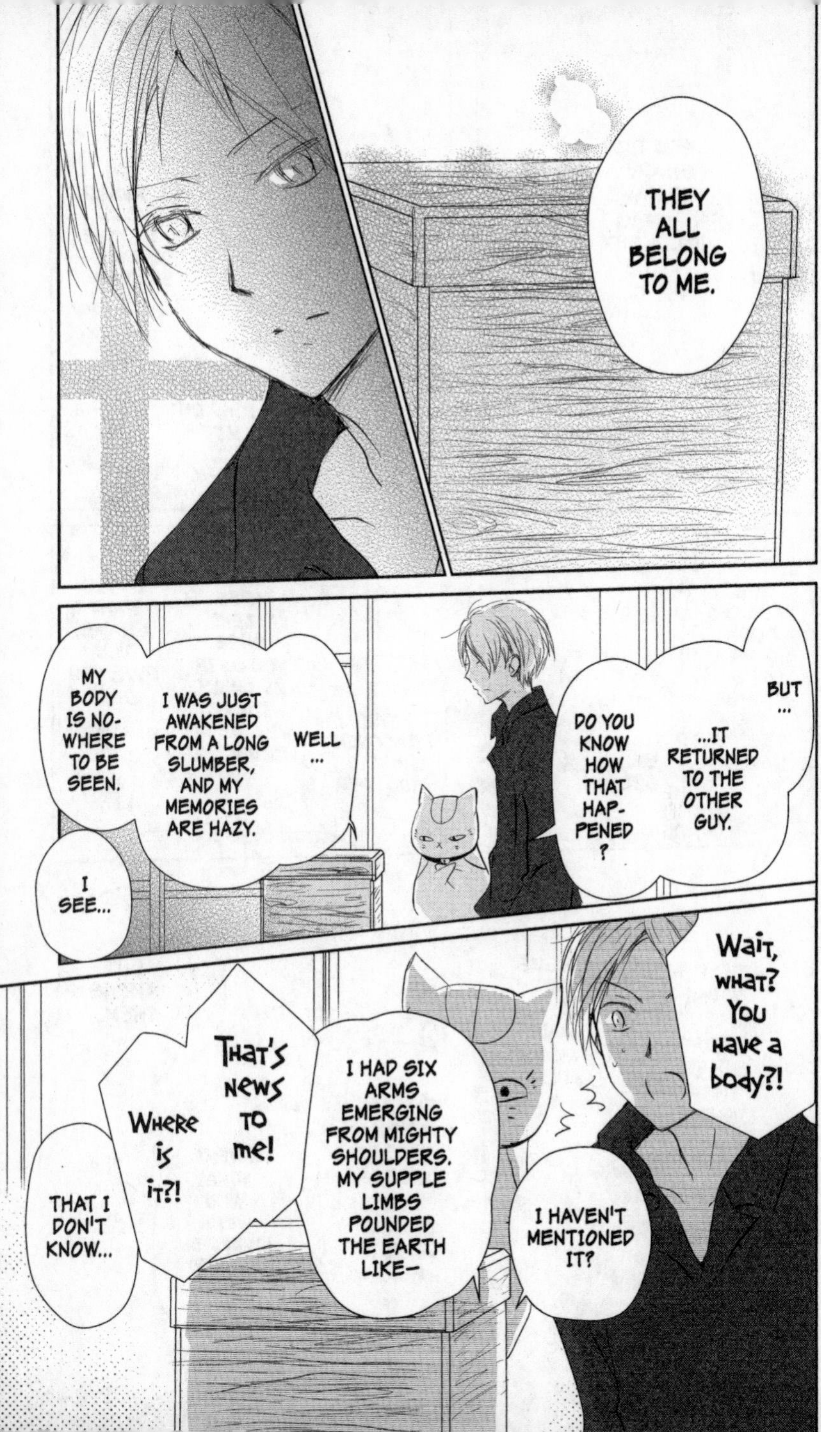
THEY ALL BELONG TO ME.
BUT ...
...IT RETURNED TO THE OTHER GUY.
DO YOU KNOW HOW THAT HAP-PENED?
WELL ...
I WAS JUST AWAKENED FROM A LONG SLUMBER, AND MY MEMORIES ARE HAZY.
MY BODY IS NO-WHERE TO BE SEEN.
I SEE...
Wait, what? You have a body?!
I HAVEN'T MENTIONED IT?
I HAD SIX ARMS EMERGING FROM MIGHTY SHOULDERS. MY SUPPLE LIMBS POUNDED THE EARTH LIKE–
That's news to me!
Where is it?!
THAT I DON'T KNOW...

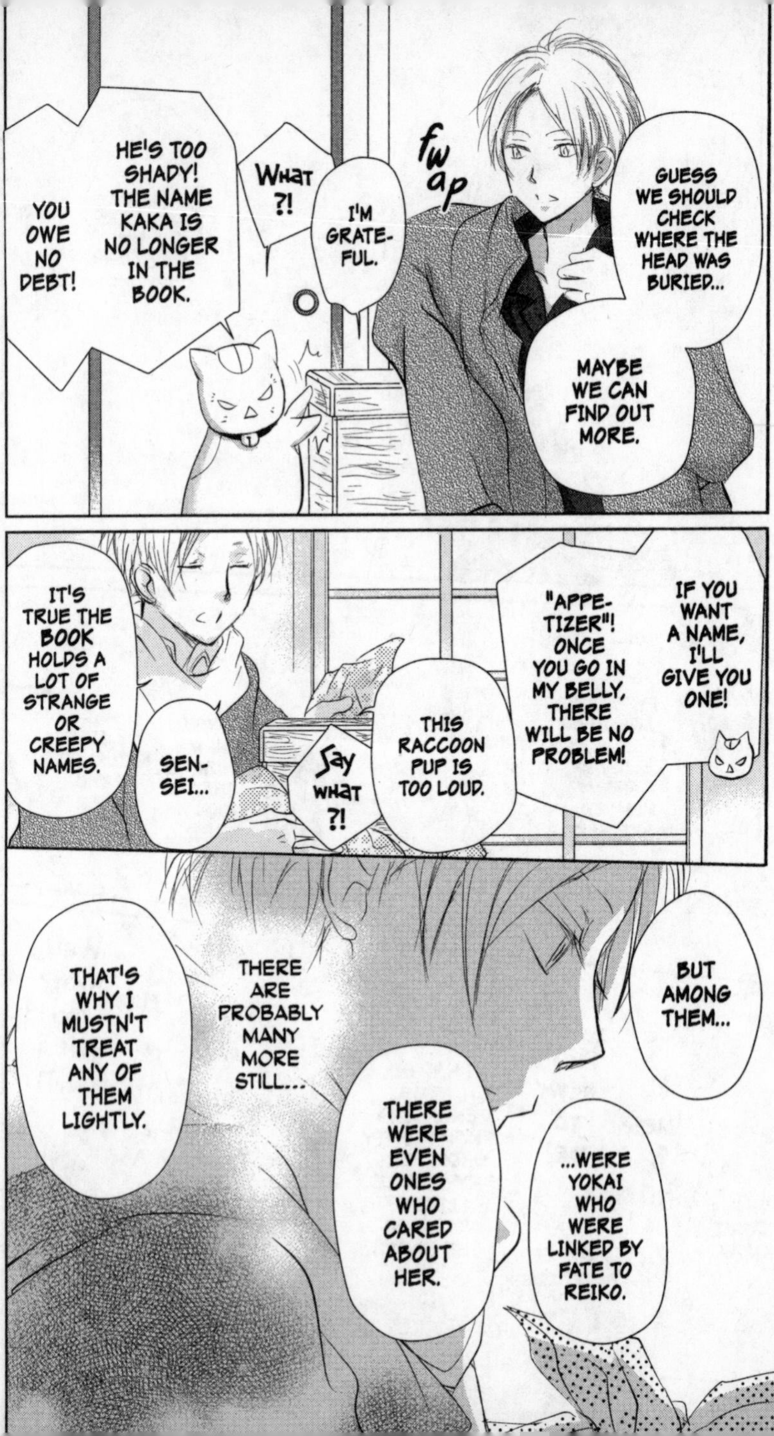
GUESS WE SHOULD CHECK WHERE THE HEAD WAS BURIED...
MAYBE WE CAN FIND OUT MORE.
fwap
I'M GRATE-FUL.
WHAT ?!
HE'S TOO SHADY! THE NAME KAKA IS NO LONGER IN THE BOOK.
YOU OWE NO DEBT!
IF YOU WANT A NAME, I'LL GIVE YOU ONE!
"APPE-TIZER"! ONCE YOU GO IN MY BELLY, THERE WILL BE NO PROBLEM!
THIS RACCOON PUP IS TOO LOUD.
SAY WHAT ?!
SEN-SEI...
IT'S TRUE THE BOOK HOLDS A LOT OF STRANGE OR CREEPY NAMES.
BUT AMONG THEM...
...WERE YOKAI WHO WERE LINKED BY FATE TO REIKO.
THERE WERE EVEN ONES WHO CARED ABOUT HER.
THERE ARE PROBABLY MANY MORE STILL...
THAT'S WHY I MUSTN'T TREAT ANY OF THEM LIGHTLY.

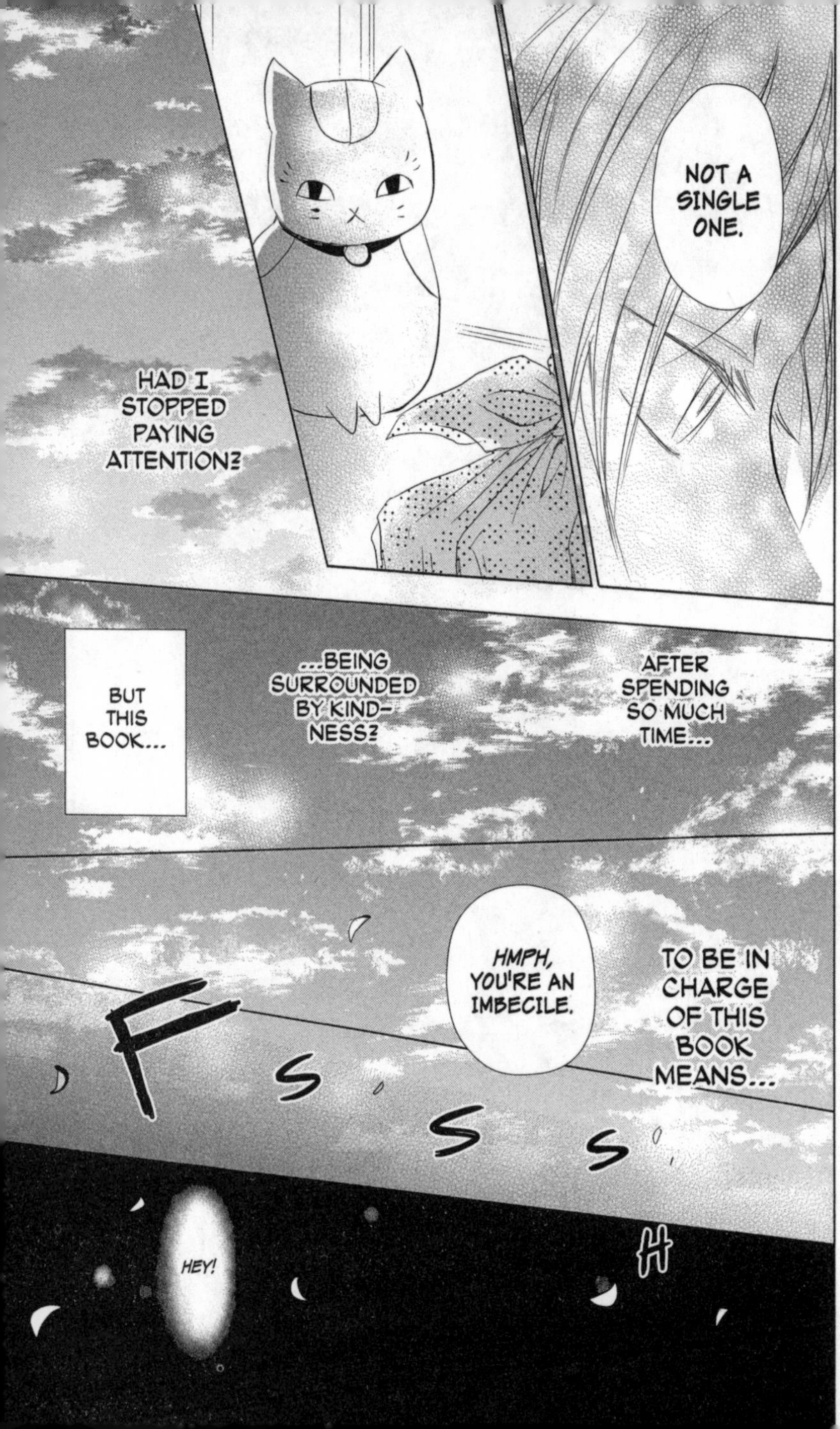
NOT A SINGLE ONE.
HAD I STOPPED PAYING ATTENTION?
AFTER SPENDING SO MUCH TIME...
...BEING SURROUNDED BY KINDNESS?
BUT THIS BOOK...
TO BE IN CHARGE OF THIS BOOK MEANS...
HMPH, YOU'RE AN IMBECILE.
FSSSH
HEY!

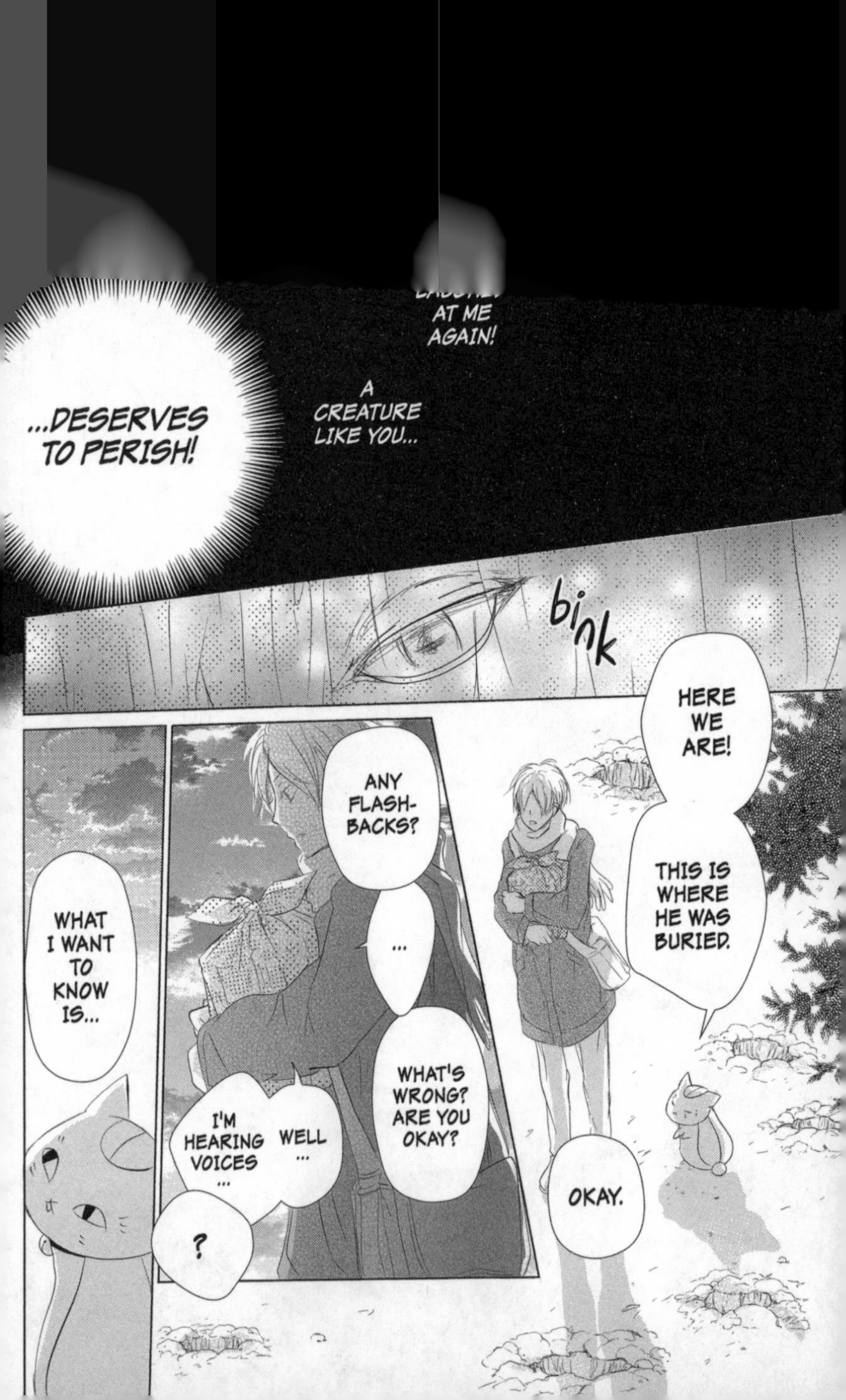
[redacted] AT ME AGAIN!
A CREATURE LIKE YOU...
...DESERVES TO PERISH!
bink
HERE WE ARE!
THIS IS WHERE HE WAS BURIED.
OKAY.
ANY FLASH-BACKS?
...
WHAT'S WRONG? ARE YOU OKAY?
WELL ...
I'M HEARING VOICES ...
?
WHAT I WANT TO KNOW IS...

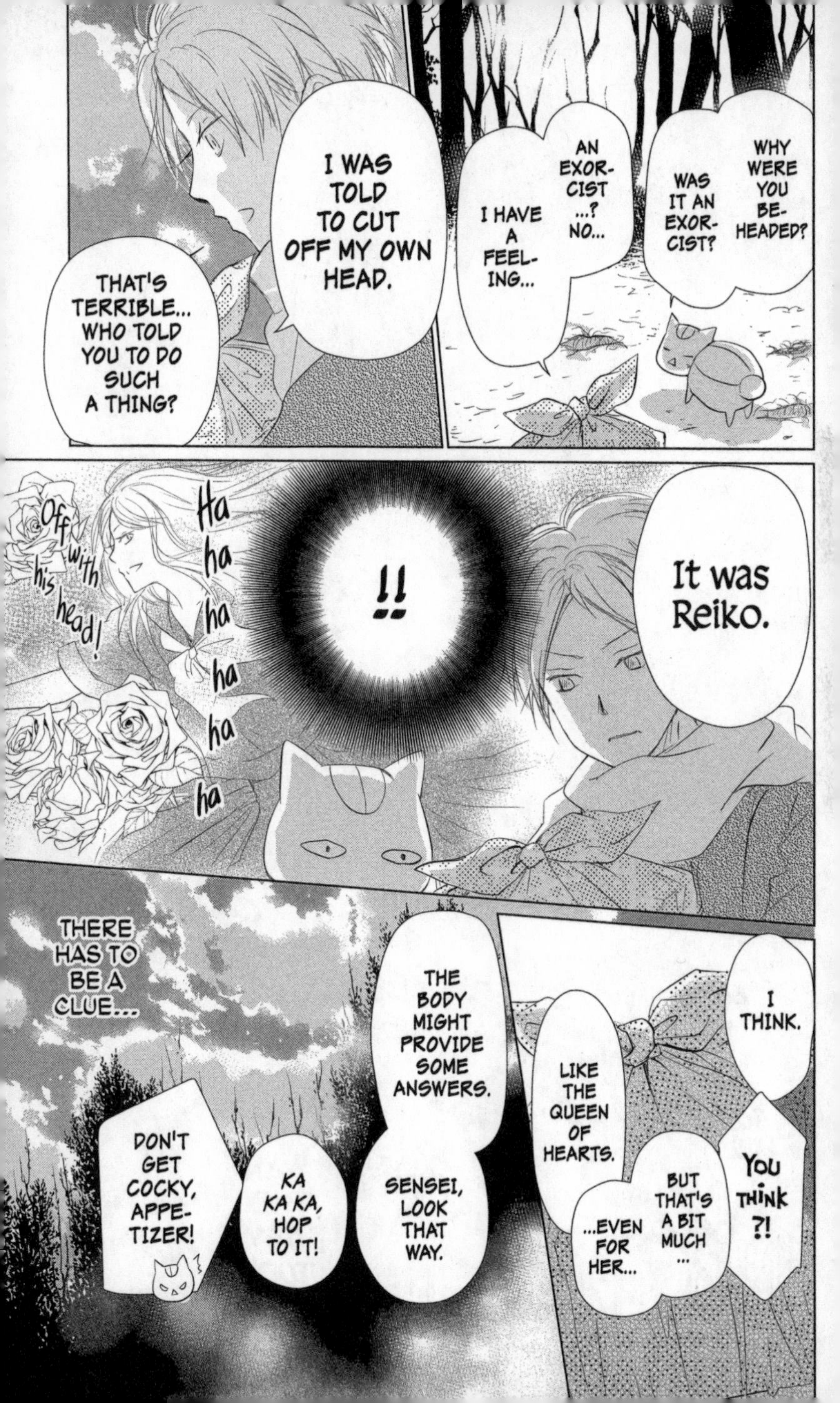
WHY WERE YOU BE-HEADED?
WAS IT AN EXOR-CIST?
AN EXOR-CIST ...? NO...
I HAVE A FEEL-ING...
I WAS TOLD TO CUT OFF MY OWN HEAD.
THAT'S TERRIBLE... WHO TOLD YOU TO DO SUCH A THING?
It was Reiko.
!!
Ha ha ha ha ha ha
Off with his head!
I THINK.
YOU THINK ?!
BUT THAT'S A BIT MUCH ...
...EVEN FOR HER...
LIKE THE QUEEN OF HEARTS.
THE BODY MIGHT PROVIDE SOME ANSWERS.
THERE HAS TO BE A CLUE...
SENSEI, LOOK THAT WAY.
KA KA KA, HOP TO IT!
DON'T GET COCKY, APPE-TIZER!

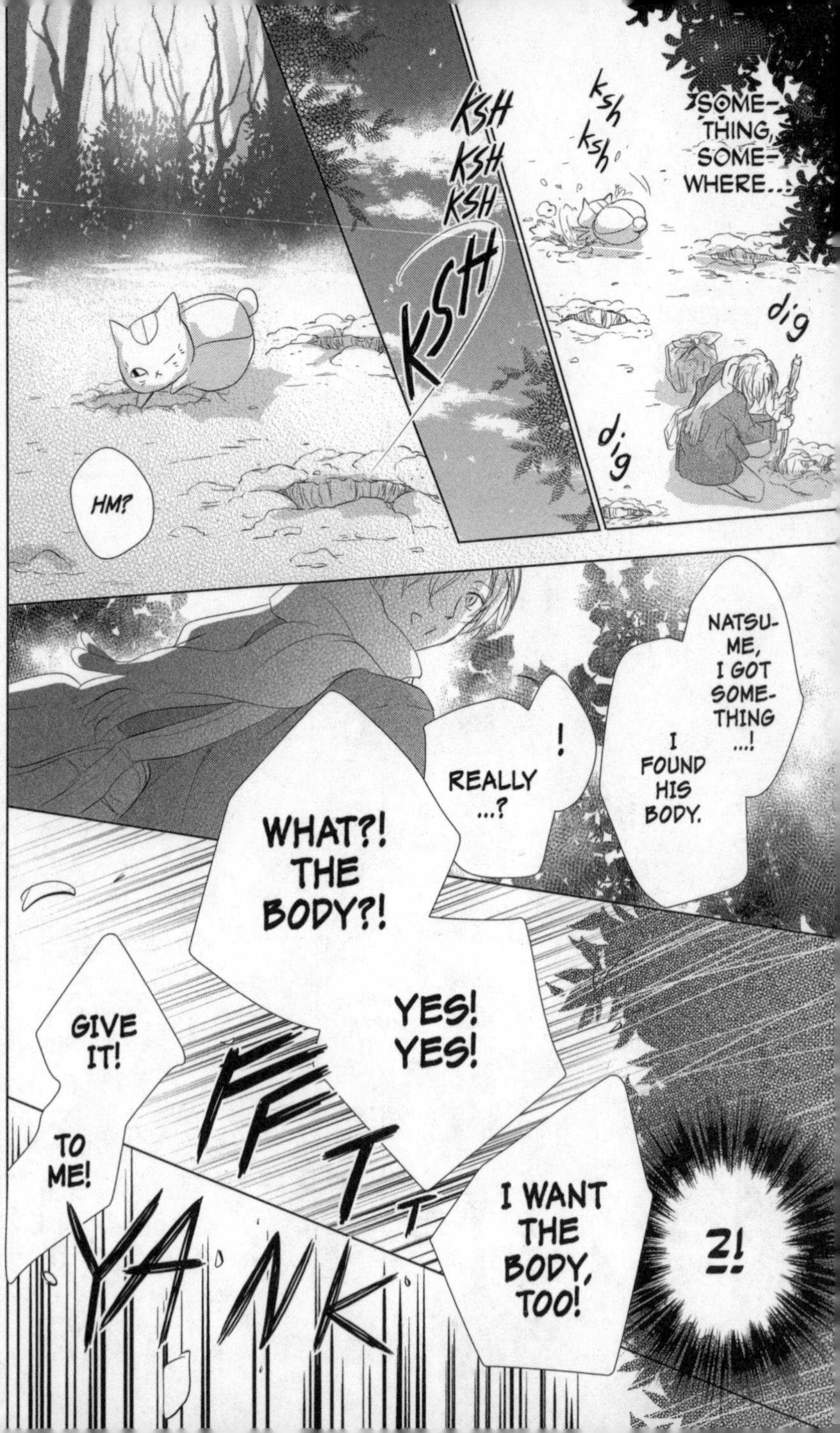
SOME-THING, SOME-WHERE...
ksh ksh
dig
dig
KSH KSH KSH
KSH
HM?
NATSU-ME, I GOT SOME-THING ...!
I FOUND HIS BODY.
!
REALLY ...?
WHAT?! THE BODY?!
YES! YES!
I WANT THE BODY, TOO!
Z!
FFT
GIVE IT!
TO ME!
YANK

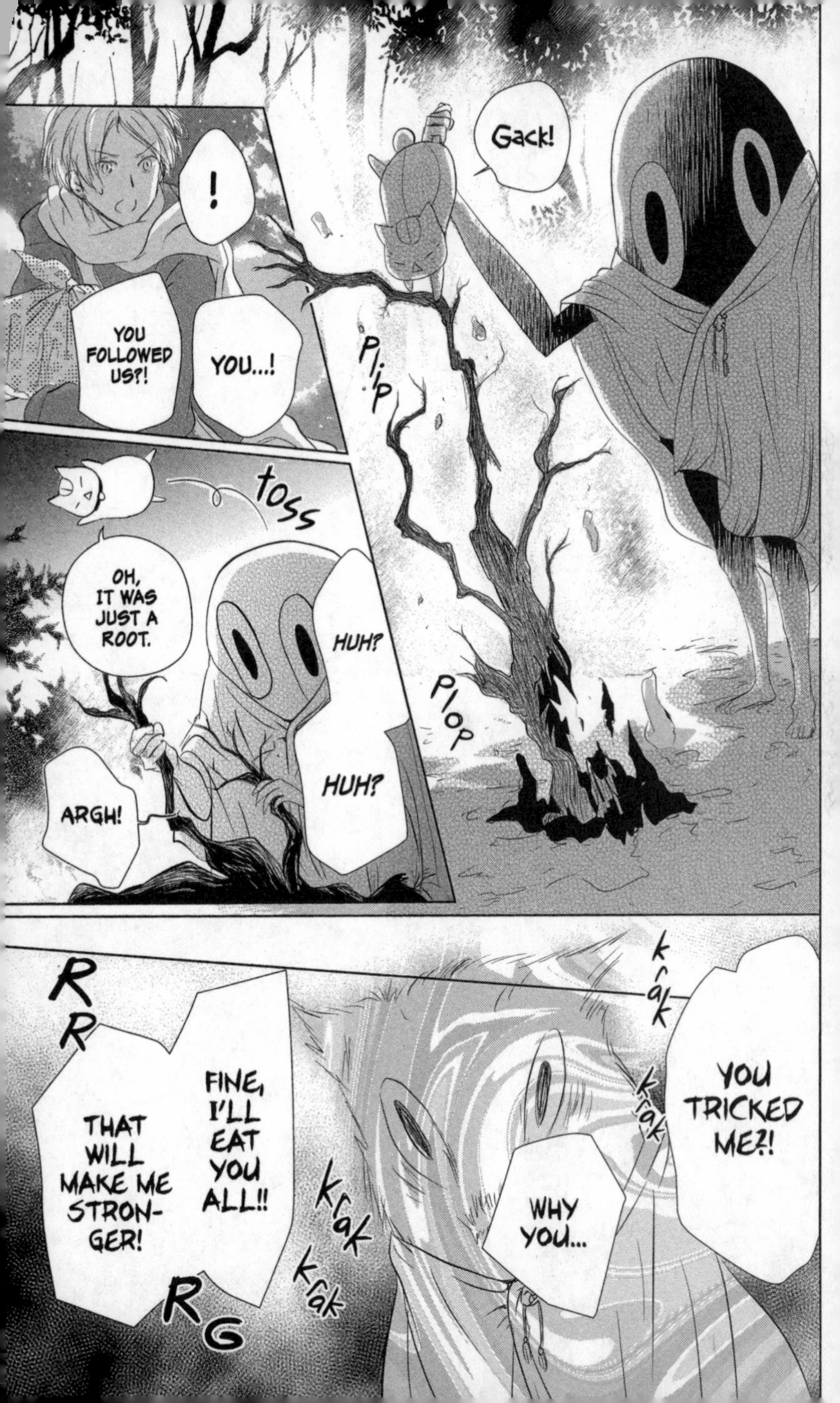
Gack!
Plip
Plop
!
YOU...!
YOU FOLLOWED US?!
toss
HUH?
HUH?
OH, IT WAS JUST A ROOT.
ARGH!
krak
krak
YOU TRICKED ME?!
WHY YOU...
krak
krak
FINE, I'LL EAT YOU ALL!!
THAT WILL MAKE ME STRONGER!
RR
RG

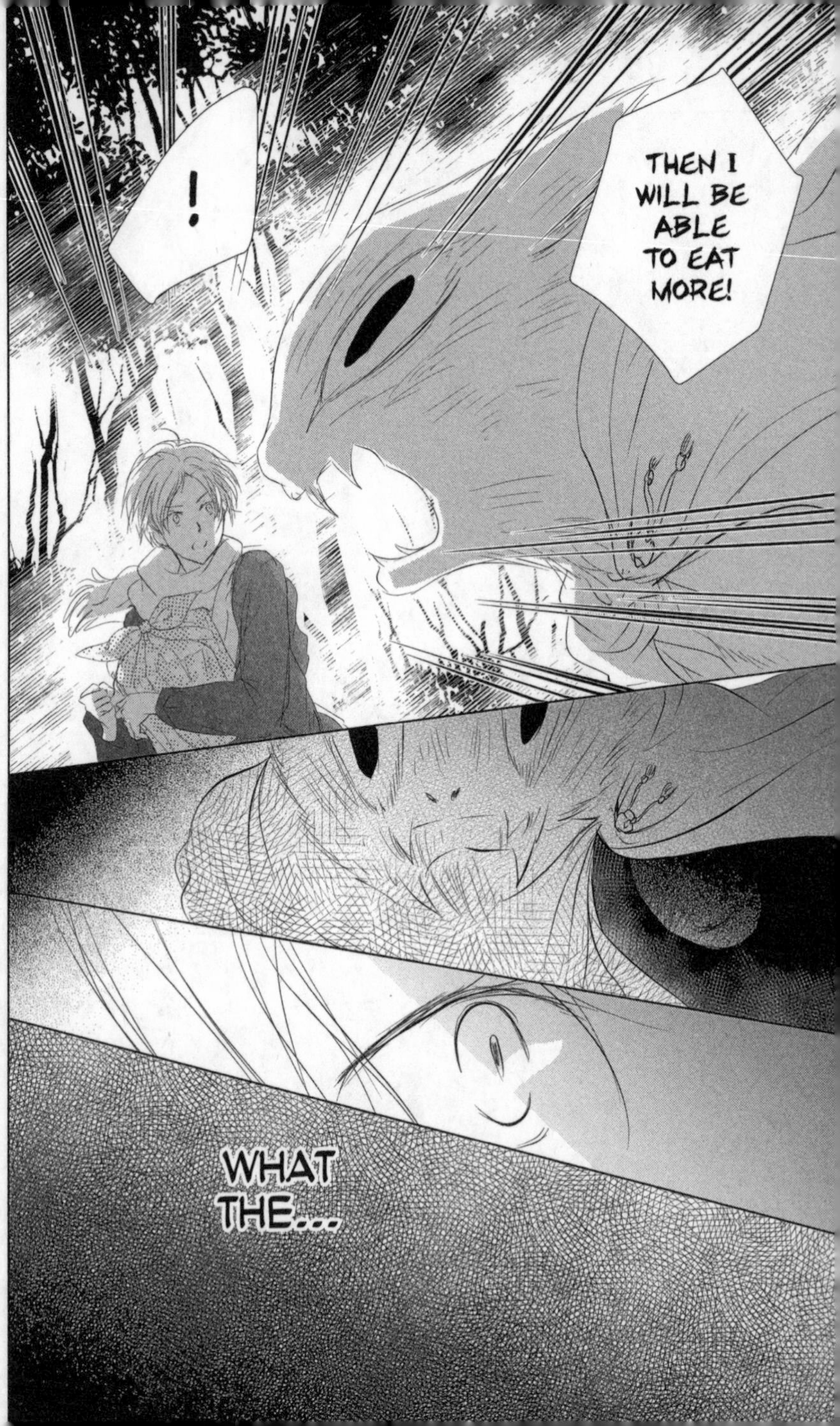
THEN I WILL BE ABLE TO EAT MORE!
!
WHAT THE...

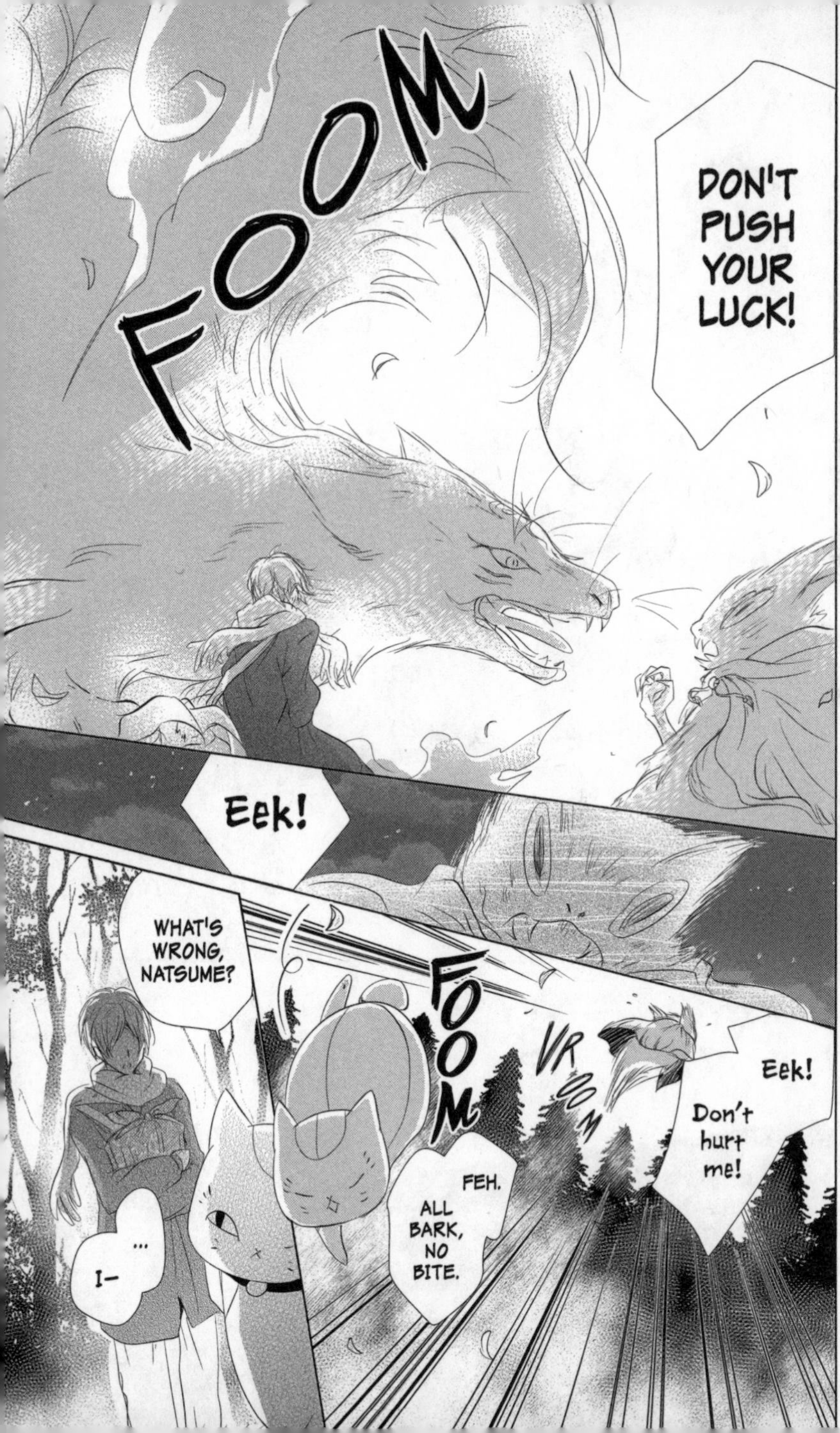
DON'T PUSH YOUR LUCK!
FOOM
Eek!
Eek!
Don't hurt me!
VROOM
FOOOM
FEH.
ALL BARK, NO BITE.
WHAT'S WRONG, NATSUME?
...
I–

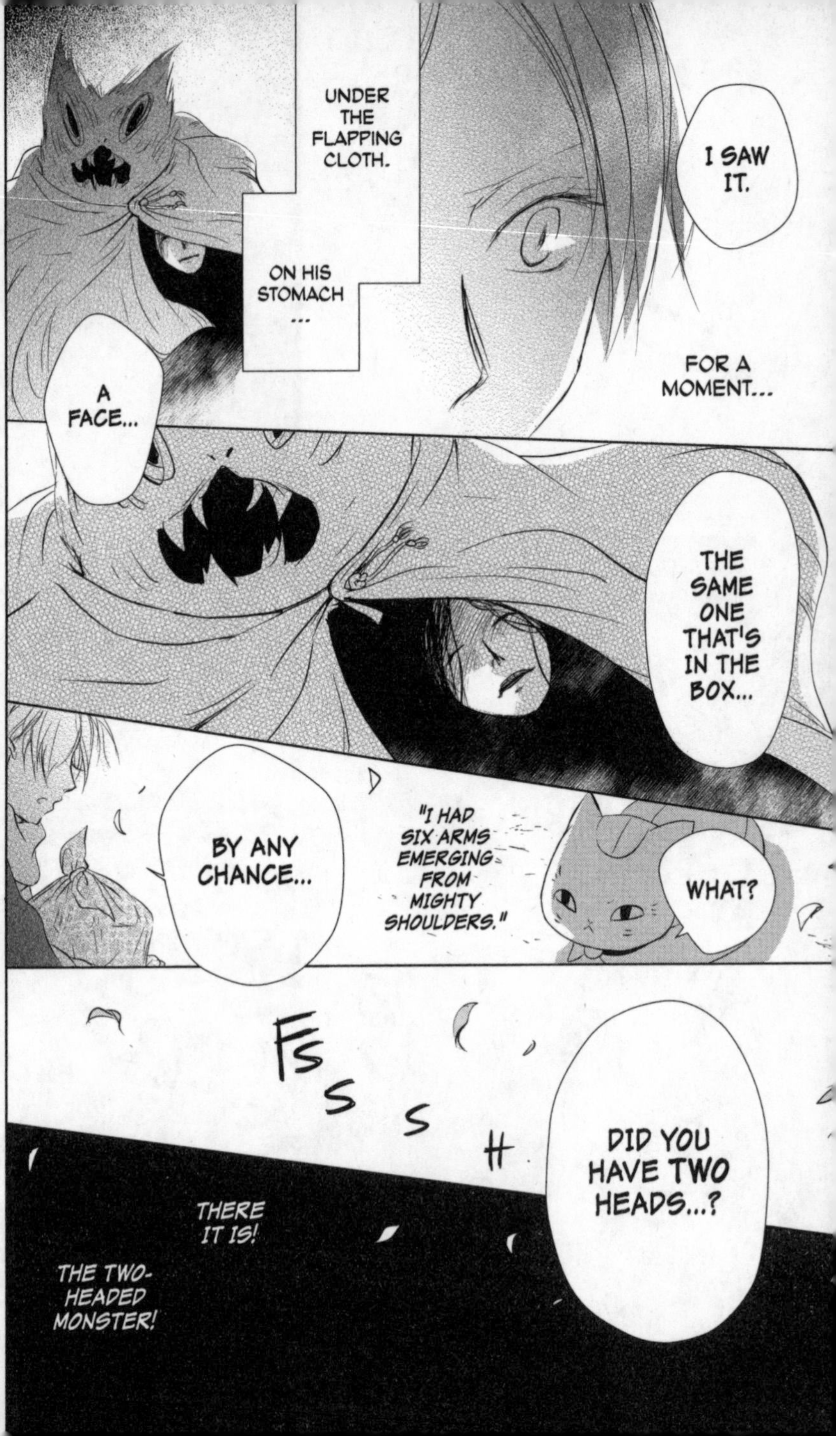
I SAW IT.
FOR A MOMENT...
UNDER THE FLAPPING CLOTH.
ON HIS STOMACH...
A FACE...
THE SAME ONE THAT'S IN THE BOX...
WHAT?
"I HAD SIX ARMS EMERGING FROM MIGHTY SHOULDERS."
BY ANY CHANCE...
DID YOU HAVE TWO HEADS...?
FSSSH
THERE IT IS!
THE TWO-HEADED MONSTER!

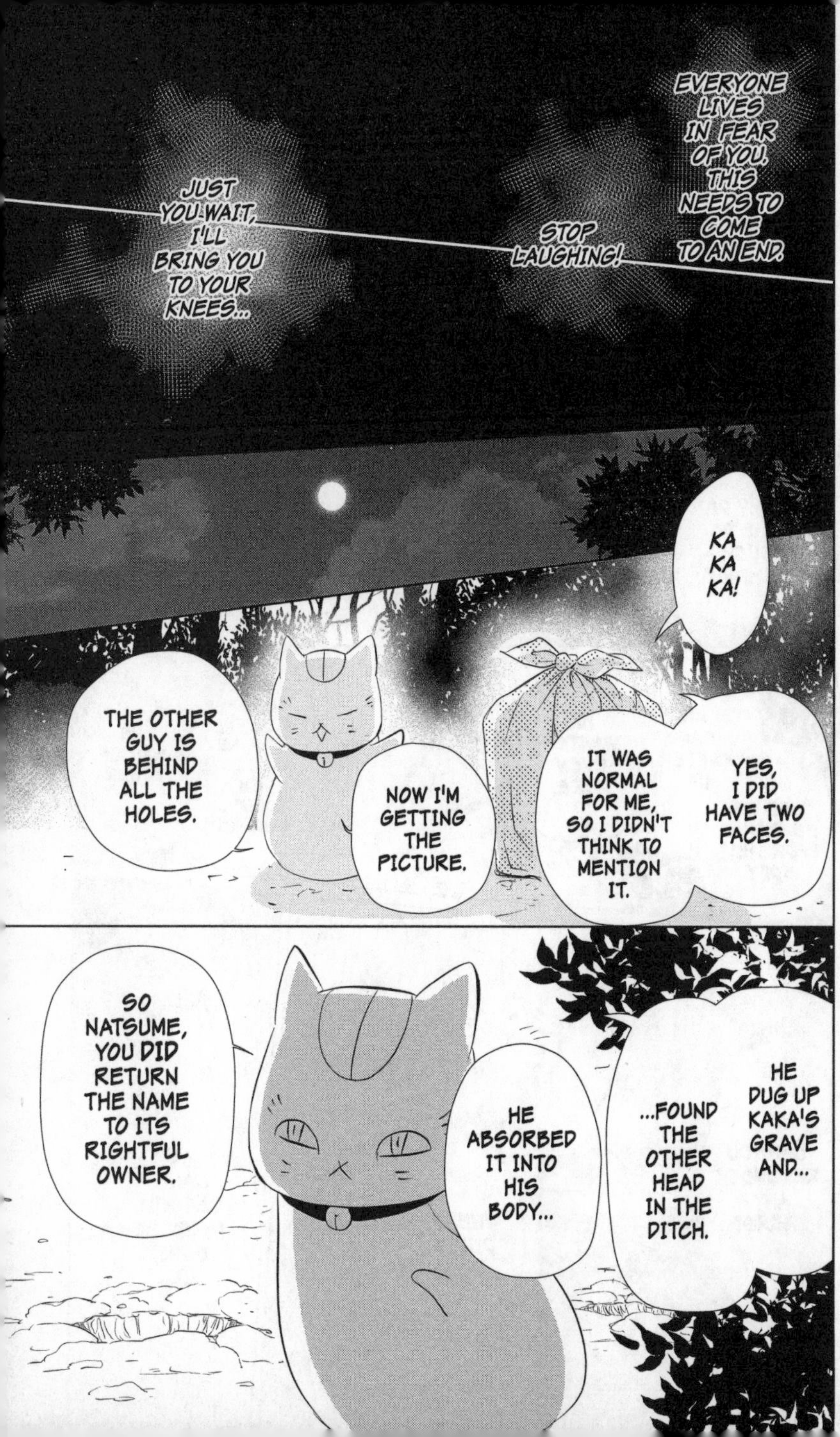
EVERYONE LIVES IN FEAR OF YOU. THIS NEEDS TO COME TO AN END.
STOP LAUGHING!
JUST YOU WAIT, I'LL BRING YOU TO YOUR KNEES...
KA KA KA!
YES, I DID HAVE TWO FACES.
IT WAS NORMAL FOR ME, SO I DIDN'T THINK TO MENTION IT.
NOW I'M GETTING THE PICTURE.
THE OTHER GUY IS BEHIND ALL THE HOLES.
HE DUG UP KAKA'S GRAVE AND...
...FOUND THE OTHER HEAD IN THE DITCH.
HE ABSORBED IT INTO HIS BODY...
SO NATSUME, YOU DID RETURN THE NAME TO ITS RIGHTFUL OWNER.

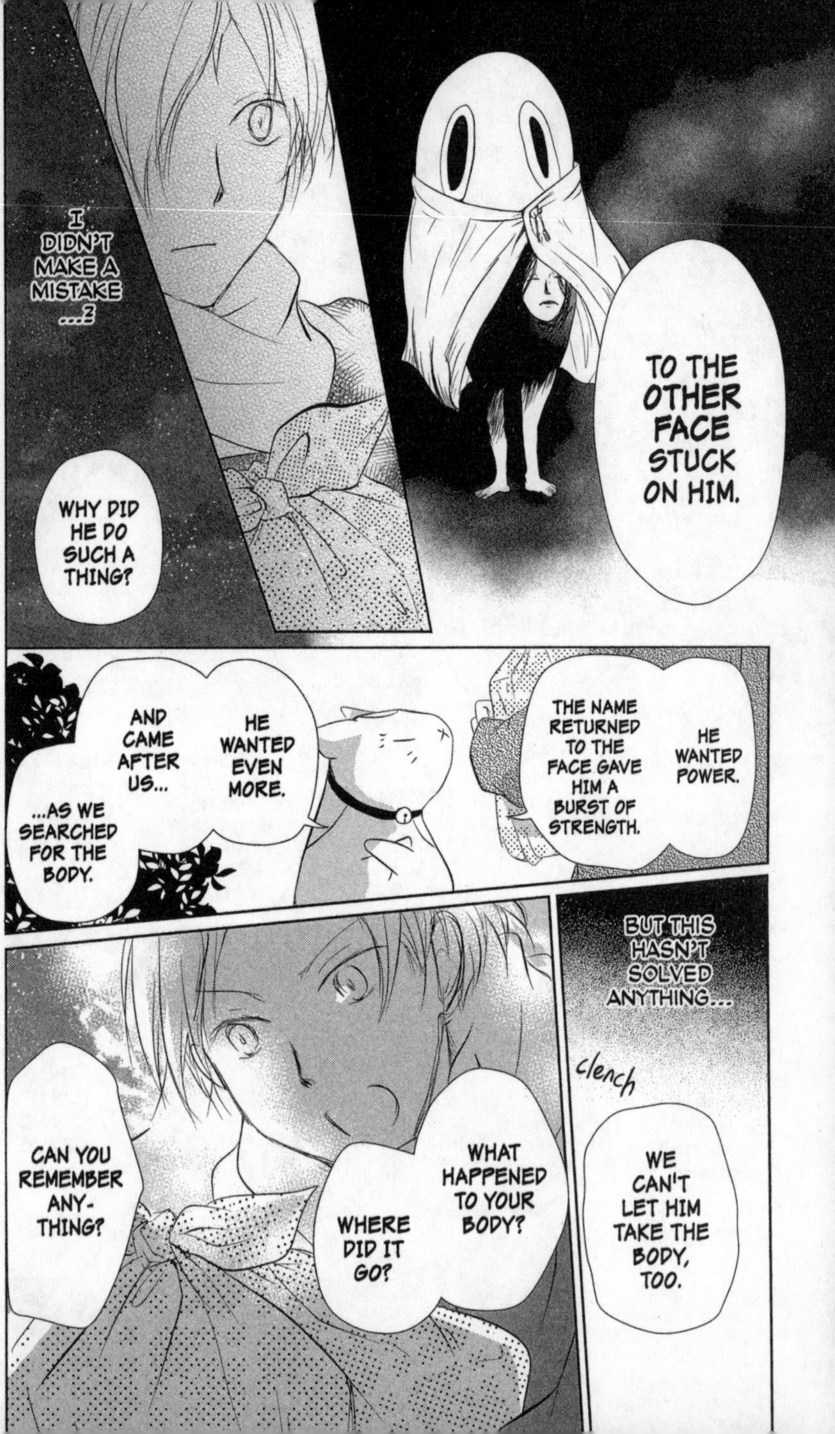
TO THE OTHER FACE STUCK ON HIM.
I DIDN'T MAKE A MISTAKE ...?
WHY DID HE DO SUCH A THING?
HE WANTED POWER.
THE NAME RETURNED TO THE FACE GAVE HIM A BURST OF STRENGTH.
HE WANTED EVEN MORE.
AND CAME AFTER US...
...AS WE SEARCHED FOR THE BODY.
BUT THIS HASN'T SOLVED ANYTHING...
clench
WE CAN'T LET HIM TAKE THE BODY, TOO.
WHAT HAPPENED TO YOUR BODY?
WHERE DID IT GO?
CAN YOU REMEMBER ANYTHING?

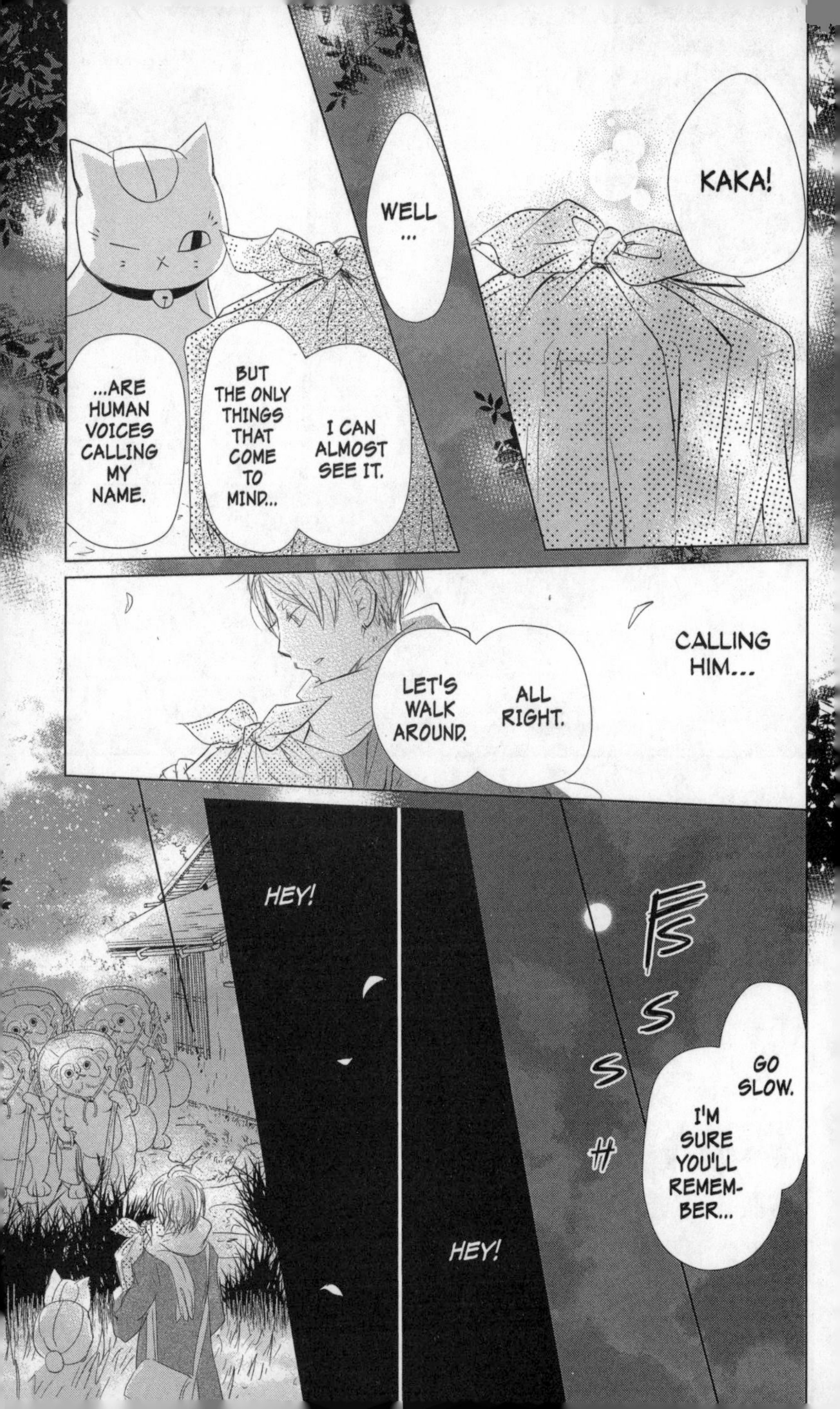
KAKA!
WELL...
I CAN ALMOST SEE IT.
BUT THE ONLY THINGS THAT COME TO MIND...
...ARE HUMAN VOICES CALLING MY NAME.
CALLING HIM...
ALL RIGHT.
LET'S WALK AROUND.
FSSSH
GO SLOW.
I'M SURE YOU'LL REMEMBER...
HEY!
HEY!

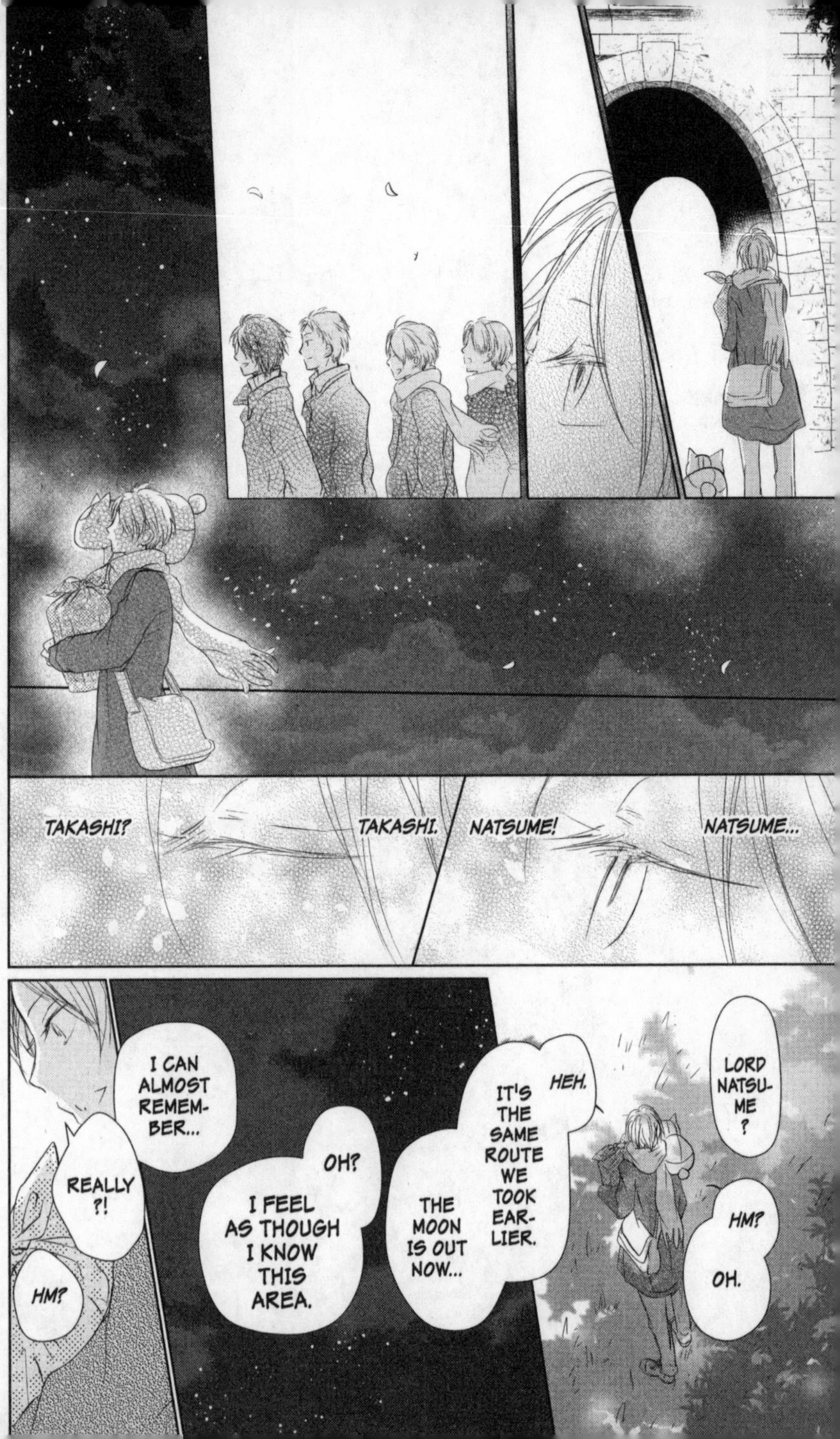
NATSUME...
NATSUME!
TAKASHI.
TAKASHI?
LORD NATSUME?
HM?
OH.
HEH.
IT'S THE SAME ROUTE WE TOOK EARLIER.
THE MOON IS OUT NOW...
OH?
I FEEL AS THOUGH I KNOW THIS AREA.
I CAN ALMOST REMEMBER...
REALLY?!
HM?

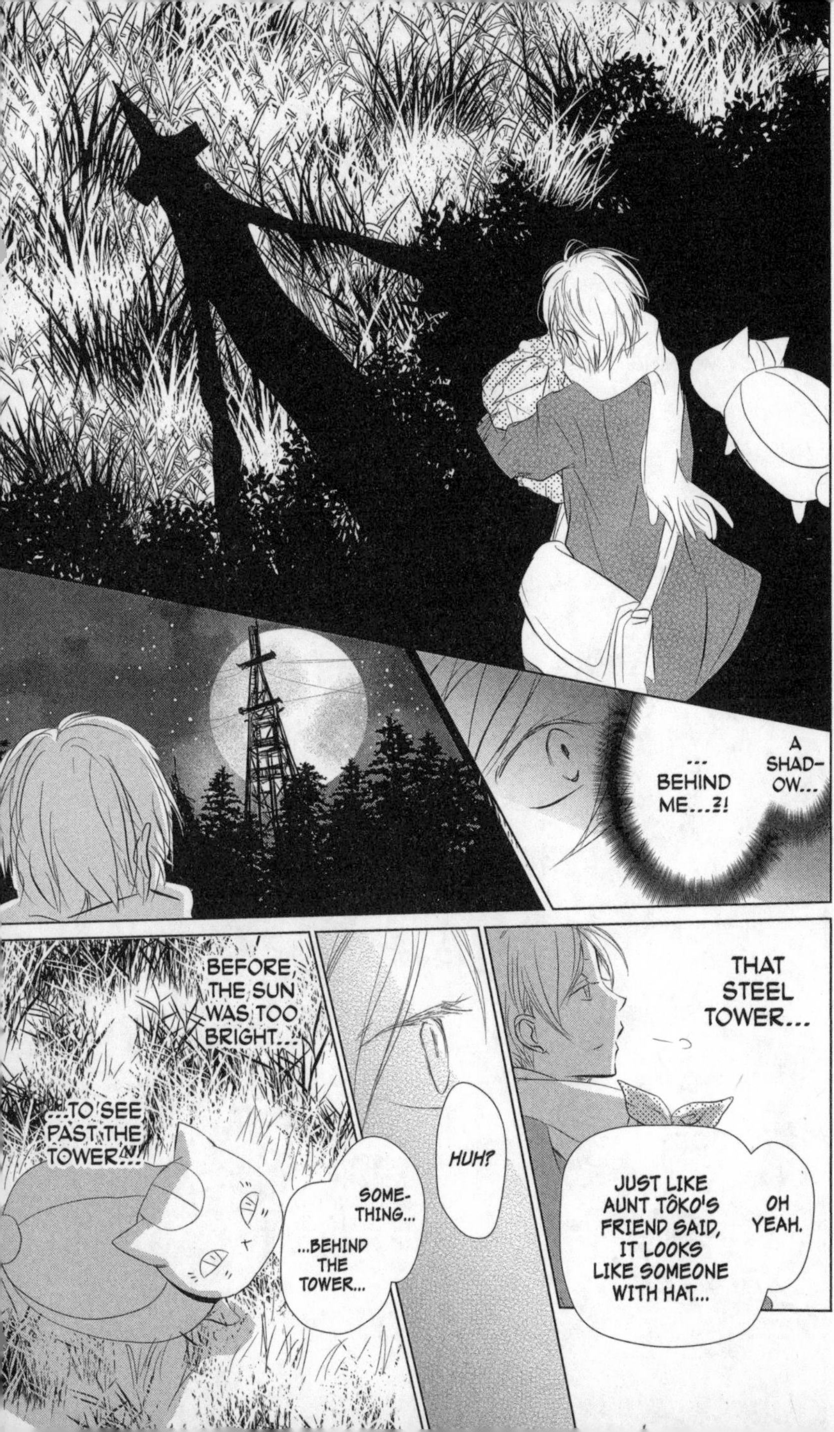
A SHADOW...
...BEHIND ME...?!
THAT STEEL TOWER...
OH YEAH.
JUST LIKE AUNT TÔKO'S FRIEND SAID, IT LOOKS LIKE SOMEONE WITH HAT...
HUH?
SOMETHING...
...BEHIND THE TOWER...
BEFORE, THE SUN WAS TOO BRIGHT...
...TO SEE PAST THE TOWER...!!

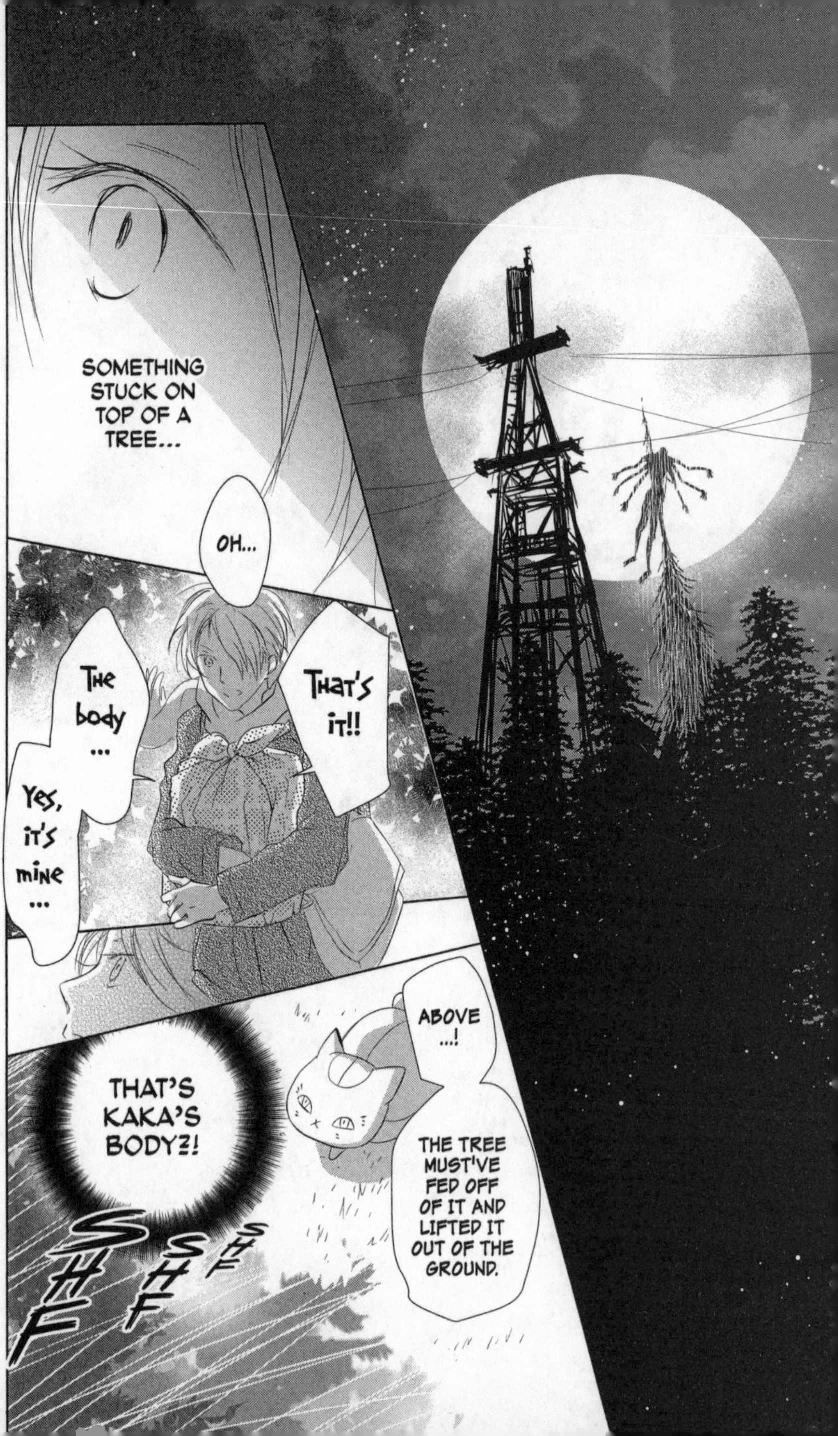
SOMETHING STUCK ON TOP OF A TREE...
OH...
THAT'S IT!!
The body ...
Yes, it's mine ...
ABOVE ...!
THE TREE MUST'VE FED OFF OF IT AND LIFTED IT OUT OF THE GROUND.
THAT'S KAKA'S BODY?!
SHF SHF SHF

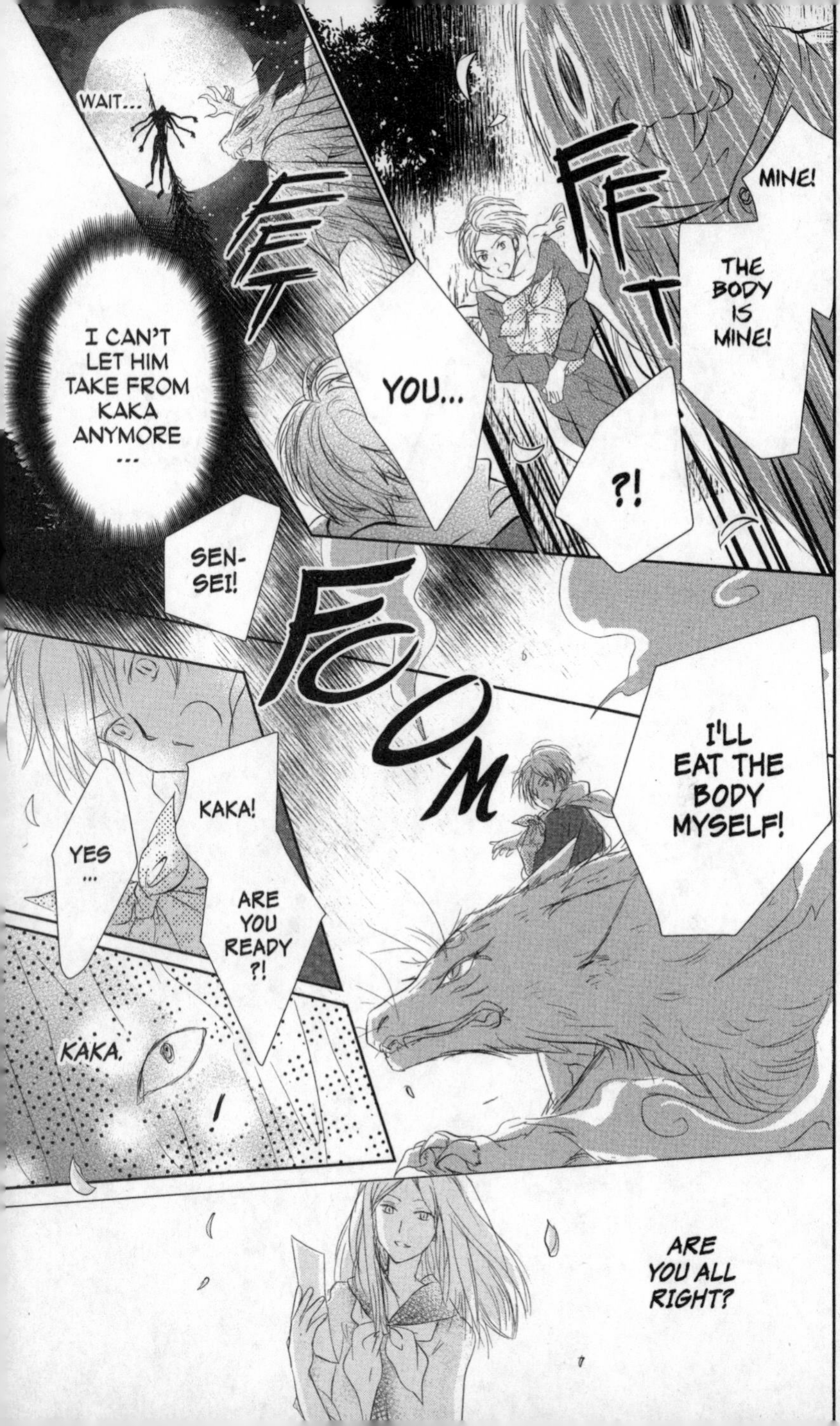
MINE!
THE BODY IS MINE!
FFT
?!
YOU...
FFT
WAIT...
I CAN'T LET HIM TAKE FROM KAKA ANYMORE ...
SEN-SEI!
FOOM
I'LL EAT THE BODY MYSELF!
KAKA!
YES ...
ARE YOU READY ?!
KAKA.
!
ARE YOU ALL RIGHT?

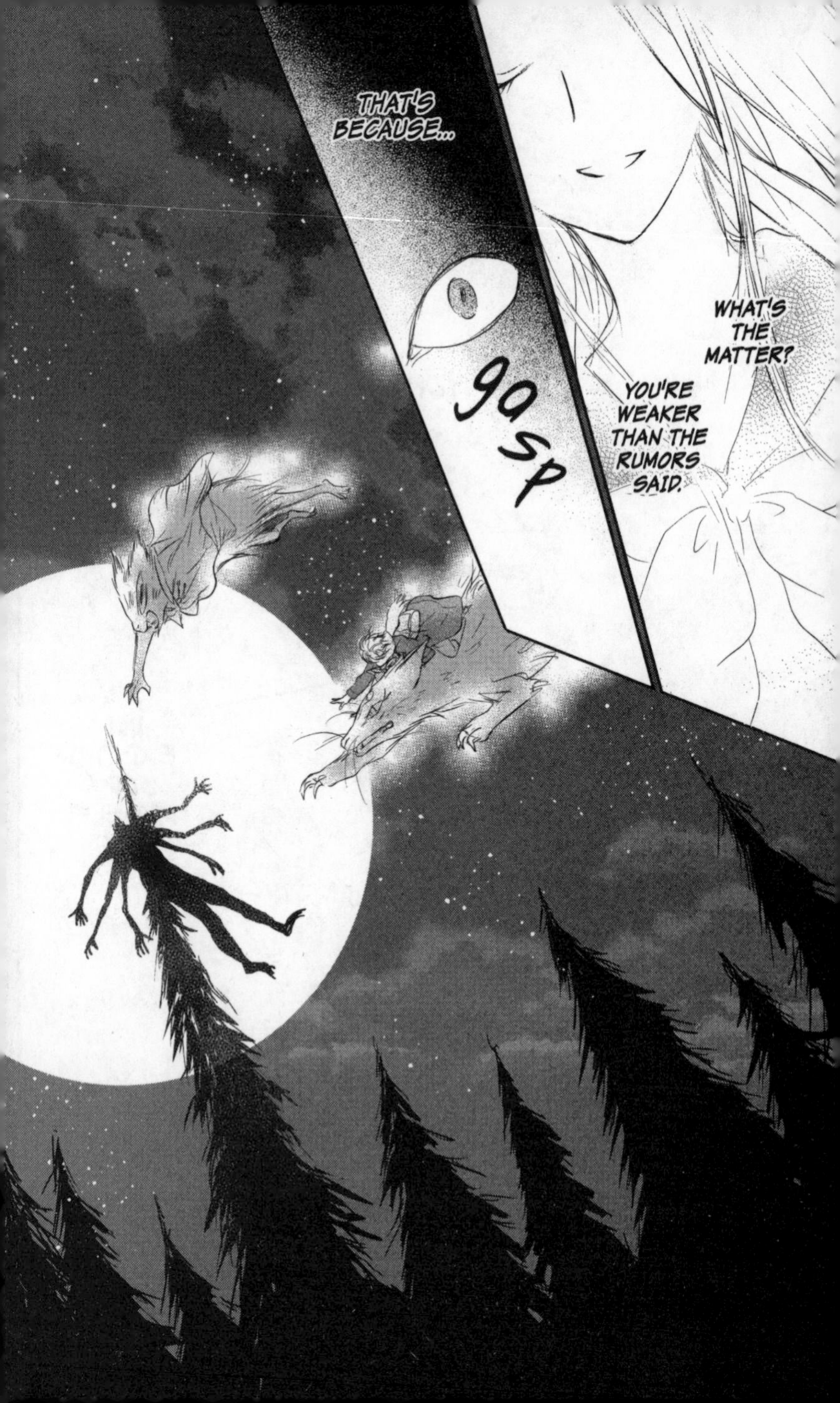
WHAT'S THE MATTER?
YOU'RE WEAKER THAN THE RUMORS SAID.
THAT'S BECAUSE...
gasp

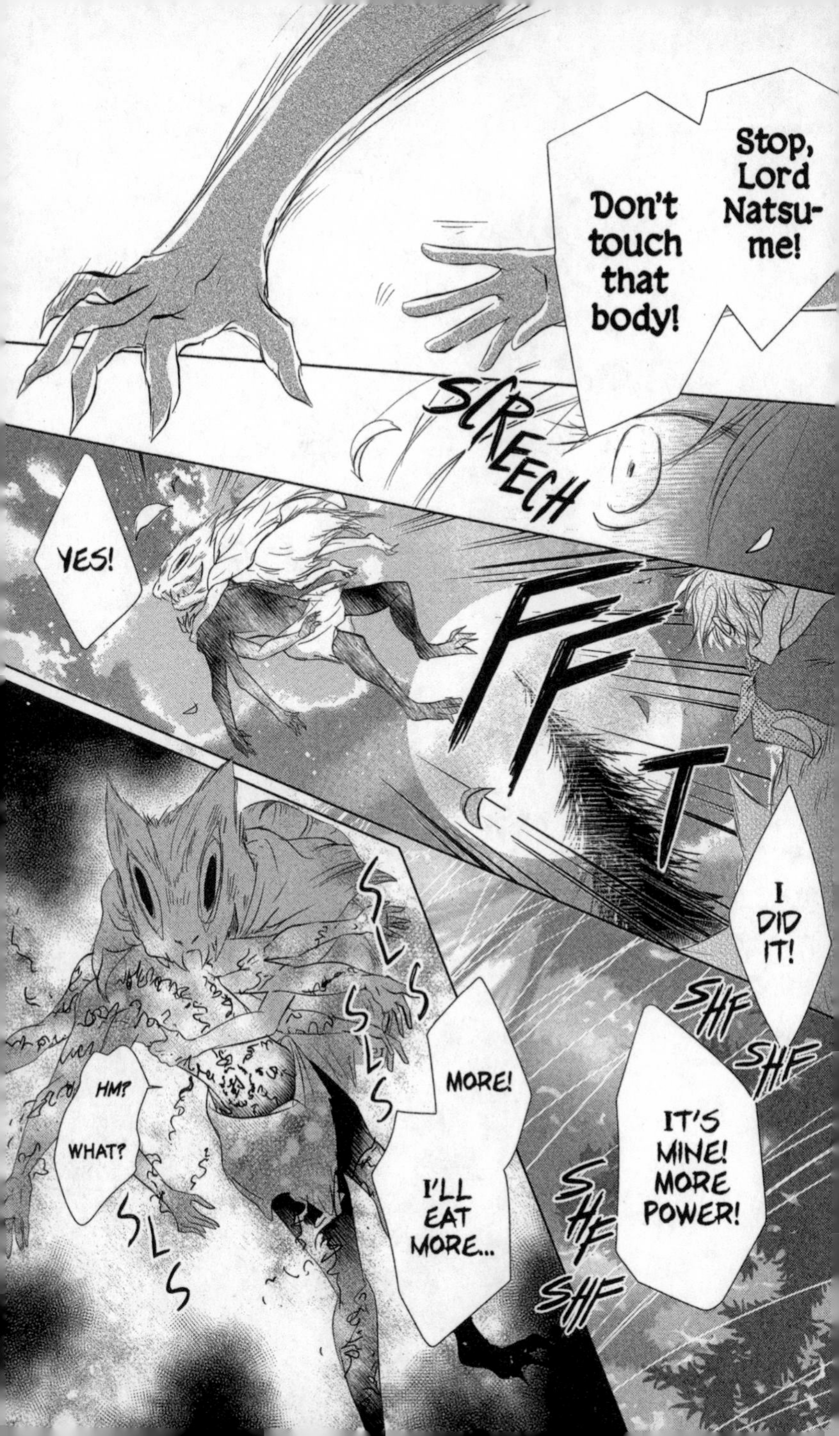
Stop, Lord Natsume!
Don't touch that body!
SCREECH
FFT
YES!
I DID IT!
SHF SHF
IT'S MINE! MORE POWER!
SHF SHF
MORE!
I'LL EAT MORE...
SLS
SLS
HM?
WHAT?
SLS

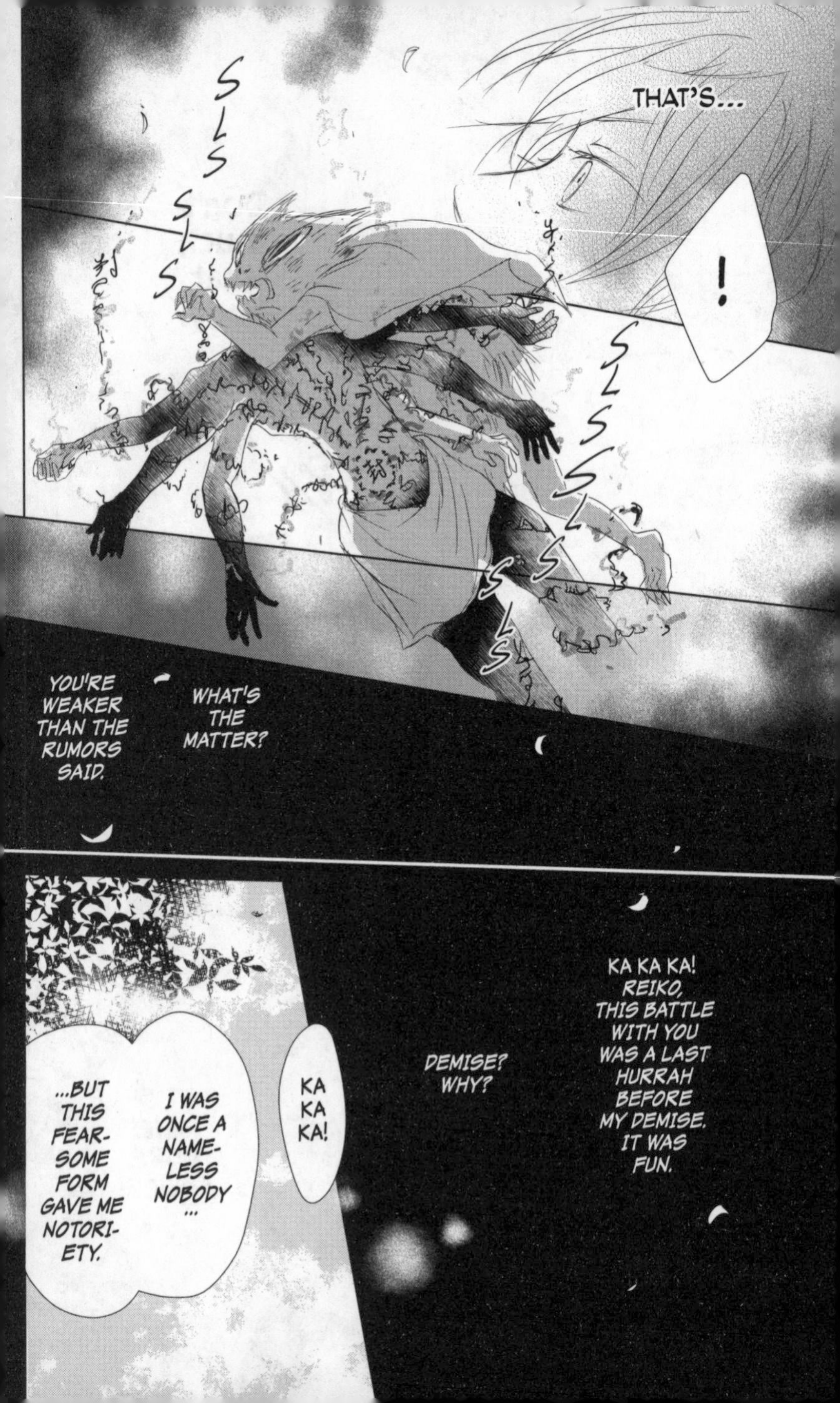
THAT'S...
!
SLS SLS
SLSS
SLSS
SLS
WHAT'S THE MATTER?
YOU'RE WEAKER THAN THE RUMORS SAID.
KA KA KA! REIKO, THIS BATTLE WITH YOU WAS A LAST HURRAH BEFORE MY DEMISE. IT WAS FUN.
DEMISE? WHY?
KA KA KA!
I WAS ONCE A NAME-LESS NOBODY...
...BUT THIS FEAR-SOME FORM GAVE ME NOTORI-ETY.

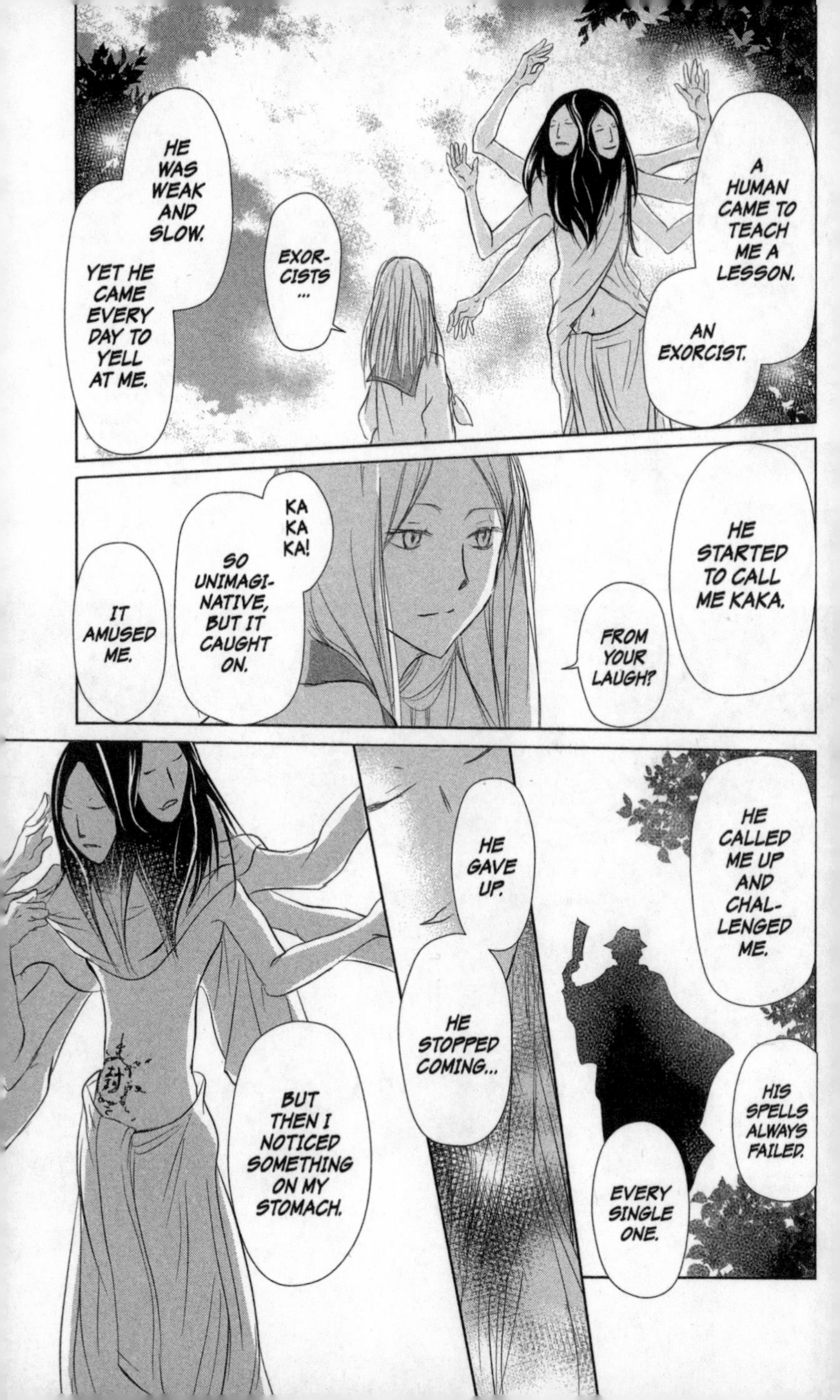
A HUMAN CAME TO TEACH ME A LESSON.
AN EXORCIST.
EXORCISTS...
HE WAS WEAK AND SLOW.
YET HE CAME EVERY DAY TO YELL AT ME.
HE STARTED TO CALL ME KAKA.
FROM YOUR LAUGH?
KA KA KA!
SO UNIMAGINATIVE, BUT IT CAUGHT ON.
IT AMUSED ME.
HE CALLED ME UP AND CHALLENGED ME.
HIS SPELLS ALWAYS FAILED.
EVERY SINGLE ONE.
HE GAVE UP.
HE STOPPED COMING...
BUT THEN I NOTICED SOMETHING ON MY STOMACH.

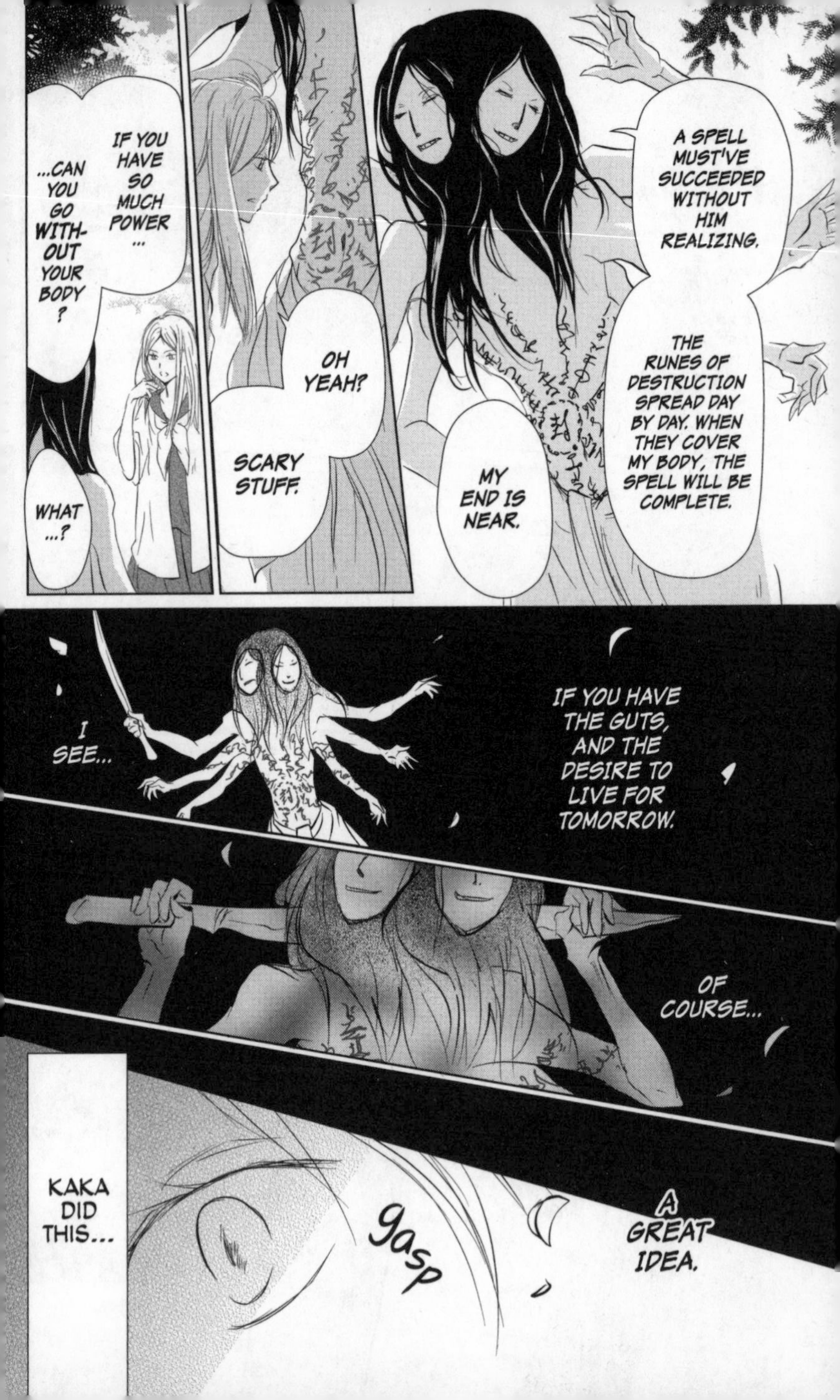
A SPELL MUST'VE SUCCEEDED WITHOUT HIM REALIZING.
THE RUNES OF DESTRUCTION SPREAD DAY BY DAY. WHEN THEY COVER MY BODY, THE SPELL WILL BE COMPLETE.
MY END IS NEAR.
OH YEAH?
SCARY STUFF.
IF YOU HAVE SO MUCH POWER...
...CAN YOU GO WITH-OUT YOUR BODY?
WHAT...?
IF YOU HAVE THE GUTS, AND THE DESIRE TO LIVE FOR TOMORROW.
I SEE...
OF COURSE...
A GREAT IDEA.
gasp
KAKA DID THIS...

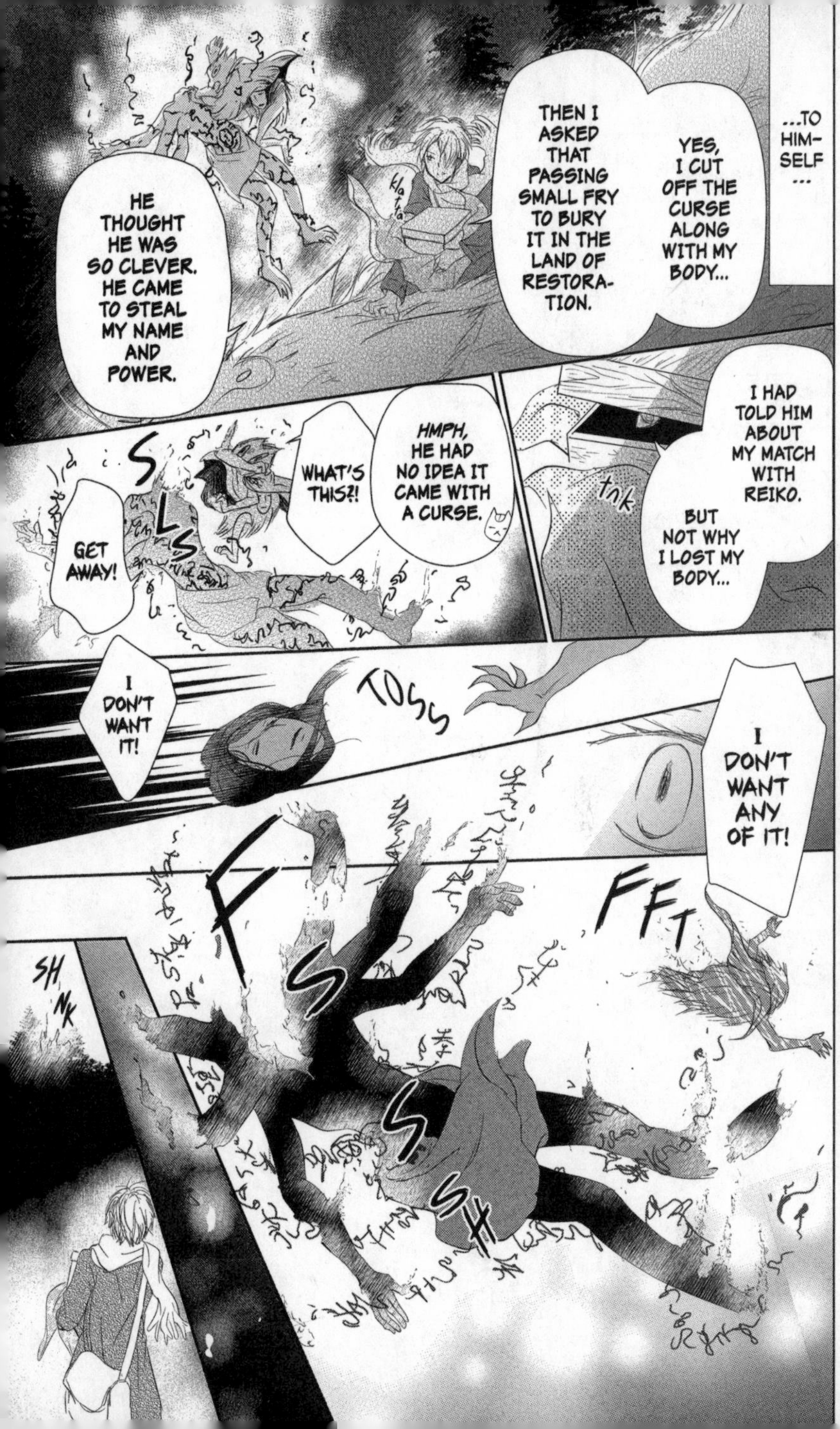
...TO HIM-SELF...
YES, I CUT OFF THE CURSE ALONG WITH MY BODY...
THEN I ASKED THAT PASSING SMALL FRY TO BURY IT IN THE LAND OF RESTORA-TION.
HE THOUGHT HE WAS SO CLEVER. HE CAME TO STEAL MY NAME AND POWER.
I HAD TOLD HIM ABOUT MY MATCH WITH REIKO.
BUT NOT WHY I LOST MY BODY...
TNK
HMPH, HE HAD NO IDEA IT CAME WITH A CURSE.
WHAT'S THIS?!
SLS
GET AWAY!
I DON'T WANT ANY OF IT!
TOSS
I DON'T WANT IT!
FFT
FSSSH
SHNK

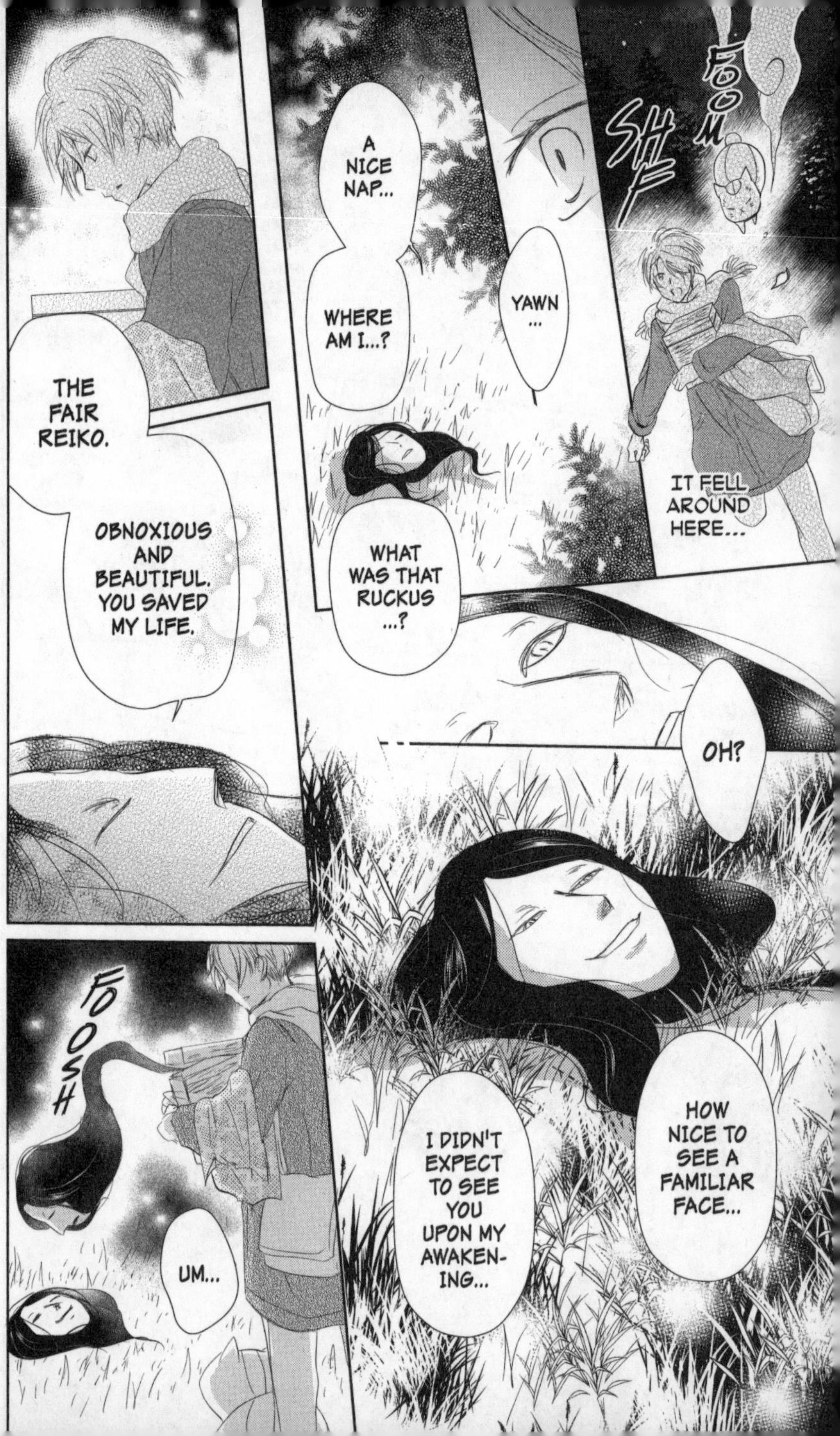
FOOM
SHF
IT FELL AROUND HERE...
YAWN...
A NICE NAP...
WHERE AM I...?
WHAT WAS THAT RUCKUS...?
OH?
HOW NICE TO SEE A FAMILIAR FACE...
I DIDN'T EXPECT TO SEE YOU UPON MY AWAKENING...
THE FAIR REIKO.
OBNOXIOUS AND BEAUTIFUL. YOU SAVED MY LIFE.
FOOSH
UM...

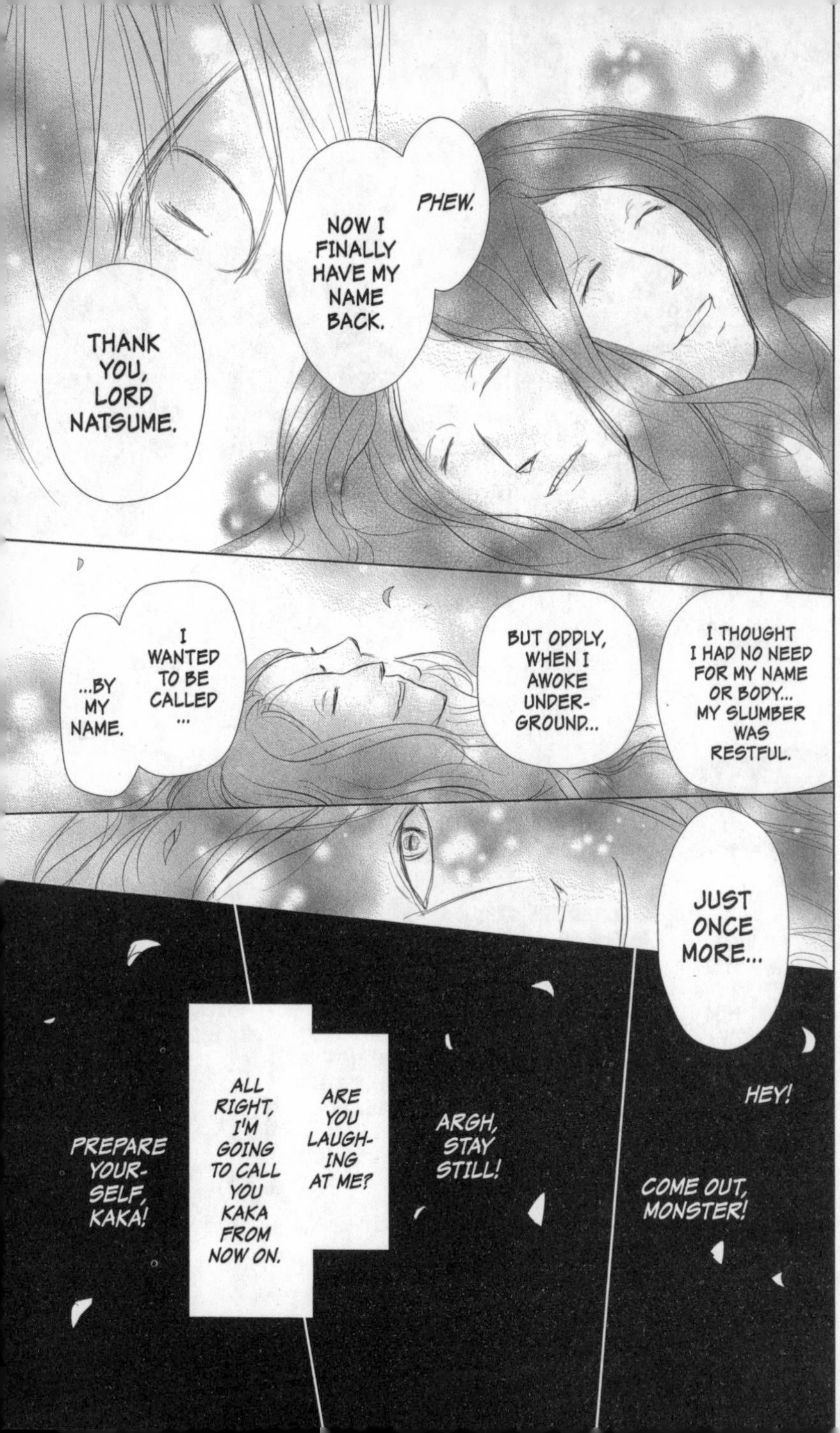
PHEW.
NOW I FINALLY HAVE MY NAME BACK.
THANK YOU, LORD NATSUME.
I THOUGHT I HAD NO NEED FOR MY NAME OR BODY... MY SLUMBER WAS RESTFUL.
BUT ODDLY, WHEN I AWOKE UNDER-GROUND...
I WANTED TO BE CALLED...
...BY MY NAME.
JUST ONCE MORE...
HEY!
COME OUT, MONSTER!
ARGH, STAY STILL!
ARE YOU LAUGH-ING AT ME?
ALL RIGHT, I'M GOING TO CALL YOU KAKA FROM NOW ON.
PREPARE YOUR-SELF, KAKA!

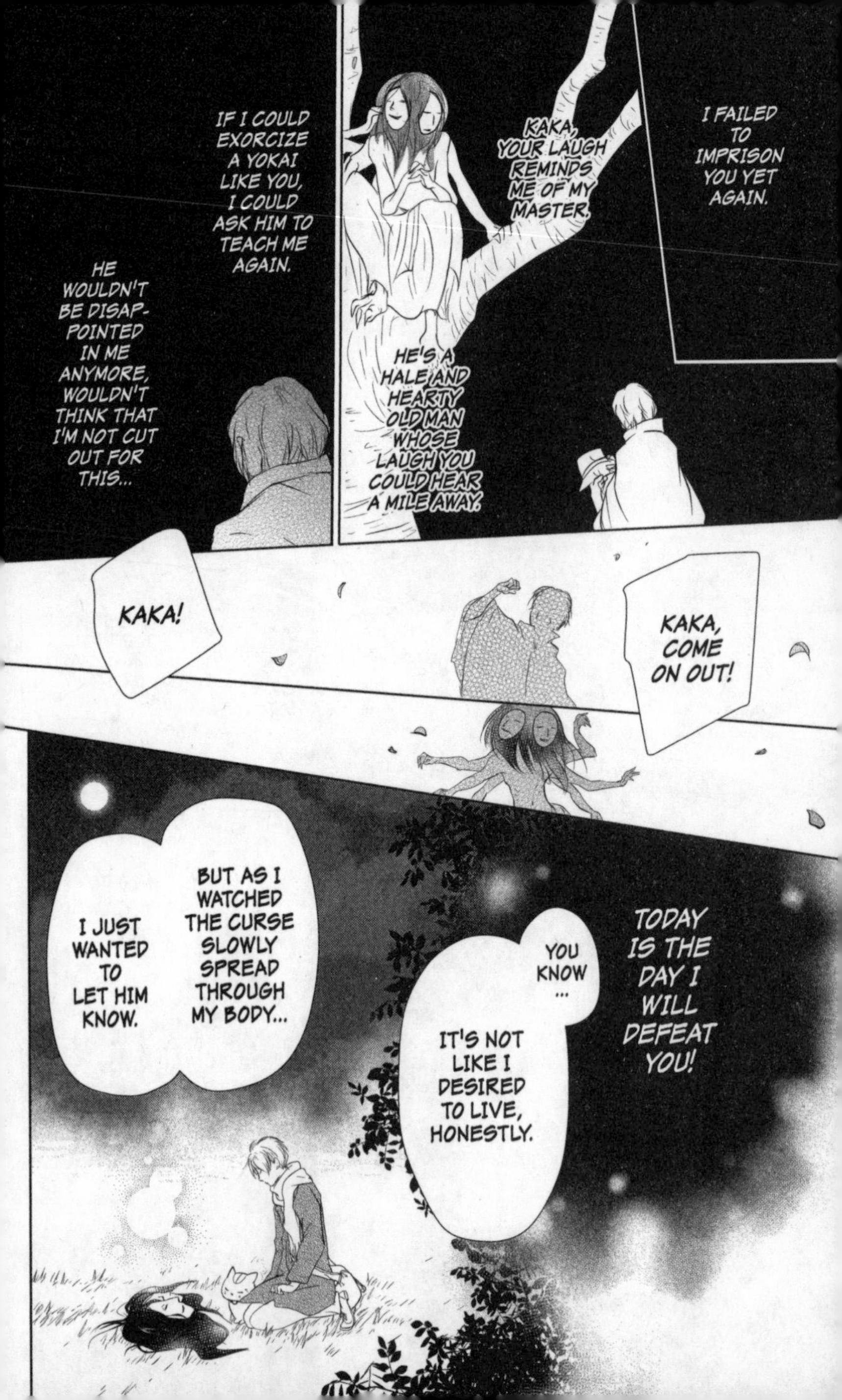
I FAILED TO IMPRISON YOU YET AGAIN.
KAKA, YOUR LAUGH REMINDS ME OF MY MASTER.
HE'S A HALE AND HEARTY OLD MAN WHOSE LAUGH YOU COULD HEAR A MILE AWAY.
IF I COULD EXORCIZE A YOKAI LIKE YOU, I COULD ASK HIM TO TEACH ME AGAIN.
HE WOULDN'T BE DISAP-POINTED IN ME ANYMORE, WOULDN'T THINK THAT I'M NOT CUT OUT FOR THIS...
KAKA, COME ON OUT!
KAKA!
TODAY IS THE DAY I WILL DEFEAT YOU!
YOU KNOW...
IT'S NOT LIKE I DESIRED TO LIVE, HONESTLY.
BUT AS I WATCHED THE CURSE SLOWLY SPREAD THROUGH MY BODY...
I JUST WANTED TO LET HIM KNOW.

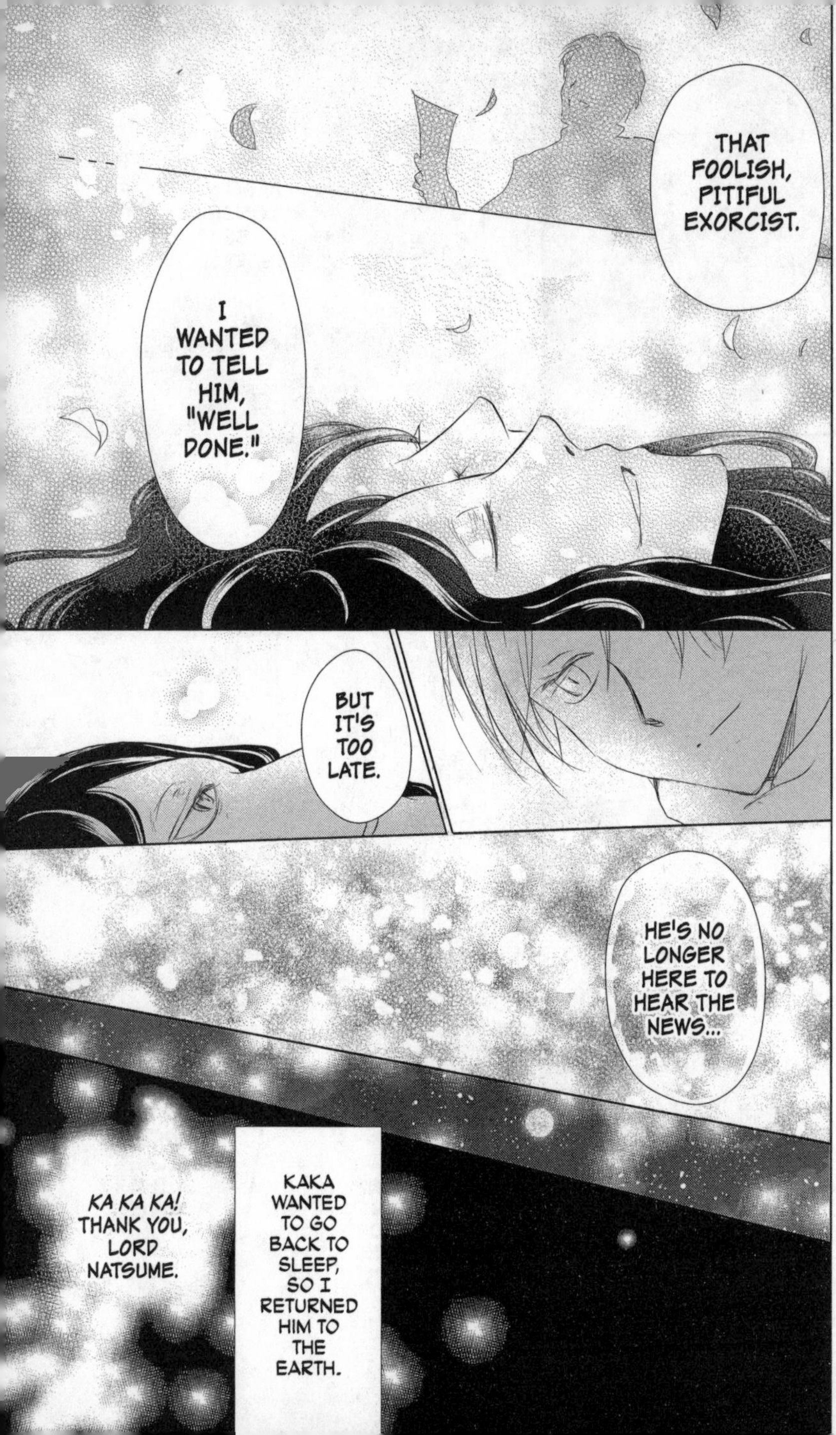
THAT FOOLISH, PITIFUL EXORCIST.
I WANTED TO TELL HIM, "WELL DONE."
BUT IT'S TOO LATE.
HE'S NO LONGER HERE TO HEAR THE NEWS...
KAKA WANTED TO GO BACK TO SLEEP, SO I RETURNED HIM TO THE EARTH.
KA KA KA! THANK YOU, LORD NATSUME.

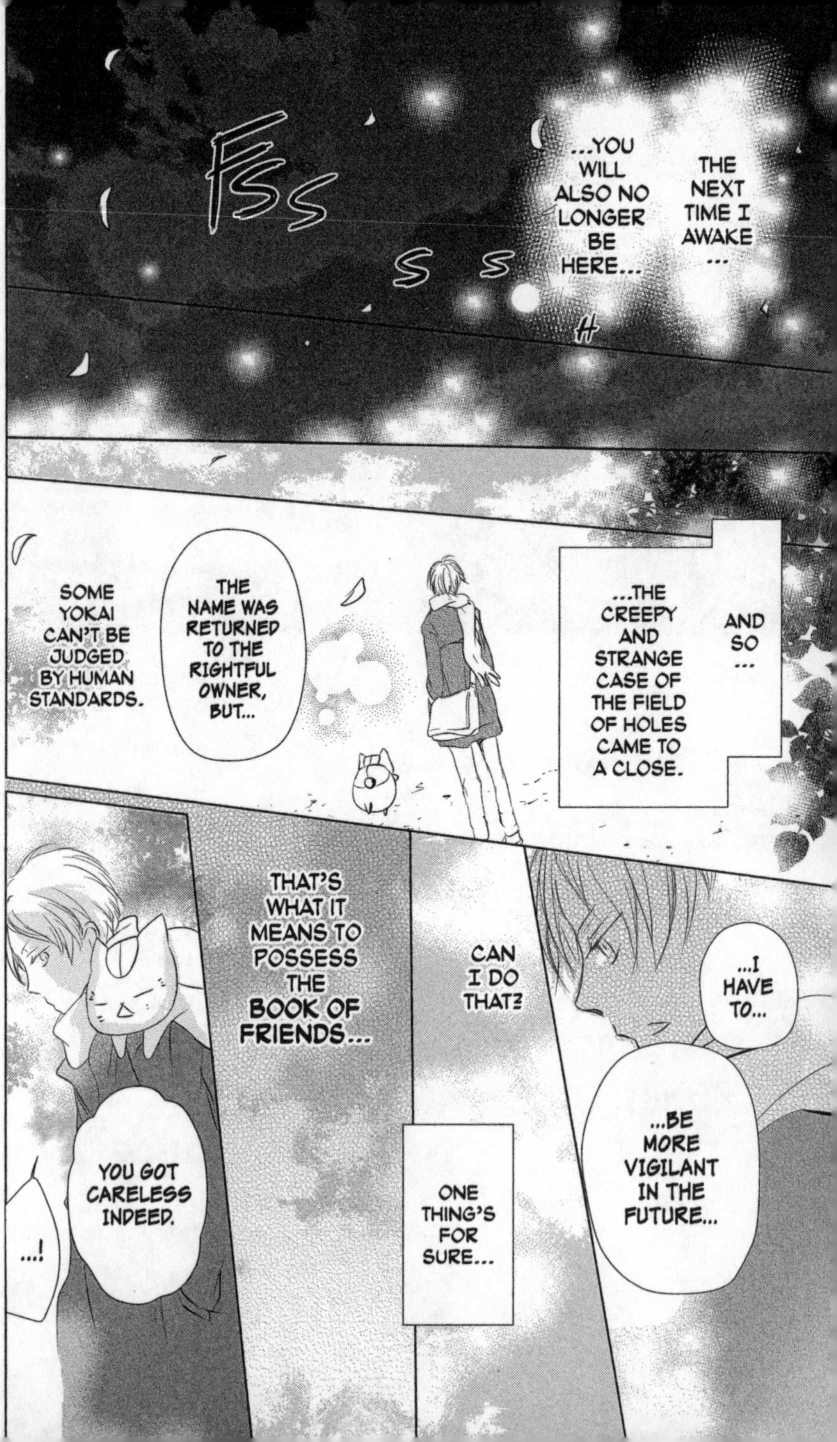
THE NEXT TIME I AWAKE...
...YOU WILL ALSO NO LONGER BE HERE...
FSSSSH
AND SO...
...THE CREEPY AND STRANGE CASE OF THE FIELD OF HOLES CAME TO A CLOSE.
THE NAME WAS RETURNED TO THE RIGHTFUL OWNER, BUT...
SOME YOKAI CAN'T BE JUDGED BY HUMAN STANDARDS.
...I HAVE TO...
...BE MORE VIGILANT IN THE FUTURE...
CAN I DO THAT?
ONE THING'S FOR SURE...
THAT'S WHAT IT MEANS TO POSSESS THE BOOK OF FRIENDS...
YOU GOT CARELESS INDEED.
...!

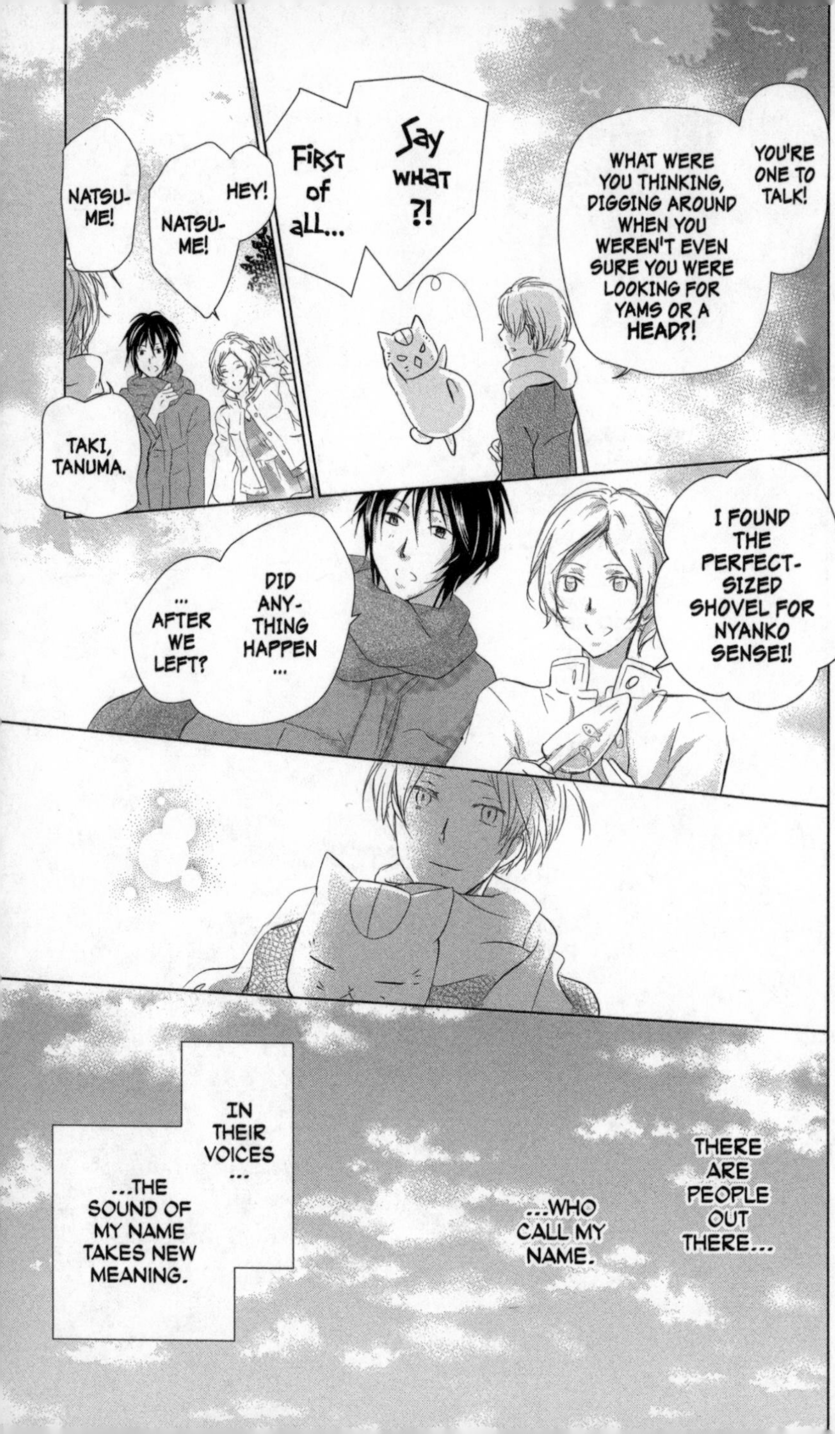
YOU'RE ONE TO TALK!
WHAT WERE YOU THINKING, DIGGING AROUND WHEN YOU WEREN'T EVEN SURE YOU WERE LOOKING FOR YAMS OR A HEAD?!
Say what ?!
First of all...
HEY!
NATSUME!
NATSUME!
TAKI, TANUMA.
I FOUND THE PERFECT-SIZED SHOVEL FOR NYANKO SENSEI!
DID ANYTHING HAPPEN...
...AFTER WE LEFT?
THERE ARE PEOPLE OUT THERE...
...WHO CALL MY NAME.
IN THEIR VOICES...
...THE SOUND OF MY NAME TAKES NEW MEANING.

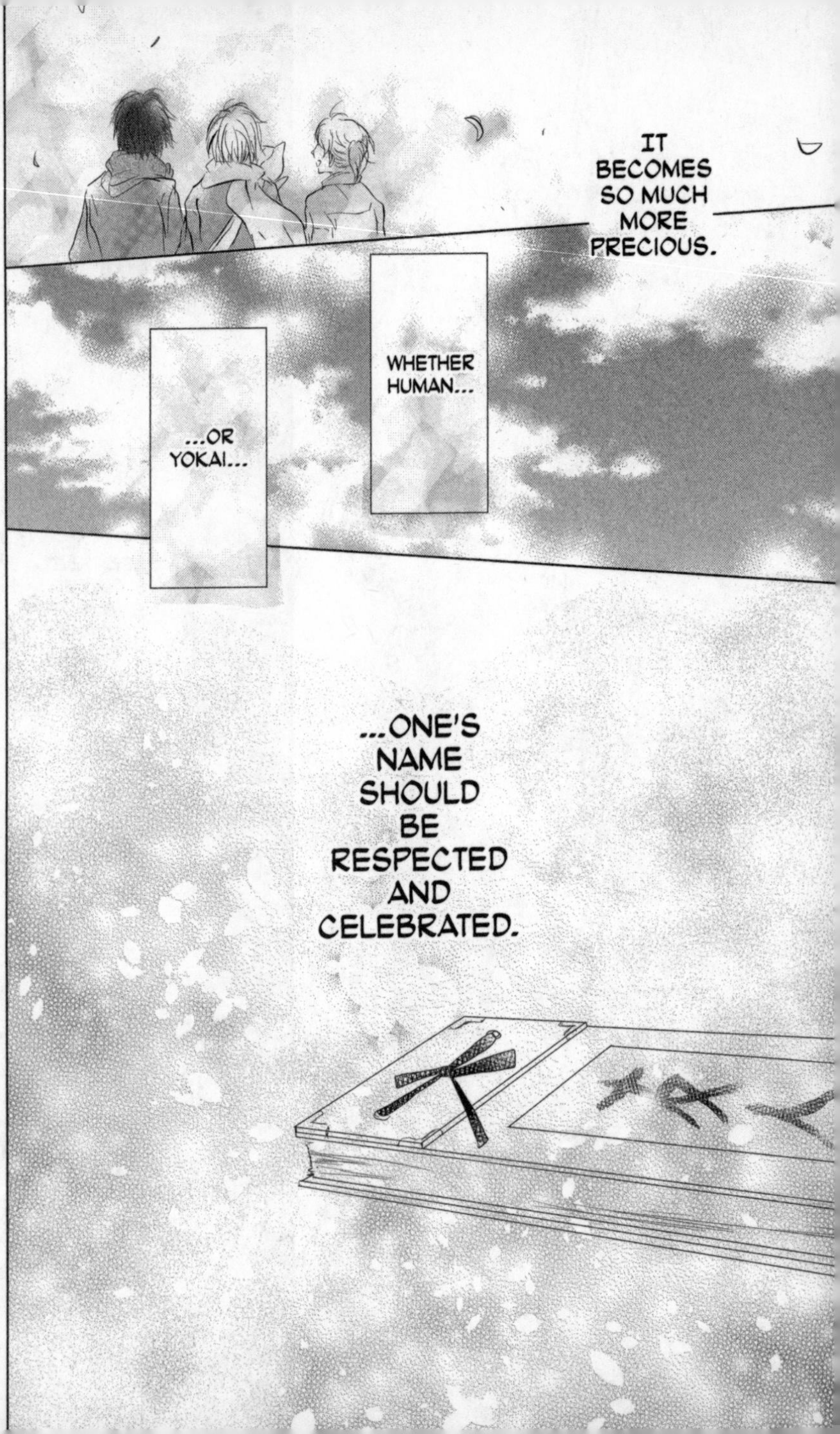
IT BECOMES SO MUCH MORE PRECIOUS.
WHETHER HUMAN...
...OR YOKAI...
...ONE'S NAME SHOULD BE RESPECTED AND CELEBRATED.

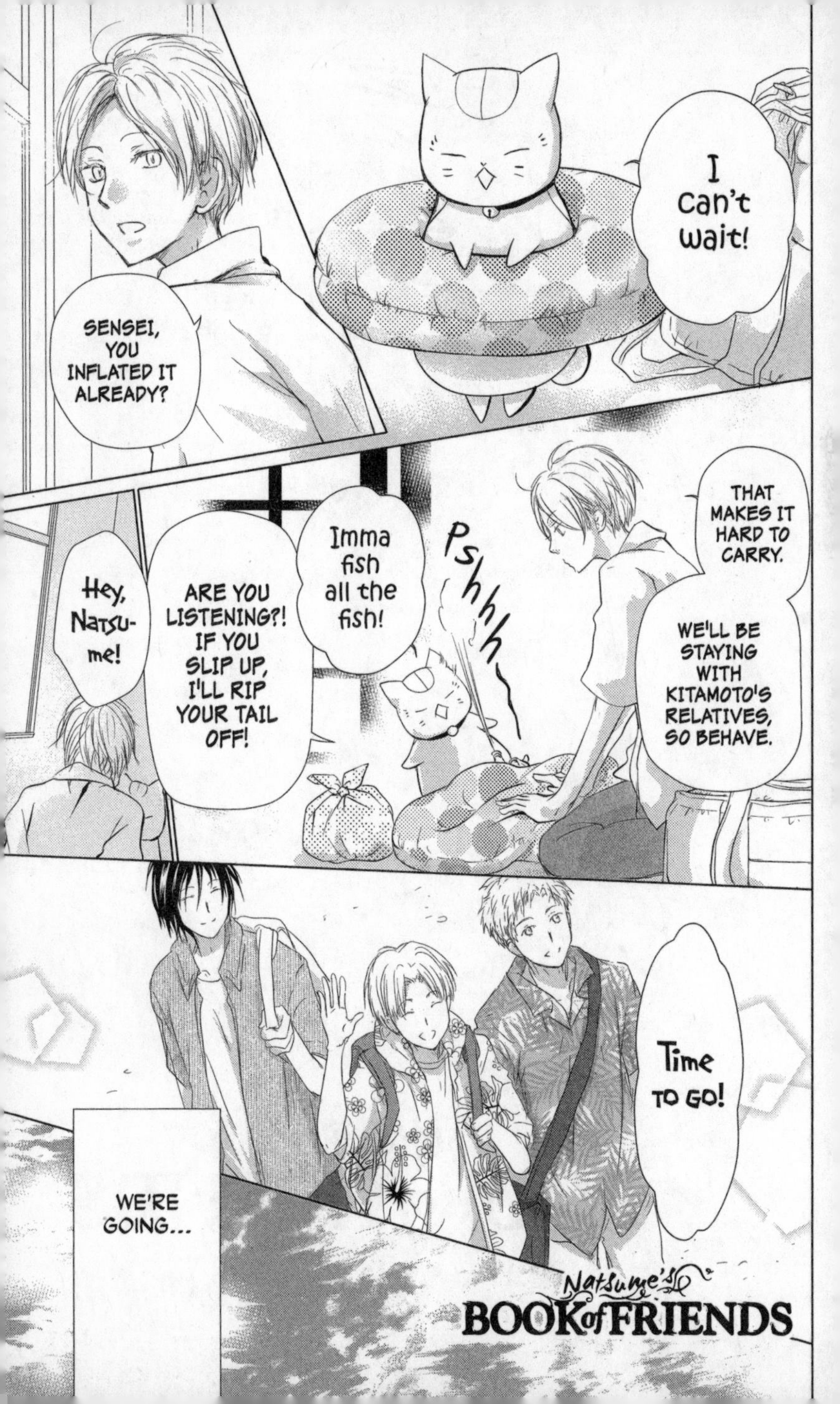
I can't wait!
SENSEI, YOU INFLATED IT ALREADY?
THAT MAKES IT HARD TO CARRY.
WE'LL BE STAYING WITH KITAMOTO'S RELATIVES, SO BEHAVE.
Pshhh~
Imma fish all the fish!
ARE YOU LISTENING?! IF YOU SLIP UP, I'LL RIP YOUR TAIL OFF!
Hey, Natsume!
Time to go!
WE'RE GOING...
Natsume's BOOK of FRIENDS

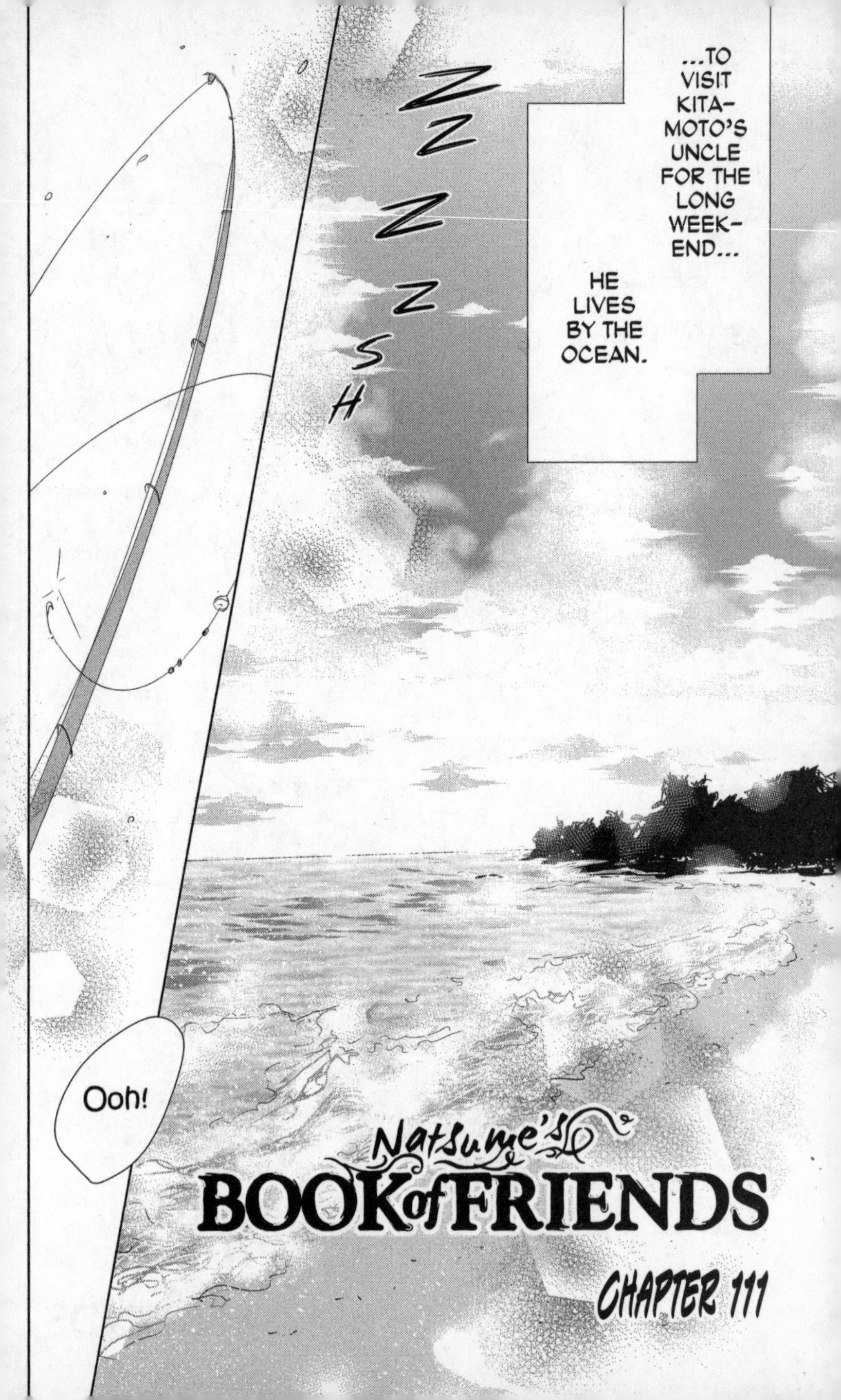
...TO VISIT KITA-MOTO'S UNCLE FOR THE LONG WEEK-END...
HE LIVES BY THE OCEAN.
ZZZZSH
Natsume's BOOK of FRIENDS
CHAPTER 111
Ooh!

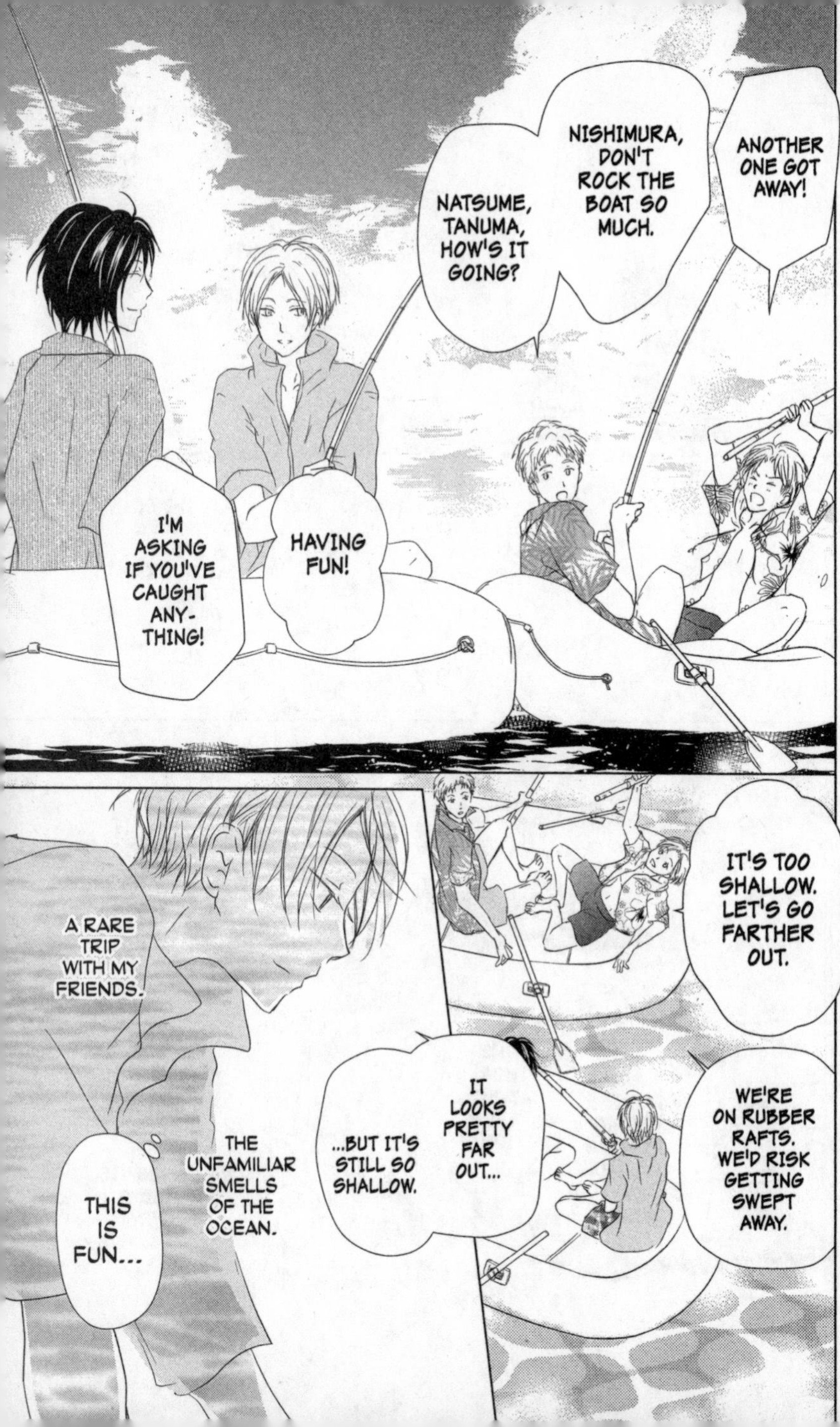
ANOTHER ONE GOT AWAY!
NISHIMURA, DON'T ROCK THE BOAT SO MUCH.
NATSUME, TANUMA, HOW'S IT GOING?
HAVING FUN!
I'M ASKING IF YOU'VE CAUGHT ANY-THING!
IT'S TOO SHALLOW. LET'S GO FARTHER OUT.
WE'RE ON RUBBER RAFTS. WE'D RISK GETTING SWEPT AWAY.
IT LOOKS PRETTY FAR OUT...
...BUT IT'S STILL SO SHALLOW.
A RARE TRIP WITH MY FRIENDS.
THE UNFAMILIAR SMELLS OF THE OCEAN.
THIS IS FUN...

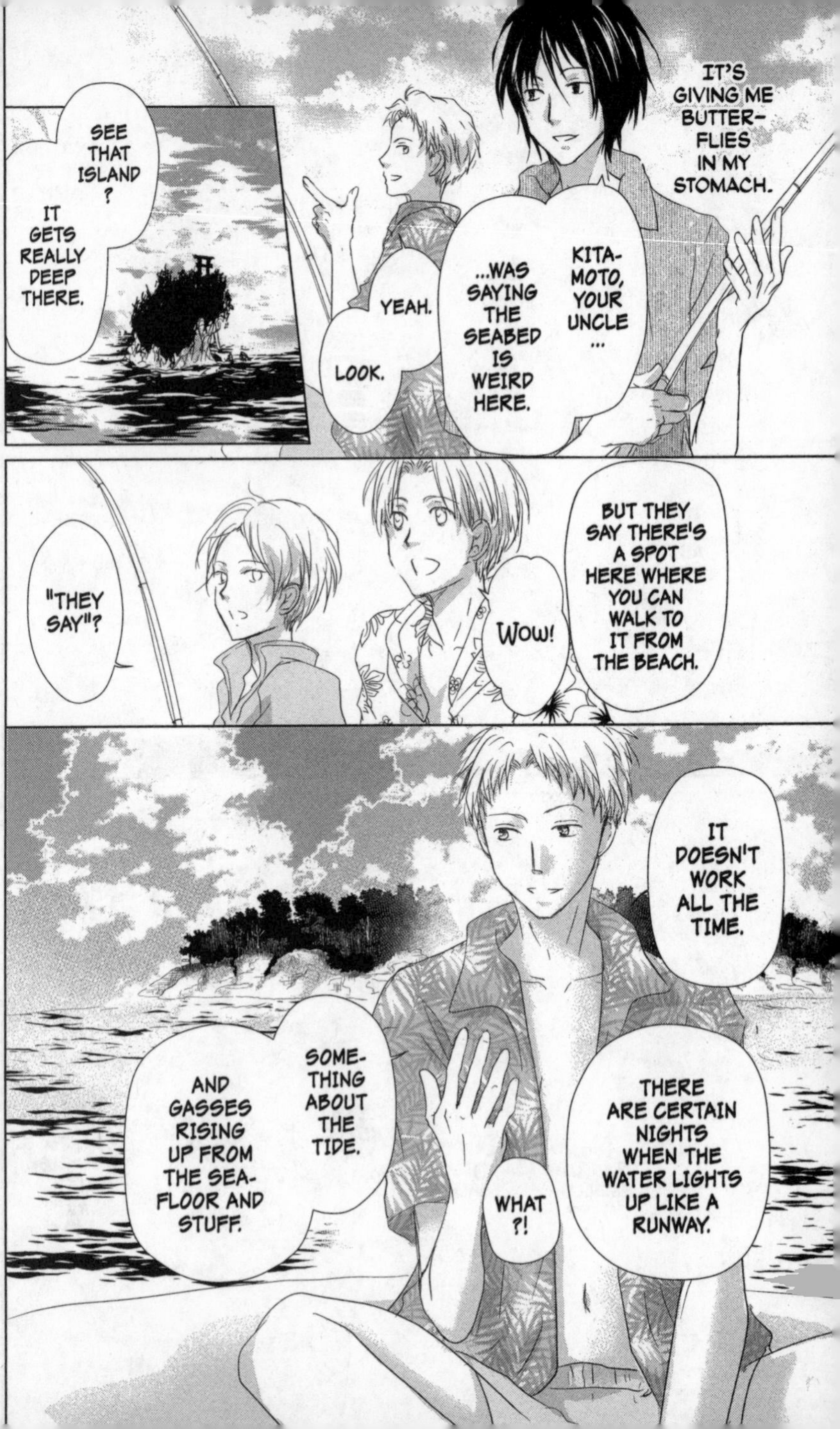
IT'S GIVING ME BUTTER-FLIES IN MY STOMACH.
KITA-MOTO, YOUR UNCLE ...
...WAS SAYING THE SEABED IS WEIRD HERE.
YEAH.
LOOK.
SEE THAT ISLAND ?
IT GETS REALLY DEEP THERE.
BUT THEY SAY THERE'S A SPOT HERE WHERE YOU CAN WALK TO IT FROM THE BEACH.
WOW!
"THEY SAY"?
IT DOESN'T WORK ALL THE TIME.
THERE ARE CERTAIN NIGHTS WHEN THE WATER LIGHTS UP LIKE A RUNWAY.
WHAT ?!
SOME-THING ABOUT THE TIDE.
AND GASSES RISING UP FROM THE SEA-FLOOR AND STUFF.

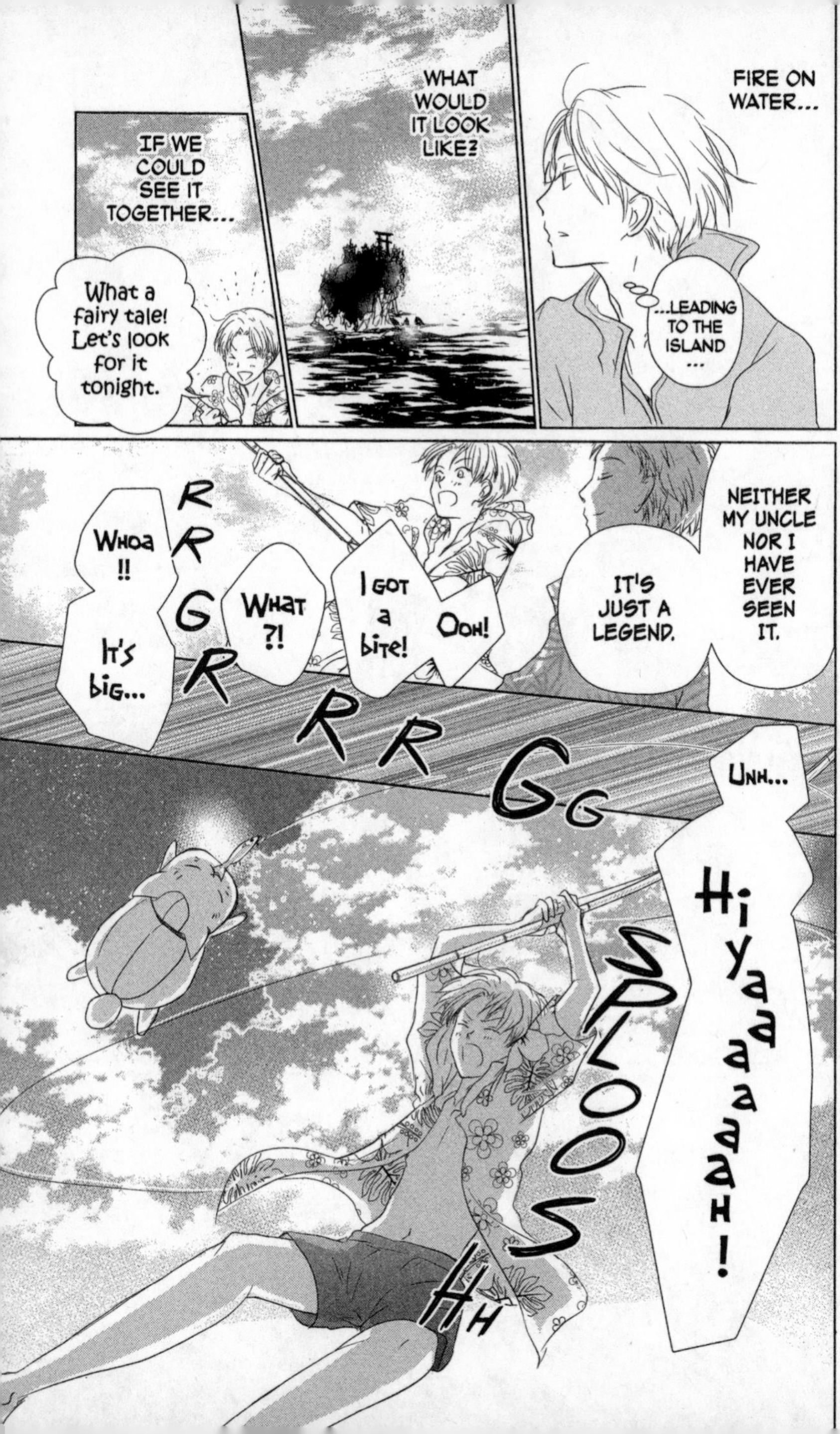
FIRE ON WATER...
...LEADING TO THE ISLAND...
WHAT WOULD IT LOOK LIKE?
IF WE COULD SEE IT TOGETHER...
What a fairy tale! Let's look for it tonight.
NEITHER MY UNCLE NOR I HAVE EVER SEEN IT.
IT'S JUST A LEGEND.
Ooh!
I got a bite!
What?!
RRGR
Whoa!!
It's big...
RRR
GG
Unh...
Hiyaaaaaaah!
SPLOOSHH

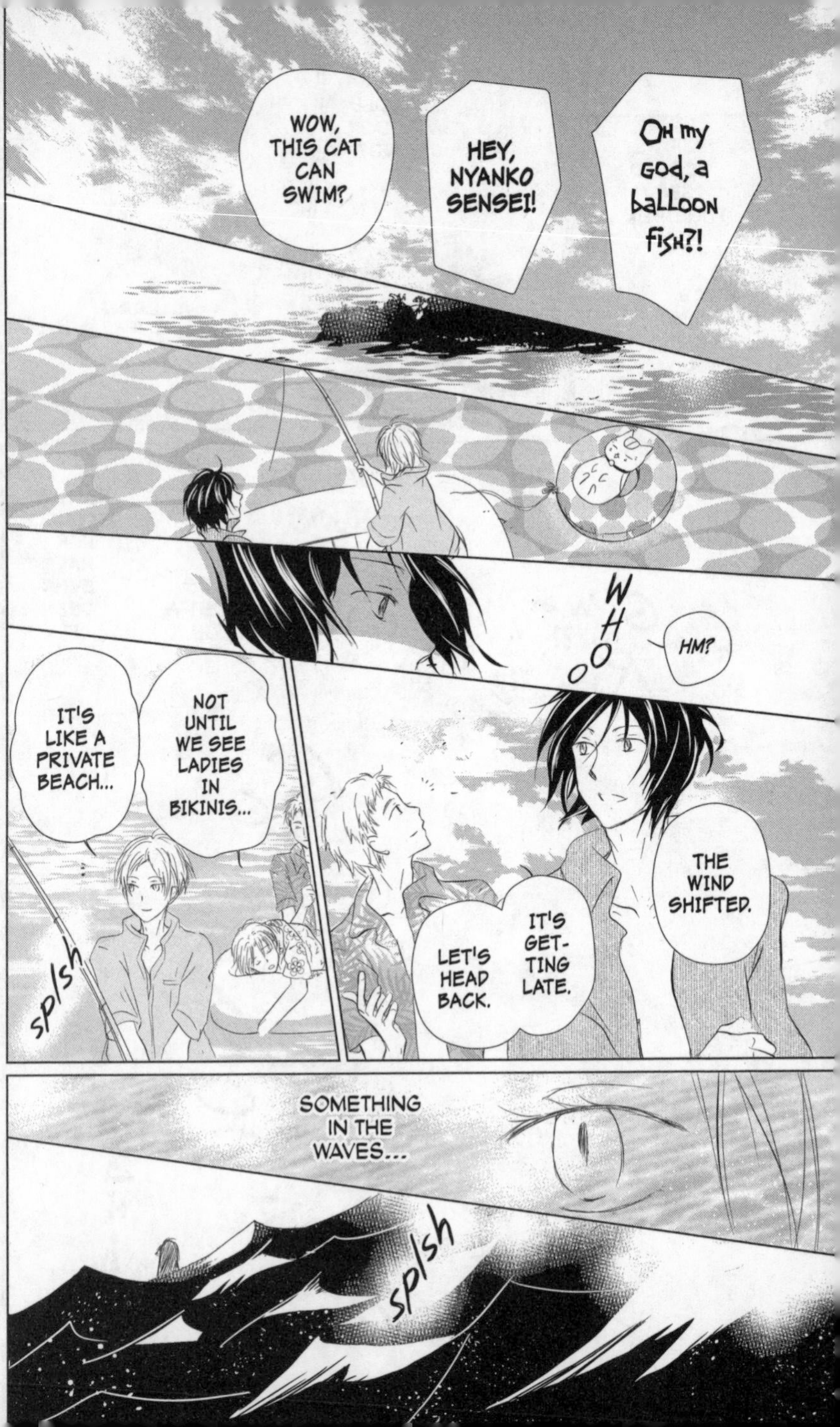

Oh my god, a balloon fish?!
HEY, NYANKO SENSEI!
WOW, THIS CAT CAN SWIM?
WHOOO
HM?
THE WIND SHIFTED.
IT'S GETTING LATE.
LET'S HEAD BACK.
NOT UNTIL WE SEE LADIES IN BIKINIS...
IT'S LIKE A PRIVATE BEACH...
splsh
SOMETHING IN THE WAVES...
splsh

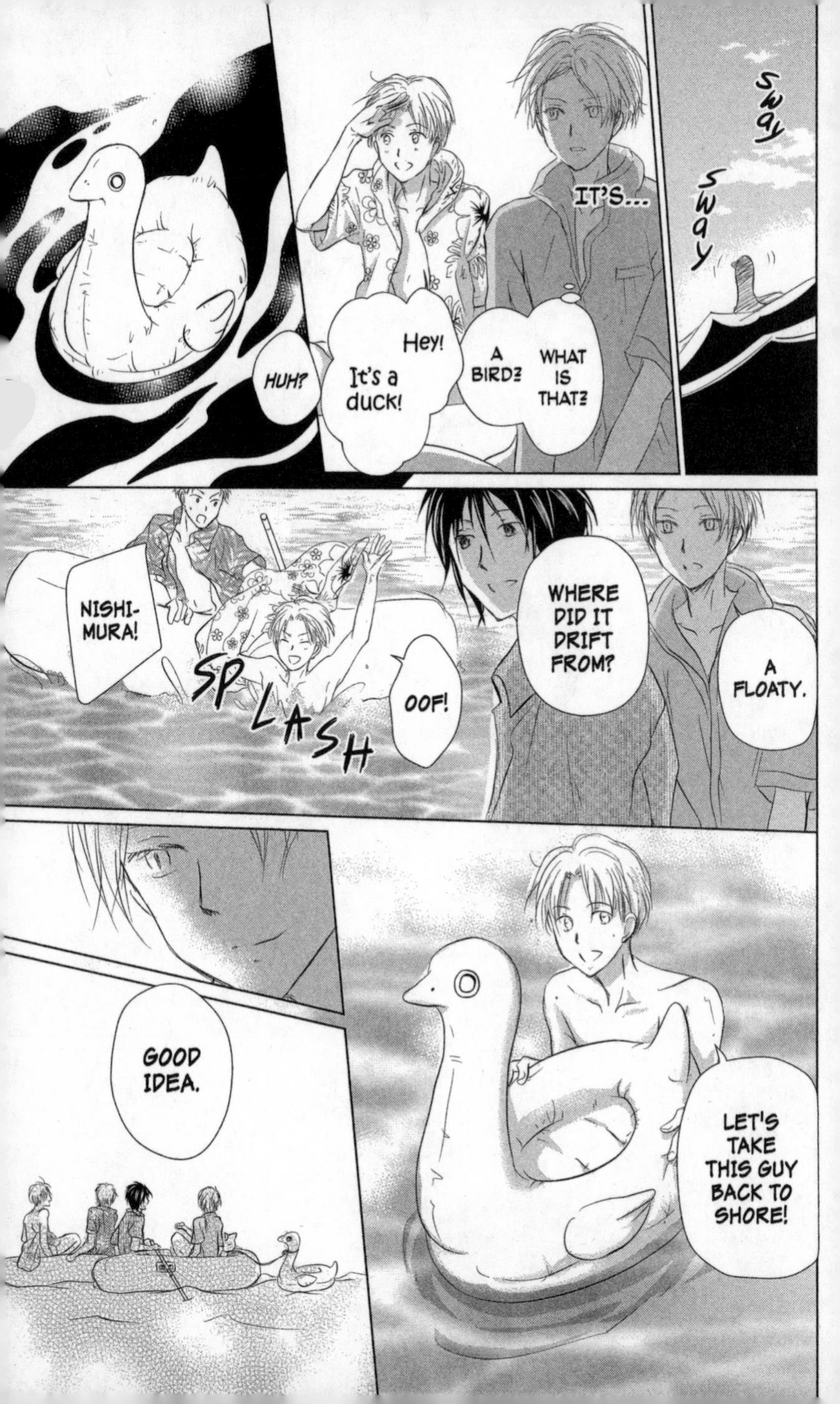
SWAY
SWAY
IT'S...
WHAT IS THAT?
A BIRD?
Hey! It's a duck!
HUH?
A FLOATY.
WHERE DID IT DRIFT FROM?
OOF!
SPLASH
NISHIMURA!
LET'S TAKE THIS GUY BACK TO SHORE!
GOOD IDEA.

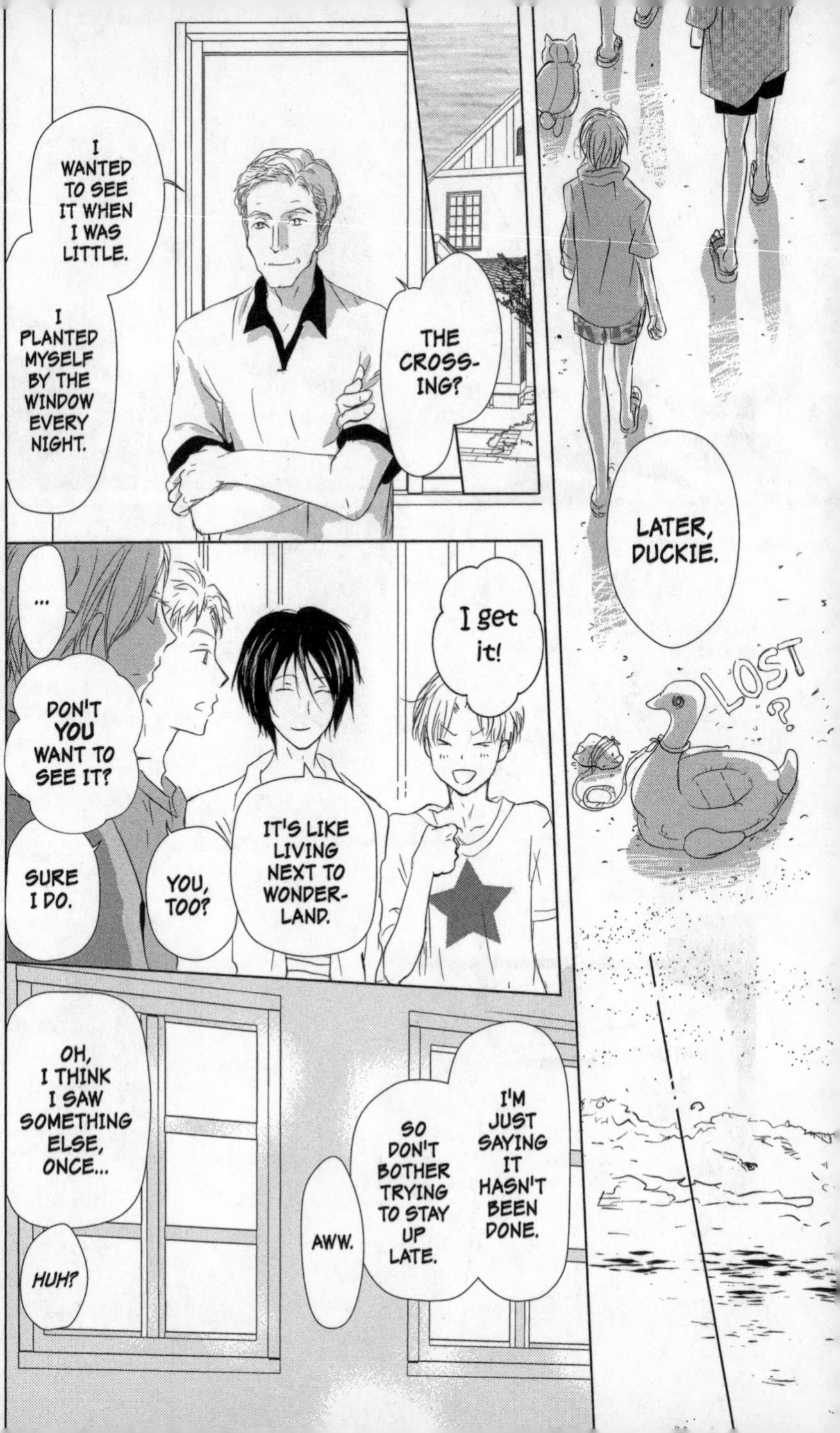
LATER, DUCKIE.
LOST
?
THE CROSSING?
I WANTED TO SEE IT WHEN I WAS LITTLE.
I PLANTED MYSELF BY THE WINDOW EVERY NIGHT.
I get it!
IT'S LIKE LIVING NEXT TO WONDERLAND.
...
DON'T YOU WANT TO SEE IT?
YOU, TOO?
SURE I DO.
I'M JUST SAYING IT HASN'T BEEN DONE.
SO DON'T BOTHER TRYING TO STAY UP LATE.
AWW.
OH, I THINK I SAW SOMETHING ELSE, ONCE...
HUH?

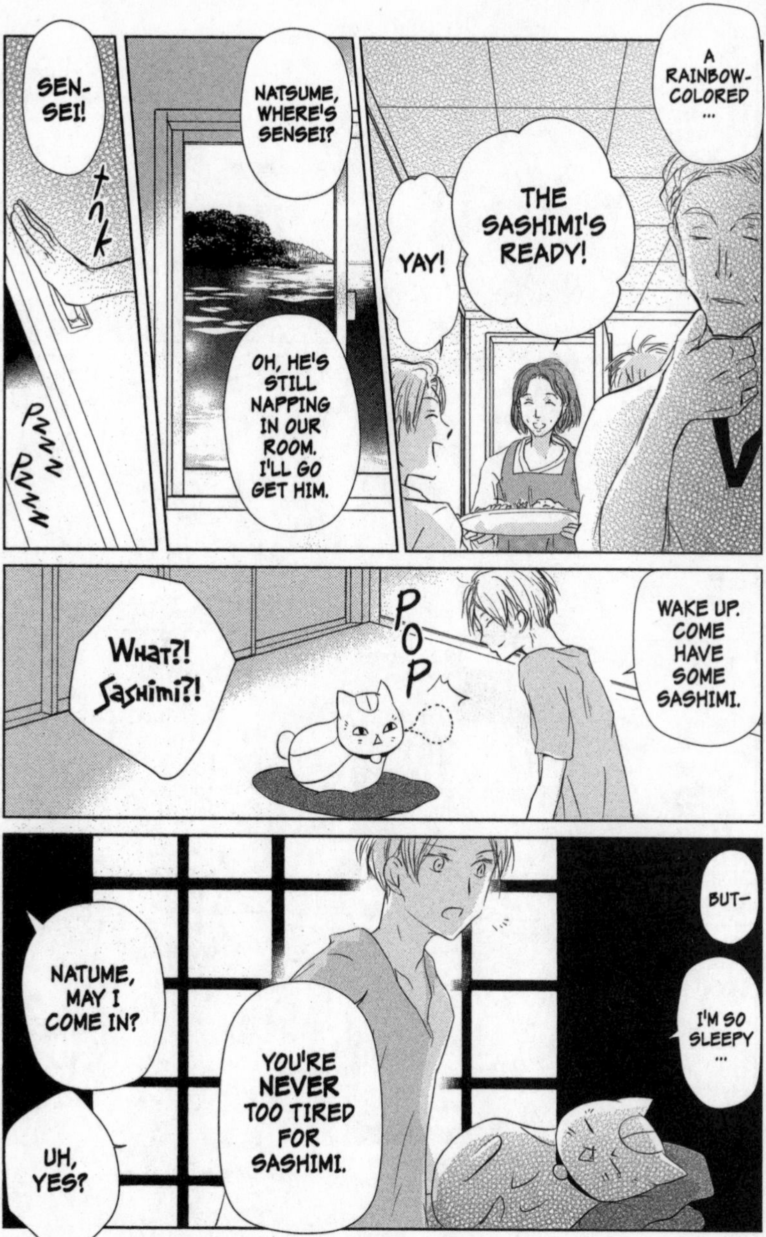
A RAINBOW-COLORED ...
THE SASHIMI'S READY!
YAY!
NATSUME, WHERE'S SENSEI?
OH, HE'S STILL NAPPING IN OUR ROOM. I'LL GO GET HIM.
SEN-SEI!
tnk
Pzzz Pzzz
WAKE UP. COME HAVE SOME SASHIMI.
POP
What?! Sashimi?!
BUT—
I'M SO SLEEPY ...
YOU'RE NEVER TOO TIRED FOR SASHIMI.
NATUME, MAY I COME IN?
UH, YES?

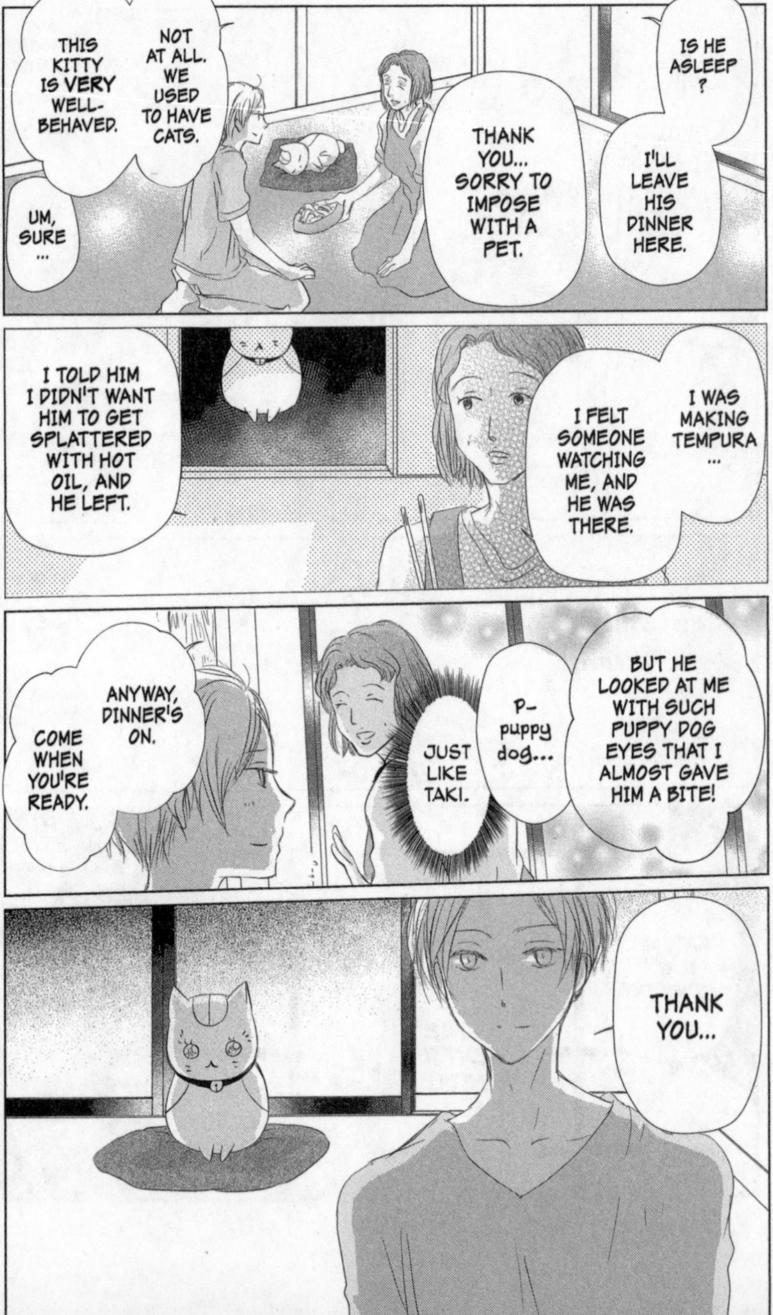
IS HE ASLEEP?
I'LL LEAVE HIS DINNER HERE.
THANK YOU... SORRY TO IMPOSE WITH A PET.
NOT AT ALL. WE USED TO HAVE CATS.
THIS KITTY IS VERY WELL-BEHAVED.
UM, SURE...
I WAS MAKING TEMPURA...
I FELT SOMEONE WATCHING ME, AND HE WAS THERE.
I TOLD HIM I DIDN'T WANT HIM TO GET SPLATTERED WITH HOT OIL, AND HE LEFT.
BUT HE LOOKED AT ME WITH SUCH PUPPY DOG EYES THAT I ALMOST GAVE HIM A BITE!
P-puppy dog...
JUST LIKE TAKI.
ANYWAY, DINNER'S ON.
COME WHEN YOU'RE READY.
THANK YOU...

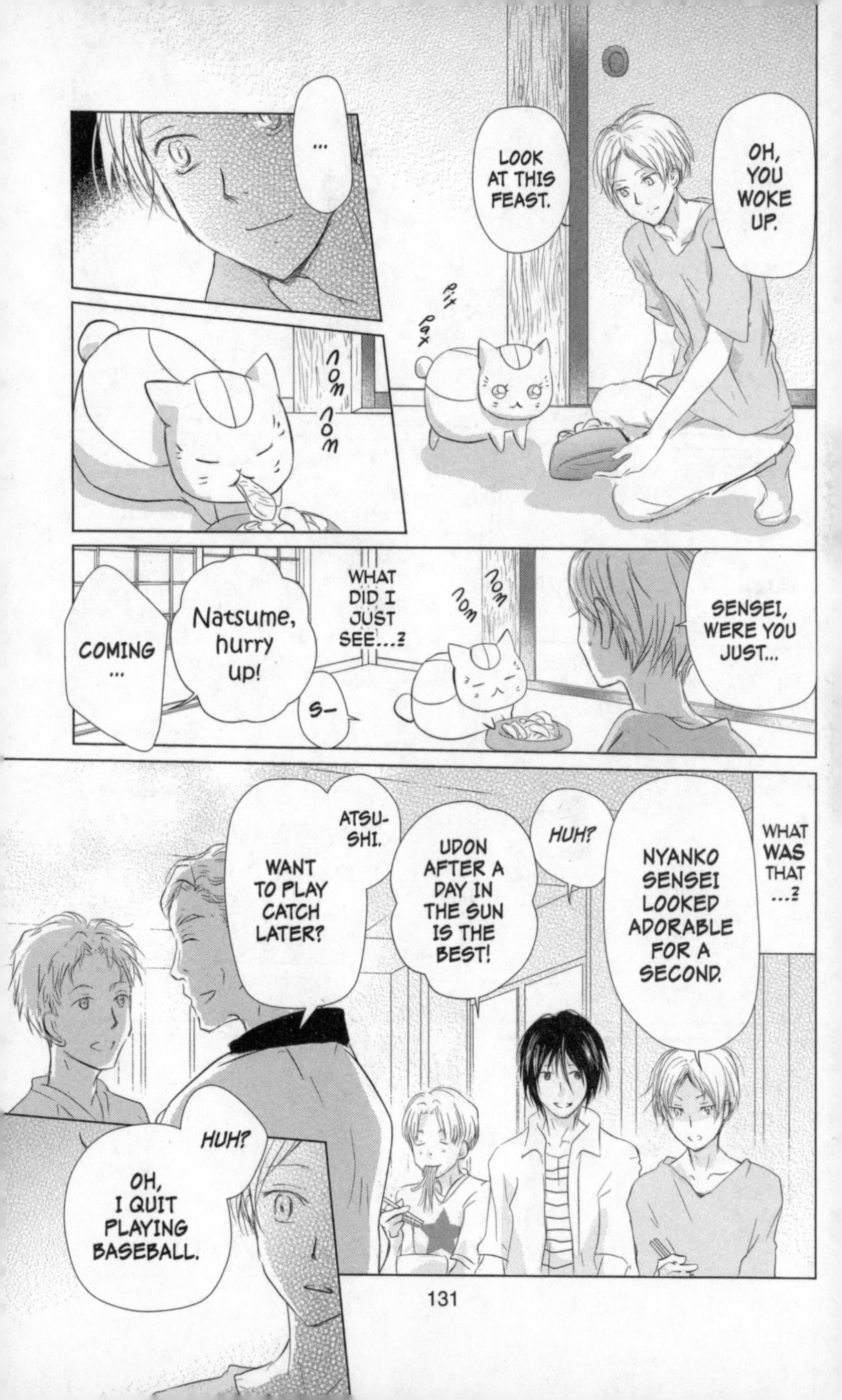
OH, YOU WOKE UP.
LOOK AT THIS FEAST.
pit pat
...
nom nom
SENSEI, WERE YOU JUST...
nom nom
WHAT DID I JUST SEE...?
S—
Natsume, hurry up!
COMING...
WHAT WAS THAT...?
NYANKO SENSEI LOOKED ADORABLE FOR A SECOND.
HUH?
UDON AFTER A DAY IN THE SUN IS THE BEST!
ATSU-SHI.
WANT TO PLAY CATCH LATER?
HUH?
OH, I QUIT PLAYING BASEBALL.

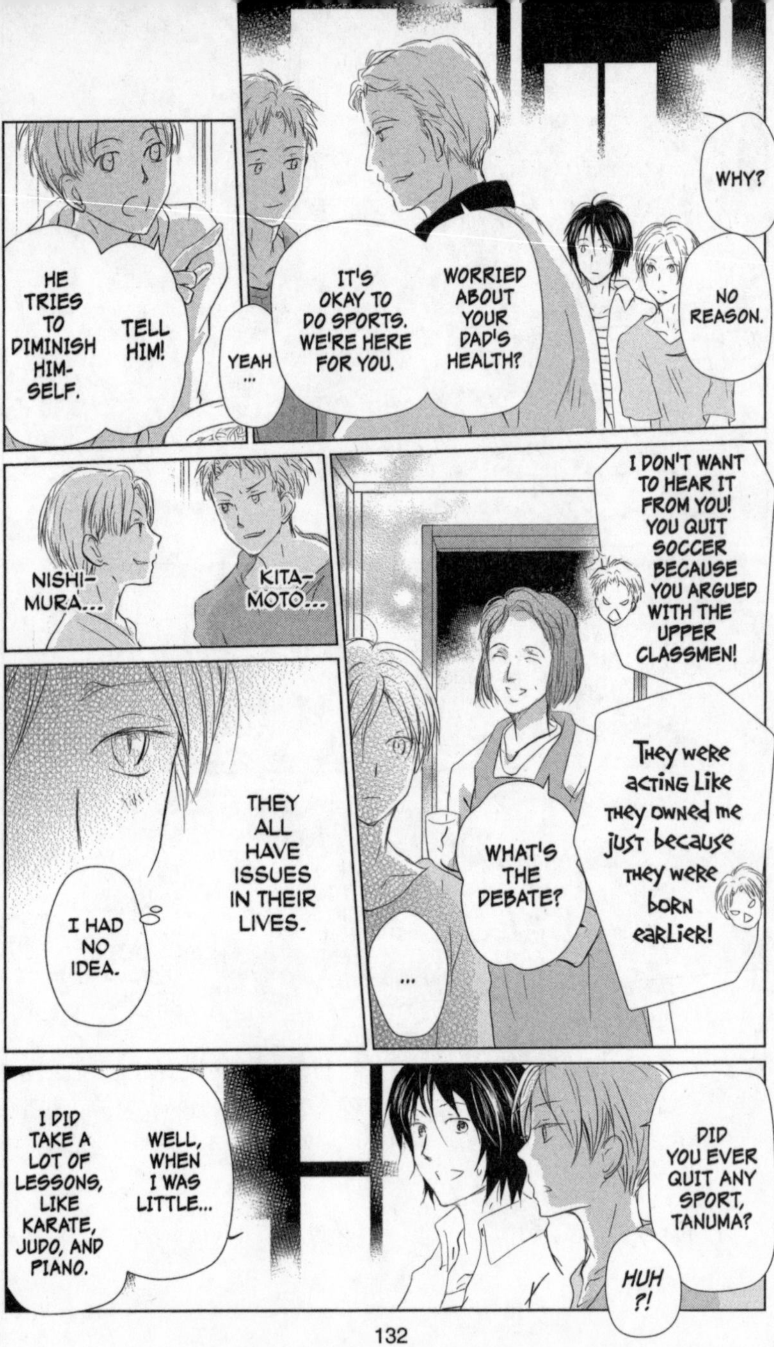
WHY?
NO REASON.
WORRIED ABOUT YOUR DAD'S HEALTH?
IT'S OKAY TO DO SPORTS. WE'RE HERE FOR YOU.
YEAH...
TELL HIM!
HE TRIES TO DIMINISH HIMSELF.
I DON'T WANT TO HEAR IT FROM YOU! YOU QUIT SOCCER BECAUSE YOU ARGUED WITH THE UPPER CLASSMEN!
They were acting like they owned me just because they were born earlier!
WHAT'S THE DEBATE?
...
KITA-MOTO...
NISHI-MURA...
THEY ALL HAVE ISSUES IN THEIR LIVES.
I HAD NO IDEA.
DID YOU EVER QUIT ANY SPORT, TANUMA?
HUH?!
WELL, WHEN I WAS LITTLE...
I DID TAKE A LOT OF LESSONS, LIKE KARATE, JUDO, AND PIANO.

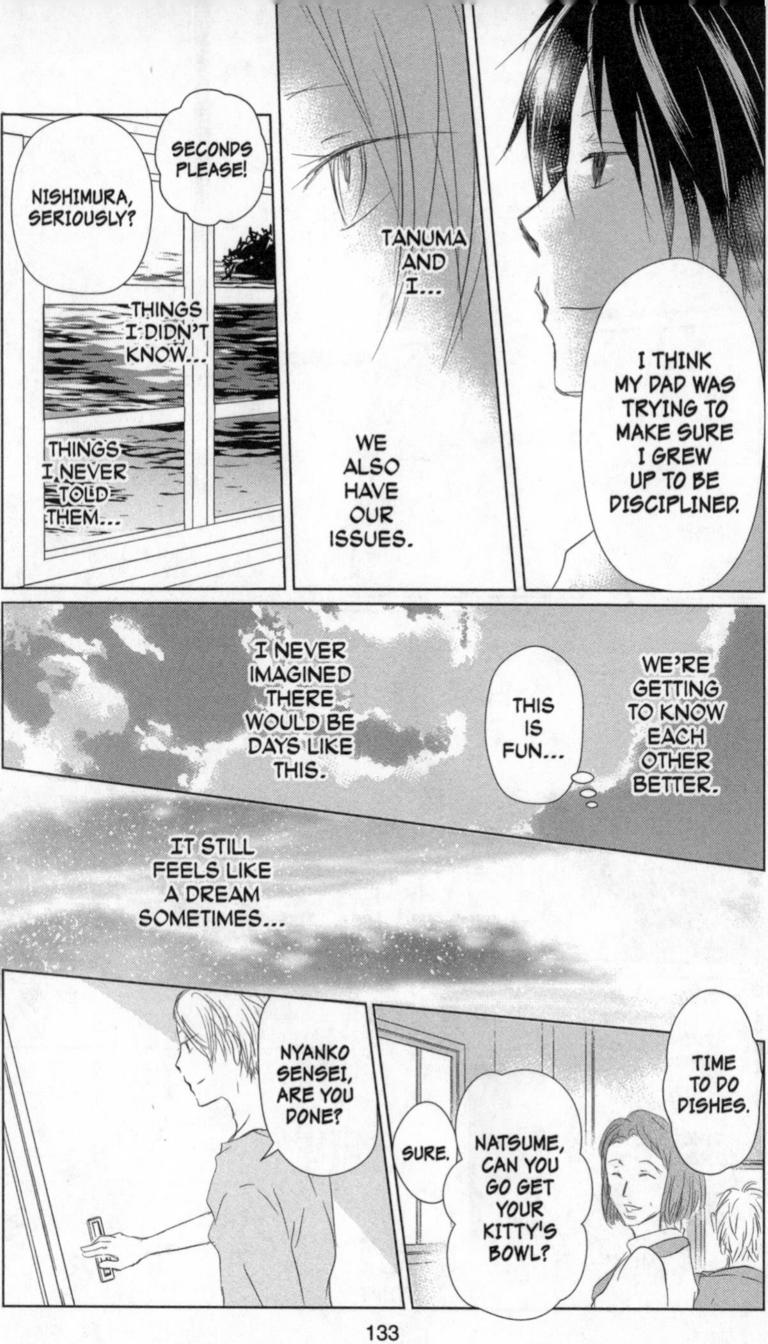
I THINK MY DAD WAS TRYING TO MAKE SURE I GREW UP TO BE DISCIPLINED.
TANUMA AND I...
WE ALSO HAVE OUR ISSUES.
SECONDS PLEASE!
NISHIMURA, SERIOUSLY?
THINGS I DIDN'T KNOW...
THINGS I NEVER TOLD THEM...
WE'RE GETTING TO KNOW EACH OTHER BETTER.
THIS IS FUN...
I NEVER IMAGINED THERE WOULD BE DAYS LIKE THIS.
IT STILL FEELS LIKE A DREAM SOMETIMES...
TIME TO DO DISHES.
NATSUME, CAN YOU GO GET YOUR KITTY'S BOWL?
SURE.
NYANKO SENSEI, ARE YOU DONE?

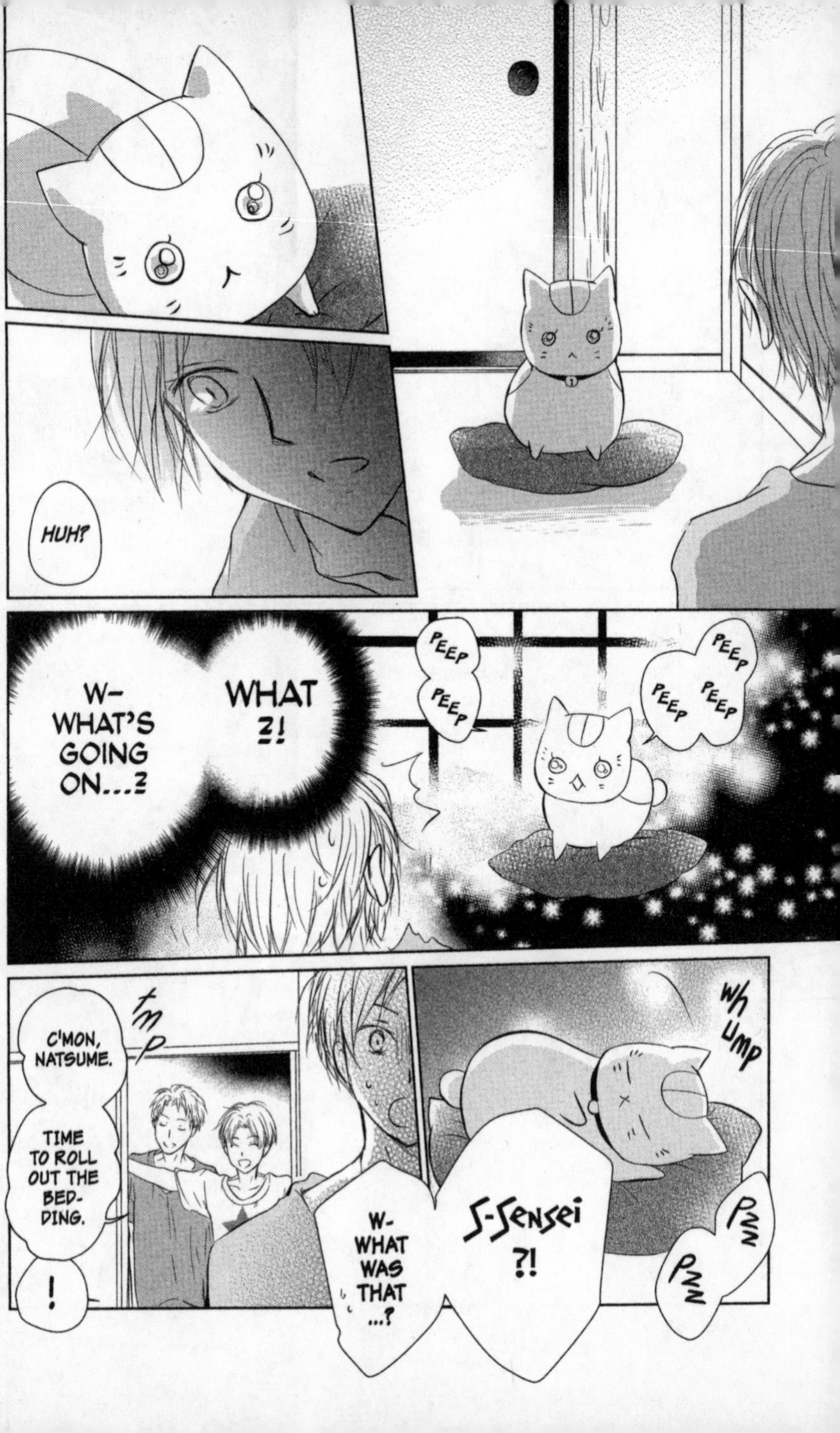
HUH?
PEEP PEEP PEEP
PEEP PEEP
WHAT?!
W-WHAT'S GOING ON...?
whump
Pzz
Pzz
S-Sensei?!
W-WHAT WAS THAT...?
tmp
C'MON, NATSUME.
TIME TO ROLL OUT THE BED-DING.
!

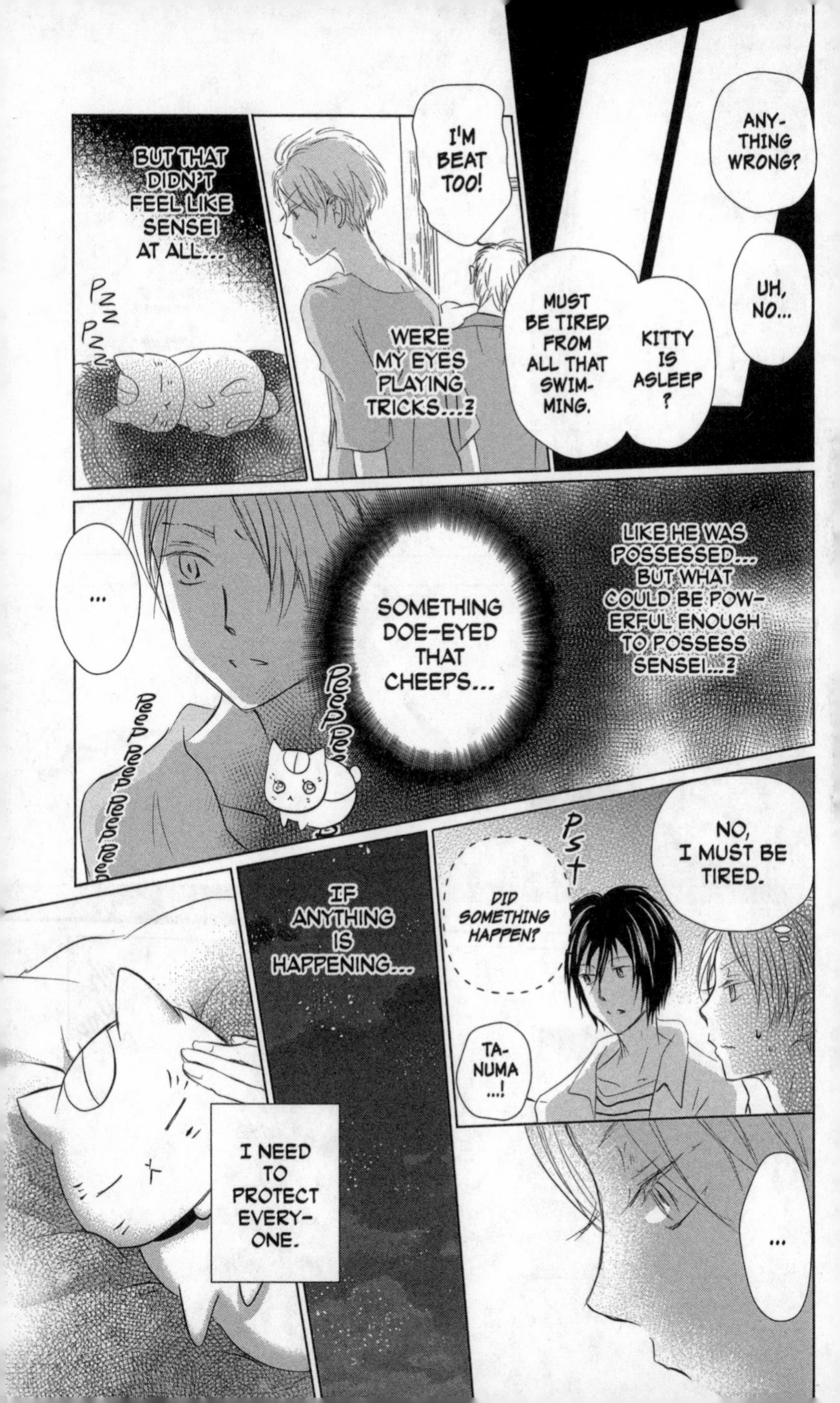
ANY-THING WRONG?
UH, NO...
I'M BEAT TOO!
KITTY IS ASLEEP?
MUST BE TIRED FROM ALL THAT SWIM-MING.
WERE MY EYES PLAYING TRICKS...?
BUT THAT DIDN'T FEEL LIKE SENSEI AT ALL...
PZZ PZZ
LIKE HE WAS POSSESSED... BUT WHAT COULD BE POW-ERFUL ENOUGH TO POSSESS SENSEI...?
SOMETHING DOE-EYED THAT CHEEPS...
PEEP PEEP
...
PEEP PEEP PEEP PEEP
NO, I MUST BE TIRED.
PST
DID SOMETHING HAPPEN?
TA-NUMA ...!
...
IF ANYTHING IS HAPPENING...
I NEED TO PROTECT EVERY-ONE.

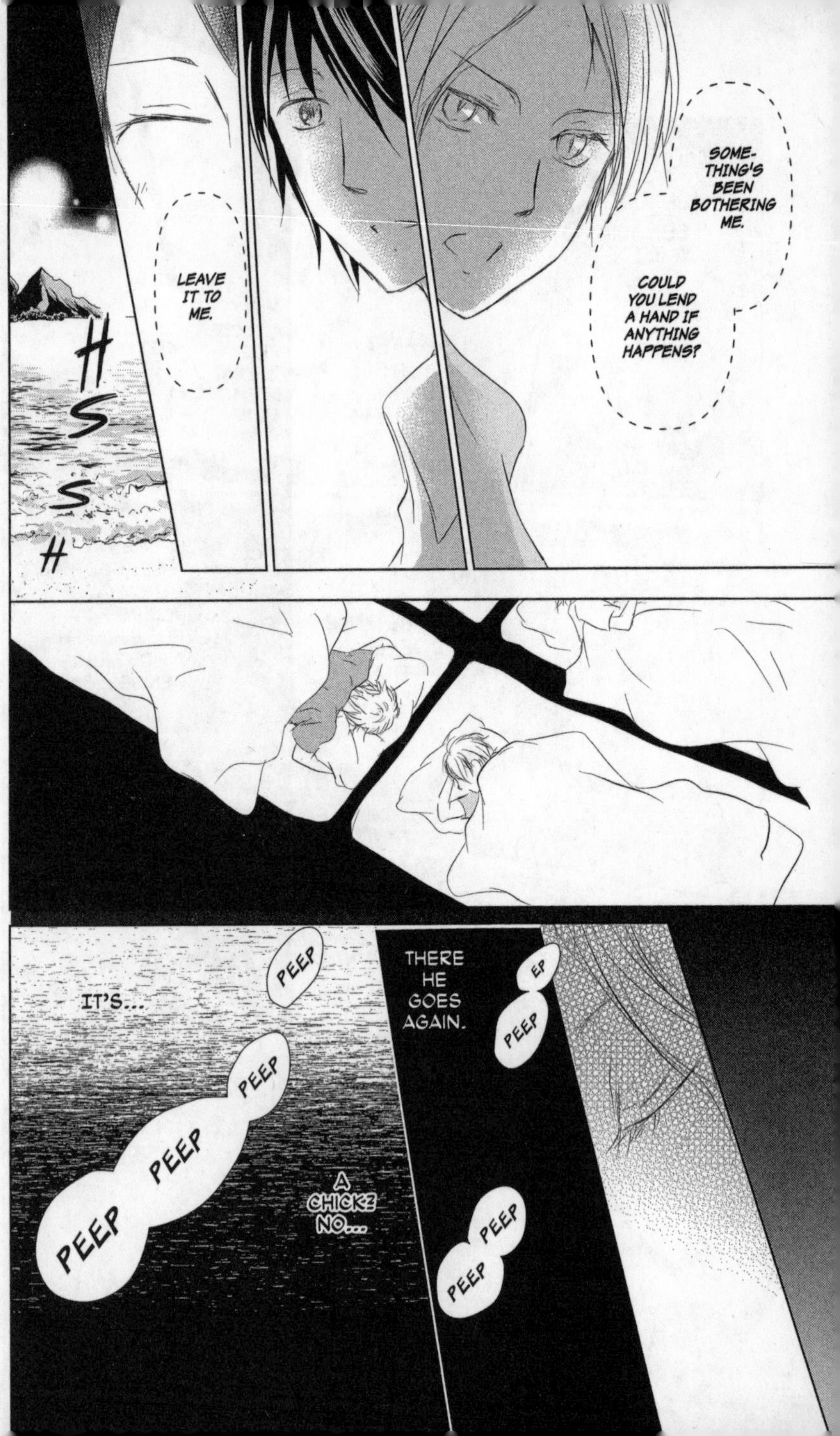
SOME-THING'S BEEN BOTHERING ME.
COULD YOU LEND A HAND IF ANYTHING HAPPENS?
LEAVE IT TO ME.
HSSH
THERE HE GOES AGAIN.
EP
PEEP
PEEP PEEP
PEEP
IT'S...
PEEP PEEP PEEP PEEP
A CHICK? NO...

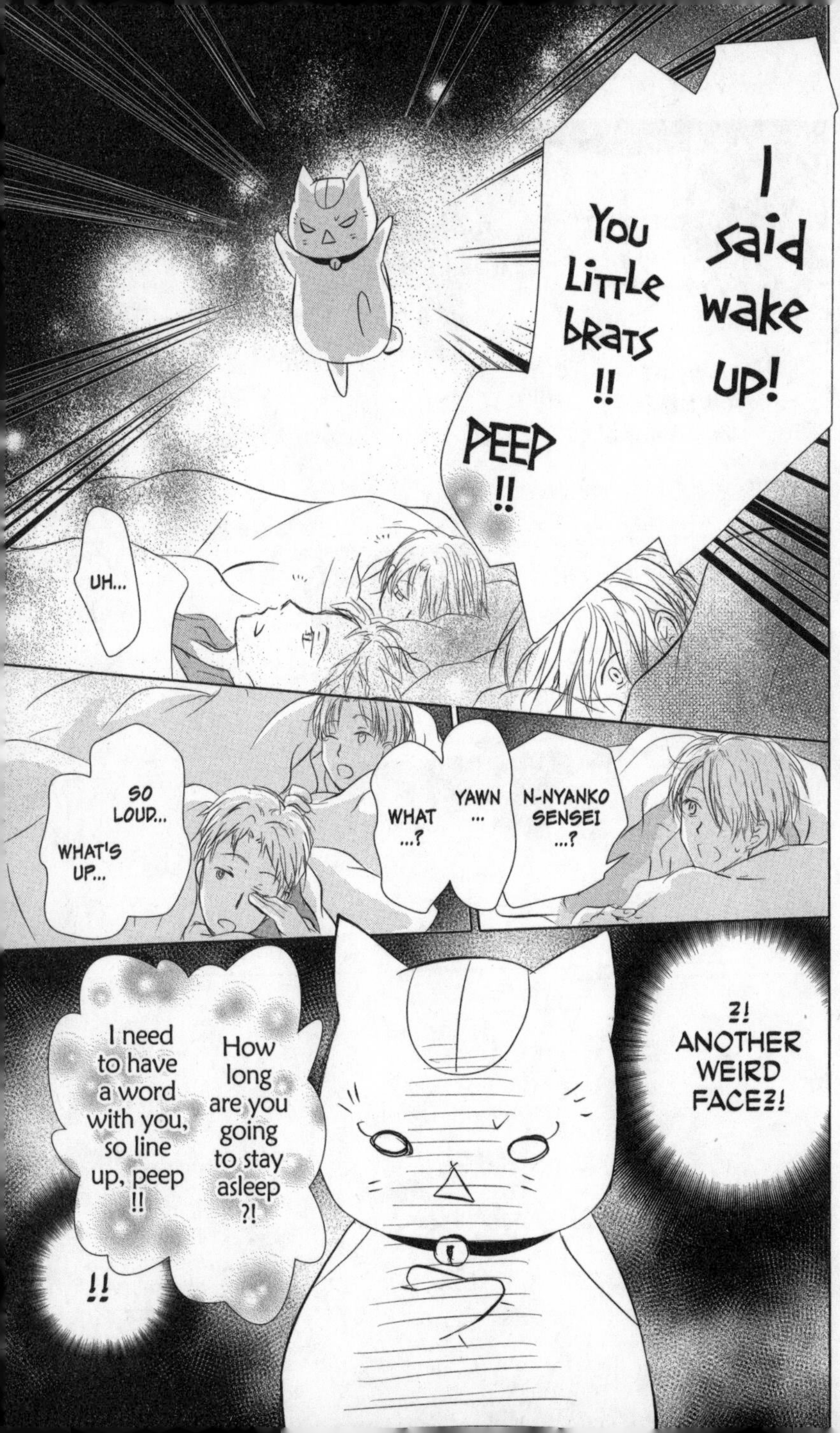
I said wake up!
You little brats !!
PEEP !!
UH...
N-NYANKO SENSEI ...?
YAWN ...
WHAT ...?
SO LOUD...
WHAT'S UP...
?! ANOTHER WEIRD FACE?!
How long are you going to stay asleep ?!
I need to have a word with you, so line up, peep !!
!!

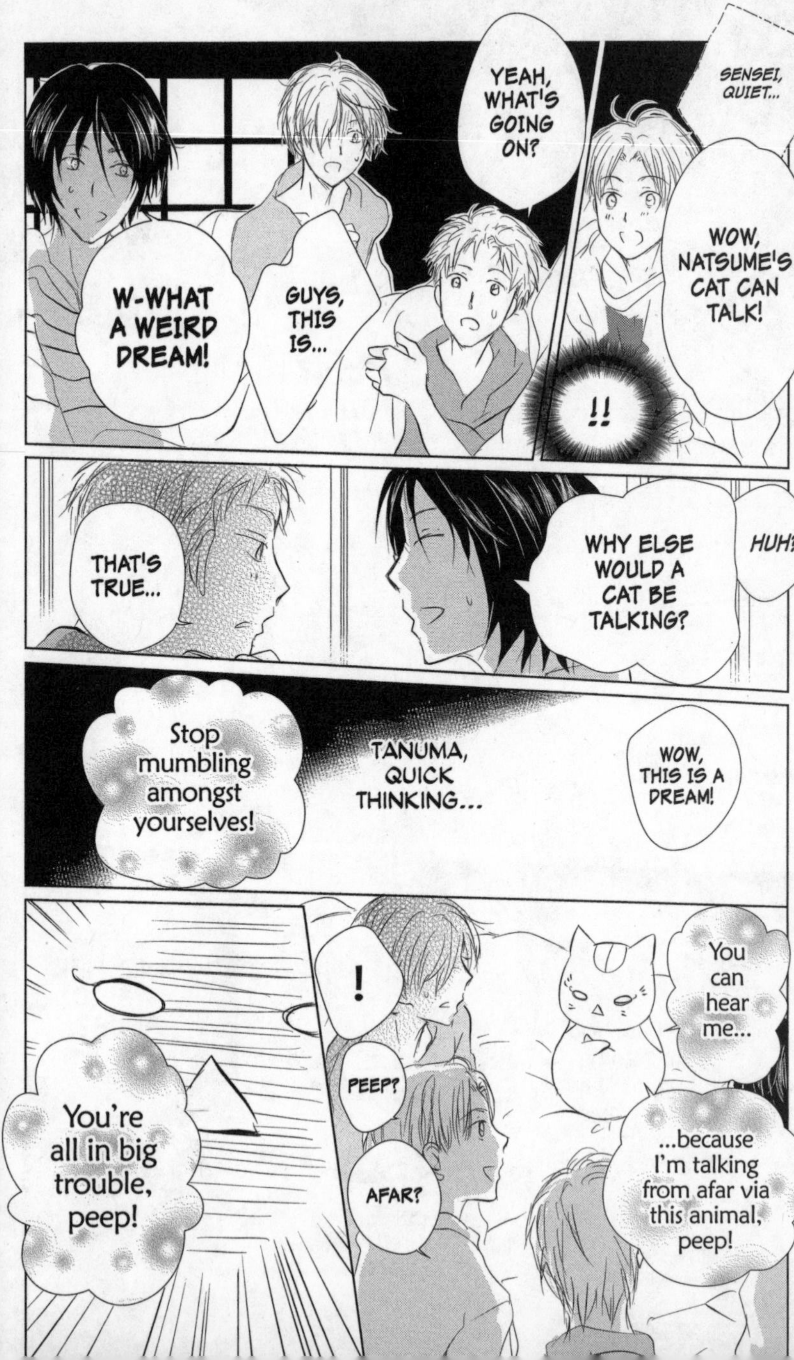
SENSEI, QUIET...
WOW, NATSUME'S CAT CAN TALK!
!!
YEAH, WHAT'S GOING ON?
GUYS, THIS IS...
W-WHAT A WEIRD DREAM!
HUH?
WHY ELSE WOULD A CAT BE TALKING?
THAT'S TRUE...
WOW, THIS IS A DREAM!
TANUMA, QUICK THINKING...
Stop mumbling amongst yourselves!
You can hear me...
...because I'm talking from afar via this animal, peep!
!
PEEP?
AFAR?
You're all in big trouble, peep!

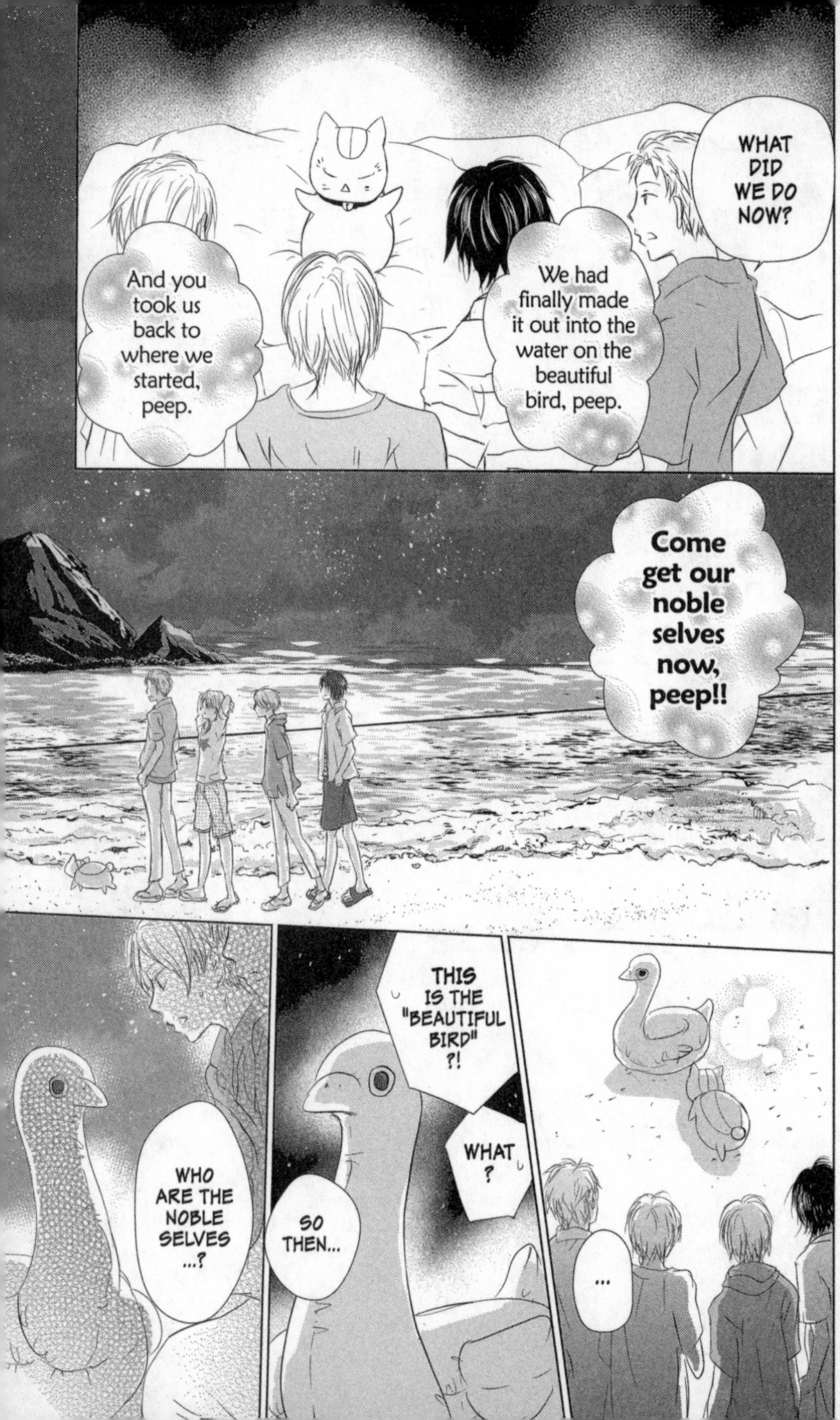
WHAT DID WE DO NOW?
We had finally made it out into the water on the beautiful bird, peep.
And you took us back to where we started, peep.
Come get our noble selves now, peep!!
...
THIS IS THE "BEAUTIFUL BIRD" ?!
WHAT ?
SO THEN...
WHO ARE THE NOBLE SELVES ...?

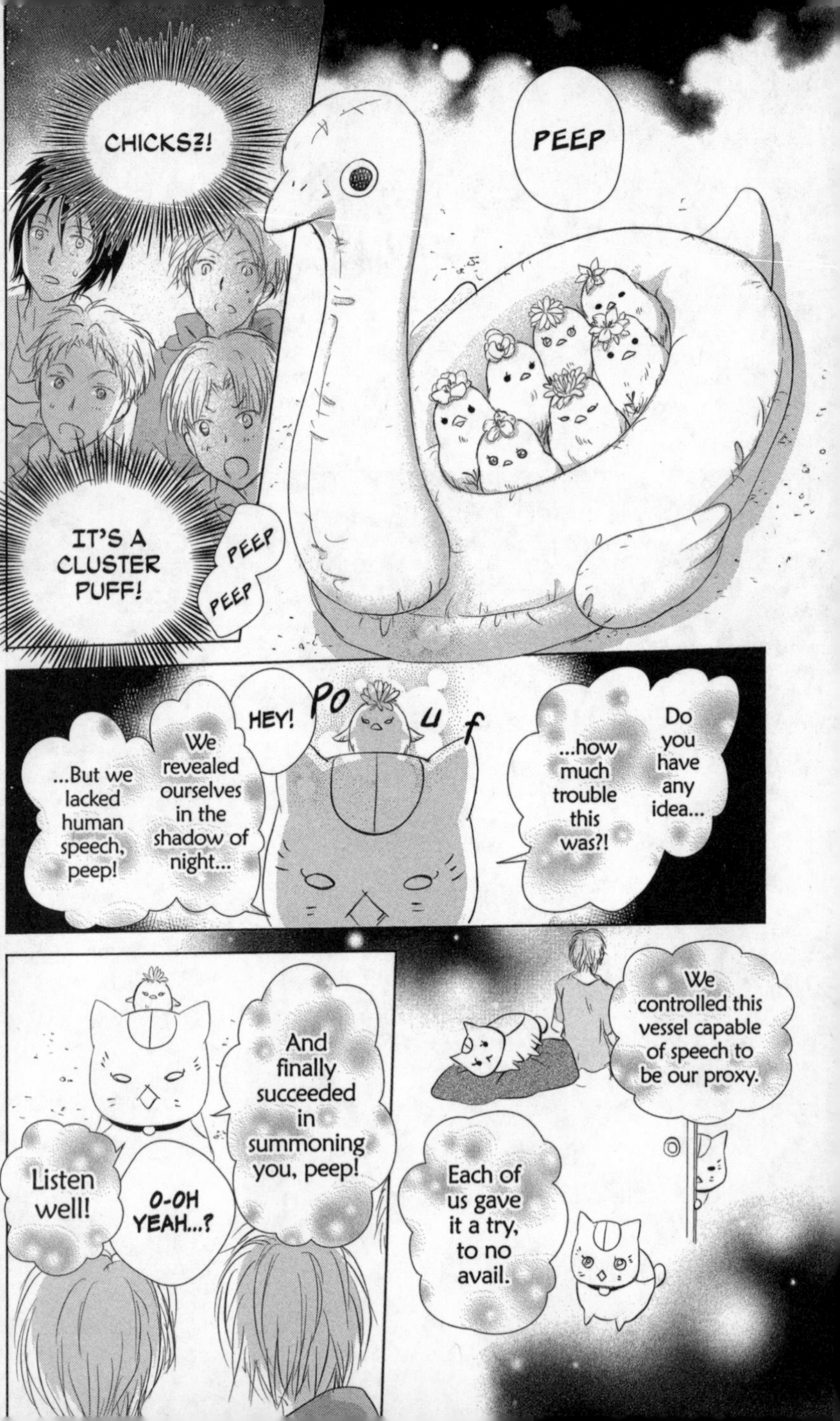
PEEP
PEEP
PEEP
CHICKS?!
IT'S A CLUSTER PUFF!
Do you have any idea...
...how much trouble this was?!
POUF
HEY!
We revealed ourselves in the shadow of night...
...But we lacked human speech, peep!
We controlled this vessel capable of speech to be our proxy.
Each of us gave it a try, to no avail.
And finally succeeded in summoning you, peep!
O-OH YEAH...?
Listen well!

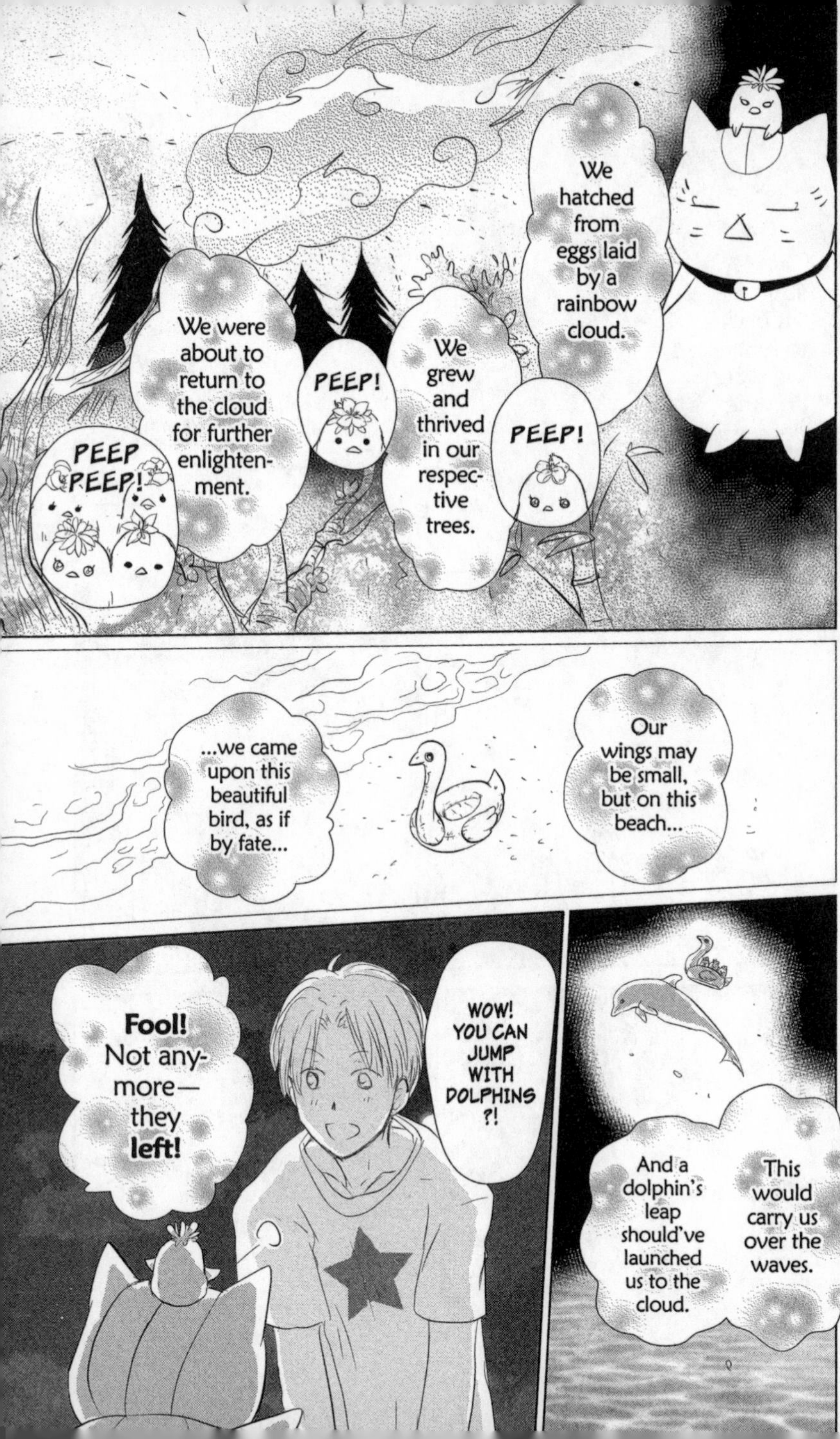
We hatched from eggs laid by a rainbow cloud.
PEEP!
We grew and thrived in our respective trees.
PEEP!
We were about to return to the cloud for further enlightenment.
PEEP PEEP!
Our wings may be small, but on this beach...
...we came upon this beautiful bird, as if by fate...
This would carry us over the waves.
And a dolphin's leap should've launched us to the cloud.
WOW! YOU CAN JUMP WITH DOLPHINS?!
Fool! Not anymore—they left!

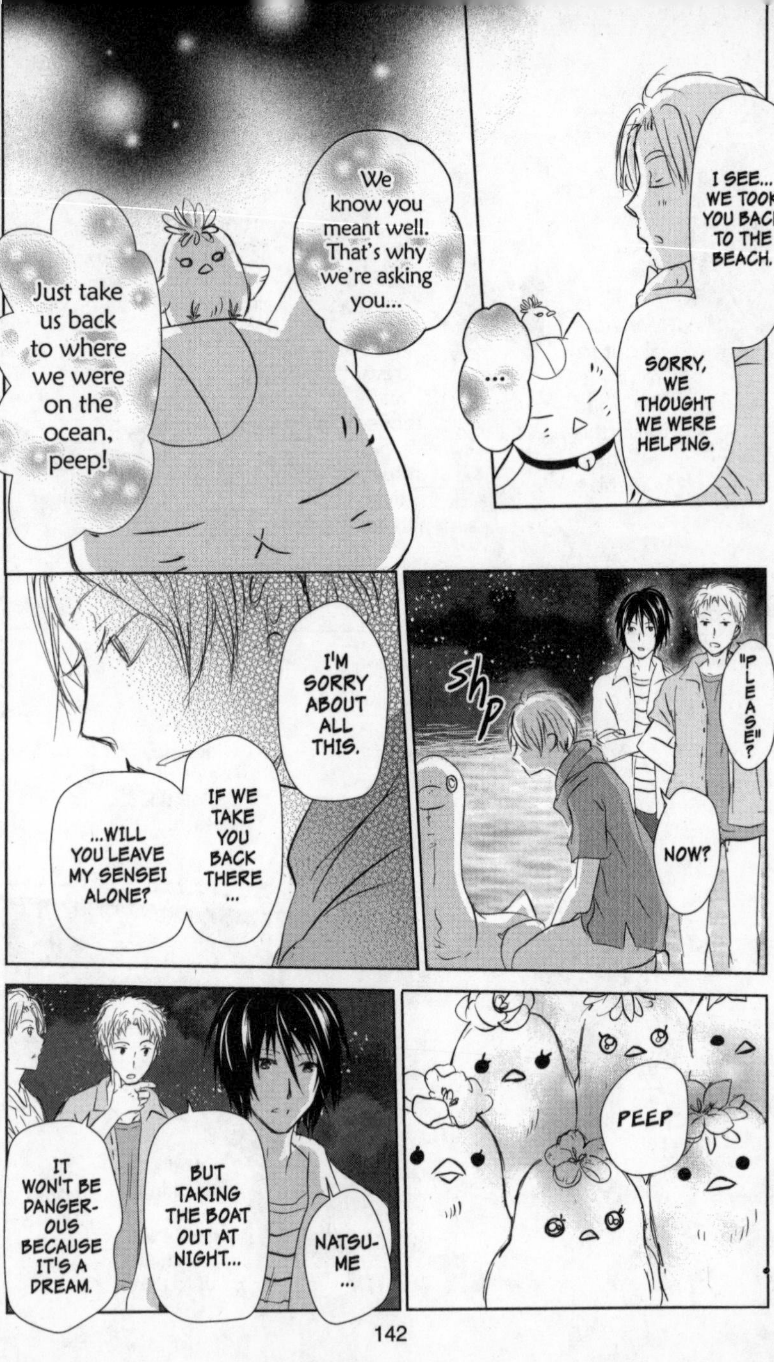
I SEE... WE TOOK YOU BACK TO THE BEACH.
SORRY, WE THOUGHT WE WERE HELPING.
...
We know you meant well. That's why we're asking you...
Just take us back to where we were on the ocean, peep!
"PLEASE"?
NOW?
SHP
I'M SORRY ABOUT ALL THIS.
IF WE TAKE YOU BACK THERE...
...WILL YOU LEAVE MY SENSEI ALONE?
PEEP
NATSUME...
BUT TAKING THE BOAT OUT AT NIGHT...
IT WON'T BE DANGEROUS BECAUSE IT'S A DREAM.

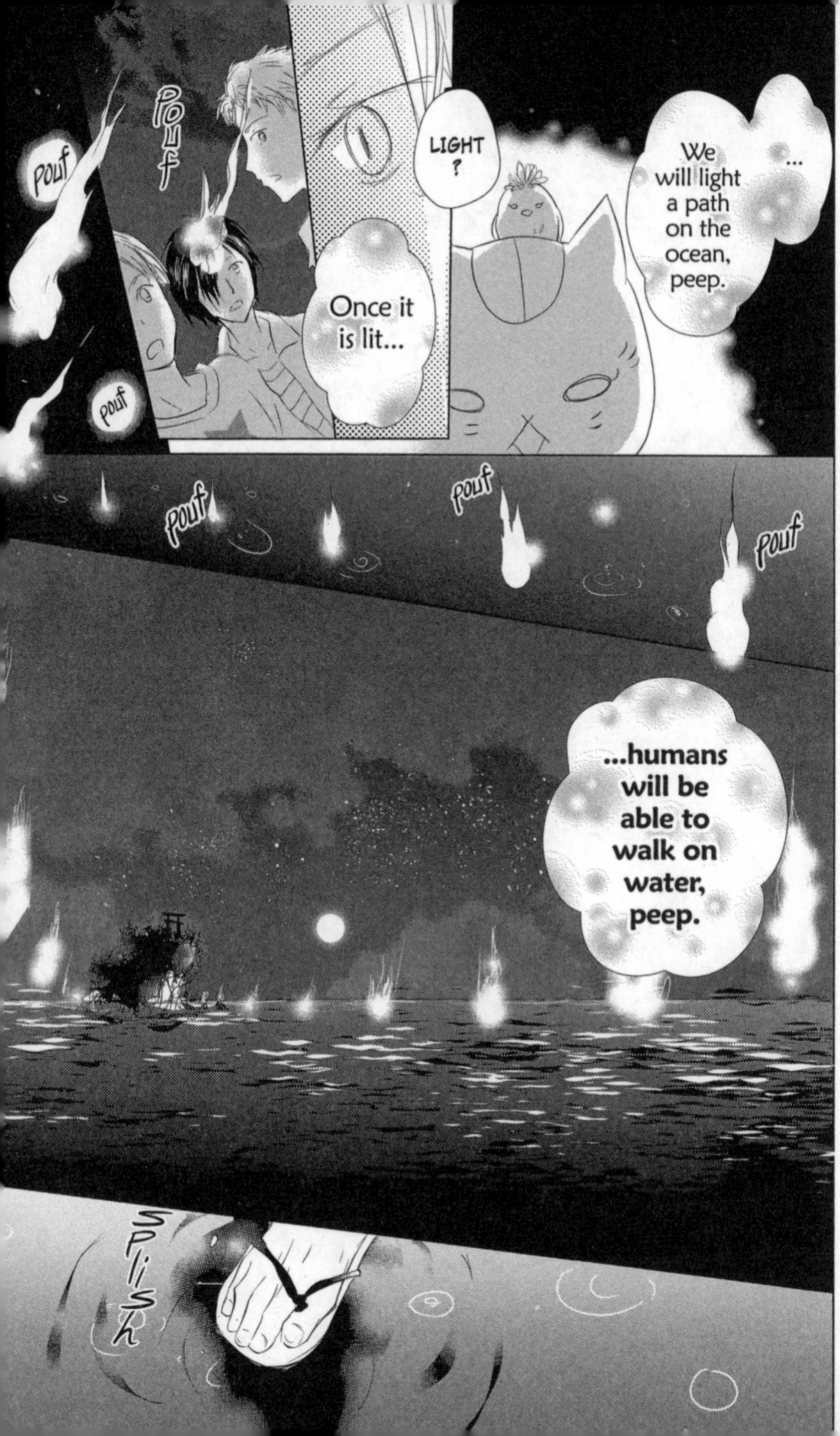
...
We will light a path on the ocean, peep.
LIGHT?
Once it is lit...
POUF
pouf
pouf
Pouf
pouf
pouf
...humans will be able to walk on water, peep.
SPLISH

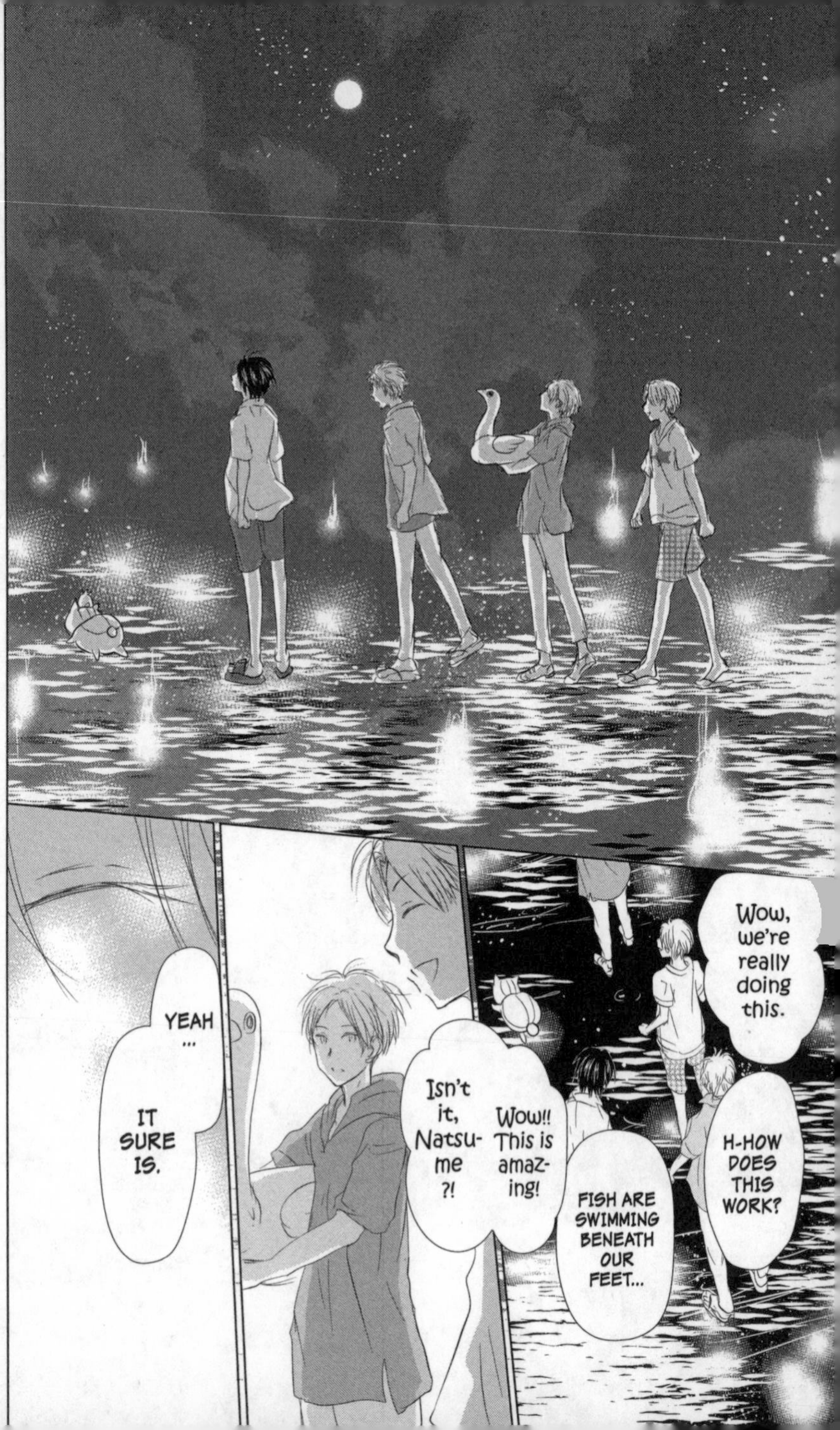
Wow, we're really doing this.
H-HOW DOES THIS WORK?
FISH ARE SWIMMING BENEATH OUR FEET...
Wow!! This is amazing!
Isn't it, Natsume?!
YEAH...
IT SURE IS.

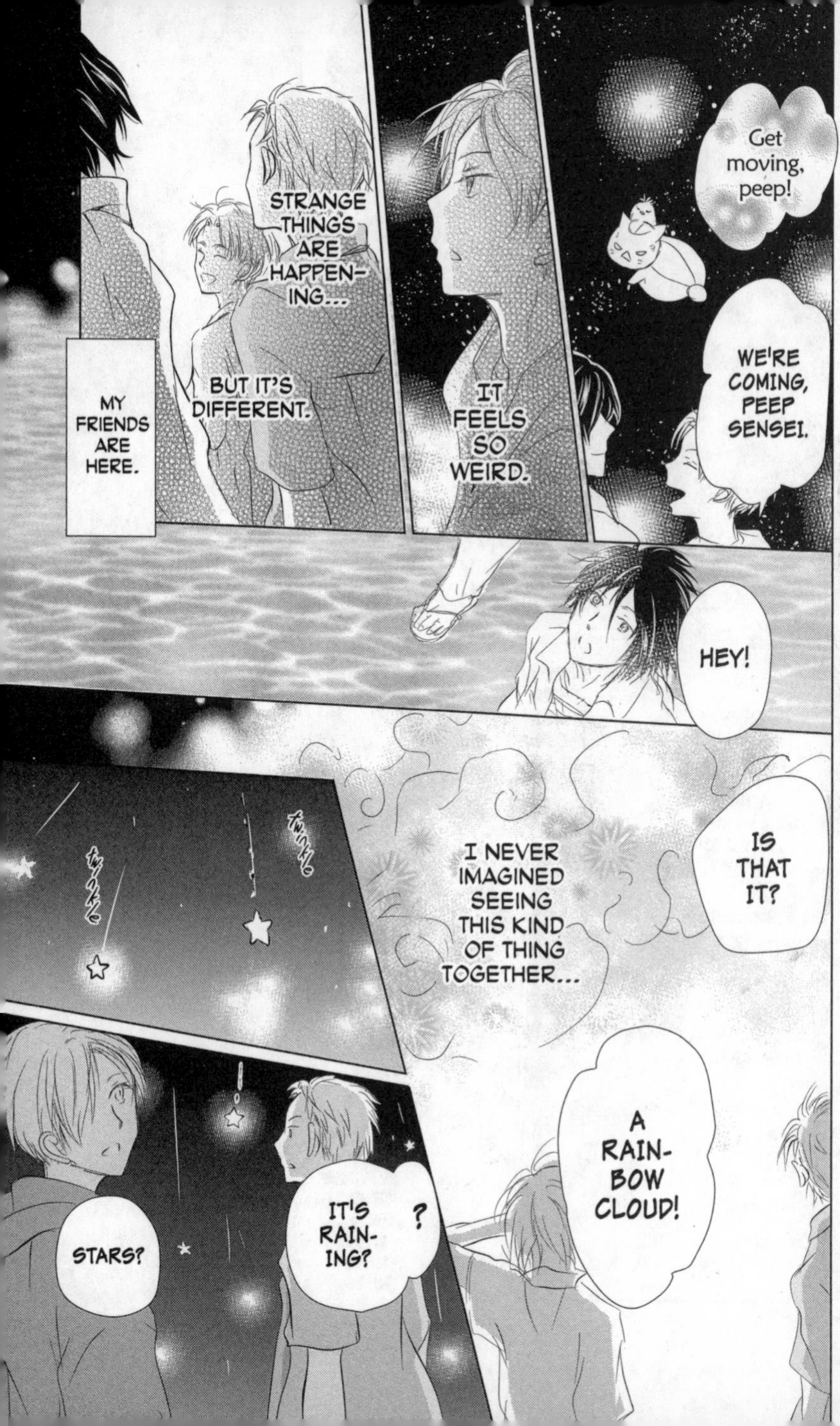
Get moving, peep!
WE'RE COMING, PEEP SENSEI.
IT FEELS SO WEIRD.
STRANGE THINGS ARE HAPPENING...
BUT IT'S DIFFERENT.
MY FRIENDS ARE HERE.
HEY!
IS THAT IT?
I NEVER IMAGINED SEEING THIS KIND OF THING TOGETHER...
twinkle
twinkle
A RAINBOW CLOUD!
?
IT'S RAINING?
STARS?

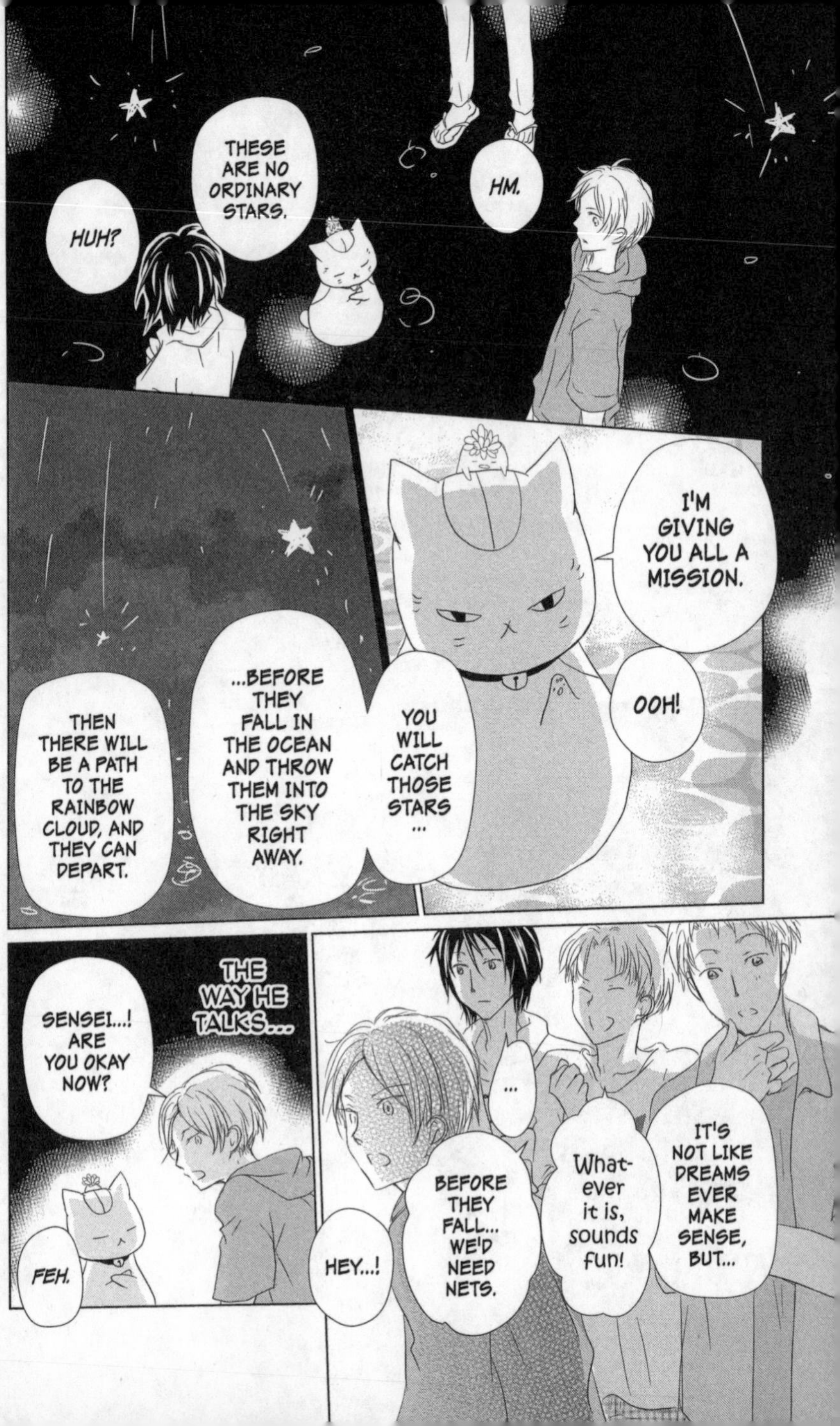
HM.
THESE ARE NO ORDINARY STARS.
HUH?
I'M GIVING YOU ALL A MISSION.
OOH!
YOU WILL CATCH THOSE STARS...
...BEFORE THEY FALL IN THE OCEAN AND THROW THEM INTO THE SKY RIGHT AWAY.
THEN THERE WILL BE A PATH TO THE RAINBOW CLOUD, AND THEY CAN DEPART.
IT'S NOT LIKE DREAMS EVER MAKE SENSE, BUT...
What-ever it is, sounds fun!
...
BEFORE THEY FALL... WE'D NEED NETS.
HEY...!
THE WAY HE TALKS...
SENSEI...! ARE YOU OKAY NOW?
FEH.

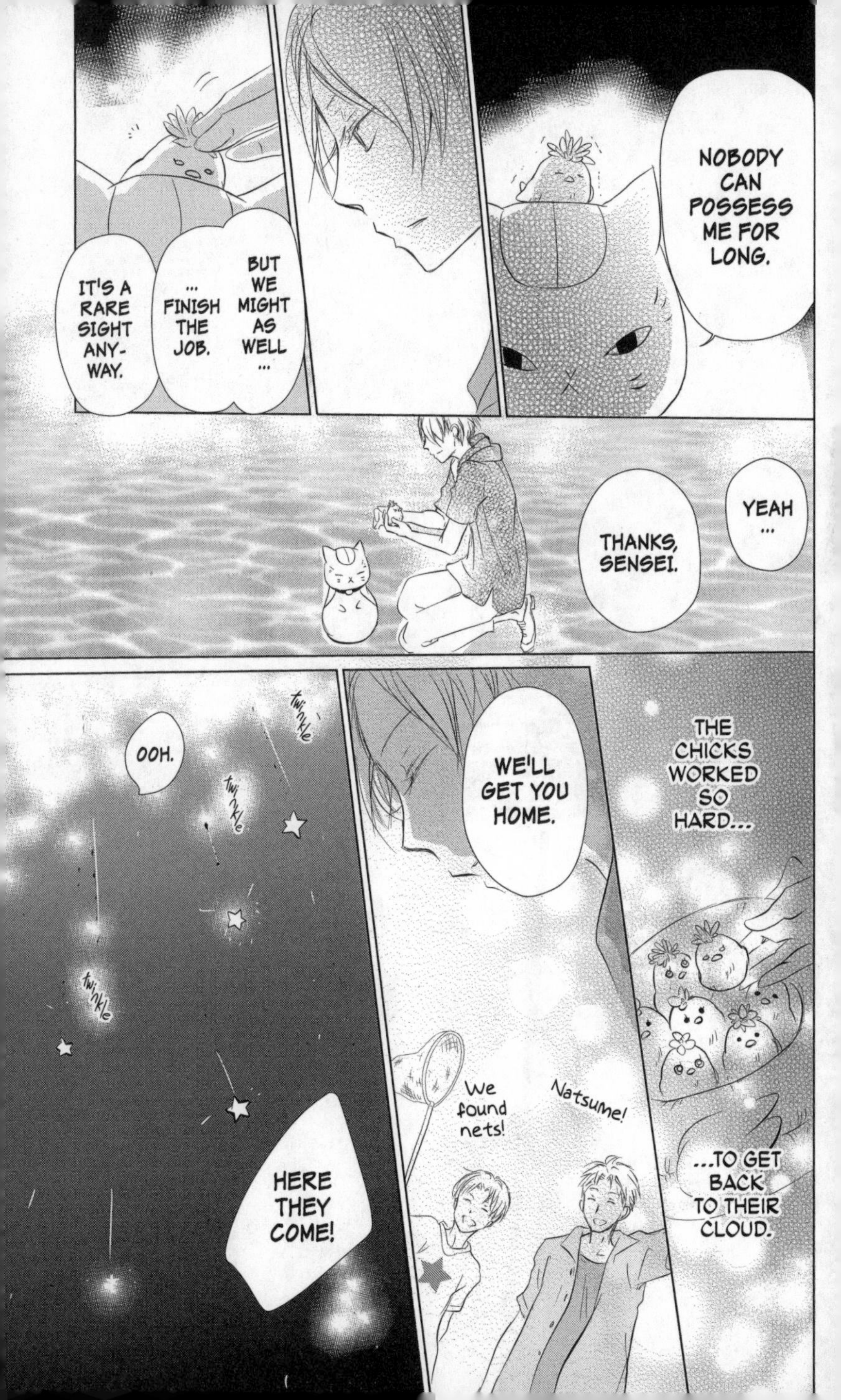
NOBODY CAN POSSESS ME FOR LONG.
BUT WE MIGHT AS WELL ...
... FINISH THE JOB.
IT'S A RARE SIGHT ANY-WAY.
YEAH ...
THANKS, SENSEI.
THE CHICKS WORKED SO HARD...
WE'LL GET YOU HOME.
...TO GET BACK TO THEIR CLOUD.
Natsume!
We found nets!
twinkle
OOH.
twinkle
twinkle
HERE THEY COME!

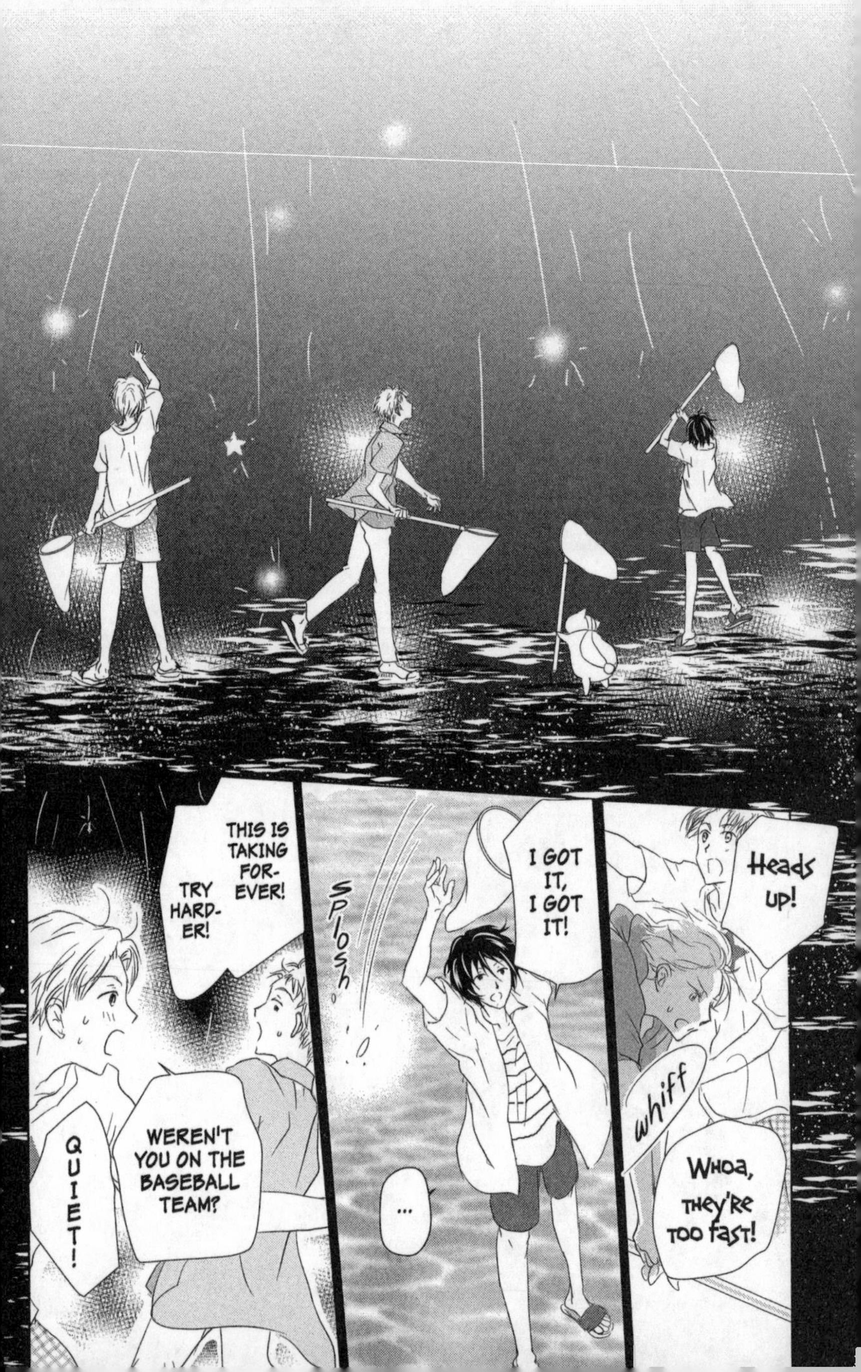
Heads up!
whiff
Whoa, they're too fast!
I GOT IT, I GOT IT!
SPLOSH
...
THIS IS TAKING FOR-EVER!
TRY HARD-ER!
WEREN'T YOU ON THE BASEBALL TEAM?
QUIET!

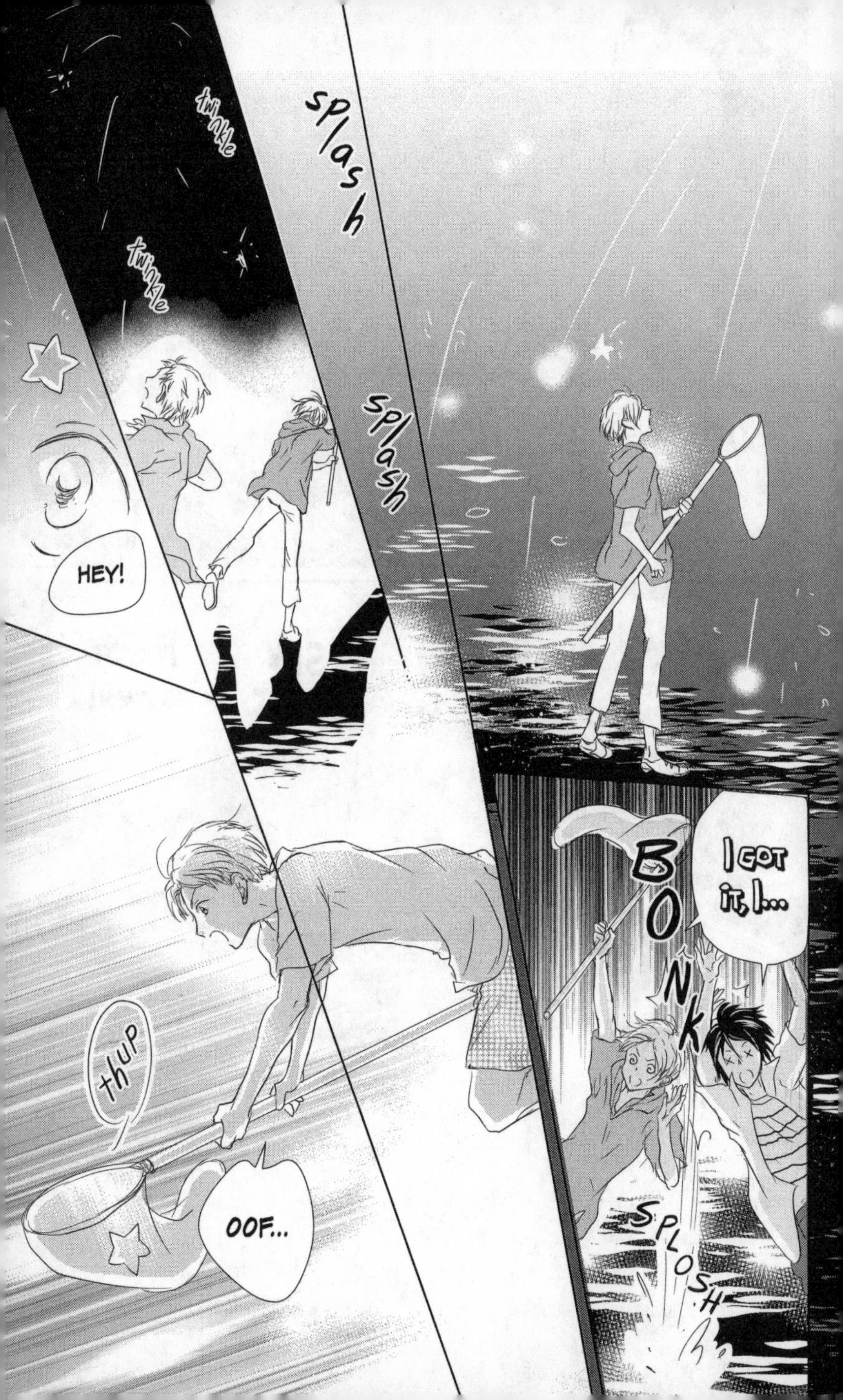
splash
splash
twinkle
twinkle
HEY!
I GOT IT, I...
BONK
SPLOSH
thup
OOF...

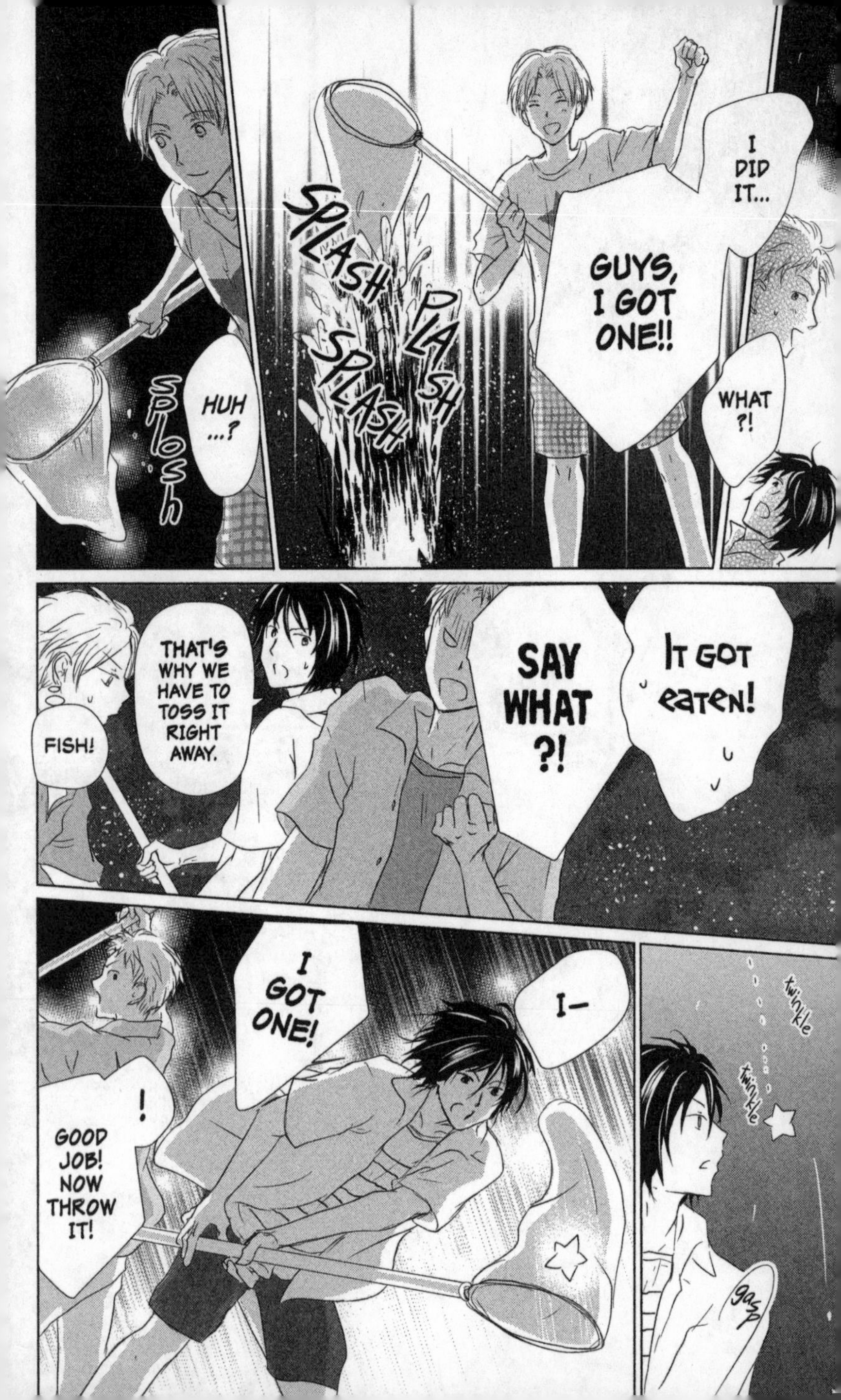
I DID IT...
WHAT ?!
GUYS, I GOT ONE!!
SPLASH PLASH SPLASH
HUH ...?
splosh
IT GOT eaten!
SAY WHAT ?!
THAT'S WHY WE HAVE TO TOSS IT RIGHT AWAY.
FISH!
twinkle
twinkle
gasp
I-
I GOT ONE!
!
GOOD JOB! NOW THROW IT!

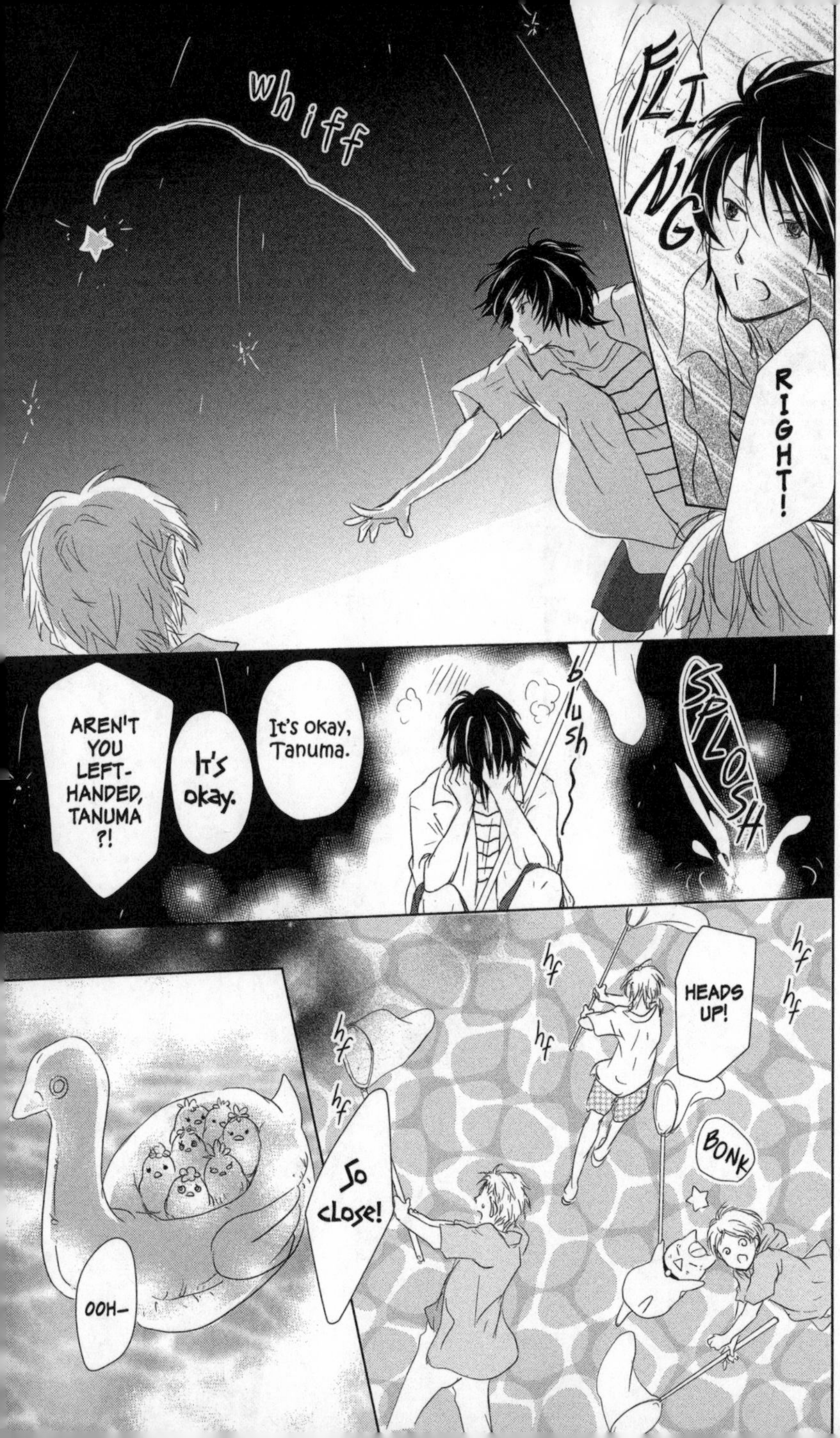
FLING
RIGHT!
whiff
SPLOSH
blush
It's okay, Tanuma.
It's okay.
AREN'T YOU LEFT-HANDED, TANUMA?!
hf hf
HEADS UP!
hf
BONK
hf hf
So close!
OOH—

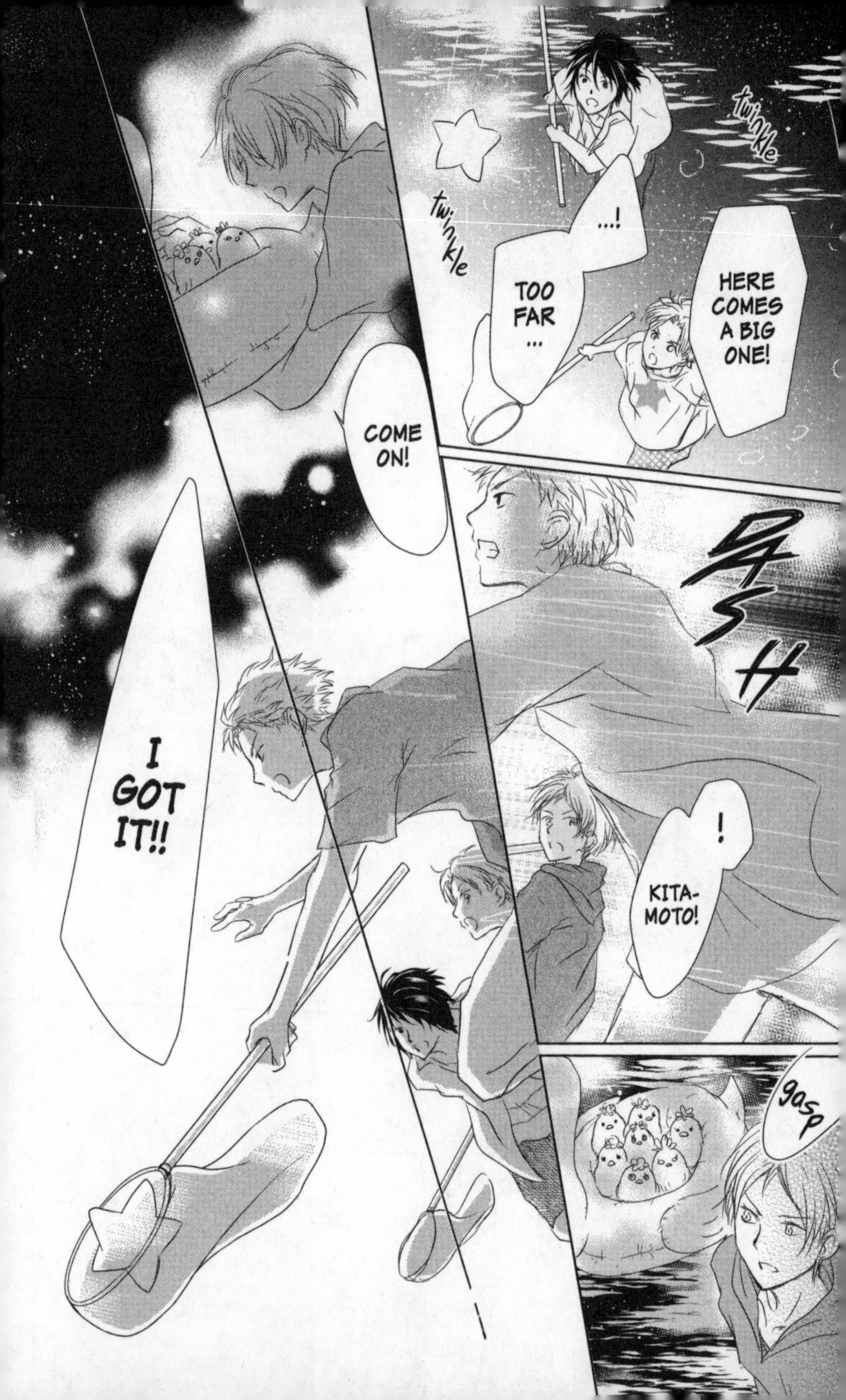
twinkle
HERE COMES A BIG ONE!
...!
TOO FAR ...
twinkle
DASH
!
KITA-MOTO!
gasp
COME ON!
I GOT IT!!

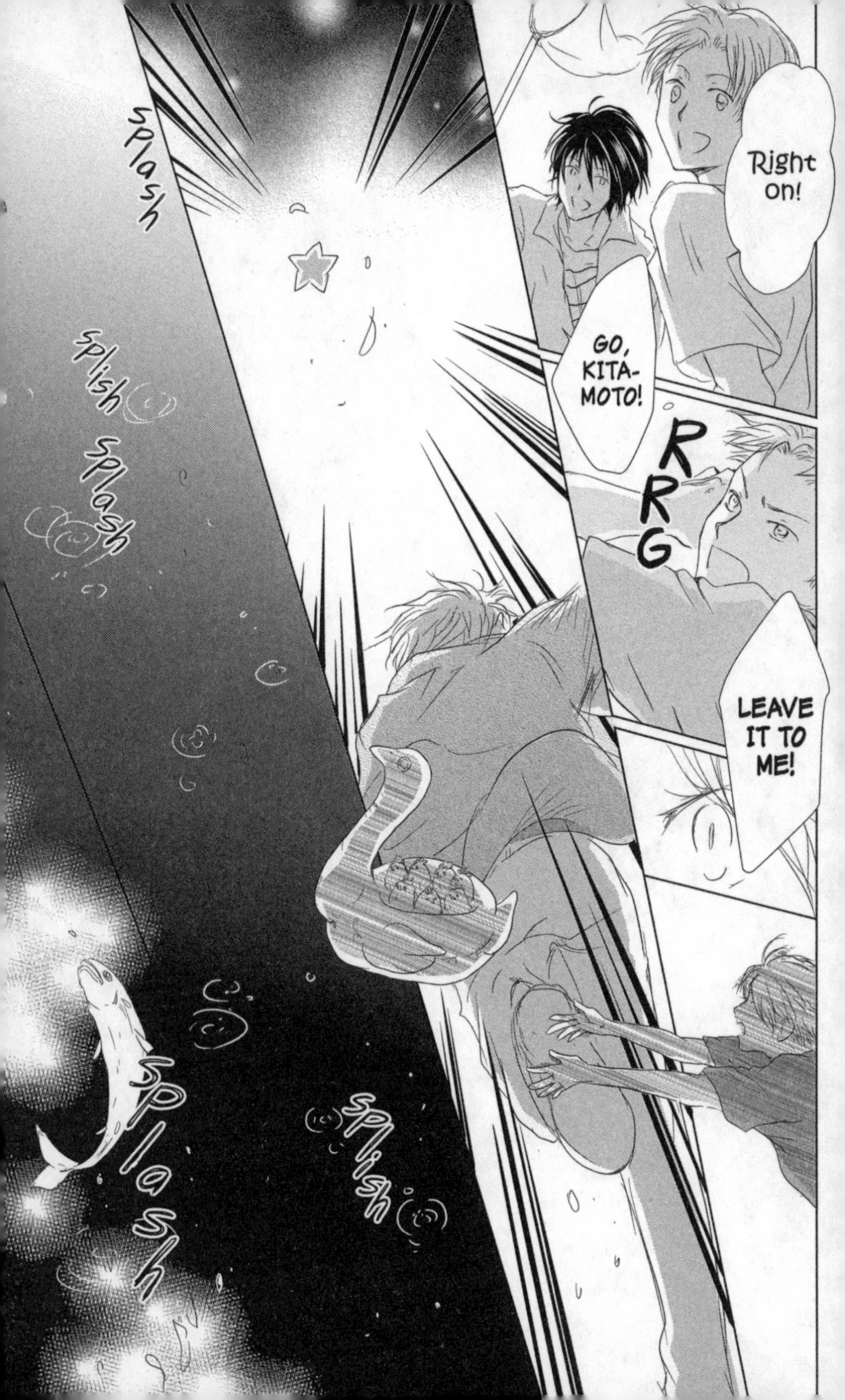
Right on!
GO, KITA-MOTO!
RRG
LEAVE IT TO ME!
splash
splish splash
splish
splash

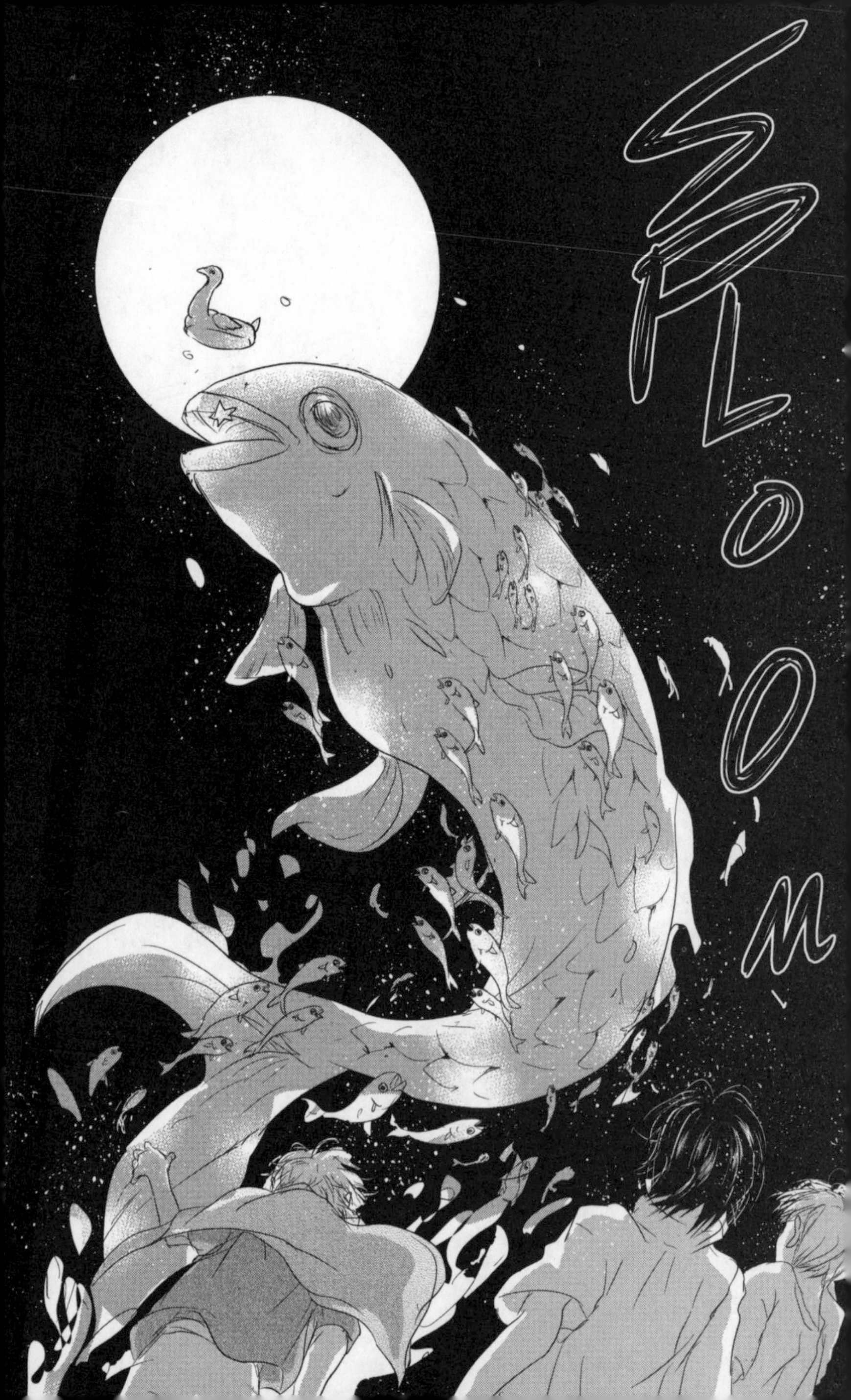
SPLOOOM

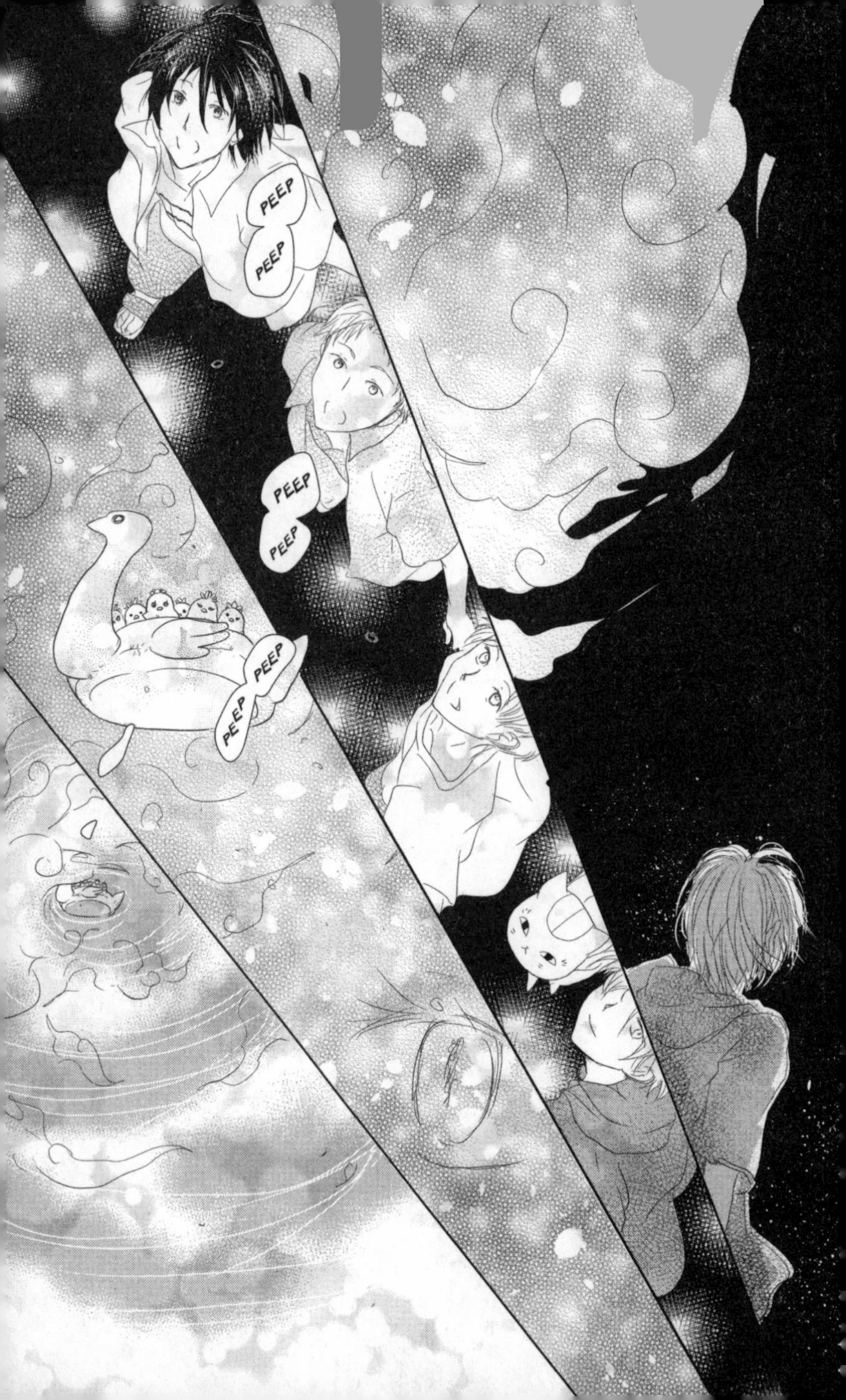
PEEP
PEEP
PEEP
PEEP
PEEP
PEEP

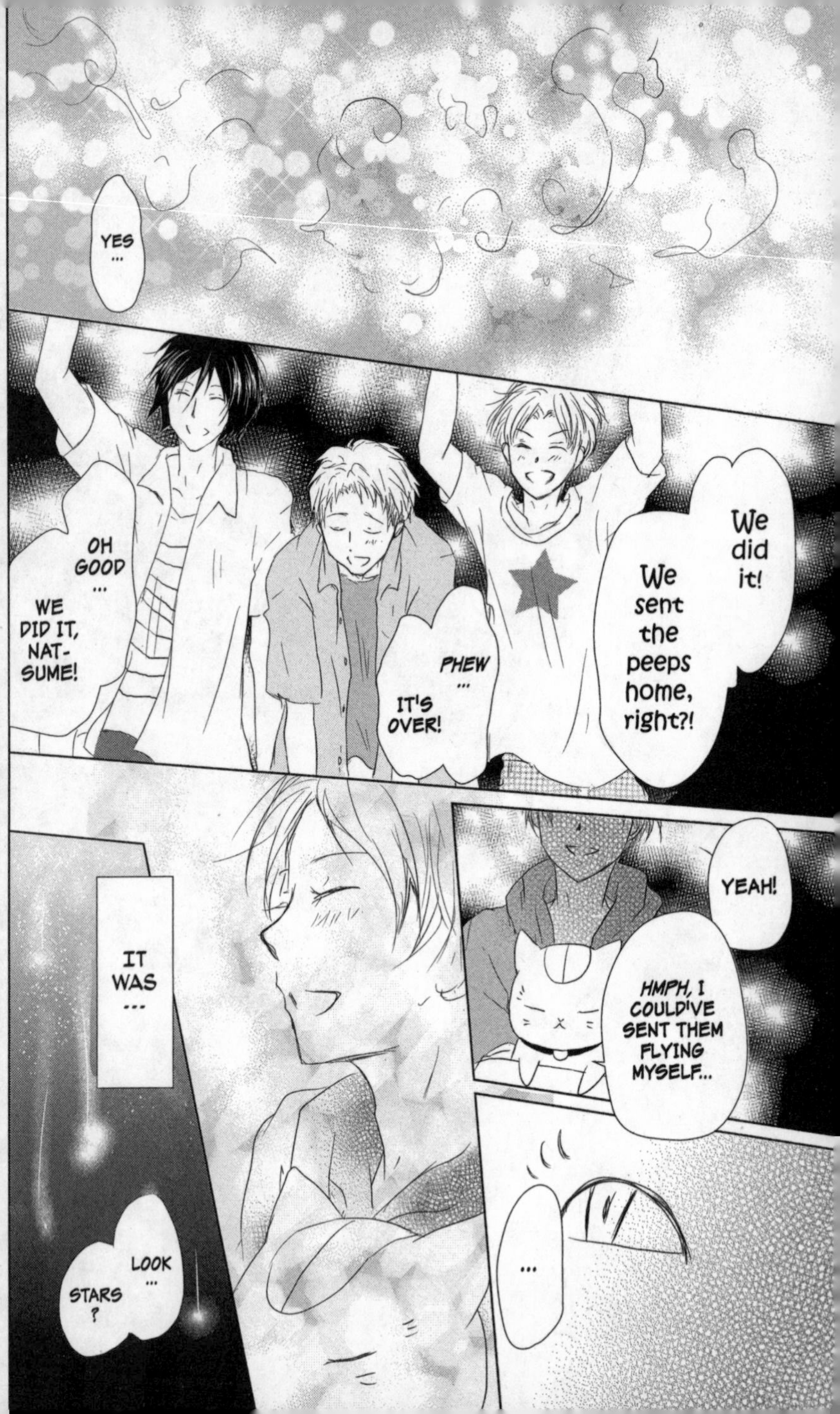
YES ...
We did it!
We sent the peeps home, right?!
PHEW ...
IT'S OVER!
OH GOOD ...
WE DID IT, NAT-SUME!
YEAH!
HMPH, I COULD'VE SENT THEM FLYING MYSELF...
...
IT WAS ...
LOOK ...
STARS?

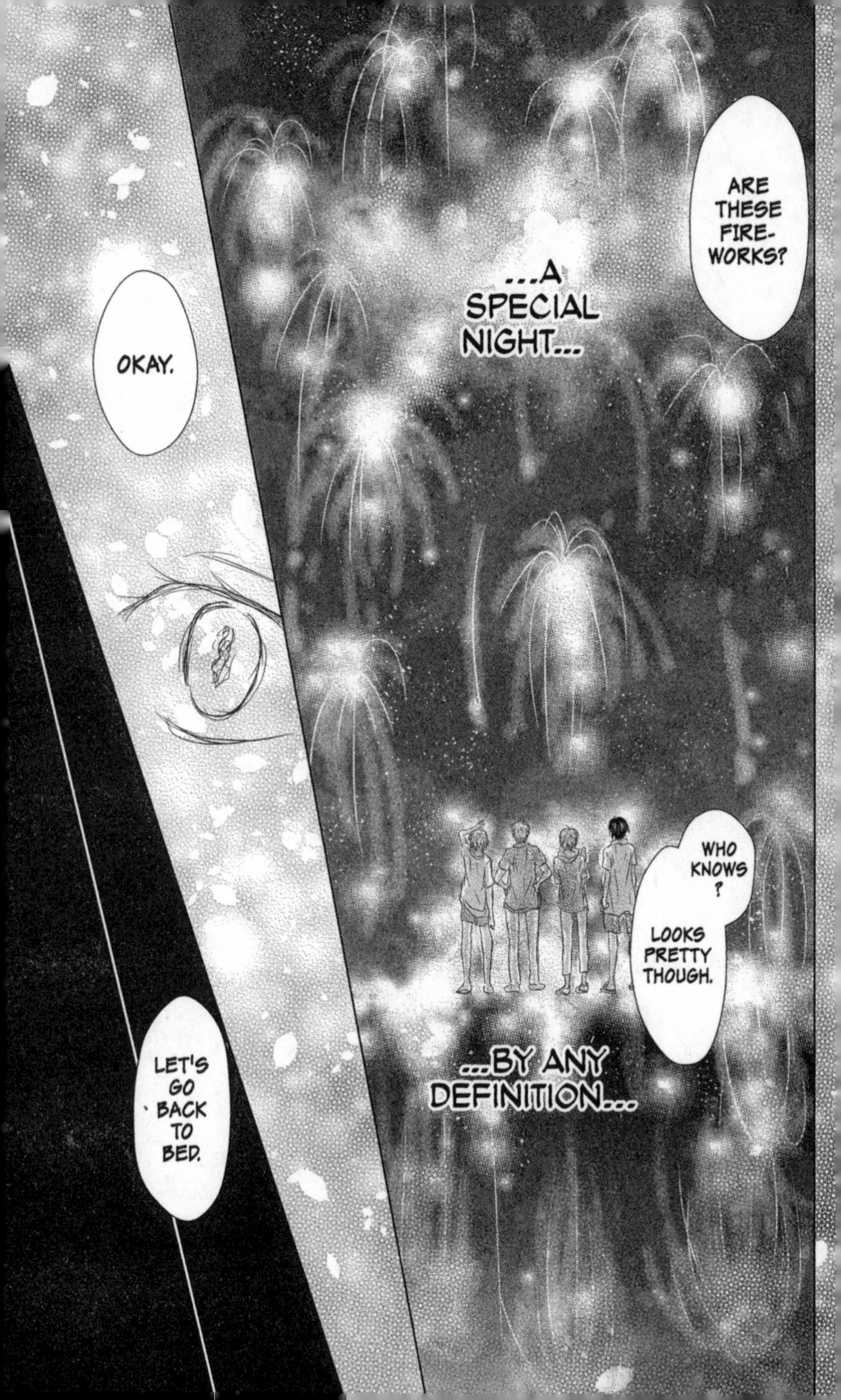
ARE THESE FIRE-WORKS?
...A SPECIAL NIGHT...
WHO KNOWS?
LOOKS PRETTY THOUGH.
...BY ANY DEFINITION...
OKAY.
LET'S GO BACK TO BED.

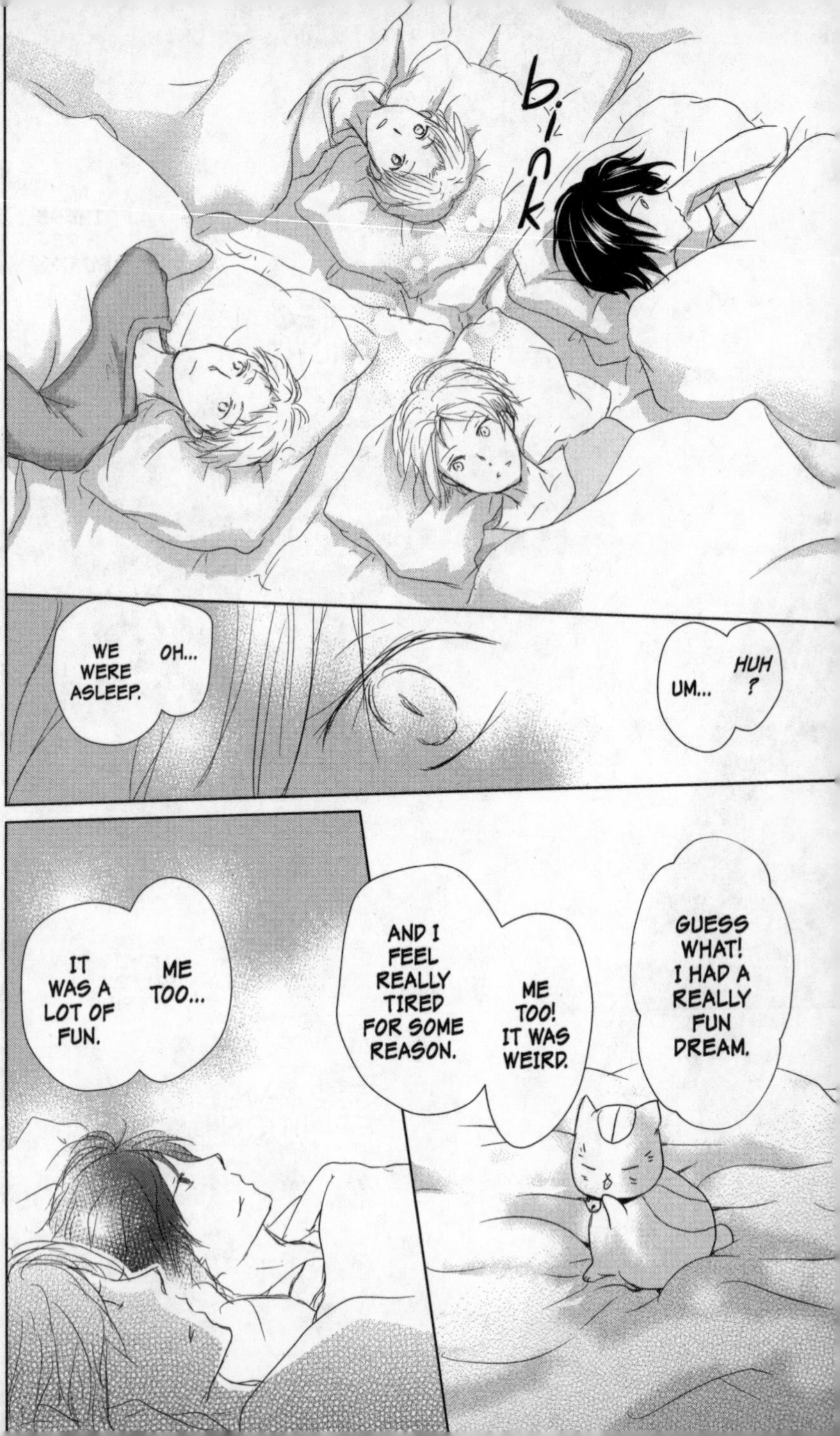
bink
HUH? UM...
OH... WE WERE ASLEEP.
GUESS WHAT! I HAD A REALLY FUN DREAM.
ME TOO! IT WAS WEIRD. AND I FEEL REALLY TIRED FOR SOME REASON.
ME TOO... IT WAS A LOT OF FUN.

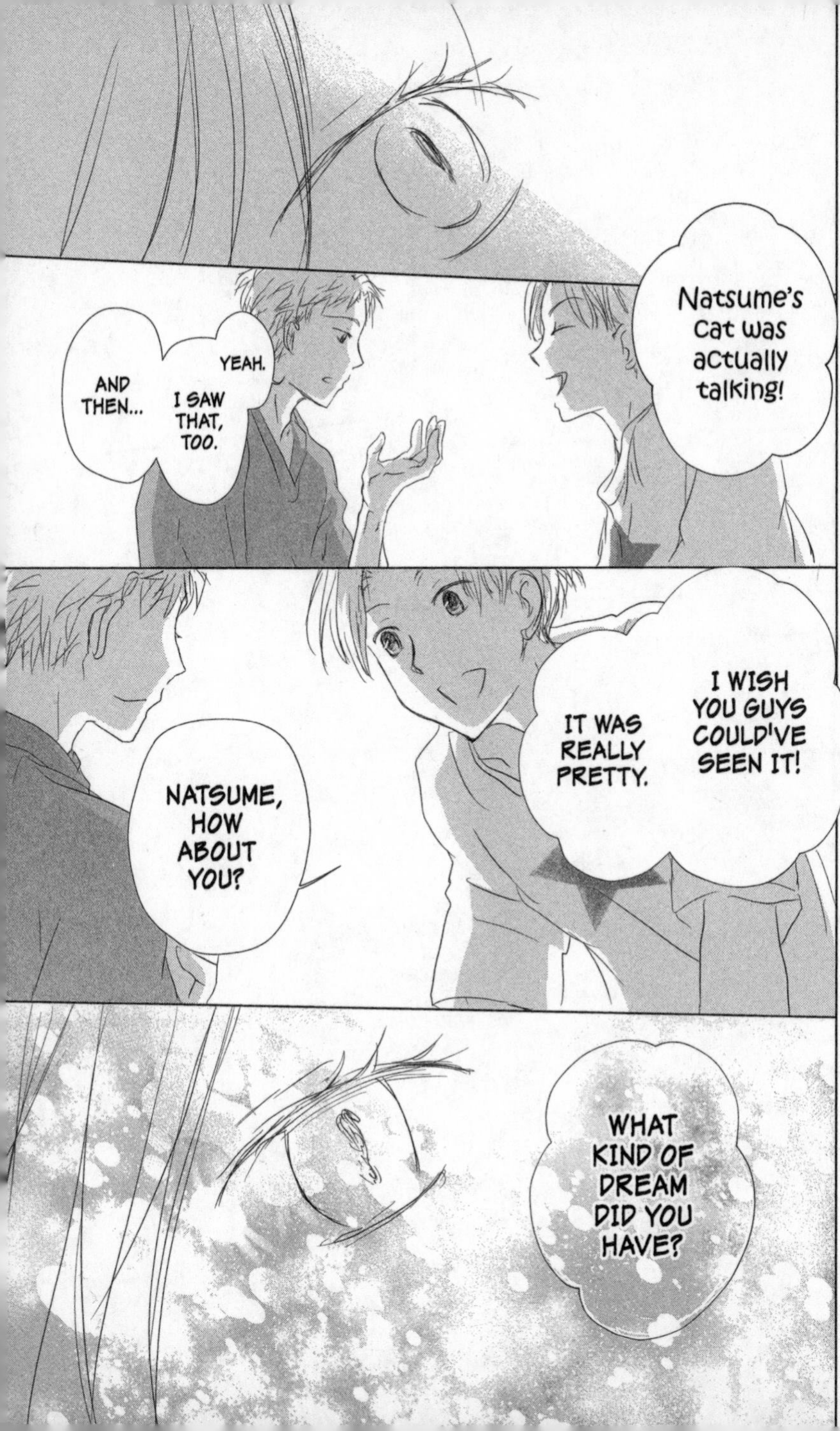
Natsume's cat was actually talking!
YEAH.
I SAW THAT, TOO.
AND THEN...
I WISH YOU GUYS COULD'VE SEEN IT!
IT WAS REALLY PRETTY.
NATSUME, HOW ABOUT YOU?
WHAT KIND OF DREAM DID YOU HAVE?

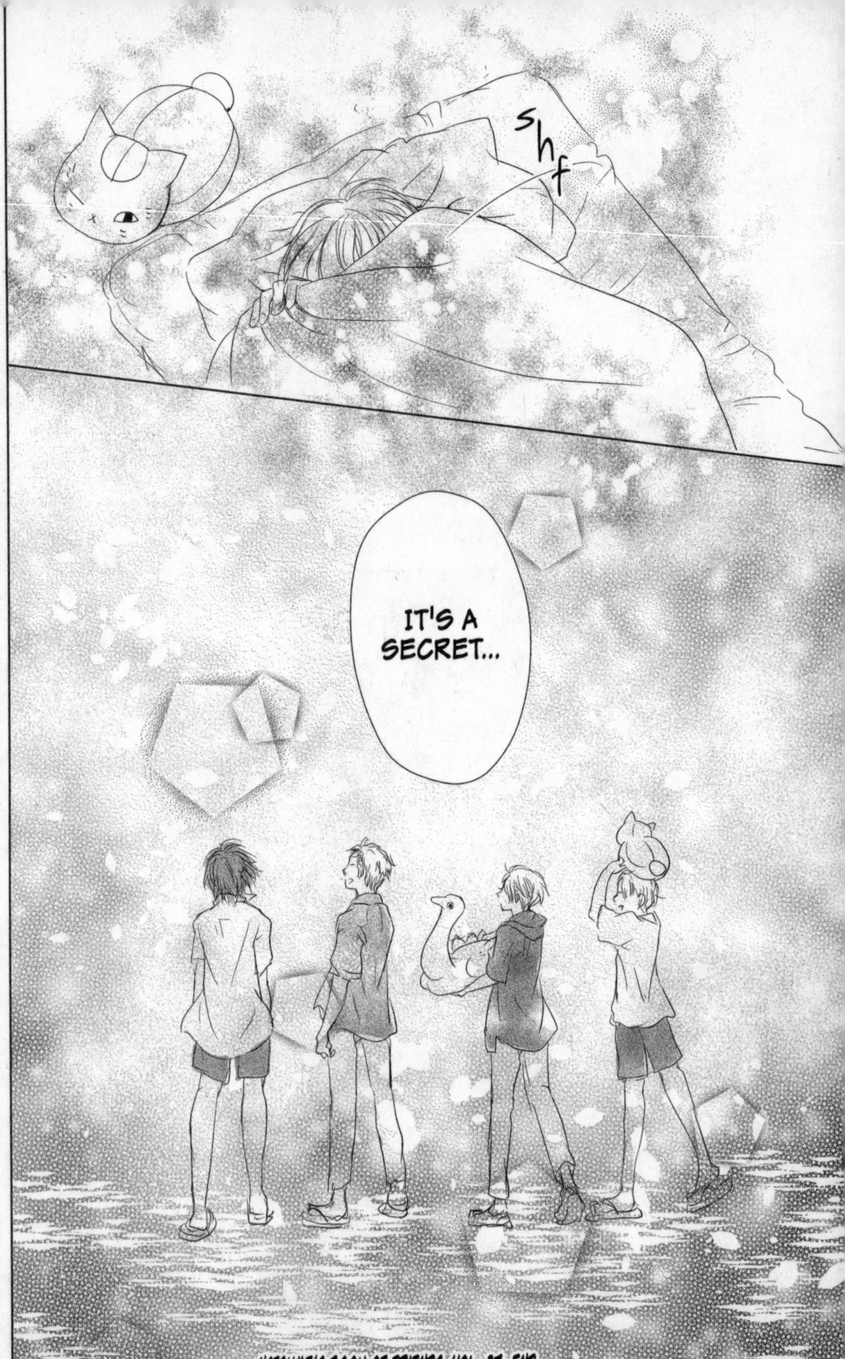
shf
IT'S A SECRET...

NATSUME'S BOOK OF FRIENDS, VOL. 27: END

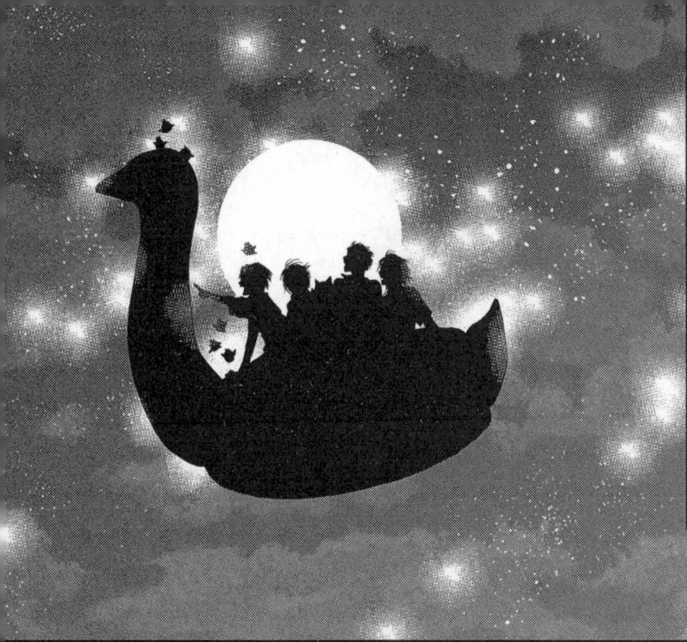

AFTER-WORD

Thank you for reading. To avoid spoilers, please read the rest of this afterword only after reading the entire volume.

Hi, Midorikawa here. This is the 27th volume of *Natsume*. I'm full of the joy of being allowed to continue for so long, and of the anxiety that I could easily topple all that I've built with a single misplaced word.

CHAPTER 108 Chobi's Precious Thing

A while ago, I was able to meet Ms. Sato, a producer at Shuka Inc. (the anime studio), and I asked her if there's any topic she'd like to read about. She was very fond of Chobi, which made me happy, and then I remembered that I had never even revealed his true form. In the episode where he first appeared, he was supposed to celebrate Taki's curse getting lifted by transforming and flying up in the air. Taki and Natsume would look up, but of course only Natsume would be able to see him. I couldn't make it fit no matter how hard I tried, and I hadn't been able to bring it up since. Then again, what was a throwaway scene back then turned into a whole story because of the relationships the characters have built over time. The purpose of his mustache was for him to transform. Like Nyanko Sensei, Chobi feels that it's easier to move about as the compact version of himself.

CHAPTER 109-110 The Name's Owner Cometh

I wanted to do a story of Nyanko Sensei catching a grave robber. Robbing a grave sounds unacceptable, but what about a yokai grave? I tried to go with a different flow than usual, so I hope it read with a different rhythm, at least for the first half. I want to do a scary story sometimes, the subject matter being what it is, but the perception of "scary" is a delicate matter. I try to balance it with the fun. I'd always wanted to tackle this topic with the *Book of Friends*.

CHAPTER 111 A Rainbow Night's Dream

It was the month where I had drawn a picture of Natsume by the ocean for the cover of the magazine, so I decided to sync the story to that image. Since I grew up in the mountains, I couldn't think of what would happen at the beach, so my editor, who did grow up by the ocean, told me some anecdotes. When she told me that things often drift in with the current, I imagined an inflatable duckie carrying some small critters. I also always wanted to draw the act of walking on water, so I feel I was able to stuff enough summery elements. And I think I was able to go right up to the edge of the fantasy element possible in Natsume's world.

It was fun drawing stories that aren't possible in real life and could only happen because of their occult-adjacent circumstances. My goal is to depict the catharsis of being able to find a common bond while living with totally different standards.

I'll keep working hard so you can pick up the next volume. Please continue with your support. Thank you so much.

Thanks to:

Lulu Eijo
Sachi Fujita
Mr. Kakiuchi
Nanao
Mr. Nakamura
Mr. Nomura
Hoen Kikaku Ltd.

Thank you.

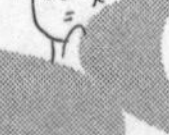

Yuki Midorikawa

is the creator of *Natsume's Book of Friends*, which was nominated for the Manga Taisho (Cartoon Grand Prize). Her other titles published in Japan include *Hotarubi no Mori e* (Into the Forest of Fireflies), *Hiiro no Isu* (The Scarlet Chair), and *Akaku Saku Koe* (The Voice That Blooms Red).

NATSUME'S BOOK OF FRIENDS

Vol. 27
Shojo Beat Edition

STORY AND ART BY *Yuki Midorikawa*

Translation & Adaptation *Lillian Olsen*
Touch-Up Art & Lettering *Sabrina Heep*
Design *Jimmy Presler*
Editor *Pancha Diaz*

Natsume Yujincho by Yuki Midorikawa
© Yuki Midorikawa 2021
All rights reserved.
First published in Japan in 2021 by HAKUSENSHA, Inc., Tokyo.
English language translation rights arranged with HAKUSENSHA, Inc., Tokyo.

The stories, characters, and incidents mentioned in this publication are entirely fictional.

Printed in the U.S.A.

Published by VIZ Media, LLC
P.O. Box 77010
San Francisco, CA 94107

10 9 8 7 6 5 4 3 2 1
First printing, November 2022

Behind the Scenes!!

STORY AND ART BY **BISCO HATORI**

From the creator of
*Ouran High School
Host Club*

Ranmaru Kurisu comes from a family of hardy, rough-and-tumble fisherfolk and he sticks out at home like a delicate, artistic sore thumb. It's given him a raging inferiority complex and a permanently pessimistic outlook. Now that he's in college, he's hoping to find a sense of belonging. But after a whole life of being left out, does he even know how to fit in?!

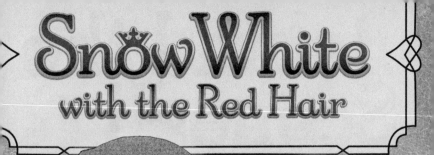

Snow White with the Red Hair

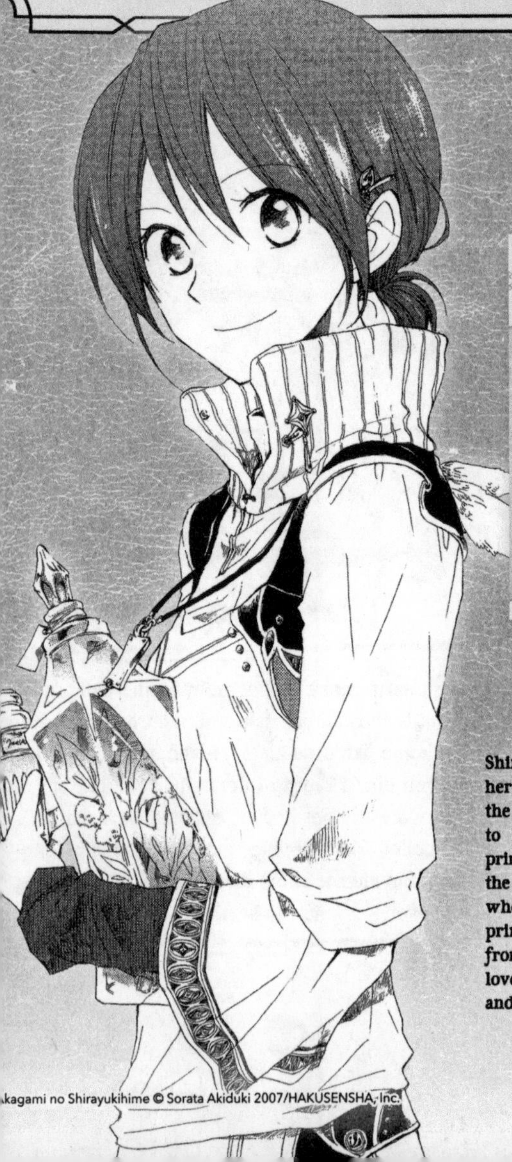

Inspired the anime!

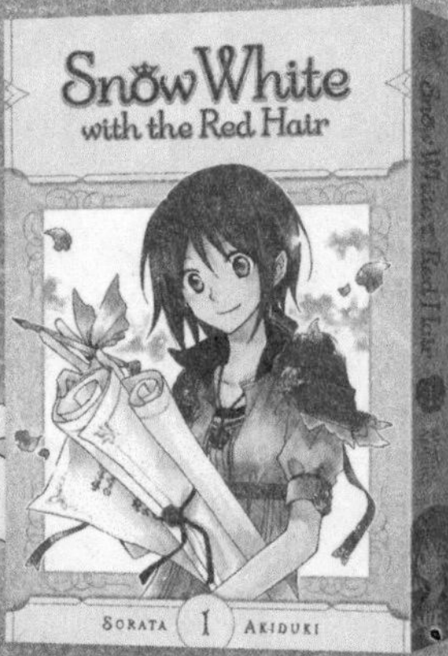
Snow White
with the Red Hair
SORATA
1
AKIDUKI

STORY & ART BY
SORATA AKIDUKI

Shirayuki is an herbalist famous for her naturally bright-red hair, and the prince of Tanbarun wants her all to himself! Unwilling to become the prince's possession, she seeks shelter in the woods of the neighboring kingdom, where she gains an unlikely ally—the prince of that kingdom! He rescues her from her plight, and thus begins the love story between a lovestruck prince and an unusual herbalist.

RATED T TEEN

VIZ

SHORTCAKE CAKE

STORY AND ART BY
suu Morishita

**An unflappable girl and a cast of
lovable roommates at a boardinghouse
create bonds of friendship and romance!**

When Ten moves out of her parents' home
in the mountains to live in a boardinghouse,
she finds herself becoming fast friends with
her male roommates. But can love and
romance be far behind?

VIZ

SURPRISE!

You may be reading the wrong way!

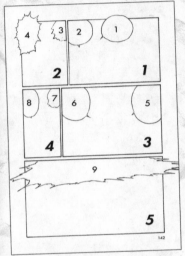

It's true: In keeping with the original Japanese comic format, this book reads from right to left—so action, sound effects, and word balloons are completely reversed. This preserves the orientation of the original artwork—plus, it's fun! Check out the diagram shown here to get the hang of things, and then turn to the other side of the book to get started!

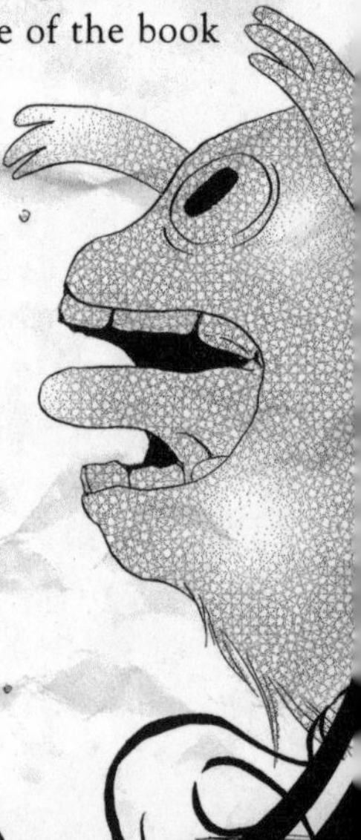